ASSESSING, DIAGNOSING, AND TREATING SERIOUS MENTAL DISORDERS

ASSESSING, DIAGNOSING, AND TREATING SERIOUS MENTAL DISORDERS

A Bioecological Approach

Edward H. Taylor

OXFORD
UNIVERSITY PRESS

OXFORD

UNIVERSITY PRESS

Oxford University Press is a department of the University of
Oxford. It furthers the University's objective of excellence in research,
scholarship, and education by publishing worldwide.

Oxford   New York

Auckland   Cape Town   Dar es Salaam   Hong Kong   Karachi
Kuala Lumpur   Madrid   Melbourne   Mexico City   Nairobi
New Delhi   Shanghai   Taipei   Toronto

With offices in

Argentina   Austria   Brazil   Chile   Czech Republic   France   Greece
Guatemala   Hungary   Italy   Japan   Poland   Portugal   Singapore
South Korea   Switzerland   Thailand   Turkey   Ukraine   Vietnam

Oxford is a registered trademark of Oxford University Press
in the UK and certain other countries.

Published in the United States of America by
Oxford University Press
198 Madison Avenue, New York, NY 10016

Library of Congress Cataloging-in-Publication Data
Taylor, Edward H., author.
Assessing, diagnosing, and treating serious mental disorders : a bioecological approach / Edward H. Taylor.
p. ; cm.
Includes bibliographical references and index.
ISBN 978–0–19–532479–2 (alk. paper)
I. Title.
[DNLM: 1. Mental Disorders—diagnosis.   2. Social Environment. WM 141]
RC455.4.E58
616.89—dc23
2014022085

This book is dedicated to Susan J. Wells, my wife and very best friend. Without her love, kindness, and reassurance, this book likely would not have been completed. She had faith that I actually had something to say, and the ability to get it onto paper. She also promised me a new barbecue grill and smoker once the book was completed. However, she is the one deserving of a very special gift.

CONTENTS

Preface   ix

Acknowledgments   xvii

Introduction: Brain, Mind, and Environment   1

1. Theoretical Foundations for Treating Bioecological Mental Disorders
    and Illnesses   7

2. The Family as Treatment Partners: Moving Beyond Education and Coping   49

3. The Comprehensive Continuous Assessment   79

4. Schizophrenia   109

5. Major Depressive and Dysthymic Disorders: Introduction and
    Comparison Between *DSM-IV-TR* and *DSM-5*   184

6. Bipolar Disorders   239

7. Anxiety Disorders   280

8. Personality Disorders   313

9. Child and Adolescent Mental Disorders: An Overview   356

10. Into the Future   376

Index   387

PREFACE

A PERSONAL STORY

Writing this book has been a journey influenced by many people and events. Certainly the hundreds of clients and families with whom I have worked have continuously shaped my intervention perspective and theoretical framework. While at the National Institute of Mental Health's Neuroscience Research Hospital, I heard the concerns and witnessed the care provided by parents of adults with schizophrenia. Often they were not only tired and worried from the struggle to help a daughter or son to make it safely through another day, but additionally felt both abandoned by the mental health care system and blamed for their loved one's disorder. I will always owe these families a debt of gratitude for what they taught me. My perceptions and knowledge have also been shaped by the numerous neuroscientists, social work clinicians, psychologists, and professors who have provided supervision, mentorship, guidance, and friendship over the years. Some I continue to have the privilege of working with to this day. However, as important as clients, mentors, and friends have been, an equally large influence has been the growth that has occurred from personal struggles.

The experience of living with what had been a hidden neurodevelopmental disorder became a shocking reality for me in the sixth grade at Aurora (Colorado) Elementary School and continues to this very day. My years from birth to the sixth grade were, I suppose, spent in a family that was often below or near the official poverty line and often economically stressed. I only suppose this is true—because life was filled with non-monetary riches and joy. As a child, doing without running water, a refrigerator, indoor plumbing, or financial security did not matter. Even enduring the Texas heat with only a homemade paper fan was not a hardship. Happiness was walking across one field to my paternal grandparents' house and going in a different direction to end up at my mother's parents' without crossing a single street. Aunts and uncles and cousins seemed to be everywhere. I had a sister I adored who was 6 years younger than myself. I was constantly playing with an aunt who was months older than I was, and another who was only about a year and half older. Along with these two, I was often in the care and orbit of an uncle who was 7 years older, and an aunt who was 8 years my senior. These were my big brother and sister role models. Today it would seem odd for one's mother and grandmother to be pregnant at the same time. If this was seen as out of step culturally by others in our community, their editorials went unnoticed by the entire family.

Until entering the sixth grade, I lived in a world of parental and extended family support. The idea of being defective, or less than anyone else, was never a thought. The summer before entering the sixth grade, my father, out of desperation for work and a determination to financially take care of the family, unexpectedly enlisted in the Air Force. He was soon assigned to an air base in Aurora, Colorado. So, we left the extended family, Texas, cats, and other animals, and traveled to an apartment complex in Colorado. This was strange, but an adventure rather than a perceived stress. After all, we were the same intact family, just minus so many extended members who had always been there, but were now far away. The real adjustment and test to my emotional stability, however, would not come until fall and the opening of school.

As September arrived, I was apprehensive but excited about starting the sixth grade in a new school. After all, this was my last year of elementary schooling. The school was much larger than the one I had previously experienced. The relief of finding my assigned room immediately evaporated upon realizing that the teacher was a man. Teachers were supposed to be women. At this young age, and previously having seen only women in teaching positions, I could only wonder what would make a man become a teacher. Upon starting class, the teacher handed out several textbooks. I sat in amazement. In Texas we had never had our own books. At the end of the day, textbooks were neatly stacked on the teacher's desk. With what I am sure was over-animation in my voice, I asked, most likely without raising my hand, "We keep these?" The expression on the teacher's face and his words told me that even though I did not understand, nonetheless, that was strike one. It took only a short time for strike two to occur. A sign-out paper was passed around, and students were asked to write their name and the number on the back of each textbook. Since I had never done this before, it was explained in the most serious of tones that if the books were lost or damaged, payment would be expected. I think I was the only student whose name was printed.

The big strike three came when the teacher instructed us that we were to individually read from one of the textbooks when pointed to until we were told to stop. After a few students read, he pointed to me. I had no idea where in the book we were. He instructed for me to find my place and that I would be called on again later. Later came all too soon, and again I was lost and could not respond. I was given the same instructions with a stern warning to pay attention. After a short period, the teacher's finger was once again pointing to me, and I once again could not respond. This time the teacher walked over to me, rapidly turned the pages, took my hand and placing it under a line of print, said in a harsh voice, "Now, read!" Immediately, both he and I discovered that I could not read a single word. Being a wise instructor, he gently closed my book and said, "I think we have done enough of this," and without missing a beat carried on with his teaching. Until that moment, neither I nor my parents had any idea that I could not read. I would later find that I could perform only the most simplistic math. Soon I was in strange little offices taking psychological tests, and without explanation I was placed in a special education room.

Attempts were made to teach me basic reading and math skills. By the end of sixth grade, I still was not reading anywhere near the sixth grade level, but had matriculated to the seventh grade, and that experience magically turned into eighth grade. These were painful years, knowing that I was different from the others, sometimes trying, and at other times simply giving up. In the eighth grade I developed severe pneumonia and missed 6 weeks of school. Upon returning to school, a note from my mother stating that I had been ill was given to the homeroom teacher. Neither I nor the note was questioned, and I was admitted back to the classroom. I honestly recall thinking, "They know I am stupid and mentally retarded, and do not care that I missed weeks of school." My insight proved to be at least partially correct in that neither the homework nor instruction were caught up, but as in previous years, eighth grade was passed.

As the result of an inability to academically achieve, I became convinced that I must be mildly mentally retarded. This stuck with me until I was in the Army, where I was selected from basic training for Officers Candidate School and became an infantry second lieutenant. In Vietnam I became an extremely successful combat officer, decorated four times for valor. One day while on combat patrol in the jungle, I literally said to myself, "If I am this good of a lieutenant, and selected over others to lead difficult missions, then I cannot be mentally retarded!" Upon this self-discovery, I concretely decided that my new goal was to learn how to learn and to get a doctorate. Sharing this discovery and decision was neither possible nor wise. After all, how does a person who barely is able to read, who received a "socially granted" high school degree, who failed out of Bible College (a story for another day), and who is in the middle of the jungle share this type of revelation? Knowing that one does not announce having gone from worries of mild mental retardation to a decision to gain a doctorate in an unknown subject does not require a great amount of social intelligence. This was a secret to keep from the Army, my parents, and even my sister. Upon my safe return to the United States after a year in Vietnam, I quietly started night classes. As I struggled with English literature, an observing professor suggested that I go to the learning center and have a complete academic screening. The suggestion sent waves of anxiety. I felt like a successful warrior who was about to be rejected again by academia, labeled, and pointed back to special education. At that time I was not sure if colleges had special education classes, but if they did, I was certain that was my destiny. After the third reminder about the learning center, and being informed that I was failing, an appointment was painfully made. The testing identified that I have a severe learning disability. Once I was assured that learning disorders are not related to intelligence, the diagnostic label provided an interesting sense of calm, relief, and hope.

Over many years of part- and full-time education, I gained my degrees. The struggle was often marked with setbacks as well as victories. There were professors who encouraged me, as well as those who suggested I leave college and find a trade. One professor, who knew that my wife at the time was an ethnic minority person, formally accused me of having her write my paper. He was certain that no native English-speaking person could have written such a fragmented, misspelled, run-on-sentenced, grammatically incorrect paper. However, if my wife had written the paper, it would have been far better. Out of embarrassment and dismay over a professor assuming that because my wife was a minority she could not possibly be literate, the incident was never shared with her. I simply did not want to add to the weight of discrimination that she experienced almost daily. While pursuing my doctorate, a social work professor humiliated me in front of the class because I would not follow his instructions and write on the chalkboard. During those days I was too embarrassed to let anyone know that I had a learning problem, and I certainly was not going to expose myself by writing on a board in front of everyone. However, to this day I will not, and almost cannot, serve as a group recorder during brainstorming sessions. My doctorate was completed before word processing and spell check software were commonly available. As a result, I literally looked up every word in the dictionary for each required paper. Nonetheless, I persisted and earned a BA in psychology, then an MSW, and finally a PhD in social work. Throughout my studies I had the opportunity to learn about the brain, the environment, systems, and bioecological concepts. The evidence seemed incomplete, but clear, that learning disorders, schizophrenia, and all major mental disorders have a foundation within the brain and generally react and interact with the environment. Certainly the environment had been both helpful and hurtful in my personal struggle.

A quick analysis illustrates the impact of biology and environment in my life. As will be described in Chapter 9 on child and adolescent mental disorders, evidence supports the assumption that learning disorders are biologically based but are highly impacted by interactions with the environment. My family provided attachment, support, and structure. An uncle throughout the years repeatedly stated that grades had no meaning. There was no pressure from my parents to make high grades. The fact that my sister was a high academic achiever never jeopardized my place of belonging in the family. We simply agreed across the extended family that my sister was good at school stuff, and I, less so. The family and school environments also prevented me from moving forward. My parents were not highly educated, and had no idea how to help me. Reading was not an important skill in our house. The schools had yet to develop a curriculum for special needs children who learned differently. Kids who caused no trouble were tolerated, overtly labeled, and socially passed from grade to grade. Behaviorally troubled youth were expelled and pushed out of school. Learning disorders have a higher probability of improving when a child's family and school tailor academic experiences to address the child's specific skills, deficits, and interests. Considering that the school had no tools for enriching my learning, I was fortunate to have a family where accumulating a grade point average between a D- and D+ made no real difference.

Looking back, there were a number of object lessons learned from these experiences that reinforce my social work perspective. Perhaps most important is that one cannot be "loved" out of a disorder, and that neurobiological problems generally are not simply outgrown. I neither developed a learning disorder nor was cured because of parental actions. I did, however, survive social harassment, labeling, and self-doubt by clinging to the social support, acceptance, and love provided by a large extended family. The Army placed me in physical risk, but validated that I had skills and allowed me to realize that if I could lead troops in combat, I surely could academically learn. Nonetheless, validation, awards, and acceptance did not make a neurobiological disorder disappear. A caring and observing professor identified the problem, but learning did not suddenly become easy. What did help was a correct diagnosis, guidance in how to learn, computers and spell check, years of practice, support, and a wife with patience and knowledge. I met my second wife while in the doctorate program. From the very beginning, she started tutoring and helping me learn how to learn. This was not and continues not to be an easy task for her. In the early years, I would come to her after trying to write and with sincerity say, "See what you think of this paper and my ideas." She would start reading and marking problems line after line. It would become painfully clear that she was correcting grammar and sentence structure. As I watched, my anxiety and self-doubt roared out of control until I would angrily yell, "Just throw the damn thing away," rush out of the house, slamming the door behind me. When I returned, she would sit down with me and go over, line by line, the strength and weakness of every sentence in the paper. Without her supportive teaching, reassurance, and belief in me, publishing and academic achievement would not have occurred. She will testify that the help I needed was not for just a brief period. She continues to mentor and reassure me to this very day. Yes, I have vastly improved, and I no longer charge out of the house slamming doors, but the learning disorder and writing problems remain. The dedication and support provided by my partner have helped me to not only publish, but also understand how a neurobiological disorder stresses and emotionally costs family members. For this reason, I have tried to emphasize throughout this book the importance for social workers to listen, validate, and gently work with families. I do not believe that my personal struggles compare with the hardships and disappointments experienced by families facing psychoses, autism, mood disorders, anxiety, and other major neurobiological problems. However, my personal experiences have assisted me in understanding stigmatization, frustration, failure, and the feeling of being discounted and overlooked. Equally important, I have learned through personal and professional experience the need for people with neurobiological disorders and their families to be truly heard and treated with empathy, professionalism, evidence-based methods, and respect.

My personal challenges and 35 years of social work have fostered a desire to help professional clinicians understand the importance of uniting evidence-based diagnostic information, research-oriented treatment, and compassion for mentally ill clients and their families within a bioecological practice model. Additionally, there is a desire to underscore that the wrong diagnostic and treatment theory can result in clients experiencing increased symptoms, emotional hurt, family disruptions, and, for some, self-harm and suicide. The "biology first" concept presented in Chapter 1 is not an attempt to undermine the importance of environment, nor to deny that we all, with or without a mental disorder, have a mind and psychological self that are mysterious and in urgent need of being researched. I am concerned, however, that the biological foundation of mental disorders becomes clouded when the emphases are placed on one-dimensional environmental explanations, singularly focused strengths models, and complex but unproven psychological theories. Life has taught me that environments are extremely complex, often hidden and changing, and constantly interacting with each other and our neurobiology. Life and studies have taught me that what is obvious and logical seldom explains behavior or mental disorders. The goal for this text, therefore, was to translate insights from my individual, educational, and professional experiences into a work emphasizing the neurobiological foundation of mental disorders—a conscious attempt to address a perceived gap in social work education—by highlighting neurobiology as a primary factor in mental illness. The book also attempts to underscore that once the neurofoundation is formed, interacting social environments may help or hurt recovery, but seldom independently cure or make the disorder disappear. Determining whether biology causes people to gravitate to and interact with certain environments, or whether complex ecological systems shape biology, is basically beyond the scope and knowledge of the author, and appears to be a topic greatly in need of an empirical rather than philosophical answer. Finally, a secondary purpose of this book is to help readers conceptualize psychopathological theory and social work practice as interlocking and interdependent professional competences—that is, one biases how the other is framed and used. Theory, however, dictates to a greater extent the selection of methods, and shapes how we perceive mental disorders. A better understanding of the theory-practice gestalt is desperately needed within social work and mental health professions as a whole.

ACKNOWLEDGMENTS

I wish to thank Oxford University Press for making this book possible. I especially owe gratitude and thanks to Dana Bliss and his OUP team. The number of times they had to extend the deadline is embarrassing. Thank you, Dana, for your guidance, advice, and patience. In addition, I would like to thank the professionals who reviewed my manuscript and offered excellent suggestions. Their efforts greatly improved a number of sections within the book. This book would not have been possible had it not been for all of the clients and their families who over many years taught me about mental illness, and how to listen. Their strength, spirit, and willingness to share have inspired and motivated me throughout my career. Finally, I must thank Seana Dombrosky. Seana has critically read every chapter and provided meaningful editorial advice. I am not sure what I would have done without her eagle eye for grammatical requirements that escaped my vigilance. I greatly appreciate her attention to detail and meaningful feedback. Seana is completing her master's degree in English at the University of British Columbia. Thank you, Seana, for all of your work and quick responses.

BRAIN, MIND, AND ENVIRONMENT

By design, this book reinforces the assumption that mental disorders are highly associated with altered brain structures and functioning. This premise, however, does not undercut the role that environment plays by interacting with neurobiological factors, possibly initiating or triggering illness, and providing a dynamic source of treatment. Nevertheless, environment is assumed by this book to be multidimensional, expanding beyond social relationships, visible systems, and traditional power structures. This book also assumes that environments are both inclusive and exclusive and interact within and across systems differentially. Traditionally, social work education has researched and taught the power of environments to enhance or jeopardize the health, rights, and well-being of individuals and groups; indeed, our strength as a profession lies in understanding people within an environmental context. This book simply expands this traditional concept of the intersection of biology, psychosocial functioning, and environment, especially in the study of mental disorders, to include human neurobiology.

An attempt is made to illustrate that both symptoms and disorders relate to the complex interactions among multiple internal biological and external social systems. A human mental problem may be rooted mostly in biological or social ecological systems, but always involves both brain functions and societal factors. Our job as social workers is to engage with clients and families to discover how the difficulties relate to these internal and external environments. However, neither the neurobiology nor the environment is always dominant or most important. This book proposes that in most cases either internal brain functioning or external social environments become primary, while the other is a secondary contributing factor to the client's symptoms. Because an interactional model for describing mental disorders is employed, Bronfenbrenner's "bioecological" term is adopted (Bronfenbrenner & Morris, 2006). As used in this book, bioecological simply means that there are reciprocal interactions within and among biological and social systems. Furthermore, bioecological interactions have the ability to create change across the internal and external systems. However, the power to direct or create change is not distributed equally across systems, and consequently either the biological or social environment becomes, at differing points in time, a dominant agent for change.

Still, more emphases have been placed throughout this textbook on neurobiological contributions to mental disorders, rather than on the social environment. This is because social work has only recently started to incorporate brain factors into our teaching of human development and mental disorders. In the past, our textbooks and research have had very little to say about the brain. There are numerous textbooks focused on environment, trauma, and oppression, but only a small number of writings emphasize what social workers need to know about neurobiology. If we accept that environment extends beyond the social milieu, than we must stretch our learning and psychosocial education to include the client's biological systems. In order to accomplish this, the neurobiology of disorders has been highlighted.

This book thus has been written to help social workers and other mental health clinicians increase their knowledge of how the brain forms a foundation for both mental health and mental disorders. As will be discovered throughout the chapters, researchers have yet to identify precisely what causes mental disorders. As a result, it is beyond the scope of this book to explain how the brain's foundation for supporting mental illness or wellness is shaped or formed. It is, however, an obvious bias of this book that mental illness is best explained as atypical brain activity that differentially interacts and responds to social environments. It is important to note, though, that this assumption does not preclude the idea that in some situations environmental interventions represent the best practice treatment, while in other cases medical interventions or medications are more effective.

A fundamental perspective of this book is that there is always a need for social environmental interventions, and that medication treatment is dependent upon the type of disorder and the severity of the illness. Identifying the brain as a foundation for mental disorders neither explains causation nor disqualifies social-environmental interventions. Indeed, the social worker's responsibility for assessing and treating the person within a social context is expanded, rather than diminished, by the bioecological model. Knowledge about brain functioning can assist us in measuring and evaluating how clients with mental disorders perceive, experience, and respond to their social environments.

For many years, mental disorders were more understood from theoretical models that placed the causation for illness completely outside the person. That is, symptoms were thought to stem largely from parental-caused internalized conflicts, learned behavioral responses to environmental stimuli, or internal thoughts triggered by social events. Today, few professionals endorse a social-psychological model as a principal explanation for the cause of mental disorders (Paris, 2005). There is little evidence that unconscious or other internal dynamic factors create or initiate mental illness, and it is not productive to interpret or label symptoms from a psychoanalytic perspective (Paris, 2005). In fact, the idea that our brain activity interacts with social environments has even begun to be adapted into psychoanalytic theory (Sergerie & Armony, 2006). The value of studying major psychoanalytic concepts from a neuroscience perspective is yet unknown. Nonetheless, psychoanalytic theorists' movement toward neurobiology signals the importance of understanding the brain's relationship to mental disorders. While traditional psychodynamic theory offers little for understanding mental illness, it would be shortsighted not to remind ourselves that many of our concepts for forming client relationships and many of our intervention methods have been pioneered by psychoanalytic practitioners.

The "biology first" concept of mental illness may seem foreign and counterintuitive to some social workers as, without question, the concept underscores the neurobiological foundation of mental disorders. This was purposely done—to remove stigma and to reframe how client and family education is presented. There is now ample evidence that mental disorders are associated with changes in brain functioning and structure. For example, as presented later in the book, schizophrenia is thought not only to be biological in nature, but also possibly to be a neurodegenerative developmental disorder.

A consideration of heart disease is helpful in illustrating the biology first concept. For some, the disorder occurs at birth from genetic or unknown factors. Others are predisposed, and the illness is triggered by numerous biological and environmental possibilities; yet another group increases their probability for heart problems by eating fatty foods, smoking, gaining weight, and failing to properly exercise. A more fortunate group of individuals, regardless of their dietary, smoking, and exercise habits, appear immune to heart problems. For these individuals, the environment does not appear to affect their cardiovascular system.

No matter how a person develops heart disease, our first attitude or perception is that the individual has a biological disorder. Seldom do you hear a social worker say, before assessing and knowing the facts, "The heart attack must have occurred because the person or family was doing something wrong in the environment." Yet this process and type of thinking have historically been the message communicated to clients with mental disorders. Meanwhile, for cardiology clients we first identify the cardiovascular problem, reduce the immediate crisis, provide appropriate medical treatment, and then, or parallel with medical treatment, intervene environmentally.

Thus the biology first concept guides social workers to (1) not assume causation; (2) resolve the immediate crisis; (3) remove stigma by not purposefully or accidentally signaling blame; (4) understand environments as potentially helpful, hurtful, or neutral; (5) assure clients and families that they did not cause mental illness; and (6) identify whether environmental and talk therapies should be a primary or secondary intervention. The biology first concept does not automatically mean that medication or other medical devices are the first and most important form of intervention. Treatment decisions are dictated by the type of disorder, severity of symptoms, level of crisis, and environmental circumstances. Psychosis, for example, requires immediate medication, whereas anxiety may best be treated with cognitive and environmental interventions. An environmental intervention becomes a priority, however, for a person with most any disorder living in a state of physical danger. The biology first concept shapes the clinician's attitude toward and understanding of mental illness. It does not remove or diminish the importance of environmental assessments, client relationship building, client and family treatment planning participation, talk therapies, case management, or environmental interventions.

Clients have a right to know how a social worker professionally frames mental illness. They additionally expect clinicians to employ models and interventions that are up to date and founded on sound research. It is therefore the social worker's responsibility to know and communicate with clients the level of evidence documenting the assessments, educational information, and interventions that are recommended. When evidence-based interventions either are not available or have failed to help, clients deserve an explanation and alternative assessment or treatment choices. This book mostly provides evidence for assessing, diagnosing, and understanding mental illness and educating clients about the disorders they face. Examples of evidence-based interventions are provided, but not in a detailed manner. It has been the author's experience that if social workers learn to perform competent assessments, they will in most cases develop successful treatment plans. The steps and art of treatment are best learned through readings dedicated completely to specific methods, observation of interventions, excellent supervision, and practice. Within the structure provided by evidence from research, social workers need to find their own therapeutic artistic skills and boundaries.

To help clinicians improve their assessment skills, a chapter on the topic (Chapter 3) and a suggested diagnostic outline have been provided. The assessment outline is designed to serve as a model and will always need modification to fit the needs of specific clients and situations. However, hopefully it will help social workers consider the range, scope, and depth that an assessment needs to cover before a diagnosis can be determined. The family chapter (Chapter 2) additionally provides assessment information. Clinicians may want to combine items from both chapters when organizing a multidimensional comprehensive assessment. A principal point made throughout the book is that assessment never ends, and is the foundation for therapeutic decision-making. Illustrations to help one recall key diagnostic criteria and symptom clusters are included for a number of disorders. Lists and items are sometimes easier to recall when they are part of our visual memory.

For every disorder overviewed by the *Diagnostic and Statistical Manual of Mental Disorders* (4th ed., text rev.; *DSM-IV-TR*), diagnostic criteria have been included, along with a brief statement of any changes that were made in the new *DSM-5*. Unfortunately, the rights to publish the *DSM-IV-TR* criteria had been arranged prior to the introduction of *DSM-5*. Nonetheless, the diagnostic standards for most disorders were either not changed by the *DSM-5* review committees, or were given only minor revisions. The *DSM-IV-TR* diagnostic criteria, along with clarification of the *DSM-5* changes, have been included so that individuals who are not planning mental health careers and professors focusing less on diagnosis would not require the *DSM-5* as a supplement to this textbook. Individuals planning to work in any health, mental health, or child welfare agency will, however, find the *DSM-5* helpful.

Readers will find that the personality chapter (Chapter 8) provides diagnostic criteria, but at the same time challenges whether many of the difficulties relate to abnormalities in personality development or should more appropriately be seen as within the spectrum of other mental disorders. There is growing concern among researchers that we know very little about classifying normal—let alone abnormal—personality structures. Because of the influence that culture, economics, opportunity, oppression, health, crises, and multiple other factors have on one's temperament, personality theories and disorders need to receive more critical consideration by social workers.

Finally, it is hoped that this book plays a small role in stimulating the profession of social work's interest in neuroscience. The brain is a key factor in how we develop, perceive the world, and become mentally ill or remain well. We have no state of mind without a living brain. Learning how the brain incorporates genetic messages, ecological input, and cognitive thoughts into a dynamic problem-solving human mind is an important social work issue. This book was specifically planned and written to increase the conversation about the role that brain development and neurological changes play in mental illness. It is sincerely hoped that the chapters motivate readers to further explore brain functioning and structure as the foundation for mental disorders and mental health.

REFERENCES

Bronfenbrenner, U., & Morris, P. A. (2006). The bioecological model of human development. In W. Damon & R. M. Lerner (Eds.), *Handbook of Child Psychology* (6th ed., Vol. 1, pp. 793–828). New York: John Wiley & Sons.

Paris, J. (2005). *The Fall of an Icon: Psychoanalysis and Academic Psychiatry*. Toronto: University of Toronto Press.

Sergerie, K., & Armony, J. L. (2006). Interaction between emotion and cognition: A neurobiological perspective. In M. Mancia (Ed.), *Psychoanalysis and Neuroscience* (pp. 125–150). Milan, Italy: Springer.

/// 1 /// THEORETICAL FOUNDATIONS FOR TREATING BIOECOLOGICAL MENTAL DISORDERS AND ILLNESSES

Although conceptualizing treatment was much easier when a single developmental theory was thought to explain most human psychological functioning, one theory cannot accurately describe human behaviors, symptoms, or individual strengths. Today, social workers must simultaneously coordinate interventions that target biological, environmental, social-cognitive, and emotional domains while continuously ensuring that the client's differential needs and unique characteristics are addressed. Failure to incorporate multi-theory clinical models will lead to flawed interventions that may harm clients and their families. This chapter is designed to highlight the important interactions among theory, research, and creativity in the professional art of treating people who experience serious mental illness. Specifically, an attempt is made here to explain key biological, ecological, and social learning concepts that provide a foundation for the bioecological clinical framework used throughout this book. The term "bioecological" is utilized to emphasize that rehabilitation for clients with serious mental illness requires coordinated treatments that target precise interactions among neurological, ecological, and social-cognitive systems. Furthermore, a bioecological framework underscores that biological and environmental systems are always important, but often impact a person differently. A central theme of this text is that while causation of mental disorders cannot yet be identified, neurobiology, nonetheless, forms the foundation for the expression of mental health or illness. Therefore, the term "bioecological" refers to the assumption that behavior, health, and mental health indicators are created or triggered by interactions among multiple biological and external ecological factors.

THE "BIOLOGY FIRST" PERSPECTIVE

The author's perspective is that all serious long-term mental illnesses not directly related to extensive trauma, abuse, or neglect occur because of irregularities in the brain's structure and chemical functioning. The book therefore addresses neurobiological disorders that may range in intensity from almost unnoticeably mild to extremely severe and debilitating. Referring to the illness as a "neurobiological disorder" does not diminish the role of environmental interaction, nor does it identify causation. The term does, however, place biology as the foundation, but not the complete explanation, for observable changes in a person's social, cognitive, behavioral, and perceptual functioning. Moreover, identifying disorders as neurobiological removes the stigma and the idea that either the client wants to be ill or that the difficulties are directly resulting from mothering or parenting deficiencies. All neurobiological disorders, regardless of severity, are labeled serious mental illness. Just as mild heart disease or diabetes can be manageable or ultimately deadly, mild neurobiological illnesses can remain stable or can lead to symptoms that bring about suicide, accidental death, homelessness, poverty, or even institutionalization. Terminology for mental disorders varies across authors and researchers. The terms "bipolar disorders" and "manic depressive illness" continue to be used interchangeably. While mental disorders range from very mild to extremely disabling, schizophrenia is considered a severe disorder regardless of a client's level of illness. Severe mental illness is also often referred to by authors as serious long-term disorders, neuropsychiatric disorders, neurodevelopmental disorders, or neurobiological illnesses (E. Taylor, 2003). There are slight technical differences among these terms. However, in this textbook they each refer to mental illness resulting largely from abnormal changes in the brain. Generally most researchers agree that mental disorders result from an interaction among neurobiological and environmental factors (E. Taylor, 2003; US Department of Health and Human Services, 1999). Table 1.1 lists most of the neurobiological disorders.

TABLE 1.1 Neurobiological Disorders

- Attention deficit hyperactivity disorder (ADHD)
- Anxiety disorders (generalized and obsessive-compulsive disorders, panic, PTSD)
- Borderline personality and schizophrenia-related personality disorders
- Major mood disorders
- Developmental disorders (autistic spectrum disorders, and all early onset developmental disorders)
- Schizophrenia and schizoaffective disorder

While environment often plays a role in how neurobiological symptoms are expressed, the illnesses must first and foremost be understood using neuropsychiatric research and theory. This is not to say that social workers are expected to become neuroscientists; however, they are responsible for developing skills and knowledge that permit them to accurately translate key neurological concepts to clients, families, and communities. Because the symptoms of serious mental disorders are primarily biologically determined, psychiatric symptoms may increase, plateau, or decrease independently, regardless of psychological and ecological forces. Another physical disease analogy highlights the importance of this assumption. Cardiovascular problems, for example, are influenced by numerous environmental elements: a person may have never smoked and may have eaten low-fat food, exercised, and meditated daily, but nonetheless may have a deteriorating cardiovascular system due to other factors.

The idea that symptoms of major mental disorders develop from a biological foundation does not alter the need for completely examining how ecological factors, including system interactions, influence symptoms, treatment, and recovery. Many times a client's cultural history or social setting will explain behaviors and symptoms or will significantly change how they are understood. The importance of cultural learning, customs, social environments, and behavioral influences must be incorporated in every social work assessment and treatment plan. That social workers are trained to understand behavior and symptoms within a social context is therefore of great benefit. A major segment of the bioecological approach is the assessment of the client's historical and current cultures. Nonetheless, it is paramount to underscore that symptoms caused by serious mental illness do not always have contextual meaning. Bioecological social workers are open to the idea that symptom changes and plateaus may stem more from brain abnormalities than psychosocial elements. That is, a bioecological model neither discounts the importance of environment nor obligates clinicians to interpret, explain, or link every symptom to a social, cultural, or historical event. The reverse, however, is also assumed. Changing the environment may directly affect a person's symptoms or level of functioning. Therefore, from a bioecological perspective, the environment is neither discounted, nor automatically assumed to explain mental illness symptoms.

By recognizing biology as the first element for assessment responsibility, we are not disregarding a client's environment or internal perceptions, but rather ensuring that the pathology is not automatically blamed on the individual, family, or community, thus avoiding a common pitfall of previous treatment perspectives. Diagnostic and treatment frameworks frequently condition social workers to develop habitual responses. For many years, most mental health clinicians automatically assumed that unconscious conflicts, personal behavior choices, cognitive thinking, or interpersonal relationships explained the onset and continuation of serious mental illness. As a result, the paramount objective for diagnostic and treatment assessments was to determine either why the client chose to be symptomatic or how inadequate parenting or relationships injured the individual's psyche. The biology first theory, on the other hand, starts by assessing a client's neurocognitive condition and then determines whether environmental factors support or detract from the person's current neurobiological health status. Consequently, acceptance of this treatment perspective obligates social workers to extend their knowledge base and forge a working relationship with the medical and neuroscience professions.

The bioecological perspective recognizes that environmental events both trigger and play a major role in the creation of trauma-induced disorders. Abuse, war, disasters, threats, and loss are real and have the ability to damage the mental stability of children and adults. In cases involving post-traumatic stress, biology most likely plays either a secondary role to environment or fails to protect the individual from ongoing distress. We also know that poverty can have a detrimental effect on a child's brain. One study that is particularly interesting for social workers found that stress related to poverty can alter a child's hippocampus structure. However, the abnormal brain development was mediated by positive caregiving. The researchers suggest that enhanced parenting and caregiving skills should become the focus of public health policy and community intervention (Luby et al., 2013). Obviously, the study requires replication and further evidence before the findings are incorporated into public policy. Nonetheless, the research illustrates how environments and neurodevelopment have the potential for dynamic interaction.

Discussion of these treatment issues is elaborated throughout this text in conjunction with specific biosocial research, assessment issues, and treatment interventions. The author, however, does acknowledge that this book focuses heavily on the neurobiological foundations of mental disorders. This is, first, an attempt to at least partially address gaps in this vital academic and practice area. Social work education has historically emphasized the ecological concepts of mental illness in a rather narrow, blaming manner. That is, environment has been overly defined in terms of one-dimensional variables, such as "bad" parenting and abuse, rather than both observable and invisible complex ecological factors. Only recently has our profession started to prepare students for addressing the biology and environmental elements of severe disorders. Second, my personal bias is a belief that science currently indicates that serious long-term mental disorders result more from a neurobiological foundation that interacts with and most often, but not always, reacts to environmental and psychological issues. The role that environments play in establishing the neuro-foundation is less personally clear. The chicken-egg debate of genetic-environmental causation remains an enigma.

HAS THE PSYCHOSOCIAL MODEL BEEN CORRUPTED AND OUTDATED?

Yes. Unfortunately, most ecological perspectives are used more in social work for guiding discussions than for creating actual clinical interventions. That is, ecological theory is used for communicating the importance of environment and culture to individuals, but seldom becomes the actual foundation for clinical assessments and interventions. When used in this manner, ecological theory becomes a supporting clinical value system that influences rather than directs multiple levels of intervention. A more dynamic perspective would be to view the components of neurobiological, ecological, and social learning theories as an interlocking and interactional theory for diagnosing and treating serious mental illness. This purposefully is not referred to as a biopsychosocial model. Clinicians have historically been trained to perceive psychosocial concepts as an extension of psychoanalytic or ego psychological theories. The psychosocial model cues clinicians to focus on abstract terms symbolizing internal psychological conflicts, deficits, or strengths. The language of psychoanalytic theories has primarily evolved from philosophy, clinical observations, and research with extremely limited generalizability (Haight & Taylor, 2007; Johnson, 2004; E. H. Taylor, 2006b).

This textbook argues that far too many clinicians continue to concern themselves with identifying symbols of ego and unconscious injuries rather than applying evidence-based assessments and interventions. From Freud to current times, the concepts of ego and unconscious motivation have remained intangible concepts, defined slightly differently by competing psychoanalytic theorists (Davison, Neale, Blankstein, & Flett, 2002). Still, Freud's broad abstract brain model (id, ego, superego, and unconscious energy), along with Eric Erikson's developmental stages, continues to find high acceptance among many mental health professionals, teachers, and religious leaders. Consequently, many professionals have developed a tradition of diagnosing mental health problems based on clinician-interpreted psychological abstractions. For these clinicians, a client's lack of self-integration or unconscious conflict becomes the explanation for dysfunction, and the target for change-producing interventions (Gazzaniga & Heatherton, 2009; Paris, 2005; Sue, Sue, & Sue, 2006; Westen, 1999). Keep in mind that we are discussing whether psychoanalytic theories adequately explain and define mental disorders, not whether psychodynamic interventions have efficacy. The theory we adopt largely dictates how one understands and educates clients and families about mental illness. This makes social workers' selection of a theoretical framework extremely important. Psychodynamic, cognitive, behavioral, environmental, and feminist theories have limited scientific evidence for explaining mental disorders; their interventions, however, are known to decrease many, but not all, mental illness symptoms (Hubble, Duncan, & Wampold, 2010). Certainly, some methods work better than others for differing disorders, but most interventions appears to have some evidence of efficacy. Therefore, how one theoretically understands mental illness is arguably more important than the clinician's selection of an intervention. As will be shown, this is not completely true for all diagnostic categories. The wrong talk therapy, for example, for a person experiencing psychosis or mania can increase symptoms. Generally, one's theoretical perspective predicts or guides the type of interventions that are used.

Early psychoanalytic cognitive and behavioral theories largely separated mental illness symptoms from a person's biology and placed them, or explained them, primarily from a social context. Though the concepts sound logical, they often do not hold up under scientific examination. Mental health workers find it tempting to define and interpret a client's response to environmental factors at least in part through logic, or through a psychoanalytic or a one-dimensional lens. The term "psychosocial" was thus rejected for describing interactions between the human mind, emotions, or psyche and the social environment in this text because we have been conditioned to automatically link psychosocial assessments with constructs that

- overly emphasize poorly researched, abstract psychological concepts for explaining behaviors and symptoms;
- view abstract unconscious constructs as over-riding mental structures that have the power to independently control and explain behavior;
- minimize the role of neurodevelopment, brain functioning, and sociocultural context for explaining behavior;
- interpret past experiences into broadly defined explanations of illness causation that cannot be validated;
- universalize the meaning of behavior, past experiences, and psychological structures with little regard to culture and social context;
- overly permit clinicians to label, stereotype, and interpret (according to the clinician's biases) the "secret" mental or unconscious meaning of behaviors; and
- always use retrospective interpretation, often made by a single office-based professional using incomplete data, in order to produce explanations of social-environmental causation and unconscious conflict.

Clearly, a basic bias of this textbook, then, is that when psychodynamic-ego concepts are included with psychosocial assessments, clinicians focus more on interpreting unconscious conflicts than on measuring how ecological and neurobiological factors are interacting. As a result, empirical measurement of the current biosocial context becomes a secondary goal, subordinate to a therapist's generated insights and explanations.

One may argue that the psychosocial model assesses psychological constructs within the dynamics of the client's environment. This is sometimes true. Traditionally, however, psychosocial models assess the client's environment as a means of explaining how ecological stressors cause the development of psychopathology, rather than considering a two-way interaction between the environment the client is in and the illness she experiences.

Environmental elements are also frequently used to validate logical, but unprovable hypotheses. For example, a clinician may hypothesize that a depressed client's symptoms arise from unconscious and unresolved anger at her father. Within her daily life, the young person avoids men, and often gets into power struggles and heated arguments with men who are in authoritative positions. The client is clinically pictured as unconsciously angry at her father, but afraid of the anger. Therefore, her rage is pushed into the unconscious, which then creates depressed symptoms. Her environmental behavior illustrates the concept of transference. That is, she unknowingly approaches all men, especially those in authority positions, as though they were her father. This in turn is seen as proof, or an explanation, of her avoidance of men.

This scenario has a number of problems. First, statistically, association does not prove causation. Individuals often have numerous unrelated positive and negative events occurring simultaneously in their lives. Second, the hypothesis creates a self-fulfilling prophecy. After labeling or giving symptoms meaning, such as unconscious anger at a client's father, the therapist is predisposed to observe validating behaviors. Interpretation of unconscious conflict is often made before the environment is assessed. This assures that environmental links will be found that validate the therapist's perspective. The therapist is expected to present a logical link between internal dynamics and current behaviors. The difficulty is that neurobiological disorders often fail to follow or create logical patterns. Additionally, behaviors are often interpreted with the clinician having made no actual environmental observations, and having conducted only limited collaborating interviews. Psychosocial therapists seldom assess how a client interacts, behaves, and experiences each environmental setting in which the client participates. Consequently, rather than environments being assessed, they are simply screened and considered in global terms. Furthermore, many therapists assign intrapsychic and environmental labels without talking to anyone other than the client. It is difficult to comprehend how a client can be understood within an environmental context without involving the person's family and community, as these people constitute a significant portion of this context. Finally, the psychosocial scenario for depression given above fails to consider the person's biology and genetic history.

The propensity for conceptualizing and assessing human problems as hypothetical psychological structures is so culturally ingrained for Western social workers that the psychosocial model and terminology should be abandoned rather than modified and fixed. Social workers are encouraged to develop biosocial assessments that are based on measurable evidence. Rather than labeling and treating abstract psychological constructs, the bioecological model views behavior and emotion as observable elements created by physiology and contextual environmental factors. Figure 1.1 illustrates how human problems may be more biological, ecological, or interactional. Does this mean that within the bioecological framework unconscious activities do not exist? To this the response is a definitive, "it depends."

For some, ecological concepts serve as a structure that facilitates an understanding of dynamic interactions between ego and environmental settings (Farmer, 2009). When used in this manner, traditional psychological and ego-psychodynamic concepts are often strongly considered. Ecological theory as used here, however, redefines the meaning and role of intra-psychological structures or activity. Labeling behavior as motivated

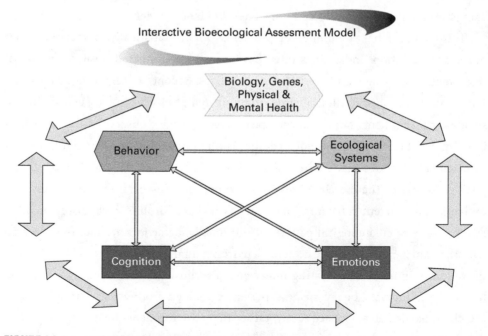

FIGURE 1.1 Interactive Bioecological Assessment Model.

by unconscious conflict or psychological defense mechanisms is at best unproductive and most likely inaccurate. There is little scientific evidence that the unconscious as proposed by Freud exists. A child, for example, at either the psychosexual pre-Oedipal or Oedipal stage has not developed the necessary brain connections and myelination required for producing the Freudian-assigned emotions and ego activities (Fabiani & Wee, 2001; Sampaio & Truwit, 2001). In fairness, as mentioned in the Introduction, psychodynamic theory has moved beyond Freud's conceptualizations. Modern psychoanalytic theorists are attempting to develop a concept of the unconscious that is testable and supported by neuroscience. If this is accomplished, clinicians and researchers will need to reconsider their assumptions, perspectives, and understanding of the unconscious mind.

Unconscious mental activity can, nevertheless, shape behavior. Few would argue that traumatic events like child abuse do not impact a person's emotions and behavior. However, devastating events are most often held as active memories rather than unconscious activity. Neuroscientists have found that the human unconscious allows for automatic behavior such as reading. In one's mind, one unconsciously decodes letters into words, and words into sentences that have meaning. All of this work is done without conscious knowledge (Kihlstrom, 2002). It does appear that some emotions and thoughts are both triggered and mediated by unconscious activity. This occurs when the amygdala automatically links to subcortical structures and influences the working memory (Kihlstrom, 2002). In many ways we are constantly moving information from unconscious to conscious awareness. However, this process does not represent the dynamic emphasis given to the unconscious by Freud and others (Hobson, 1994 J. LeDoux, 2002). Few argue that there is no unconscious, though modern neuroscience indicates that unconscious influences are explained by science, and are not forces attempting to control or take over our cognitive life. While the world of unconscious activity does exist, its role is far more limited in purpose, scope, and power than that advocated by psychoanalytic theorists (Gazzaniga, 1985; Gazzaniga & Heatherton, 2009; Kihlstrom, 2002; J. LeDoux, 2002; Marshall, 2003).

The questions for social work, then, are, how do we understand or explain behavior that does not come from cognitive awareness, and how are these psychological structures addressed in treatment? Conceptually, we do not think or assess in terms of unconscious processes. Behaviors performed without forethought or cognitive awareness occur from encapsulated neurosystems resulting from

- neurobiological chemical reactions that exist outside awareness;
- over-learned or over-practiced ecological experiences; or
- an interaction between neurosystems and over-learned social experiences.

Encapsulation refers to the brain's ability to develop extremely fast processes that bypass cognitive neuronetworks and automatically produce emotions and behaviors (Gazzaniga, 1985; Gazzaniga & Heatherton, 2009; Lieberman, 2007). That is, certain stimuli can cue the brain to bypass the steps, considerations, and memory normally used for processing information and decision-making. When this occurs, the brain's chemistry produces extremely quick and often intense responses. If a speeding car approaches while crossing a street one experiences increased heart rate, motor activity, and emotional responses. There is little or no process, or careful weighing of choices, in this type of situation. We move toward safety and then process the event. This type of encapsulation also happens on the interpersonal and emotional levels. Through constant cognitive practice we learn to act without awareness or cognitive choice (Gazzaniga, 1985; Lieberman, 2007).

Ecological and social learning experiences are constantly influencing encapsulated thinking. Our culture often trains us to have automatic religious beliefs that remain throughout life. Religious encapsulation can be so strong that even when a person has denounced these beliefs for an extended period of time, they may, nonetheless, reappear without forethought during a natural disaster or frightening experience (Haight & Taylor, 2007). Automatic or encapsulated behavior also occurs from genetic predeterminates and mental illness. Our personality and temperament, for example, appear to be in part biologically controlled. Research has found that, beginning in infancy, genetics highly influence temperament and personality development (Ebstein, Benjamin, & Belmaker, 2003). Furthermore, there is growing evidence that our genetic predisposition helps to determine the environments we self-select (Kalidindi & McGuffin, 2003). Genetics direct us to attend to certain environmental cues and disregard other events. Over time, cues constantly observed and processed within selected environments develop into encapsulated personality traits and temperament. Once this occurs, one is chemically programmed to instantly respond with sadness, anger, kindness, empathy, fear, or happiness when certain cues appear. However, mental illness can block neuronetworks and can replace behaviors that previously would have been well thought out with new automatic and rigid encapsulated behaviors. This again illustrates how labeling behavior as the result of unconscious conflicts or defense mechanisms is simplistic, unproductive, and punitive.

THE BIOECOLOGICAL FRAMEWORK

Clinicians using a bioecological framework neither interpret nor use a client's unconscious processes for stimulating psychological and behavioral change. This is illustrated in Box 1.1.

BOX 1.1

CINNAMON BREAD DREAM

A client reports the following reoccurring dream. The individual dreams that he has half a loaf of cinnamon bread somewhere in the house. His dream consists of an endless but unproductive search for the sweet bread. It is known that the individual has a history of dysthymia (mild depression) and anxiety, and within the past 2 years his mother passed away. It is also known that the middle-aged adult loved his mother, but always characterized her as distancing, rigid, and having difficulty accepting or expressing warmth.

EGO PSYCHOLOGICAL PERSPECTIVE

A dream analysis may attempt to look at the symbolic meaning of the sweet bread and endless search. Perhaps the bread represents the deceased mother, and the searching represents the individual's lifelong struggle to gain recognition from his mother. The fact that it is a half loaf that is lost may have even deeper unconscious meaning. The adult son may unknowingly recognize the need for important attachments and experiences that were never provided by his mother. Unfortunately, the mother's death prevents this client from ever receiving the longed-for warmth and parental relationship. He can no longer even pretend that one day his mother will validate his emotional needs—half of the loaf is gone. Furthermore, one may even hypothesize that this person's depression is explained by unconscious anger. The depression and anxiety serve as dysfunctional defense mechanisms that protect him from discovering and aggressively acting on his parental hatred. In addition, if these interpretations are accepted, one could also hypothesize that this person cannot complete the grieving process until insight into the unconscious and incomplete process is gained. Finally, one may also evoke Eriksonian theory and declare that negative parental experiences prevented this client from resolving an early developmental crisis and advancing smoothly from one growth stage to another. He therefore became stuck in an endless search for intimacy that caused symptoms of depression and anxiety.

BIOECOLOGICAL INTERPRETATION

The bioecological clinician's interpretation is more focused on immediate contextual behavior. The depression and anxiety are not directly related to the reoccurring dream. It is assumed that these problems are related to neurobiological and ecological factors. Therefore, no symbolic relationship between the cinnamon bread dream and psychiatric symptoms is hypothesized. The dream is interpreted as being linked to current social and environmental issues that are stimulating the brain's memory and creative systems. In addition, the biology of depression and anxiety, along with medications and personal behaviors, are creating sleep disturbances. The therapist using bioecological concepts would argue that there are no researchable grounds for interpreting the dream components symbolically, and further that symbolic interpretations reflect both incorrect information about the origins of depression and incorrectly use the therapist's power. Interpreting the dream gives a seductive meta or unspoken message that a therapist has the ability or power to understand the hidden meanings of behavior. This seductively places the social worker in a powerful, almost omnipotent, position over the client. The claim to have knowledge and insight that is unconsciously hidden from the client is very empowering for the therapist. The interpretation can also be viewed as placating the client and possibly causing the person to become dependent on the clinician. More important, however, the psychodynamic interpretation labels the problem of depression and anxiety as being produced and actually psychologically needed by the client. It is saying to the client, "you choose to be depressed because the alternative choices are too frightening." In contrast, the bioecological perspective proclaims that depression is coming from biological abnormalities that have little relationship to the dream.

While education and knowledge are viewed as important treatment goals, little or no effort is made to help clients gain insight into their early developmental stages or conflict (E. H. Taylor, 2006b). The bioecological model according to Taylor (2006) believes that psychological and behavioral change is produced by

- modifying the environment;
- altering the client's environmental perceptions;
- improving social cognitive information-processing skills;
- decreasing unproductive encapsulated emotional and behavioral responses;
- reducing symptoms and enhancing personal strengths;
- assisting or improving the client's neurological functioning;
- supporting both the client and the client's social relationships; and
- using medication when appropriate for changing the client's neurobiological systems.

In order to use these elements for creating change, the client's behaviors must always be understood within a biological, social, and cognitive context. Bioecological social work treatment plans tend to emphasize ecological and cognitive variables that support the client's current neurological and medical status. If a client, for example, has difficulty complying with her or his medications, the social worker would use ecological and cognitive assessments that specifically target methods for increasing compliance.

Generally an assessment of this type attempts to look equally at the client's behavior, symptoms, skills, and the environment's structural components. This requires gaining an understanding of the person's

- environmental settings, climate, and structure (boundaries, goals, roles, rules, and energy);
- beliefs, roles, perceptions, and goals within each environmental setting;
- perceptions, and the perceptions and beliefs of significant others within each setting;
- client's information-processing style within each setting; and
- distribution of the responsibilities of the client, significant other, and system.

After the assessment data is collected the components or separate domains are analyzed individually and as a gestalt.

Social learning and information-processing skills play a major role in understanding a client's strengths, symptoms, and behavioral style. Ecological, social learning, and other cognitive-oriented concepts overlap and share many common theoretical boundaries. Clinically it is often difficult to determine if behaviors and temperament are reinforced more by ecological systems or cognitive elements. From an assessment perspective, this is not an empty philosophical question. Most assessments attempt to define whether a person's behavior is more driven by biology, cognition, or environment. The point of entry of assessment biases the social worker's perception and guides both the emphasis and selection of intervention methods. Ecological interventions are generally selected when an environment is targeted for change rather than the client, or when experiential learning and social support activities are employed. Social cognitive methods most often focus on altering incorrect environmental perceptions, internal "self" messages, beliefs and knowledge, information-processing skills, false memories, or problem-solving strategies.

Whether a social worker uses an ecological or social learning intervention is related to how a client's behavior is labeled and targeted. However, identifying whether a client's behavior is influenced more by ecological or social learning variables is difficult. Often the value of one method over another can be determined only by introducing change into the environment or to the client's social learning style while attempting to hold all other variables constant. In other words, the social worker uses a series of single-subject research designs to measure which assessment and treatment technique is more effective for a specific client.

Social cognitive theories teach that learning and behavior are stimulated by thinking, behavior, and environmental influences (Haight & Taylor, 2007). Thus, a single behavior or series of actions can create or modify a person's next set of behaviors. When this occurs, the person's cognitive processes may or may not change. The theories equally teach that cognition (thinking) can cause a continuation or formation of new thoughts, and has the ability to modify behaviors (Haight & Taylor, 2007; Johnson, 2004; E. H. Taylor & Cadet, 1989). As we have learned from ecological theory, the environment is in a reciprocal relationship with the client's cognition and behaviors. A change in one influences the other. Often, however, we have thoughts that are not behaviorally acted upon, and we perform behaviors that have only minor impact on our thoughts, beliefs, or cognitive style.

Today, many researchers are adding emotion as a fourth force that has the ability to create, sustain, and modify behavior, cognition, and environmental climates (Barlow, 2002; J. E. LeDoux & Phelps, 2000). However, as pointed out by Farmer (2009), there is no central "emotional" processor in the brain. Emotions are labels that have personal cognitive and physical meaning (Farmer, 2009). Social work assessments are improved by determining how major emotions (joy, surprise, fear, sadness, anger, disgust/contempt, and interest) are triggered by environmental cues and either create or prevent cognition (Brown, 2000; Forgas & Vargas, 2000). Modern research supports the idea that emotions stem from neurological and ecological factors. Additionally, cognition can stir emotions, and emotions can both block and create thoughts (Johnson-Laird & Oatley, 2000; J. E. LeDoux & Phelps, 2000). Mental illness often causes a person to become hypersensitive or hyposensitive to environmental cues. The hypersensitive person will react overly emotionally, whereas the hyposensitive individual has a reduced or blunted emotional response. Furthermore, damage to the brain's amygdala and limbic system can alter emotions without the client being cued or stimulated by environmental cues (E. H. Taylor, 2006a).

In the most simplistic explanation, social learning is stimulated by observing the performance of others (Haight & Taylor, 2007). As behaviors are modeled, information is incorporated and a cognitive problem-solving script or schema is created. These abstract structures are at first incomplete memory maps that will be forgotten unless they are behaviorally practiced and modified to fit the observer's personal skills and personality style. Through trial-and-error behavioral experiments, we incorporate, modify, or reject observed methods for negotiating social systems and completing individual goals. The flexibility needed for positively incorporating schema, as well as learning from experiential behaviors, can be blocked by serious mental illness. Social learning avenues for the client with mental illness are often blocked because the

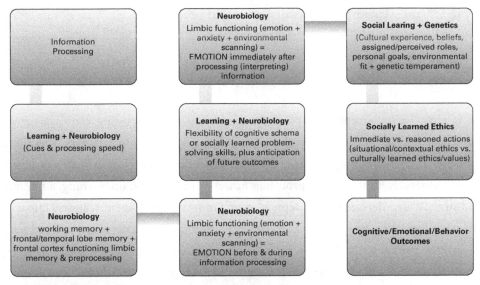

FIGURE 1.2 Complex Interactions Required for Information Processing.

There are no arrows indicating directions or systematic linkages. The processing actions do not necessarily occur in any specific order, nor is one step dependent on the previous occurrence of a specific step. The interactions are more like a deck of cards that can shift from position to position depending on ecological situations and brain activity. Additionally, cards can drop out of the deck and have no influence on how information is processed. Emotion and beliefs, as an example, may in some circumstances block cultural learning, or genetics may automatically predispose certain actions.

neurological structures and chemicals controlling attention, memory, abstract thinking, reality testing, anxiety, and cognitive processing speed have been disrupted (E. H. Taylor & Cadet, 1989). When these and other key neurological activities fail to function, the client's information-processing skills are decreased. Figure 1.2 illustrates the complexity of information processing. How one interprets signals, abstractions, and concrete data requires interactions among brain activity, genetics, learning, social situations (ecology), beliefs and ethics, trait and state emotions, and cultural biases.

Social information processing is one of the cognitive and learning concepts that explains how environmental data are identified, filtered, and converted into behaviors. Before individuals respond to information and interact with social events, a number of neurological functions are rapidly triggered. Social information processing can globally be hypothesized as requiring the following six cognitive steps (Haight & Taylor, 2007):

1. Attention is focused on selected cues from the social environment.
2. Cues are cognitively transformed or encoded into symbols that have personal and cultural meaning.
3. Encoded symbols are decoded into cognitive scripts or a schema.

4. Schema is cognitively translated into social behaviors.
5. Environmental feedback cues are used for evaluating the behaviors' effectiveness and appropriateness.
6. Behavior is either accepted, modified, rejected, or forgotten.

It must be underscored that deficits in information processing can occur from numerous social, cultural, general medical, and neurobiological factors. Identified problems in information processing do not independently serve as evidence of severe mental illness. Neurobiological problems, however, including mild learning, attention, and anxiety disorders, as well as depression and most severe disorders, always impact a client's information-processing skills. Faulty neurological systems at any age can temporarily or permanently alter how a person processes information.

Consider how critical attention is to correctly interpreting social cues. In any environmental setting, numerous related and unrelated cues are transmitted. How successful would you be if, while reading this text, unrelated cues automatically flooded your awareness and competed for your attention? Conversely, picture how you would feel and look to others if important ecological cues were often missed and were outside your awareness. Identification of too many cues can disrupt cognitive processing, whereas failure to identify cues may prevent one from making logical connections (E. Taylor, 2003; E. H. Taylor & Cadet, 1989). Both problems decrease an individual's ability to function and adapt to the social environment.

Culture plays an additional important role in social cognitive information processing. Through experiential learning and observations we incorporate rules concerning which cues are attended to, and what symbolic meanings are encoded (Haight & Taylor, 2007; Johnson, 2004). These cues and symbols are sensitive to the social context. That is, identical cues will be selected more or less quickly and will be assigned greater or lesser symbolic importance within differing social contexts. For example, society often teaches that the symbol "Ph.D." represents academic accomplishment and knowledge, yet the prestige and authority provided by the Ph.D. to a person will vary according to the environmental context. Within the university setting the symbol gains importance, while at the supermarket it has less influence. Few of us, for example, pattern our grocery buying after our favorite professor. This ability to flexibly fit cue selection and symbolic encoding into a contextual framework is often disrupted by mental illness. Misperceptions and incorrect information processing can also occur during cross-cultural exchanges. Communicating is very difficult when individuals within the same setting observe different cues and assign the cues different symbolic meanings. Obviously, it is extremely important that clinicians have the skill to assess when communications and behavioral patterns represent neurological deficits rather than cultural differences in information-processing styles.

The numerous cognitive functions required for processing information stretch far beyond the scope of this chapter. Nonetheless, a few concepts need to be briefly highlighted. Serious mental illness consistently interferes with one or more of the following neuroprocesses: working memory, social memory, problem-solving, short-term and long-term memory, sequencing, simultaneous processing, gestalt development, abstraction, processing speed, and attention (Farmer, 2009; Johnson, 2004). Difficulties in these areas substantially alter how social information is processed and how the environment is perceived. As these alterations occur, clients with serious mental illness usually have no alternative but to behave differently than they and society would desire.

The impact of mental illness over memory is particularly troubling, as all forms of memory are required for processing information. We must make sense and meaning of our world through previously learned knowledge and experiences. Working memory is the cognitive function that organizes information from long-term memory and allows a person to systematically move from one problem-solving step to another without forgetting contextual meaning and goals (Haight & Taylor, 2007; E. H. Taylor & Cadet, 1989). Information is retrieved into the working memory from numerous chemical memory networks. The working memory is then responsible for locking the recalled knowledge in place, which allows an individual to consciously manipulate or use the information. Working memory is like the brain's teleprompter. As we attempt to problem-solve or perform a task, the brain moves information step by step into our conscious awareness. This process must continue until the task is completed. If our teleprompter fails and the recalled data blink off our screen, we will appear confused, forgetful, or unknowledgeable. Permanent working memory problems often appear in individuals with learning disorders, attention deficits, and schizophrenia, while clients with mood and anxiety disorders seem to experience temporary memory disruptions (Barlow, 2002; E. H. Taylor, 2006a).

Through experiences, observations, and teaching from authority figures, social-cultural memories become part of an individual's encapsulated neurological system. Often without awareness or cues from the environment, social-cultural memories influence how individuals process information, perceive interactions or social events, and eventually behave (Gazzaniga, 1985). Go to a fast food restaurant and observe how people approach the counter. Without signs or instructions, customers form lines behind cash registers and space themselves in somewhat of an equal distance, one behind the other. One can often see signs of agitation and stress if a customer in line lags behind or moves unacceptably close to another individual, talks loudly, or takes too long placing an order. However, except in our social-cultural memory, there are no rules dictating how one stands and communicates while in line for fast food. Social-cultural memory, then, is used to process over-learned environmental cues. In an office, there are locations that appear more private or public than others. We gravitate toward certain people and away from others when seeking information. Our tone, volume, and voice inflections automatically change as we transition from one setting to another. Asking directions to a public restroom seems easy and appropriate in one setting and an imposition in another. Each of these examples represents practiced memories that occur automatically.

An individual's social-cultural memory also helps the person guess or problem-solve how to negotiate a strange building or neighborhood with minimum increased anxiety. Certain building or area layouts, decor, equipment, residents, and human activities send cues that stimulate social memory and allow one to draw conclusions and behave in a controlled manner. Encapsulated social memories may direct us to perceive a location as safe or dangerous, regardless of the activity and interactions that are immediately occurring.

Serious mental illness often blocks, distorts, or changes a client's social memory. Individuals experiencing reduced social memory may appear to be unaware of rules, exhibit high anxiety, and lack common sense. They may also demonstrate unusual dependent or avoidant behaviors in an environment that others perceive as easy to negotiate and completely secure. Issues other than mental illness, however, can also cause social memory deficits and create information-processing problems. Social workers therefore need to ensure that a client's symptoms are not resulting from cultural conflicts, power disparities, temporary situations, or other environmental factors before applying mental illness labels.

The creation of multiple solutions from social cues and determination of which behavioral response best fits the immediate situation require critical analysis skills. This type of abstract problem-solving is performed mostly by the brain's frontal cortex (E. H. Taylor, 2006a). Our brain must weigh alternatives and determine how each possible solution will immediately benefit or cost us, or how it could influence future events. We critically analyze how much data, truthfulness, assertiveness, emotion, persistence, and personal energy is appropriate for responding to interpersonal situations. Social problem-solving and interpersonal relationships require an ability to develop alternative solutions, alter emotions, and predict the current and future impact of behaviors. Imagine how distressing it must be to have only one or two solutions and emotional responses for every social situation. Mental illness, unfortunately, limits a person's ability to perform critical analysis. As a result, individuals with neurobiological disorders may demonstrate social responses that fail to appropriately address environmental cues and social expectations.

Sequential and Simultaneous Processing

Some ecological situations require information to be processed in a step-by-step cognitive sequence, while other circumstances force us to rapidly consider multiple cues simultaneously. An algebra problem cannot be solved unless the steps are performed in a specific sequence. Likewise, attaining a job or college admission requires one to follow a series or sequence of rules and requirements. Even a child's birthday party calls on the participants to use their social-cultural memory and to follow defined steps. The host's schedule for gift opening, cake eating, game playing, and free time is adapted to and accepted by the children. Corrections are usually quickly made if a child decides to change the sequence independently.

Other social situations require the use of simultaneous processing. We quickly determine if a person is speaking seriously or lightly by concurrently measuring the individual's words, tone, voice inflections, posture, gestures, facial expressions, knowledge, authority, and past communication history or style. When a person is unable to engage in such processing, it can result in a number of communication problems and other related issues. For example, a parent of a 9-year-old, learning-disordered child reported that her son often misunderstood and misinterpreted satirical statements. He was constantly unable to determine when his playmates were exaggerating and when they were serious. Soon his peers created a cruel game, competing to see how often the boy could be made to appear gullible and stupid. A client's inability to simultaneously process multiple and partial cues result not only in social difficulties, but also cause unaware social workers and educators to inappropriately label the individual's symptoms and behaviors.

Individuals with mental illness also sometimes make incorrect decisions because they are unable to cognitively incorporate numerous cues, incomplete information, and knowledge into a meaningful mental gestalt. The person may separately understand each interlocking segment, but may be unable to conceptualize how the parts form an abstract dynamic whole. The impact and significance of the social transaction is overlooked, while a single isolated part is overemphasized. An inability to develop social-cognitive gestalts also limits the client's use of abstract concepts and planning. In addition, disrupted abstract thinking and problem-solving skills may indicate that a client has difficulty processing incomplete social cues, or systematically focusing his or her attention (E. Taylor, 2003; E. H. Taylor & Cadet, 1989).

Finally, the speed at which an individual processes information can be changed by mental illness. Depression and anxiety often disrupt and slow cognitive processes. These individuals may need to have information repeated and presented in briefer segments. For many individuals, depression not only creates attention deficits, but also increases the amount of time needed for considering routine information (Johnson-Laird & Oatley, 2000; Johnson, 2004; E. H. Taylor, 2006a). It is therefore important to determine whether the client's lack of response relates more to cognitive blocking, confusion, attention to internal processes such as anxiety or hallucinations, or reduced processing speed. The term "cognitive blocking" is used when clients suddenly lose their immediate thought and cannot keep in mind the topic or concept being deliberated during a discussion. The information is no longer locked in the person's working memory.

Clients with schizophrenia and manic episodes may have either extremely fast or slow processing styles. Both are biologically produced deficits that result in a person overlooking numerous cues, misinterpreting social transactions, and experiencing increased anxiety (E. H. Taylor, 2006a). Some of these clients will rapidly respond before a complete question or problem has been presented. The person fires an answer without waiting for additional information or properly processing the preceding events. Additionally, the client may repeatedly respond with the same or similar verbalizations and may become agitated if clarification is requested. Information processing will also be slowed, increased, or disrupted when an individual is having hallucinations and delusions.

ENVIRONMENTAL THEORY AND ITS RELATION TO THE BIOECOLOGICAL PERSPECTIVE

Environmental factors influence all human intra- and interpersonal activities. This is not a contradiction to the "biology first" rule. Human behaviors are created either from neurobiological factors that are largely free of immediate environmental influences or from bioecological interactions; however, in either case, the behavioral outcome is interpreted by the individual and others within an environmental context. Very frequently this interpretation then influences the next chain of internal and external perceptions, which in turn stimulates additional reactions (Bargh, 2007; Gazzaniga & Heatherton, 2009; Howard, 2006; Stoerig, 2007; Westen, 1999). A client's symptoms therefore may be generated almost completely by internal chemical activities, but may take on environmental characteristics. Paranoia, for example, is neurologically generated, but is expressed by the client in terms of suspicion. The interaction between abnormal brain functioning and ecological learning can result in issues such as a client believing that the government has placed microchips in her heads. The paranoia is caused by brain dysfunction, but the individual expresses the abnormal fears and beliefs in terms that link to the environment. However, it would be incorrect to interpret ecological factors as the cause of the paranoid thoughts in this example. Social workers should, however, attempt to determine if providing environmental supports together with doctor-prescribed medications help reduce the person's symptoms and distress.

When assessing environmental supports, it is important to remember that there may be other influencing factors, particularly when these supports do not produce the desired or expected results. When environmental manipulations fail, practitioners sometimes blame the client, family, or supporting agency without assessing alternative hypotheses for why the clinical efforts were unsuccessful. Social work interventions can also become ineffective because of biological or ecological variables. Often, environmental manipulations, skills training, education, or other therapies fail to work because

- the client's symptoms are driven principally by biology and do not respond to environmental supports;
- psychotropic medications are incorrectly prescribed, or the dosage needs to be adjusted;
- psychotropic medications are interacting with other substances;
- psychotropic medications have not had time to take effect;
- psychotropic medications cannot be taken without severe side effects;
- none of the psychotropic medications at any dose level reduces the person's symptoms;
- the individual and family were not given enough support, education, clear communications, or assistance to incorporate the environmental changes;
- the environmental task is too large, or requires more energy to perform than the client or family currently is able to generate;
- the suggested environmental changes violate the client's or family's cultural practices or belief systems;
- interacting systems exert power, place impermeable boundaries, or erect barriers that negate the positive environmental changes;
- the environmental manipulation targeted the wrong ecological system;
- the client does not have the cognitive skills or enough community support to carry out the environmental recommendations; or
- the client, family, and agencies have given up and no longer believe that positive change will occur.

Clinical ineffectiveness can be minimized when we use evidence-based assessments, actively listen to our clients and their families, and treat both a person's neurobiological illness and surrounding environments. The bioecological model helps social workers focus and plan interventions that continuously address a client's brain disorder and interacting home and community settings.

Ecological theory incorporates the major concepts found in general and open systems theories and establishes assumptions for identifying how living organisms develop, behave, and change (Haight & Taylor, 2007). It hypothesizes that growth, development, behavior, and learning occur from interactions among neurobiological and social-environmental systems and encoded memory. Together the interacting bioecological systems, along with memory, learned beliefs, creative thinking, and experience shape perceptions and psychological responses.

Only a thin line separates ecological and social learning theories (Haight & Taylor, 2007). From a clinical perspective, the two are separated more by their points of emphasis or focus than by clear rules. Perhaps the most important contribution made by ecological theory has been the recognition that social systems from the smallest to the largest influence each other's behavior: all activity creates some type of reciprocal impact throughout the systems (Haight & Taylor, 2007). Therefore, from an ecological perspective, observing internal relationships alone cannot assess a family because while a family has its own unique boundaries, communication style, relationships, and rules, it is not a "closed" system. Ecological theory teaches that individual and group behaviors can be more precisely understood by examining reciprocal responses that are shaped from interactions within and across other systems. The boundaries and influences of a parent's work or client's day care do not end when the individuals enter their home, yet many therapies treat individuals and families as if a solid, impregnable boundary exists between them and their related systems. Ecological theory challenges clinicians to assess how family behavior is shaped or influenced by public policies, economics, and support or stress from community systems, as well as events within the immediate family. Therefore, while severe mental disorders may stem largely from neurobiological abnormalities, the assessment and treatment of these illnesses always include ecological perspectives and interventions.

Ecological theory's relative newness, overly broad scope, and multiple perspectives have created differing points of emphasis among the professional communities (Bronfenbrenner & Morris, 1998; Germain, 1991; Germain & Gitterman, 1996; Gibson, 1979; Johnson, 2004; Moos, Finney, & Cronkite, 1990). This is not unusual; both psychoanalytic and cognitive theories are subdivided into numerous competing yet similar perspectives. Therefore, it is important to briefly and somewhat critically review how the differing environmental and systems treatment perspectives apply when treating serious mental illness.

CRITICAL PERSPECTIVES AND CONCEPTS: A REVIEW IN RELATION TO THE BIOECOLOGICAL PERSPECTIVE

Harriette Johnson (2004) was among the very first social work theorists and writers to link neurobiology and ecological systems for explaining mental disorders and to help establish ecological theory as one of the bioecological clinical model's cornerstones; however, Germain (1991) was one of the first to clearly incorporate ecological theory into social work practice and literature, nearly a decade earlier. This author's dissertation and professional development were greatly influenced by Carol Germain's (1991) pioneering work. Germain and Gitterman (1996) extended ecological theory into a social work practice model focused on human exchanges or interactions across the life course. These authors reject the idea that humans develop in linear time-ordered stages. People are not viewed as part of a life cycle, but rather as participants in a life built through interactional experiences. As a result, they hypothesize that development and behavior cannot be understood when separated from a person's history, culture, or social context. For these authors, pathology is almost completely explained by the impact of difficult or punishing environmental transactions, lost or unavailable resources, a poor fit between the client and social climate, oppression, and perceived or real social stress. This is an extremely useful model for treating clients who are not suffering from serious mental illness, such as new immigrants, and the assessment and intervention methods are extremely helpful for individuals who have problems stemming directly from social transactions, limited resources and power, underemployment, and a lack of acceptance by the majority culture, rather than neurobiological disorders. However, while the Germain and Gitterman model includes biological and cognitive systems, in practice it moves the social worker's assessment focus away from personal deficits to an examination of social interactions.

Germain at first viewed ecological concepts as a framework for guiding social work assessments and practice, rather than as an independent theory. In her early work she collaborated with Carol Meyer, who linked the ecological framework to traditional ego psychology and the psychoanalytic assessment process. This model permitted ego and unconscious psychological structures to be assessed within an interactive environmental context (Meyer, 1970).

Later, Germain shifted her focus to client strengths and moved away from pathology- or deficit-oriented models. Human problems were conceptualized as stemming from a client's inability to cope with stress. Germain and Gitterman (1997) believed that physical and emotional stress results when an individual's personal or environmental resources cannot resolve life events. Thus, from this perspective, a social work assessment is designed to measure environmental exchanges or interactions that explain the person's strengths, degree of environmental fit, and stress-related difficulties. The identified ecological stressor and nonadaptive coping skills are then treated by altering the environment or enhancing the client's personal strengths and power. Like the "strengths" model, Germain and Gitterman believe that through empowerment and enhancement of existing healthy skills, a client's problems can be resolved (Saleebey, 2011).

Building on these two ideas, the bioecological framework emphasizes treating the client's deficits or pathology, as well as focusing on the person's strengths. However, unlike either the Germain-Gitterman ecological framework or the "social work strengths" model, the bioecological approach teaches that deficits or pathology can stem from within the individual, environment, or both (E. H. Taylor, 2006b). When treating serious mental illness, deficits must be taken seriously and are often, though not always, treated before attention is given to the client's strengths. Some clients are so controlled and limited by psychosis, depression, or anxiety that meaningful strengths interventions cannot be applied until medications or other interventions have decreased the symptoms. In many cases, both strengths and deficit symptoms are treated simultaneously. Nonetheless, from a bioecological perspective, one almost always starts with treating symptoms and adds interventions for enhancing strengths as the client improves.

The concept of empowerment also takes on a different meaning when working with the seriously mentally ill. For severely mentally ill clients, empowerment is most often a treatment goal or outcome measurement rather than an intervention. Clients cannot actualize or use self-determination and empowerment interventions until evidence-based treatments have successfully reduced their symptoms and internal pain. When treating mental disorders, one cannot automatically accept the strengths model assumption that clients know what they need, but are prevented from succeeding because of poor technical skills, or social-economic barriers (Cowger, 1994). Self-empowerment and self-determination are important goals, but must often be achieved indirectly, particularly when an individual is severely ill. Moreover, acts of empowerment do not resolve neurobiologically related symptoms, nor do all seriously mentally ill individuals continuously have the cognitive capacity for decision-making, planning, and abstract problem-solving. Assuming that a person has the ability to make healthy choices, perceive realistic goals or needs, process alternatives, and use personal strengths for resolving problems could result in tragedy or death for a seriously mental ill client (E. H. Taylor, 2006b). Self-determination and empowerment

goals are dictated by the client's degree of illness, cognitive orientation and awareness, social judgment skills, and treatment responsiveness. Helping the client move
into the least restrictive environment required for treatment, obtain social justice,
and participate meaningfully in the treatment process are important social work
interventions. These acts do not in themselves, however, move the mentally ill client
toward empowerment, nor will they overcome the symptoms stemming from neurobiological illnesses. Nonetheless, helping clients move toward independence, assertive decision-making, self-actualization and control, and personal authority over their
lives is always a paramount treatment goal. The goal simply cannot outpace the individual's cognitive skills and psychiatric status.

The bioecological model also differs in that the primary efforts or focus of empowerment often shift among the client and that person's family, treatment facility, living
setting, or support group. Often, clients cannot be empowered until those who emotionally, financially, and physically support them are given personal and systems power.
This is not suggesting that client participation and empowerment is unimportant. It
does reflect two basic principles of this textbook. Clients with severe mental illness,
however, must first be protected and their symptoms reduced before vocational rehabilitation, self-determination, and empowerment become realistic intervention goals.
Second, the client's family and support systems may need to be empowered ahead of
the ill person. When clients cannot adequately care for themselves, others need tools,
creativeness, support, economic stability, and sanction to protect and nurture the individuals within a safe therapeutic environment. In addition, empowerment is viewed
as a goal that is achieved through decreasing the client's psychiatric symptoms, as well
as improving the person's strengths, quality of life, and socioeconomic opportunities.
This often, but not always, involves helping clients receive and take psychotropic medications. Treatments designed to empower or increase the mentally ill person's strengths
without first decreasing psychiatric deficits may not only fail, but may create additional
hardships for the client and family (Johnson, 2004; E. H. Taylor, 2006b). Unlike the
conditions of many other clients helped by social workers, serious long-term mental illness does not originate, nor does it usually continue, solely because of cultural, social,
political, or economic oppression (Johnson, 2004). Nonetheless, socioeconomic factors can decrease the effectiveness of medications and other interventions (Johnson,
2004; E. Taylor, 2003). For this reason the bioecological framework is equally tied to
the medical and social-interaction models.

Much of Germain's (1991) interactional framework can be traced back to the work
of Uri Bronfenbrenner. He and his associates demonstrated that social systems directly
influence how humans develop and behave throughout their lives (Bronfenbrenner,

1979; Bronfenbrenner & Morris, 1998). Building upon general and open systems theories, they hypothesized that social systems create hierarchical relationships. Smaller systems are conceptually seen as nesting, like Russian dolls, within larger systems. The nesting relationship symbolizes how systems are interdependent, maintain equilibrium, and incorporate or create power, boundaries, and mechanisms for exchanging energy. The role that social systems play in directing or causing behaviors through an environment's social climate has also been illustrated (Haight & Taylor, 2007; Moos et al., 1990).

Like individuals, ecological systems have common and unique factors that constitute their temperament. The ecological social climate is often described as the setting's "personality." From a bioecological perspective, the environment's personality is separate and distinct from the personality or temperament of the individuals acting and interacting within a defined social setting (Bronfenbrenner, 1979; Haight & Taylor, 2007). As a result, the setting's social climate and participating individuals within the setting are always in a reciprocal relationship and, to some extent, are changing each other (Bronfenbrenner, 1979; Bronfenbrenner & Morris, 1998).

Most of us accept that culture plays a key role in explaining how human behavior and temperament develop. Bronfenbrenner (1979, 1998), however, defines culture as an actual social system that plays a major role in forming personal and family growth. Dynamic interactions, along with individual and group experiences, are thought to explain how cultural systems shape social functioning. That is, cultural experiences define "truth," goals, roles, problem-solving methods, authority, rights, and social expectations, from conception to death (Haight & Taylor, 2007). Cultural-political systems, for instance, largely dictate how a woman cares for herself and her fetus during pregnancy. The force and power of experiential culture direct what the expecting mother eats, how much she works, how emotions are understood and handled, how the fetus is talked about, from whom medical help is received and when, and numerous other communicated rules of pregnancy.

Cultural expectations are also expressed and enforced through macro policy. Whether childbirth is the responsibility of a private individual or a community, for example, is dictated by the social context, rules, availability, and type of public support systems provided for the pregnant woman (Bronfenbrenner, 1979; Haight & Taylor, 2007). Likewise, macro systems determine the mentally ill person's right to treatment, as well as its availability, assessment methods, and interventions; they also determine how psychiatric problems are socially classified.

How these macro and micro cultures affect a person is furthermore determined, in part, by the occurrence of significant point-in-time or clusters of events (Bronfenbrenner, 1995). We would anticipate that early onset mental illness would affect the client and family differently than onset occurring later in life. In addition, because mental illness is less stigmatizing than it was 10 or 20 years ago, treatment received today is hopefully experienced more positively. Whether biological, cognitive, or environmental factors increase or decrease specific symptoms can also vary from one point in time to another. Therefore, how clients experience shifts in their biological and social systems partly depends on when the changes take place. Both positive behavior and symptoms are better understood when events are clearly placed in a cultural and point-in-time context.

The impact of culture is also modified by the amount of social density experienced by an individual at critical points in time. Social density is a measurement of the number of people who can meaningfully give an individual support and increased social skills (Haight & Taylor, 2007). As social workers, we need to keep in mind that enjoyable ongoing contact with others does not necessarily constitute expected clinical or treatment-oriented social density. From this textbook's perspective, clinical or treatment-oriented social density requires the following six continuous elements from professional, community, peer, and family helpers:

1. Client accepts helper as having authoritative information, meaningful skills for providing relief from pain and concerns, or an ability to provide meaningful resources.
2. Helpers must have the ability to develop a therapeutic relationship rather than a simple friendship with the client.
3. Throughout the relationship, the helpers must remain linked and must be able to survive disagreements with the client over time.
4. Helpers must possess, model, and teach social skills needed by the client.
5. Helpers must have an ability to differentially teach the needed skills in a manner that is both accepted and employed by the client.
6. Helpers must have the time and willingness to provide clinical social density to the client.

A good social work treatment plan assures that clients experience both social non-treatment and clinical social density.

Elevating culture to a social systems level has helped to clarify how environments influence human development. Unfortunately, how these dynamics are assessed and clinically used for either supporting the client's strengths or decreasing symptoms remains more philosophical than empirically documented. Social work has long realized that an individual's cultural experience is not always congruent with society's dominant culture. This is particularly true for disenfranchised and socially or economically oppressed clients whose cultural system is nested within the majority culture. Cultural variables that interact, compound, and sometimes conflict with dominant social norms can both positively and negatively shape a minority individual's attitudes, perceptions, beliefs, self-efficacy, and behaviors.

Assessing culturally learned issues on an individual level, however, becomes much more difficult and is susceptible to clinician bias. No measurement instrument or structured clinical interview currently exists for determining how cultural experiences are positively or negatively influencing a client's current behaviors. We also lack assessment tools for identifying learned behaviors that serve a cultural or beneficial purpose, but that may appear unusual or dysfunctional to untrained clinicians. Some Okanagan Band Aboriginal people in Canada experience guidance from animals that directly speak to them. Numerous Christians report having out-of-body spiritual occurrences, and experiencing the Holy Spirit speaking in unknown tongues through their personal voice. The social worker is obligated to identify and separate culturally induced behaviors such as these from neurobiological disorders. At a minimum, a social work cultural assessment can clarify the client's

- historical and current cultural beliefs, experiences, and learning;
- whether identified behaviors are symptoms of mental health needs or are anchored in a minority culture tradition;
- whether the behavior in question supports the client's well-being, or as a whole the person's social skills and abilities have decreased;
- goodness-of-fit within the person's culture among expressed goals, roles, social position, power, values, and beliefs;
- conflict and incongruence between learned cultural beliefs and social rules and majority community rules and expectations;
- social competence across historical and current ecological systems;
- learned skills and how these assets are valued by the historical and current cultures;
- goodness-of-fit among his or her problem-solving, perceptual, and communication styles within the historical and current cultures; and
- ability to transition between historical and original minority culture, current minority communities, and the dominant macro culture.

Historical culture refers to the original social styles, structures, conventions, rules, expectations, and systems experienced by an individual during key periods of life. We often have a dominant historical cultural system, but never a single continuous system. A person may live and die in a single community yet may have many overlapping, sometimes similar, but nevertheless different historical cultural systems. Simply labeling a person's historical culture as African-American, or Asian, or rural is misleading and indicates stereotyping. What must be assessed is how the client experienced, perceived, and interacted with past cultural systems at specifically identified periods of time. In addition, the social worker must contrast the client's historical or original cultural dynamics with behaviors, self-efficacy, beliefs, and perceptions that occur in the current majority ecological systems. Furthermore, a cultural systems assessment must consider interactions and the social impact created by prescribed social perception, goals, and roles.

Families, social classes, and macro policies define and, in some cases, dictate the goals, roles, social perceptions, and beliefs that an individual is expected to be incorporate. We all grow up experiencing, modifying, and sometimes emotionally battling these cultural expectations. Cognitive, emotional, and sometimes behavioral conflicts occur when an individual's goals, role perceptions, and beliefs substantially differ from those prescribed by the interacting micro and macro cultures.

While cultural conflicts can be painful, can cause negative emotional responses, and can decrease a person's productivity and quality of life, they cannot independently cause serious mental illness in most people. They can, however, increase and in some cases trigger biologically rooted symptoms. Conversely, serious mental illness alters how individuals experience, perceive, label, and recall cultural conflicts. A primary goal of the social work assessment, then, is to determine whether conflict between the person's historical culture and current social settings is increasing illness symptoms.

Through comparisons made by assessing an individual's historical and current cultural systems, the clinician may determine

- which personal strengths, deficits, goals, and role perceptions have changed;
- whether the person previously had, and has maintained, an ability to flexibly transition from one cultural setting to another;
- which behaviors, personality temperament traits, and cognitive styles have remained constant across multiple historical cultural systems;
- whether unique behaviors represent symptoms or relate to cultural experiences;
- how the dominant macro culture's power and influence have interacted with the client's historical and current cultural systems; and
- whether specific majority policies, diagnostic methods, professional biases, or other barriers are preventing fair, accurate, and adequate clinical treatment.

In addition to the concept of culture, it is important to understand how ecological theory explains or accounts for developmental growth and behavioral changes. Bronfenbrenner (1995) states that growth, change, and behavior result from reciprocal interactions that occur knowingly and unknowingly among individuals and their social systems. Reciprocal interaction implies that any activity impacts and changes both the individual involved and the environmental climate or setting in which the activity takes place. Forces of power and volatility then alter this dynamic interaction. While social exchanges truly create change in all of the actors, the power within and across systems is not distributed equally. Individuals cannot always independently overcome the powerful will and control exerted by a stronger system, subsystem, or individual. However, disproportional power can foster either a positive or negative force. Most cultures agree, for example, that it is unhealthy if children become more powerful than their parental caretakers. Conversely, a majority culture can use rules, laws, and customs to exclude, oppress, or harmfully control individuals belonging to a less powerful minority. For numerous reasons, people cannot always extract themselves from such pathological environments. Serious mental illness, for instance, can disrupt an individual's power and can entrap the person in a toxic punitive environment.

Social workers also need to understand that changes created from reciprocal interactions are volatile and therefore by nature often unpredictable. Specifically, this means that an observed change may be neither permanent nor present from one setting to another. Additionally, many clinicians have relied too heavily on the assumption that change within one part of a system creates change throughout the system. Not all social, emotional, and physical boundaries are permeable, nor does every new adaptation have the force, access, or influence required for fostering a meaningful system-wide change (Haight & Taylor, 2007). We must also keep in mind that a system may react or respond to internal shifts without fundamentally changing. Furthermore, complete systems can be subservient to the energy and power of much larger systems. Consequently, when treating serious mental illness, environmental and biological interventions may suddenly stop working or may have a positive result in one setting, but fail to decrease the client's symptoms within similar or overlapping ecological systems. Unfortunately, environmental treatments continue to be guided more by clinical wisdom, intuition, and through the problem-solving of trial and error than by researched indicators. As a result, more often than not, we cannot predict if manipulating a client's social environment will increase or decrease neuropsychiatric symptoms.

A relevant sociocultural approach which social work has yet to incorporate is that espoused by Vygotsky and his followers. This Russian researcher studied how environment shaped individuals and communities before World War II. More than any other theorist, Vygotsky attempted to bridge and unify biological, ecological, and cognitive-learning conceptualizations. He and his famous student Luria rejected psychoanalytic developmental explanations and focused on the importance of group interactions, culture, experiential learning, conscious cognition, and language for explaining behavior and growth (Wertsch, 1991). Vygotsky believed that our life skills result from interactions among genetics, social life, and the human's unique ability for using technical and psychological tools to accomplish complex abstract learning.

For Vygotsky, behavior is created from individual and group actions experienced within a social-cultural context and mediated or modified by the use of technical tools (Wertsch, 1991). "Technical tools" refers to societal support systems that help provide overt structure, meaning, and direction. For example, workers may use a labor union as a technical tool for discovering and creating new protective or economically sound behaviors. The individual removed from the labor union "tool" would become less dynamic and less socially developed.

Psychological skills and supports, on the other hand, are considered to be "sign tools." Included in the psychological or sign tools are cognitive processes like language, counting and mathematics, algebraic and symbolic thought, art, diagrams, writing, and other activities (Wertsch, 1991). While these are internal psychological and cognitive tools, they can develop and take on meaning only within a sociocultural context. Serious mental illness often decreases clients' ability or prevents them from learning to use both technical and psychological sign tools.

Vygotsky's conceptualization underscores the importance of concretely including cultural and social setting climates as key parts of an assessment. Mental capacities and symptoms may dramatically improve or decrease within the context of differing socio-cultural environments. This does not mean that given the right social context any person can perform any activity. It does, however, reflect a belief that abilities are neither concretely present nor depleted. Human skills, even in the presence of serious mental illness, shift and take different forms in relationship to genetic predisposition and environmental fit. Vygotsky taught that (1) the person's genetic and biological development must always be considered or analyzed; (2) higher mental functioning is developed from social-cultural interactions; and (3) human actions on individual and group bases are mediated or facilitated by tools and signs (Wertsch, 1991).

To illustrate this concept, Vygotsky suggested that skills be measured from what became known as the zone of proximal development (ZPD). The original intent of the ZPD was to establish a child's natural or independent problem-solving skills and then determine the youth's higher or upper potential for problem-solving when guided by an adult or more capable peer (Wertsch, 1991). This technique attempts to measure intelligence and social skills from an achievement or functional perspective, rather than through a test of previously or independently learned knowledge. The zone of proximal development assigns a task to an individual and measures the difference between what is accomplished before and after expert teaching or problem-solving assistance is provided (Hedegaard, 1992). Vygotsky believed that true intelligence was reflected by the amount a person improved within an enriched or positively controlled environment. The zone of proximal development can be creatively adapted for assessing a seriously mentally ill client's current and potential social or vocational functioning across environmental settings. Why social workers have not developed or standardized Vygotsky-type instruments for assessing a client's goodness-of-fit and potential for negotiating multiple settings and cultural change is puzzling.

Another early pioneer who recognized the interdependence between biology and society was the Russian neuropsychologist Luria, who spent much of his life exploring how the human brain works and interacts with the environment. He was one of the first researchers to hypothesize that the brain cannot be studied or understood outside the social context (Luria, 1976). Today this appears to be only partly true. The living brain's structure and function can now be actively studied with magnetic resonance imaging (MRI) and other scanning instruments. Furthermore, both Luria and Vygotsky found that the direct relationship between neurodevelopment and environment does not always exist (Luria, 1976; Wertsch, 1991). There are few indications, for example, that shared or unique social environments stimulate the brain to dysfunction and cause schizophrenia (E. Taylor, 2003; Torrey, Bowler, Taylor, & Gottesman, 1994). One must also remember that the brain is changing as a person develops severe mental illness, and symptoms may not reflect or respond to the social environment.

This is not to say that the environment is not without power, but it is by no means consistent. Studies demonstrate that enriched and impoverished environments affect the neurological functioning and behavior of animals (E. H. Taylor & Cadet, 1989). These neurological changes, however, do not resemble the brain abnormalities generally documented in humans with serious mental illness. The word "generally" is used here because there have been some similarities between changes in the brains of mistreated animals and the neurological structures of people with post-traumatic stress disorders (Farmer, 2009; Haight & Taylor, 2007). Furthermore, child maltreatment not only has the possibility of abnormally altering the brain, but can also trigger hyperarousal and dissociative behaviors (Farmer, 2009).

Both the social environment and the brain appear to interact with and have an impact on the other (Farmer, 2009; Haight & Taylor, 2007). Additionally, one of these forces will often dominate, control, or offset the other's influence (Bronfenbrenner, 1979;

Farmer, 2009; Gibson, 1979; Haight & Taylor, 2007). We have all impulsively bought products because advertising created an environment that momentarily reduced our attention to our social judgment. Yet, at other times we cleverly employ knowledge and experience from our memories in order to escape the most seductive sales pitch.

It is important to keep in mind that the client's biological and environmental systems do not share equal power and influence. As the severity level for any serious mental illness increases, the ability for environmental treatments to create significant change decreases. Sometimes it is helpful to picture mental illness creating a dynamic unpredictable biosocial gestalt that can suddenly shift and change the client's strengths, symptoms, and treatment response patterns. Without warning, medications or previously positive environments may cease being helpful. In part, social work is responsible for quickly detecting changes in the client's biosocial gestalt and immediately refocusing the treatment goals and targets. This requires a flexible clinical assessment style that views the client's biological and social systems as interacting but unequal forces.

Between the late 1970s and early 1990s, Gibson performed research that greatly advanced the ecological approach, and specifically documented how human "actions" serve as a developmental catalyst. Like Vygotsky, Gibson teaches that experiential learning, guided by actions that interact within a social context, directs and "pushes" development. Her studies demonstrate that infant motor skills improve more from ever-increasing environmental actions and experiences than cognitive knowledge or random learning (Gibson, 1979).

Perhaps more important for social work is Gibson's hypothesis that social skills develop and change. Throughout our life we must learn to shift our behavior and appropriately participate within multiple systems. By performing actions within an environmental setting, we learn the accepted and anticipated behavioral boundaries. This process may be thought of as identifying a setting's perceived or defined variance (Haight & Taylor, 2007). Children, for example, learn that the defined variance for playing with toys is much wider than experimenting with matches. They may also quickly identify that the defined variance for making noise is greater at their grandparents than at home, place of worship, or preschool. Identifying, acting on, and adjusting to defined variance within and across environmental systems stimulates social development. We are "forced" to grow and change when the defined variance is expectedly or unexpectedly shifted. Furthermore, over time every environmental setting will modify the expectations and rules for participation and behavior. The ecological system's shifting and redefining of variance starts at birth and continues through the life course. Regrettably, severe mental disorders often limit our clients' ability to shift and adjust their behavior to fit the changing ecological boundaries and variance.

TURNING THEORY INTO PRACTICE: APPLYING THE BIOECOLOGICAL TREATMENT MODEL

The bioecological model provides a framework for treating serious mental illness across diagnoses without sacrificing individualized client needs. It also defines social work as the treatment team member most responsible for understanding symptoms within an environmental context, assessing the client across family, community, and other micro-systems, and directing non-medical interventions. This section briefly examines how ecological and social learning theories are translated into clinical interventions.

The first step in the bioecological treatment process requires social workers to examine their own beliefs concerning serious mental illness. Ideas and beliefs can become automatic and neurologically encapsulated when they have been extensively practiced and cognitively rehearsed. In the past, we have allowed numerous incorrect psychological theories to cloud our clinical judgment and stigmatize the client. Social workers have a professional obligation to ensure that outdated and punitive concepts are not shaping treatment responses or attitudes.

Beliefs

It has long been known that culture, education, information, and personal experiences shape our beliefs, goals, and values. These cognitive beliefs in turn guide our social perceptions and modify our ability to incorporate new information (Smith & Kosslyn, 2007). Furthermore, beliefs have the ability to justify goals and selectively reject factual information that contradicts our cultural or learned perspective (Gazzaniga, 1985; E. H. Taylor & Cadet, 1989). Successfully treating individuals with serious mental illness requires understanding and assessing the relationships among contextual social behaviors and beliefs held by the social worker, treatment team, community, and family. From an ecological and social learning perspective (E. Taylor, 2003), beliefs largely define a therapeutic environment's

- purpose and ecological boundaries (treatment scope);
- responsibilities and rules;
- worker, client, and family roles;
- interventions;
- focus of treatment and change agents; and
- each system specific and shared power and responsibility for accountability to others.

Social workers need to keep in mind that we assess, understand, and treat behavior not only with researched facts, but also with culturally and educationally learned biases. A clinician's interventions, empathy, and communication style will largely depend on how mental illness is defined and understood. Furthermore, our clinical beliefs are overtly and covertly transmitted to clients and their families. Before a single verbal statement is made by the treatment team, families often sense that they are being blamed rather than being given advice for improved relationships with the ill member. Imagine that you are a family member of a seriously mentally ill person. How will you emotionally respond to a social worker who implies that your behavior may have caused the mental illness, or at least is perpetuating the pathology? Most of us would prefer for the clinician to clearly articulate how the person's neurobiological disorder causes him or her to incorrectly interpret information, or to use poor judgment when certain stressors appear. As a clinical social worker, this author has consistently found that families want to be supportive, but need help understanding how mental illness changes what a person perceives, understands, and experiences. Clinical relationships always improve when individuals are convinced that they are not viewed as having caused the mental illness (E. Taylor, 2003; Torrey et al., 1994).

Using a bioecological model also requires understanding that micro systems, organizations, and community agencies develop their own beliefs about mental illness. Therefore, a social worker's responsibility is not only to assess an individual, but also to analyze the communities, agencies, schools, workplaces, and religious organizations that interact with the client and family. We do not want clients engaged by agencies that blame the family, prescribe inappropriate treatments, or create frustrations. The bioecological model requires that we frame the neurobiological disorder as helped or hurt by overlapping cultural settings. Our clients and families want us to understand and proactively help them negotiate ever-changing treatment and support environments.

Western culture has taught that mental illness is a reflection of inadequate parenting, poor values, lack of religious training, or self-choices. Historical beliefs make it difficult for families, educators, and religious leaders to accept that behaviors related to a mental disorder are symptoms of a treatable neurobiological illness (E. H. Taylor, 2006b). This is especially true when young children and adolescents develop a disorder (E. Taylor, 2003). In part, punitive attitudes occur because neurobiological explanations for mental illness are relatively new and have not become a part of our national culture. Therefore, social workers are responsible for assessing the beliefs about mental illness among professional service providers, communities, educators, agencies, families, and extended family members. Furthermore, supervisors are encouraged to survey how clients and families perceive their clinicians' beliefs about mental disorders, treatment, and recovery. New information becomes part of one's belief system only through practice, examination, and social support. A social worker may intellectually accept the newer neuropsychiatric information, but may knowingly or unknowingly rely on outdated beliefs for developing practice interventions. This becomes an even greater possibility when clients and families are difficult or distant, or when they are responding from a different cultural paradigm. Treatment organizations must also provide a structure for helping clinicians and support staff actualize positive beliefs concerning serious mental illness. The social worker and supervisor are jointly responsible for ensuring that therapeutically sound methodology, rather than previously learned injurious belief, is guiding the clinical interventions. Formal and peer social work supervision seldom includes neurobiological information and new research.

Perceived Variance

Within each environmental setting, clients learn to anticipate a range of expected behaviors and responses that are enforced by more powerful individuals. Ecologists refer to this as the "defined variance" or "expected-perceived variance" (Gibson, 1979; Haight & Taylor, 2007). It is hypothesized that the defined variance concept explains how human development and behavioral changes occur throughout the life cycle (Gibson, 1979). A person's behavior will change if the allowed normalized responses within an environment increase, decrease, or are redefined (Gibson, 1979; Haight & Taylor, 2007). A toddler, for example, may perceive that the variance for pulling kitchen pots and pans from the cabinet and onto the floor is very narrow at home, but widens when visiting his grandmother. Ecologists argue that learning to adjust behavior from one setting to another develops into an internalized sense of system boundaries and rules. The child learns to automatically regulate behavior as the variance shifts within and across different settings. As a result, human neurodevelopment occurs experientially. Furthermore, ecologists argue that this represents an intrinsic assimilation of environmental information rather than classical cognitive learning (Bronfenbrenner, 1979; Gibson, 1979; Haight & Taylor, 2007). It is thought that we ecologically learn by assimilating experiences that either match or conflict with our historical and current cultural perceptions.

Severely mentally ill clients frequently cannot interpret the defined variance or spontaneously alter their behaviors in order to adjust to changes, which may explain why some client's symptoms improve when they are hospitalized or placed in day treatment programs. Treatment centers provide a manageable concrete environment that limit shifts in the defined variance. The reduced variance may help clients decrease symptoms, better predict acceptable behaviors, and gain a sense of personal control. Theoretically, the interaction between the therapeutic environment and the client's neurobiological systems creates a dynamic intervention and decreases the person's symptoms.

Assessing and Changing Perceived Variance

Regardless of whether facing physical or neurobiological challenges, families are forced to learn new ways of communicating and working together. Illness disrupts a system's equilibrium, which in turn makes changing boundaries and perceived variance a necessity. In most cases, families need help to overcome obstacles and learn new boundaries. After all, change is difficult, and even harder during a crisis created by the onset of a mental disorder. Changes in perceived variance, however, can be assisted if the family is gently guided by the social worker. It is helpful, for example, to simply ask the family the following:

1. What do they know or think about the client's situation?
2. What have professionals told them about mental disorders?
3. What do they as a family believe about mental illness?
4. Are there extended family members or important friends who have a different belief?
5. How has the mental illness of a family member created special or new problems for the family?
6. What is their biggest worry or concern?
7. What they have tried?
8. What has worked or failed?
9. What family rules must be followed, and what rules can be set aside?

Once it is clear that the family has experienced contradictory and disruptive variance, the social worker needs to stop the client assessment and focus on the family's experience. Interpreting the observed conflict or concerns helps some families. Simply stating "you feel confused and frightened" can provide comfort and move the family and worker a step closer to a relationship. We also want to assure that each family member's feelings, beliefs, and concerns are identified and are provided meaningful attention. In a stressful meeting, it is easy to overlook children or more silent members. In addition, every family member deserves knowing the social worker's treatment responsibilities, limitations, and guiding beliefs. When negative emotions are expressed about the assessment process as well as the need for change, a clinician may want to slow the assessment process and listen. Increasing emotions and anger can sometimes be defused by stating, "It seems like my questions are hurtful; that is my fault, something I do not want to do. Help me understand your perspective; I want to listen. Have discussions with mental health workers in the past helped or disappointed you?"

It is also helpful to have each family member identify his or her concerns and difficulty in defining the variance within the mental health community. When the family quickly wants to move to the client's symptoms and behavior, it is useful to state, "But I am also concerned about you, and our ability to understand each other. I really want to learn about the problems facing your family member, but first tell me a little about how your previous experiences with mental health clinics or therapists have affected each of you—Mr. Jones, would you be kind enough to go first?" These methods help family members identify a new therapeutic variance and assist the social worker to more rapidly understand and empathize with each individual.

Assessing Social Climate

Settings, such as homes, schools, religious centers, treatment agencies, and shopping malls, develop their own individualized "personality" or ecological climate (Bronfenbrenner & Morris, 1998; Haight & Taylor, 2007; Moos et al., 1990). A setting's climate may be similar to that of other settings but is always unique and is considered separate from the temperament and skills of the individuals interacting within the setting. A climate is defined by concrete physical characteristics, which are generally visible and consist of elements like size, space, structure, furnishings, color, sound levels, and location, and abstract factors including the intangible rules, goals, power distribution, role expectations, cultural beliefs, allowed variance, and conflict tolerance found within the setting. We assess each setting to discover how the social climate is differentially impacting the family as a unit and the members as individuals. The bioecological model assumes that a setting's climate changes human behavior, and the individuals in turn alter the environmental climate. From a treatment perspective, we want to determine the amount that social climate accounts for symptoms and unacceptable behaviors.

A client's ability to tolerate social climates is disturbed by mental disorders. The amount of experienced difficulty, however, is not equal across all settings, and some environments may be neutral or even increase wellness. Minor changes within a poorly tolerated setting may decrease the client's behavioral symptoms, but most often will not completely resolve the person's symptoms.

It is important to assess symptoms and strengths within and across all settings that are negotiated by the client. Discovering which environments are the most helpful, or toxic, for the client may aid the family and treatment team to manipulate symptoms, prevent hospitalizations, and decrease medication requirements. An ecological climate assessment has the potential for identifying specific settings that provide the best thera-peutic fit and for decreasing the client's need for hospitalizations. This also gives the social worker specific information that can be used for teaching interventions to the family, school, case managers, and community agencies. We cannot forget, however, that neurobiological problems can be progressive and may increase even in ideal envi-ronments. Therefore, ecological climate assessment needs to be repeated at approxi-mately 6-month intervals or after each hospitalization. Both the person's illness and the social climates can be in constant change.

A serious mental illness can also cause individuals to form false beliefs and incor-rect perceptions about their settings. What an individual reports to have witnessed or experienced in a setting may or may not be correct. Distortion of beliefs occurs not only with clients who have hallucinations. In varying amounts, all forms of mental ill-ness can change perceptual skills, abstract thinking, problem-solving skills, memory, and information processing. Additionally, it is not uncommon to encounter clients who develop perseveration problems within some settings, but not in others. Perseveration symptoms consist of repetitive responses to unrelated stimuli or repetitive behaviors that the client cannot voluntarily stop (Barlow, 2002; E. H. Taylor, 2006a). It is possible for these symptoms to be unrelated to the social climate and unresponsive to ecological manipulations. Nonetheless, a clinical decision of this type can only be made after an environmental assessment across all settings has been completed. Often symptoms can be reduced by creating an improved fit between the client and environmental setting.

Change Agents

Understanding how a theory hypothesizes that behavior changes and human develop-ment occurs is exceedingly important. Without this information, one cannot develop specific interventions and target the factors responsible for the dynamic change. Social learning techniques attempt to modify, remove, increase, or create new thinking pat-terns (E. H. Taylor, 2006a, 2006b). Change is hypothesized to occur when the environ-ment, behavior, emotions, or cognitive thoughts stimulate new learning or reinforce previously unused healthy knowledge. To accomplish these goals, social workers employ methods that incorporate cognitive rehearsals, practice, role-play, imaging, suggestions, advice, education, and observations.

Social ecologists believe that positive change is brought about by one or a combination of the following (Haight & Taylor, 2007):

- interactions among individuals, subsystems, and system;
- power and energy held by individuals, subsystems, or systems being directed toward or removed from a more vulnerable person or system;
- the defined or perceived variance within a subsystem or system changing; and
- environmental experiences altering an individual's internal self-perceptions and external systems perceptions.

Interventions

Neither the etiology nor illness course for serious mental illness can be explained by ecological theory. It does, however, provide an excellent framework when combined with medical interventions for directing the client's rehabilitation treatment, organizing case management priorities, and supporting the family. The bioecological model approaches assessment and treatment differently than traditional psychosocial and many ecological perspectives. Behavior is not considered a byproduct of psychological conflict, but rather as a dynamic interaction among a person's neurodevelopmental status, cognitive skills, physical health, affect, and immediate and past environmental systems. That is, the interventions attempt to modify behavior by altering a client's current biological, cognitive, and social contextual functioning. One component may be emphasized, but both the biological and social realities must be manipulated before treatment will produce maximum outcomes. The bioecological model assumes that treatment will be less successful if environmental manipulations are overemphasized and the neurobiology of an illness is minimized.

The ability for either biological or social components to influence behavior suggests several rules for treating seriously mentally ill clients. Deterioration of social skills and cognition, for example, does not independently indicate problems within the family, school, or community systems. Serious mental illness can cause the client to suddenly have increased symptoms within highly stable and supportive surroundings. Symptoms may increase and decrease independent of the client's social context (Johnson, 2004; E. H. Taylor, 2006a).

The bioecological understanding of serious mental illness provides a meaningful framework for assessing and intervening with clients and families. It simultaneously respects the treatment team and clarifies the unique aspects of the social worker's role. In addition, the model frees social workers from the expectation of "curing" serious mental illness through talk therapies. Clinicians are allowed to focus on methods for reducing symptom and pain, improving services and removing barriers, increasing quality of life, and employing evidence-based interventions.

REFERENCES

Bargh, J. A. (2007). Social psychological approaches to consciousness. In P. D. Zelazo, M. Moscovitch, & E. Thompson (Eds.), *The Cambridge Handbook of Consciousness* (pp. 555–569). Cambridge, UK: Cambridge University Press.

Barlow, D. H. (2002). *Anxiety and Its Disorders* (2nd ed.). New York: Guilford Press.

Bronfenbrenner, U. (1979). *The Ecology of Human Development: Experiments by Nature and Design.* Cambridge, MA: Harvard University Press.

Bronfenbrenner, U. (1995). Developmental ecology through space and time: A future perspective. In P. Moen, G. H. Jr. and Elder Jr. and K. Lüsher (eds), *Examining Lives in Context: Perspectives on the Ecology of Human Development* (pp. 619–647). Washington, DC: American Psychological Association.

Bronfenbrenner, U., & Morris, P. A. (1998). The ecology of developmental processes. In R. M. Lerner (Ed). *Handbook of Child Psychology* (5th ed., Vol. 1, pp. 993–1028). New York: Wiley.

Brown, G. W. (2000). Emotion and clinical depression: An environmental view. In M. Lewis & J. M. Haviland-Jones (Eds.), *Handbook of Emotions* (2nd ed., pp. 75–90). New York: Guilford Press.

Cowger, C. D. (1994). Assessing client strengths: Clinical assessment for client empowerment. *Social Work, 39,* 262–267.

Davison, G. C., Neale, J. M., Blankstein, K. R., & Flett, G. L. (2002). *Abnormal Psychology.* Etobicoke, ON: John Wiley & Sons Canada.

Ebstein, R. P., Benjamin, J., & Belmaker, R. H. (2003). Behavioral genetics, genomics, and personality. In R. Plomin, J. C. Defries, I. W. Craig, & P. McGuffin (Eds.), *Behavioral Genetics in the Postgenomic Era* (pp. 365–388). Washington, DC: American Psychological Association.

Fabiani, M., & Wee, E. (2001). Age-related changes in working memory and frontal lobe functioning. In C. A. Nelson & M. Luciana (Eds.), *Handbook of Developmental Cognitive Neuroscience* (pp. 473–488). Cambridge, MA: MIT Press.

Farmer, R. (2009). *Neuroscience and Social Work Practice: The Missing Link.* Thousand Oaks, CA: Sage.

Forgas, J., & Vargas, P. T. (2000). The effects of mood on social judgment and reasoning. In M. Lewis & J. M. Haviland-Jones (Eds.), *Handbook of Emotions* (2nd ed., pp. 350–367). New York: Guilford Press.

Gazzaniga, M. S. (1985). *The Social Brain: Discovering the Networks of the Mind.* New York: Basic Books.

Gazzaniga, M. S., & Heatherton, T. F. (2009). *Psychological Science* (3rd ed.). New York: W. W. Norton.

Germain, C. B. (1991). *Human Behavior in the Social Environment: An Ecological View.* New York: Columbia University Press.

Germain, C. B., & Gitterman, A. (1996). *The Life Model of Social Work Practice* (2nd ed.). New York: Columbia University Press.

Gibson, J. J. (1979). *The Ecological Approach to Visual Perception.* Boston: Houghton Mifflin.

Haight, W., & Taylor, E. H. (2007). *Human Behavior for Social Work Practice: A Developmental-Ecological Framework.* Chicago: Lyceum Books.

Hedegaard, M. (1992). The zone of proximal development as basis for instruction. In L. C. Moll (Ed.), *Vygotsky and Education* (pp. 349–371). Cambridge, UK: Cambridge University Press.

Hobson, J. A. (1994) *The Chemistry of Conscious States.* New York: Little Brown.

Howard, P. J. (2006). *The Owner's Manual for the Brain.* Austin, TX: Bard Press.

Hubble, M. A., Duncan, B. L., & Wampold, B. E. (2010). Introduction. In B. L. Duncan, S. D. Miller, B. E. Wampold, & H. M. A. (Eds.), *The Heart and Soul of Change* (2nd ed., pp. 23–46). Washington, DC: American Psychological Association.

Johnson-Laird, P. N., & Oatley, K. (2000). Cognitive and social construction in emotions. In M. Lewis & J. M. Haviland-Jones (Eds.), *Handbook of Emotions* (2nd ed., pp. 458–475). New York: Guilford Press.

Johnson, H. (2004). *Psyche and Synapse Expanding Worlds: The Role of Neurobiology in Emotions, Behavior, Thinking, and Addiction for Non-Scientists* (2nd ed.). Greenfield, MA: Deerfield Publishing.

Kalidindi, S., & McGuffin, P. (2003). The genetics of affective disorders: Present and future. In R. Plomin, J. C. Defries, I. W. Craig, & P. McGuffin (Eds.), *Behavioral Genetics in the Postgenomic Era* (pp. 481–501). Washington, DC: American Psychological Association.

Kihlstrom, J. F. (2002). The unconscious. In V. S. Ramachandran (Ed.), *Encyclopedia of the Human Brain* (Vol. 4, pp. 635–646). San Diego, CA: Academic Press.

LeDoux, J. (2002). *Synaptic Self*. New York: Viking.

LeDoux, J. E., & Phelps, E. A. (2000). Emotional networks in the brain. In M. Lewis & J. M. Haviland-Jones (Eds.), *Handbook of Emotions* (2nd ed., pp. 157–172). New York: Guilford Press.

Lieberman, M. D. (2007). The X- and C-systems: The neural basis of automatic and controlled social cognition. In E. Harmon-Jones & P. Winkielman (Eds.), *Social Neuroscience* (pp. 290–315). New York: Guilford Press.

Luby, J., Belden, A., Botteron, K., Marrus, N., Harms, M. P., Babb, C., . . . Barch, D. (2013). The effects of poverty on childhood brain development: The mediating effect of caregiving and stressful life events. *Journal of the American Medical Association Pediatrics, 167*(12), 1135–1142.

Luria, A. R. (1976). *The Working Brain: An Introduction to Neuropsychology*. New York: Basic Books.

Marshall, W. L. (2003). Theoretical perspectives on abnormal behavior. In P. Firestone & W. L. Marshall (Eds.), *Abnormal Psychology*. Toronto: Prentice Hall.

Meyer, C. H. (1970). *Social Work Practice: A Response to the Urban Crisis*. New York: Free Press.

Moos, R. H., Finney, J., & Cronkite, R. (1990). *Alcoholism Treatment: Context, Process, and Outcome*. New York: Oxford University Press.

Paris, J. (2005). *The Fall of an Icon: Psychoanalysis and Academic Psychiatry*. Toronto: University of Toronto Press.

Saleebey, D. (2011). *The Strengths Perspective in Social Work Practice* (6th ed.). Boston: Allyn & Bacon.

Sampaio, R. C., & Truwit, C. L. (2001). Myelination in the developing human brain. In C. A. Nelson & M. Luciana (Eds.), *Handbook of Developmental Cognitive Neuroscience* (pp. 35–44). Cambridge, MA: MIT Press.

Smith, E. E., & Kosslyn, S. M. (2007). *Cognitive Psychology: Mind and Brain*. Upper Saddle River, NJ: Pearson Prentice Hall.

Stoerig, P. (2007). Hunting the ghost: Toward a neuroscience of consciousness. In P. D. Zelazo, M. Moscovitch, & E. Thompson (Eds.), *The Cambridge Handbook of Consciousness* (pp. 707–730). Cambridge, UK: Cambridge University Press.

Sue, D., Sue, D. W., & Sue, S. (2006). *Understanding Abnormal Behavior* (8th ed.). Boston: Houghton Mifflin.

Taylor, E. (2003). Practice methods for working with children who have biologically based mental disorders: A bioecological model. *Families in Society: The Journal of Contemporary Human Services, 84*(1), 39–50.

Taylor, E. H. (2006a). *Atlas of Bipolar Disorders*. London: Taylor & Francis Group.

Taylor, E. H. (2006b). The weaknesses of the strengths model: Mental illness as a case in point. *Best Practices in Mental Health: An International Journal, 2*, 1–29.

Taylor, E. H., & Cadet, J. L. (1989). Social intelligence, a neurological system? *Psychological Reports, 64*, 423–444.

Torrey, E. F., Bowler, A. E., Taylor, E. H., & Gottesman, I. I. (1994). *Schizophrenia and Manic Depressive Disorder*. New York: Basic Books.

US Department of Health and Human Services. (1999). *Mental Health: A Report of the Surgeon General*. Washington, DC: U. S. Public Health Service.

Wertsch, J. V. (1991). *Voices of the Mind: A Sociocultural Approach to Mediated Action*. Cambridge, MA: Harvard University Press.

Westen, D. (1999). *Psychology: Mind, Brain, & Culture* (2nd ed.). New York: John Wiley & Sons.

THE FAMILY AS TREATMENT PARTNERS

Moving Beyond Education and Coping

Serious mental illness crashes into each family member's reality, stressing his or her communications, relationships, work habits, beliefs, and, for some, spiritual faith and practices. Family members struggle with emotional pain, and experience hardships in nearly all of life's domains. Numerous factors (see Box 2.1) determine how mental illness affects and shapes family behaviors. Consequently, predicting where to initially start the process of helping a family is difficult.

While therapeutic guidelines are helpful, in reality what the family and ill member perceive as their most urgent problem should always direct and shape our professional methods. Often, however, a social worker's first family intervention consists of compassionately

- explaining what is known and not known about the ill member's psychiatric situation;
- addressing the family's questions and concerns about the immediate situation;
- validating each member's pain;
- reducing fears;
- assuring realistic hope;
- providing access to the treatment team;
- assessing the family's individual and collective skills;
- helping the family plan, organize, and manage the multiple tasks required to care for the ill member and each other;
- understanding each member's immediate needs;

- helping the family determine what they want to tell extended family, work/ school, and friends;
- ensuring that key family members understand immediate treatment requirements, and that the prescribed treatment regimen can be carried out; and
- providing emotional and concrete support.

BOX 2.1

FACTORS SHAPING FAMILY REACTIONS TO MENTAL ILLNESS

While this list is not comprehensive, it nonetheless highlights the number and variety of ecological factors that social workers must help families address.

- previous experience with mental illness
- number of family members experiencing mental illness
- factual knowledge of mental disorders
- religious and cultural beliefs about mental illness
- perceived stigma
- feelings of inadequacy to care for ill family member
- fears that care for the ill member will cheat or cause neglect of other family members
- disruptions and disputes among marital partners
- educational, behavioral, legal, emotional, physical, or financial needs of non-ill family members
- actual stigma in community, school, or workplace
- family and extended family's response and level of support
- demands placed by extended family, work/school, friends, and organizations
- financial support and economic stability
- health insurance coverage
- availability of transportation
- amount of time available for responding to ill family member's appointments and needs
- availability and experience of treatment providers
- personal feelings about treatment providers
- over-belief or lack of belief in treatment providers
- understanding of, beliefs about, and adherence to medication and other treatment regimens
- availability of community services
- physical health, energy, and stamina of family members
- permanency of housing
- home privacy and space issues created by or increased by mentally ill family member's behaviors or needs

- fear of being harmed by mentally ill family member
- fear that mentally ill family member will accidentally injure or kill self
- fear that ill family member will purposely self-injure or attempt suicide
- fear that ill family member will be harmed by bullies or unknown people
- fear that ill family member will run away from home and become homeless
- fear that ill family member will become disoriented and unable to find way home
- fear that ill family member will be arrested and imprisoned
- fear that ill family member's carelessness when smoking will start a fire
- fear that ill family member will do something that causes a lawsuit or loss of friends

Most families need concrete services and help, in addition to understanding and empathy. Concrete support is a clinical method that uses available services to alleviate problems and hardships. The word "clinical" is purposely used. Often social workers minimize the skills that are required in order to provide tangible services. However, concrete services are not simply handed out, but rather spring from a systematic assessment. Furthermore, timing, communication skills, and presentation methods are often needed to help families accept services. Keep in mind that families must be understood within the context of their culture (Knight & Ridgeway, 2008). Accepting help and concrete service may be a new experience for many, and it may go against their learned ideas of self and family responsibilities. The same skills used in psychotherapy, family therapy, counseling, and other clinical methods are employed when providing concrete services to support a client or family. An important mindset for social workers is believing that advocacy, psychosocial education, and concrete support are elements of clinical treatment (Taylor, 1995). In addition, like other mental health interventions, concrete services are used to foster short- and long-term positive behavioral and emotional client change. By providing needed services, we are treating the environment, which allows family members space for self-care and healing (Munger, 1998). Therefore, when used correctly, concrete services become a clinical technique employed by social workers for not only supporting, but also changing families and individuals.

For families of the seriously mentally ill, concrete services can range from ensuring survival needs, such as housing, food, and transportation, to linking individuals with empathetic, friendly visitors and appropriate religious or other spiritual leaders. Families adjusting to a mental health crisis often need assistance in helping employers, schools, or other institutions to understand why the various members must change their work hours and use personal leave and vacation time. In some cases, families must be actively represented so that they can preserve their jobs while taking leave, often without pay.

The social worker must also be available for re-explaining the illness or treatment plan on behalf of the family. Comprehending and internalizing technical information during highly stressful times are always difficult. Telling others about experiencing mental problems can be difficult and even fear provoking. Therefore, it is a good practice to always ask a family if they need help communicating clinical information to the extended family and significant individuals within the community. Communication assistance may consist of helping the family shape what to say, role rehearsing difficult verbal situations, talking on behalf of the family with identified individuals, or being with the family when a specific person or persons are told about the mental health problem. In addition, while advocacy is an important clinical technique, the therapeutic provision of concrete services requires more than simply representing the family. Essential to the intervention is a requirement for the social worker to oversee, supervise, and/or ensure delivery of required services. Though advocacy is sometimes needed as a means of gaining services, the therapeutic use of helping a family in need of transportation, for example, is not advocacy, but rather the act of providing timely and reliable transportation. It only becomes advocacy when an action plan must be developed to gain the needed service. As social workers, we often connect families to services as part of our case management responsibilities, and sometimes we must develop an assertive advocacy plan to gain appropriate support for the family. However, far too often social workers believe that because they advocated for a client their job is finished, whether or not the service is received. Advocacy without results is neither clinical nor therapeutic.

Emotional-cognitive support is as important as concrete clinical services for helping families. A primary goal of emotional supportive interventions is to help families make sense and meaning of mental illness, and regain their equilibrium. Box 2.2 lists some of the ways in which social workers provide emotional-cognitive support to families.

Emotional-cognitive assistance attempts to improve client functioning by specifically targeting each family member's knowledge, emotions, social perceptions, working memory, beliefs, or social skills. Furthermore, the intervention builds on each person's past strengths and experiences. However, emotional-cognitive work can also create client change by teaching new skills, reframing destructive thoughts and perceptions into positive cognitions, and supporting or challenging established belief systems.

Support sometimes includes planned and carefully prepared clinical case management and advocacy for either specific family members or the family as a whole.

BOX 2.2

EXAMPLES OF CLINICAL EMOTIONAL-COGNITIVE SUPPORT

Clinical emotional-cognitive support is designed to help family members
- make sense and meaning of developing a mental disorder;
- better understand mental illness and the treatment process;
- accept immediate and limited choices;
- identify personal and family strengths;
- accept limitations within family members and the family unit; accept the family member with a disorder as a unique and important person rather than as a defective individual;
- receive assistance without guilt;
- increase coping skills;
- develop realistic hope and reject unfounded interventions;
- find the right words for explaining mental illness and the current situation to employers, schools, places of worship, and extended family members;
- strengthen their personal internal confidence or spirituality.

Advocacy interventions provide professional representation and empowerment for the ill member and family. As social workers we have a choice. One can either simply link families to a service and accept what is given, or strategically plan how to maximize the relationship between the family and community agency. The latter requires agency assessments and a service intervention plan. The assessment not only ascertains what each community agency can provide, but additionally what will be required to develop a relationship and goodness-of-fit between the agency and family. This type of investigation allows clinicians to identify and prevent interpersonal and/or organizational conflicts and to facilitate cooperation and understanding between service providers and family members. Agencies, like individuals, are often under-resourced and need an outside professional to help bridge communications and plans with the family. Advocacy, therefore, requires thoughtful treatment planning and represents much more than simply connecting or introducing families to resources.

Agency and family assessments provide social workers with specialized knowledge and insights that can be used for tactical planning. By understanding an agency's behavior, the clinician gains tools for influencing the services their clients receive. Many agencies want to provide individualized assistance, make reasonable policy exceptions, and not only accept, but also work with the client's idiosyncratic behaviors. These organizations, however, often require specific information, justification, and assurance of accuracy before accommodations can be considered.

An agency assessment is an intelligence report. Before asking for assistance, the social worker needs to know the organization's mission, history, services, catchment area or targeted population, and resources. It is equally important to understand the organization's strengths, problems, decision-making process, and to know which individuals actually make the service decisions. Additionally, knowing the unique attitudes, biases, social and emotional intelligence and professional skill levels of the agency's paid professional and volunteer staff is useful. By reading agency documents and formally interviewing differing levels of personnel, one can determine

- whether the organization's stated mission matches its current service priorities, functions, and methods;
- the agency's values, goals, and strengths;
- what is viewed as offensive or unfair;
- how workers are rewarded;
- each worker's training, experience, and specific skills;
- worker caseload and work demand;
- funding sources and amounts; and
- the distribution of overt and covert decision-making power.

For social workers using the bioecological model, service unavailability is a problem shared by community, social work clinician, and family; it is not simply the client's misfortune. Through planned and informed advocacy, social workers join with support agencies and help define, organize, maximize, and find a means for families to gain community services. Our professional attitude is not "us against the service agency"; rather, with understanding, knowledge, and planned communication, we join with the agency for the sake of the family.

Another role played by bioecological social workers is helping families understand an agency's duties, methods, responsibilities, and limitations. One cannot assume that families automatically know how to use and communicate with agency services. Community programs need clients to take varying amounts of personal responsibility. This can trigger difficulties between agency workers and family members. In situations of this type, families often need coaching in how to approach the community workers and win their confidence. Our job is not to make the family fit the agency, but rather to assure that the agency and family learn to work together. Therefore, we assess, educate, and directly intervene with service providers and the families. Over the years, mental health professionals have held families responsible for receiving and maintaining community services, without helping individuals represent themselves, and without expecting a greater level of accountability from the service-delivery systems.

Our goal is to always help families quickly move from crisis to becoming a productive treatment team (Jensen, Penny, & Mrazek, 2006). One is tempted to say that the social worker's mission is to guide the family toward self-determination. In coping with serious lifelong mental illness, however, independence and self-reliance may be destructive for the family and the ill member (Taylor, 2006b). Treatment, including the ill member's living arrangements, improve when families participate in the decision-making process, but are not forced to independently shoulder caregiving responsibilities, or unilaterally accept professional recommendations (Dumaine, 2003). As a result, in the early stages of the illness, treatment choices are most often guided and negotiated rather than independently determined by the family and the ill member. This guidance is necessary because most families have little experience with mental disorders and treatment modalities. Nonetheless, all interventions need to be negotiated with the family and client whenever possible.

Families react differently to the hardships of mental illness. Emotions can quickly change from friendly and accepting to angry and demanding, or from expressive to withdrawn and silent. As families becomes less accepting, more questioning, emotional, or independent, professionals and social agencies can be tempted to identify the family system as causing or largely explaining the ill member's symptoms (Taylor, 1995). Moreover, when service providers become exasperated, bored, or angry, therapeutic communications stop and families are often harshly and incorrectly labeled (Taylor & Edwards, 1995). Verbal or nonverbal intolerance from a social worker can cause families to believe that they are seen as dysfunctional and therefore as the root of their loved one's mental illness. We must anticipate that families throughout the treatment process will have difficulties, anxieties, and may even become oppositional. These are normal reactions that deserve professional understanding, calm acceptance, and immediate social work attention, empathy, and assistance (Knight & Ridgeway, 2008; Taylor & Edwards, 1995). Negative family or individual behaviors are signals for social workers to slow the clinical process, assess the problems, actively listen, and develop interventions for resolving the issues (Taylor, 1995).

When difficulties between families and treatment teams occur, the intervention target—who or what needs to change—may be the family, the treatment team, or both. Adverse behaviors do not mean that a family's concerns are invalid. Their performance and demeanor most often reflect fear, frustration, burden, and difficulties communicating (Taylor & Edwards, 1995). They may also be trying to tell you that they are having difficulty accepting, understanding, or acting on a situation or clinical advice.

Remember, families want to let you know how sick the ill member is and how they perceive the inadequacies of both themselves and clinical treatment. Understandably, these concerns are not always diplomatically or efficiently stated (Taylor & Edwards, 1995). In these situations, the social worker gathers information and helps others understand that (1) the behaviors indicate problems and represent the family's concerns, rather than indicating that an individual is bad, hysterical, dumb, or uncaring; (2) mental health professionals, including the social worker, may have knowingly or unknowingly exacerbated the problem, and along with the family share responsibility for fixing the difficulty; (3) negative behaviors gain meaning, and become useful treatment information when understood within the family's complete social context; (4) family has important information, needs to be listened to, and is a respected part of the treatment team; and (5) family concerns deserve attention, honest complete feedback, and resolution. Additionally, assessments that include problem-solving techniques may assist the team and family in discovering previously unknown perceptions, missing data, outdated beliefs, culturally relevant issues, and unexplored treatment avenues. Therefore, during difficult periods, it is the social worker's job to offer interventions that restore the family's coping and communication skills, social competence, and power within the treatment team (Kune-Karrer & Taylor, 1995).

With few exceptions, there are no "bad" families. There are, unfortunately, many families in our mental health systems who have been poorly assessed, incorrectly engaged, given faulty interventions, misled, unfairly blamed, or ignored. Sadly, in too many cases, treatment teams have taught families that they have no voice. These families feel cut off and forced to use confrontation, placation, threats of abandoning the ill member, or other non-productive actions before mental health professionals will listen (Taylor, 1995; Taylor & Edwards, 1995). Each time a social worker states that a family is "difficult," the clinician should reframe the statement to say, "I have yet to correctly assess and understand this family's point of view and needs." Most often, families are demanding or confrontational because their emotions and cognitive perceptions of the environment have robbed them of alternative communication tools.

Part of the social work role, therefore, is to ensure that treatment teams do not become punitive when families fail to meet treatment expectations, follow institutional rules, or accept the team's viewpoint. It is extremely easy for a busy, overworked, understaffed treatment team to reinforce negative, rather than positive, elements and behaviors practiced by a family. Constantly reminding each other that a particular family is difficult to engage, lacks empathy, has poor communication skills, dysfunctional rules, low social skills, little insight, or reiterating any other negative label is counterproductive for all of the family members, including the identified patient. Social workers are to concentrate on enhancing the unit's combined skills and concerns. We purposefully reject and clinically attempt to prevent others from labeling family temperament. Our focus is consistently on the family's strengths and problems that can be resolved or reduced through education, problem-solving therapies, supportive consultations, emotional support, and community agency services. Negative attitudes about family members usually mean that we do not truly understand how they process information or perceive the current situation.

Families are often blamed when a social worker

- maintains rigid beliefs about client-family conformity and responsibilities;
- overlooks cultural factors;
- creates power struggles;
- lacks treatment skills or knowledge;
- is overly influenced by other treatment team members;
- understands pathology, personality development, family functioning, and behavior from a single theory, or an overly simple and global diagnostic model;
- fails to understand the family's perceptions, beliefs, goals, fears, or anxieties;
- does not know how the treatment team's attitude, goals, and methods are perceived by the family;
- lacks empathy and understanding for how the family members perceive their limitations (such as obligations to or for others, emotional coping abilities, physical health, housing, transportation, time, community and employment responsibilities, or economics); or
- is unaware of how the family is being influenced or guided by powerful forces such as religious leaders, self-help groups, other mental health professionals, educators, past experiences, or extended family members.

Whatever the cause, negative thoughts and feelings about a family that is supporting a member with serious mental illness signals a need for the social worker to search out supervision or consultation and to conduct more in-depth family assessments. Once behavior is truly understood, its troublesome nature lessens, and solutions for accepting and working with or therapeutically altering the difficulties become clear. Sometimes it is the responsibility of the social worker and the treatment team to recognize that a family is currently doing the best that is possible. Under these circumstances, accommodations for improving communications and goodness-of-fit among the family, the identified patient, and staff must be made by the agency, rather than the individuals.

BOX 2.3

FACTORS INFLUENCING FAMILY PAIN

- diagnosis
- illness severity, and symptoms occurring at onset or current episode
- diagnostic and treatment accuracy
- treatment response
- faith in treatment team and facility
- existing support, community alternatives
- economic stability
- medical insurance coverage
- treatment availability
- ages of ill person and other family members
- history of physical and mental illness across current and extended family
- work schedules and availability
- beliefs and experience with mental illness
- individual personality and temperament
- current and past relationships across the family system
- social perceptions
- organizational, problem-solving, and communication skills
- individual and family social competence, coping and crisis management skills
- degree, life goals, and plans that are disrupted for the ill person and other family members
- unique individual needs
- cumulative or total family burden created from all problems and stressors

---

When mental disorders strike, families are in pain, and often are confused, powerless, and desperately trying to protect the ill member and the family (Taylor, 1995). Families react differently to educational information and stressors. Simply receiving a diagnosis, for example, can be helpful for some individuals and can create anguish for others; while a diagnosis provides the hope of treatment, it can also stigmatize and usher in an unwanted reality (see Box 2.3). It is therefore always important to help families process information and have the freedom to express how they perceive and think about the clinical situation.

ASSESSING THE FAMILY

Clinicians routinely develop differential diagnoses, assessment strategies, and interventions for their mentally ill clients. Yet, treatment planning sessions seldom discuss how to systematically assess and assist the family's emotional, cognitive, economic, and community needs. Once families were no longer seen as causing mental illness, many mental health agencies discontinued, rather than refocused the purpose of, formal-systematic family assessments. Social work has always viewed families differentially rather than as photocopies of each other. Indeed, the pioneer social worker Mary Richmond spoke of our need for understanding the uniqueness of each family unit and member (Richmond, 1917). Unfortunately, our mental health practice methods seldom operationalize these values. Consequently, social work interventions must now evolve from providing "cookie cutter" basic services to an advanced family-bioecological-relationship model that

- sees families as part of the solution rather than the problem;
- assesses each family as consisting of a system and individual members who have differential strengths and needs;
- allows each family member to tell his or her own story without apology;
- assesses the individual and system needs of each family member and family system;
- provides differential education, services, training, resources, support, and treatment periodically for some families, and ongoing for others;
- ensures that families hold a meaningful role in treatment team decisions;
- provides meaningful, planned therapeutic-educational counseling for siblings, extended family members, and significant others throughout the community;
- tailors advocacy and community agency assistance to the family's specific needs;
- ensures that individual psychotherapy, family therapy, and marital therapy are provided only when needed and requested by the family or a family member; and
- provides specific training for selected families or family members to become treatment providers.

While families do not create mental illness, mental illness clearly creates a need in all families for education, differential services, and support. Additionally, some families will benefit from interventions that help them adjust to living with an ill member and to the new and historical stresses occurring within the individual, family, and marital systems.

DIFFERENTIAL FAMILY ATTENTION

A visit to nearly any support group continues to demonstrate that helping professionals far too often continue to appear either harsh or distancing. It is not uncommon to hear families complain that the social worker and psychiatrist hide behind confidentiality laws and provide no meaningful information. Nonetheless, an evolution, if not revolution, is occurring in clinical relationships among mental health professionals and families. The majority of clinicians have moved from blaming and excluding families to providing service, improving communications, endorsing self-help groups, and providing at least some psychosocial education.

Many hospital and clinic education programs either approach families informally, or present structured group education and information sessions. Informal family encounters are mostly unplanned and have little structure. Either the family approaches a clinician with a question, or one of the treatment team sees an opportunity to casually provide information or clinical advice. The encounter is often done as the family is walking in or out of the clinic. These informal quick meetings are helpful for the right client. This is especially true when family members are highly anxious and are having difficulty focusing on complicated or overly long presentations. Informal hallway chats, however, are often fragmented, and run a risk of being misinterpreted. Quick statements such as "I'm here whenever you need me" or "we are going to do everything possible for you and your son" can be perceived in many different ways. Some may find the global statements comforting, while others experience them as an attempt to avoid the family; yet others may take the statements literally, as a verbal promise. Especially in hospital settings, informal family links are normal and acceptable; nonetheless, they should not be the only method for communicating.

Sensing when to have informal family conversations and when issues need thoughtful detailed attention is an important clinical skill. Families can better attend to informal quick meetings when they are supplemented with formal treatment team and educational meetings. A formal meeting requires the social worker to prepare and plan, prior to seeing the family. Among other things, clinicians should include the following in their planning:

1. Understand the purpose of the meeting and clearly communicate this to the family before they arrive.
2. Identify what the family is most concerned about, or needs discussed, before the meeting starts.
3. Identify family trigger issues that either need to be avoided or presented in a non-threatening manner.
4. Ensure that information is accurate and can be explained in a way that is accessible and helpful for the family.
5. Identify which treatment team professionals and family members need to attend.

6. Identify who on the treatment team is best suited to present specialized or sensitive information.
7. Preplan how to help family members stay relaxed, yet focused.
8. Have discussion points planned but have the flexibility to throw the plan away if the situation warrants.

Family meetings, including educational sessions, are consultative treatments performed in a choreographed collaborative manner. Families deserve planned, informative, and accurate meetings, rather than improvised, spontaneous, almost random thoughts.

It is important to note, however, that though formal educational sessions offer participants an organized information package, when they are too structured individual and unique problems can be lost. The formal teaching method also tends to see families as similar, rather than having a unique burden, social perspective, and treatment needs. Furthermore, rigidly planned programs seldom address cultural differences and the family's cognitive belief system. Families, all too often, are forced to fit into a rigid preplanned educational curriculum, or to cling to quick, superficial informal remarks.

FAMILY HELPING FRAMEWORK

While each family's needs differ, a planned and flexible intervention framework can provide consistent yet differential assistance. Ideally, families are approached with a helping and educational model founded on respect, understanding, and a desire to meaningfully join with each member. A flexible family program starts with the unique needs and perceptions of each member and aims at improving the family unit's ability to function and cope with serious mental illness. The model requires clinicians to build a repertoire of specific communication techniques and educational methods for differentially training families.

Group education for families of the seriously mentally ill is routinely provided during the ill member's first hospitalization. It is interesting that this step is often performed informally, that is, it is not included in many community outpatient treatment centers. As a rule, comprehensive family education needs to start when a professional provider first sees the ill member. How fast or intensely information can be provided will vary among families, or even within the same family. While education needs to start at once, it nonetheless should be tailored to meet the comprehension level and emotional and cognitive needs of the family. Some families who have little experience with mental illness will initially require more support and less information. For other individuals, rapidly receiving technical information related to the illness is therapeutic. Therefore, social workers are challenged to approach family education as a form of clinical treatment requiring systematic assessments, bio-social-educational intervention plans, and differential information and support for each family. The following assessment questions can help social workers determine a family's educational and support needs. They will also help clinicians evaluate how quickly and to what degree family members are willing and able to participate in the ill member's treatment process. Before individualized or group education starts, explore with each family member

- whether the symptoms are viewed as being willful, substance related, an illness, and so on;
- how long the person believes the symptoms will last;
- what is thought to have caused the illness;
- what responses, comments, or behaviors are made for each symptom;
- how upsetting the symptoms are and how the symptoms change or impact the family, both as a unit and individually;
- what is expected from treatment and treatment team members;
- what is known or believed about medications;
- how frequently, when, and where contact with the ill family member occurs;
- how positive and strong the relationship is between the ill member and the family, both historically and currently;
- how much treatment and daily involvement is wanted, and how the ill member responds to this desire;
- to what degree the ill member has depended historically on this individual; and
- to what degree this individual has depended on the ill family member.

Educational assessments will gain in therapeutic value if the social worker communicates an authentic knowledge of serious mental illness, and clearly expresses her or his beliefs, role, and goals in the training process.

FAMILY SESSIONS

Family education and support always start prior to the individuals entering a formal training or support group. Through private family sessions, we are able to assess the needs of each member, and to establish relationships, goals, and realistic expectations. The following clinical framework provides social workers with a few key guidelines and ideas for interviewing and assessing families. How a session or series of sessions are sequenced depends largely on the situation. Families who are experiencing a first mental illness episode, for example, face a different type of crisis and have distinct emotions and questions from a family whose loved one has stopped taking medications and is once again spiraling downward. Both families are experiencing an emergency that must be robustly and adequately addressed before any other issues are presented by the treatment team, but the experiences are not only different, they will be unique to each family due to the interaction between the type of crisis and the characteristics of the members involved. Moreover, once the crisis starts to subside, there is still a high probability that the two families greatly differ with regard to training, information, and community service needs. Therefore, clinical models and frameworks are at best overly stated aids or guides that must be modified to fit the individual needs of each family member.

The right place to start with clients and families is the point that addresses their concerns and reduces their pain, worry, and burden. To productively identify these clinical keys, the social worker requires sanction and assistance from the family. That is, the family and social worker must jointly reach an agreement of how the problem or issue is identified and labeled before workable solutions can be discovered. Some emotions, beliefs, perceptions, and experiences are extremely difficult to articulate. For families who must communicate with treatment specialists under stressful and difficult situations, assistance with terms and with framing their concerns, questions, and observations can add meaningful structure and dynamically improve everyone's understanding.

This assistance can take a number of forms. Upon starting a family session, for example, try to genuinely engage each family member in conversation that is neither intense nor problem focused. Individuals can better express themselves and attend to sensitive information after they adjust to the room's climate and the worker's communication style. By slowing down the process, we literally allow individuals to reduce anxiety, push aside environmental and cognitive distractions, and organize what they want to report or ask into their working memories. One method for initiating the uniting process is to first talk informally about non-illness-oriented subjects that are of interest to the individual family members and the social worker. In a university town, for example, sports programs are often an area of shared interest. Ideally, we do not wish to start serious topics until a temporary link or relationship is formed between the social worker and the family.

This step may at first sound simplistic and overstated. After all, what is being suggested is that you, the professional, take time to chit-chat, a skill that most of us have overdeveloped. Consider, however, the difficulty of communicating when one feels like an intruder or stranger, or that he or she is working under time restraints. Furthermore, some individuals may believe themselves held under a microscope and may fear that their mental health and veracity are being examined word by word. Immediately focusing on problematic issues before connecting and uniting with the family can set in motion unwanted emotions and can prevent the family from either addressing concerns or discovering new points of view.

As the connecting process is accomplished, it is often helpful to ask family members what their past experiences have been with mental health workers, social workers, and treatment centers. Use this opportunity to discover what other professionals have done to win or lose their confidence, or to learn their fantasies and fears about mental health interventions and family meetings.

There are numerous programs available for helping one prepare family education meetings. The method represented in Figure 2.1 and discussed below was developed early in the author's career and illustrates one semi-structured process for helping

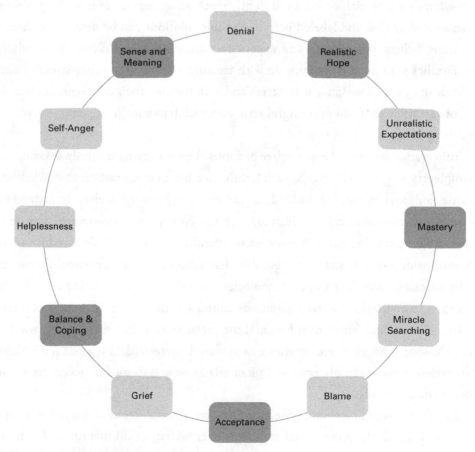

FIGURE 2.1 Family Response Wheel.

families share their concerns and victories (Taylor, 1995). The family wheel is used after a series of information sessions have been held and families have a foundational under standing of neurobiological severe mental illness.

Each month, as the families meet, they use the family response wheel to introduce how they have been reacting, both emotionally and cognitively. When using the wheel, it is important for families to understand that one does not move from point to point around the circle. Where one is emotionally may be very different from where one was a week ago or even an hour earlier. This is why it is called a response *wheel* rather than a response *cycle*. There are no set response expectations, nor any correct or set path to follow through the various points. Furthermore, when dealing with severe, long-lasting mental illness, feelings are seldom resolved forever. The feeling of grief and loss often returns just when a family believes that the emotion is behind them.

The first step, after the basic instructions about the wheel and the rules of respect have been explained, is to allow the group to warm up and join with each other. Once a level of comfort settles across the group, the social worker can ask, "Where on the wheel have you been this month?" This allows participants to understand that they are not unusual for having several different strong changes in their thoughts and feelings. In addition, the sharing process helps families understand that healing does not occur in a straight line, and that emotions can be hopeful one day and chaotic the next. The wheel also provides an opportunity for the group to softly challenge each other. A participant may be very excited about a new, but unproven vitamin supplement advertised for reducing psychotic thinking. This opens the door for individuals who are in a different place to politely ask if the person sees this as a real possibility, or more as "miracle searching" or one of the other points on the wheel. It is the social worker's job to assure that only ideas are challenged, not the individual, and that the challenge is respectful, not demeaning.

One of the positive items on the wheel is the response of "sense and meaning." This represents those breakthrough times when, rather than asking oneself, "Why me?" a moment of existential peace and understanding wafts across the mind and body. Such was the experience when a mother stated, "Schizophrenia has taken so much from our family, often it is as if my ill son is a totally different unknown person, almost like the Jason I knew died or left. Then at the most unexpected time this silly little boyish like smirk, that he never outgrew, appears, and I know that underneath all those symptoms, all the strange behaviors, is Jason and I know I still have a son and there is still hope." The wheel simply allows families a means of finding words for their experiences, and discovering that others have lived through similar situations.

FAMILY KNOWLEDGE AND STRENGTHS

While families require multiple services, support, and education, they also provide powerful resources for themselves and their ill member. Among other things, families often are the ill member's principal source of emotional support, symptom evaluation, money, housing, transportation, medication monitoring, crisis intervention, and much more. Furthermore, clinicians usually rely on the family to provide developmental data, ongoing supervision, and overall support. No mental health diagnosis should be made without family members first identifying what the client was like prior to the illness onset. Unquestionably, some families are poor informants, casual observers, excessively ruminative, unrealistically demanding, too emotional and angry (either at times or consistently), or distanced, intentionally or not, from the ill member and the treatment team. However, as stated earlier, negative family behaviors signal a need for additional assessments, changes in how the family is being approached, and additional clinician attention. A family is difficult for a reason, and for that family the behavior is perceived by the members—or at least by the member exhibiting the behavior—as justified and understandable. A family's unproductive, irritating behaviors tell us that we have failed to reduce their fears, distrust, confusion, or concerns. If I were trying to sell a car to a family that was guarded and uncooperative, my response would not be to label them as uncaring and lacking insight, and to neglect their concerns, but rather to find a means of reaching a more positive relationship and communication pattern. If salespeople can do this, surely we as social workers can do it, and in a more caring manner. After all, we asked to be social workers; the family did not place an order for a severe mental disorder.

Because of the stress created by working with the mentally ill, some clinicians develop a habit of making jokes or talking badly about families to their peers in order to alleviate their own burdens. However, declaring in the secrecy of treatment team meetings that a family is resistant and pathological, even if meant as joke, only initiates an unprofessional categorization that will ultimately injure the mentally ill client, his or her family, and the treatment providers. Labels of any kind influence our observational choices, such as which behaviors to attend to, and our interpretation of cues. Consequently, we quickly begin to observe and document the family's weaknesses, while simultaneously minimizing the members' skills, strengths, and productive works. Additionally, stereotypical clinical labeling limits the treatment team's empathy, creative problem-solving, and assessment skills. As these clinical skills diminish, mental health workers often experience anger, frustration, stress, and burnout. This, in turn, can cause the team to move away from the family and to take an anti-therapeutic approach. What we cognitively believe about a family will be ecologically confirmed. Therefore, if families are poor historians, try to see the opportunity for training and relationship building rather than inadequacy. Many adults have never considered how past developmental factors, genetic histories, social situations, economic factors, interpersonal relationships, communication styles, and observable behaviors are best organized and meaningfully portrayed. We often expect families to intuitively perform tasks that require formal education for most professionals to accomplish.

In some ways it is amazing how little families ask and expect from social workers. Mental disorders create a constant flow of needs and adjustments. Families find it extremely helpful if the social worker attempts to anticipate and prevent unseen crises and unexpected family difficulties. Consequently, an important role for the social worker is to identify and help families avert growing, but unseen dilemmas. Situations that require social workers to be proactive and to alert families that a crisis or difficulty could arise include the following:

- fatigue is becoming overwhelming, so the family needs to renew energy and gain rest;
- sadness or fear is defeating the family, so members need to control, if not resolve, personal grief, anxiety, and worries;
- it is difficult to follow treatment recommendations because the family has not developed trust in the treatment team and treatment methods;
- the illness and treatment seem like a mystery and the family is helpless against the disorder;
- the family feels defeated by the illness or the treatment team, and family members find that advocating for themselves or other family members is impossible;
- family members see no role for themselves in the treatment of their loved one, or believe that the treatment team sees no family role;
- family members fear that they cannot effectively work and live with the ill member.

Helping families recognize and overcome these and similar difficulties most often requires more than education. Families gain self-awareness, become proactive, and work closer with service providers when they are actively involved in treatment planning and informal support meetings, and when they are encouraged to initiate unplanned phone conferences with the social worker. As trust grows and the relationship improves, the family becomes more willing to engage in problem-solving, to consider the social worker's observations and concerns, and to engage in greater self-reflective conversations.

Problem-solving is not strictly the family or the client's responsibility. When offered from a perspective of shared respect, families welcome thoughtful suggestions and appropriate leadership. Families are reassured that they are not alone when social workers take the time to discover new resources, to openly become their advocate, and to seek their opinions.

We want to clearly communicate that families not only need assistance, but also play an important role in the rehabilitation process. This can occur only if each family member believes that his or her knowledge, perspectives, needs, and emotions are understood and valued. Family members need to experience validation and concern from the social worker and the entire treatment team. As the title of this chapter suggests, the clinical goal for the treatment is to move families from being sources of information and financial services for the ill member to being a actual treatment providers. The social worker is principally responsible for ensuring that team-wide respect and family participation take place. Sometimes it is helpful to ask the family for guidance and evaluation. Throughout the treatment process, one may want to periodically inquire:

- Do you see the situation differently than we do?
- What are we not considering?
- Are we overstating behaviors?
- What is not being addressed—from your perspective?
- How can we better help you?
- What do you need?

Questions probing the person's concerns, treatment satisfaction, and evaluation also need to be mixed with information and recommendations from the treatment team. Individuals feel patronized, pushed away, and frustrated when clinicians fail to engage them in a sharing, learning, planning, and treatment partnership.

The family is the most persistent advocate and the most consistent caregiver that many people with serious mental illness will have throughout their lives. 65% of all mentally ill individuals and 25% of people with serious mental illness upon discharge from inpatient psychiatric hospitalization return to their parent's or other family member's home. Furthermore, their stay is often for an extended period (Evavold, 2003; Goldman, 1982; Holden & Lewine, 1982). An unpublished survey by this author of 350 individuals with severe schizophrenia and multiple hospitalizations found that 44% returned to their parent's home for an extended stay of at least 1 year after an inpatient stay. In addition, the survey found that private psychiatric hospitals discharge approximately 77% of all individuals with schizophrenia back to a family member.

This figure combines discharges to the home of a parent, adult sibling, or spouse. In the United States, schizophrenia alone costs the nation approximately $65 billion annually (Wyatt, Henter, Leary, & Taylor, 1995). Families pay about $2 billion to $2.5 billion, or 17% of the indirect costs that are included in the $65 billion estimate (Franks, 1990; Knapp, Mangalore, & Simon, 2004). While these families save money for the nation, their willingness to support a mentally ill member is extremely costly for them in real dollars and personal sacrifice. Along with providing financial support, many families also independently, with little or no services from case managers or other professionals, ensure that the ill person remains linked to services and properly takes medications, evaluate and coordinate new treatment methods, provide transportation, assess symptoms, determine when emergency services are needed, provide emotional support and reassurance, and protect the member from outside hostile elements. It is the family who searches for the lost mentally ill person, deals with unexplained changing symptoms, or endures days, weeks, months, or even years of erratic behaviors. Furthermore, these and many unnamed tasks are done without recognition or pay, and are accomplished by trial and error. They learn and provide vital services for their loved one without the advantage of formal training, supervision, or thanks from the community.

TREATMENT TEAM PARTNERSHIP

Social work is responsible for helping all family members learn about the cause, course, and treatment options for serious mental illness. When possible, families need not only introduction to the team, but also to ways that they can appropriately become participating members. At this point of introduction, the family has moved from the perceived role of source of illness, to that of victim, resource, and advocate. The next evolutionary step is training the family members for active membership in the treatment team and as participants in the delivery of bioecological integrated interventions. Still, all families are different and must move toward treatment team participation at different speeds. Furthermore, there are some families who are unwilling and others who are not capable, or, in other cases, clients who will not allow family members to provide interventions. Additionally, it is important to remember that family members have a right to decline participation in an adult member's treatment without being made to feel guilty or punished. Nonetheless, it is this author's opinion that selected family members should clinically work with the mentally ill person.

This intervention model means that individuals who live with or near the ill person are taught and sanctioned to perform specific medication compliance strategies, as well as social, cognitive, behavioral, or supportive therapies. Moreover, when appropriate, and when agreements can be reached among the mental ill person, family members, and the treatment team, these clinical responsibilities continue during inpatient and day hospital stays. Attitudes and cooperation among family, patient, and hospital staff will in most cases improve if family members become involved and are supervised in real treatment roles. Incorporation of families in ward activities would also greatly modify the unit's social climate. A family participation model requires special attention to confidentiality issues, and individuals would need training and supervision from the hospital staff before being permitted to work with patients other than their own family member. However, family members, in many cases, would be excellent in helping with medication compliance, friendly visiting, role rehearsals, and tracking symptom changes.

Still, how involved a family becomes in the treatment process depends on numerous factors. Some families may find the stress of providing treatment beyond basic support overwhelming. When this occurs, the social worker needs to normalize the situation. Temperament and life situations do not always permit a person to be an advanced helper. There will also be families who are outstanding treatment providers that suddenly face a crisis and need to withdraw for a period of time from actively working with their family member. It's important to remember that mental illness can create a serious short-term crisis at any time. Families normally experience heightened fears and disorganization when faced with unusual events such as emergency room visits, hospitalizations, and suicidal behaviors or attempts. An unexpected crisis can also be triggered by routine events. A birthday or anniversary, for example, may trigger a rush of fears or concerns. One mother on her birthday experienced extreme anxiety and panic when she unexpectedly started obsessing about who would care for her adult mentally ill son when she passed away. Therefore, training, participation in treatment, and other services provided by the family may periodically need to be halted, reduced, or altered. Individuals must gain a sense of control and stabilization before they are involved or continue in systematic training sessions or become therapy providers. It is the social worker's job to identify when families need added support and relief from responsibilities in order to prevent or resolve a crisis. Because of the unpredictability of serious mental illness, this responsibility is ongoing and lasts throughout the relationship with the family. Some individuals, however, find it personally therapeutic and meaningful to increase their involvement when the member with mental illness has a sudden crisis, or when they as the helper are feeling upset. Likewise, some people independently know when to increase or decrease their involvement with the ill person and treatment facility, while others need help and guidance in discovering the right balance.

FAMILY ASSESSMENT, TRAINING, AND SUPPORT ARE ONGOING

A family's needs, skills, and emotions differ among members, change from one environmental setting to another, and have the ability to increase or decrease in effectiveness. As a result, there is a continuous requirement for reassessing the family unit and individual members. This requires social workers to have flexibility and skills for quickly switching roles, altering their style, and changing the family focus. Developing an ability to continuously assess and shift the social work emphases to match a family's current needs and concerns will greatly improve the goodness-of-fit between family members and the treatment team. Having a comprehensive repertoire for helping families, with the skill to strategically change and use correct methods in a timely manner, is in itself an ecological intervention. That is, professional competence provides a positive social experience that allows the family, including the ill member, to more dynamically use information and clinical assistance. Therefore, helping families move from simply surviving serious mental illness to becoming treatment providers demands skills for

- crisis and emergency management;
- advocacy and resolution of concrete economic and other "life" problems;
- genetic and biological education and counseling;
- problem-solving and relationship counseling;
- case management and coordination;
- specific advice for managing symptoms and behaviors;
- mediation between family members and treatment teams or agencies
- emotional support; and
- the ability to know when and how to shift from one intervention style to another.

Just as in good family therapy, social workers want to symbolically become part of the family and when possible anticipate, but always quickly comprehend, each member's emotional state. This type of relationship will free family members from having to endlessly justify their intentions, behaviors, and needs to the treatment team. In addition, it increases the family's ability to accept clinical decisions, poor prognoses, and difficult information. Competent practice and anticipation of needs may also help the ill family member to experience a greater sense of security, trust, and relief from stress. An ill person is always identified as being part of the family, and participates in family sessions as much as her or his mental status will permit. However, a balance must be found between inclusion and each family member's need for confidentiality.

All individuals experiencing mental illness as a patient or family member need a forum for safely expressing their concerns, emotions, worries, and hopes.

The ill member's involvement in family meetings and training depends on his or her (1) severity of mental illness, (2) concentration and attention skills, (3) ability to control anxiety and impulses, (4) comprehension skills, (5) confidentiality requirements, and (6) the family's ability to talk openly and productively in the presence of the ill member. Real or believed interpersonal situations, as well as current symptoms, may interfere with the ill member's ability to work effectively with specific family members, or with the family in general. Furthermore, the ill person's ability to participate in a family session may increase or decrease as changes occur in his or her neuropsychiatric symptoms. Therefore, screening the ill person's perceptions, concerns, social cognitive skills, and related symptoms before the person is involved in family meetings is critical. Inserting an ill person into a family session who is unable to cooperate, focus, or is not ready to face other family members will be counterproductive. As a serious illness increases, the client and other family members often need opportunities to release their emotions and address issues in private individual sessions.

It is also helpful to observe how the family unit works together. Families can be more quickly helped if the social worker understands how the family members make decisions, communicate, assign work tasks, and problem-solve in routine and unusual situations. For example, it is important to know who becomes the family leader when psychiatric symptoms increase, unexpected appointments occur, or needed services from community agencies are not provided. Treatment participation may also be altered by marital relationships, parenting styles, family belief systems, obligations to other family members, and current economic or employment responsibilities.

THE IMPORTANCE OF ACCURATE, CONVINCING, AND TIMELY KNOWLEDGE

Giving families incorrect or insufficient information can create numerous problems. Furthermore, we must be able to address questions and explain illness information in a convincing and accurate manner. This can only be done if the social worker has updated clinical and research knowledge, flexibility, and an ability to listen to what each family member is saying. Families generally want a structure that will help them meaningfully respond to the ill member's psychiatric problems and personal needs. However, they often are not in a situation to judge or explore whether information is accurate and complete. Many individuals are predisposed to concretely accept a treatment team's advice, opinions, and directions. In many ways, our society has taught us to rigidly follow instructions. We daily resolve bureaucratic difficulties, minor illnesses, computer errors, traffic jams, hostile weather, and mathematical problems by adhering to established rules or authoritative guidance. An individual's need for directions, structure, and explanatory rules understandably increase during a psychiatric crisis. Therefore, incomplete, unconvincing, or incorrect information has the potential of becoming extremely dangerous. The high rate of suicide among individuals with serious mental illness underscores the importance of accurate and convincing communications with the family (Taylor, 2006a). If for example, a life-threatening behavior is incorrectly or overly casually called a "suicide gesture" rather than a suicide attempt, the family's vigilance and willingness to use emergency assistance may decrease. Additionally, failing to help families understand suicidal indicators, prevention steps, and how to get 24-hour assistance can be equally deadly.

Introducing mental health training and information to a family is a clinical art requiring practice, expert knowledge, planning, and flexibility. Without these elements, important details will be omitted, understated, or overemphasized. Furthermore, we do not want families to experience mental health education consisting of generic or non-specific and impersonal information. This can be prevented if social workers ensure that each family member's concerns are validated and receive individualized attention. Families can be helped to become more active and more willing to self-disclose when individual and group meetings include the following elements:

- introduction of the training staff and other family participants prior to the first session;
- inviting more experienced consumers and families who are not in a state of crisis to present information and process questions;
- assigning families a consumer-mentor, and working with the mentor prior to the first session;
- ensuring that no one is blamed for the illness;
- willingness by the social worker to accept alternative perspectives, suggestions, and criticism from the family; and
- separation of research facts from personal experiences and beliefs when ideas are confronted.

Accurate and convincing presentations are worthless if they do not match the family's concerns and state of awareness. Often families are not ready to use, comprehend, or commit information to memory. Furthermore, the ability to repeat information does not ensure that the individuals are ready to emotionally and cognitively incorporate the content into their behavior. In addition to being anxious and worried, each family communicates, listens, and labels information differently. As a result, illness information and training have little value when the family is not emotionally or physically able to focus on systematic intellectual material. Often, families and patients require emotional support, distance from the presenting crisis, and rest before training can be useful.

In both health and mental health settings, families are forced to emotionally accept information and responsibilities at the staff's convenience. Little effort is made to assess the family's anxiety, home and work situations, and ability at the present moment to incorporate new information. When this author's father had cardiac bypass surgery, a well-meaning highly ranked hospital staff member "rounded" us up, and insisted that we attend a noon patient care meeting. The meeting was for patients and immediate family. The only problem was that the patients were on high dosages of pain medications, and had been out of intensive care for only a short period. Neither the families nor the patients had adjusted to viewing the raw incisions and frightening monitors. We were worried about heart failure, death, and the future care of our aging parents. How our father was to eat, exercise, drive or not drive, gauge medication responses, and care for the incision was, for the moment, unimportant. Throughout the meeting, we sat silently as our father and other patients nodded off to sleep. In addition, no attempt had been made to introduce and mix the families prior to the group session. To no surprise, the training ended without a single question from the participants, and we were mercifully dismissed.

From an ecological and social learning perspective, how a clinician approaches families will be determined in part by the individual professional's belief system. The clinicians primarily establish the social climate that experientially instructs families how to interact with the care providers. Without awareness, our beliefs can generate vocal tones, non-verbal expressions, boundaries, rigid rules, and meta-communications that define how the family is expected to behave. We must also keep in mind that carelessly used psychological terms and disparaging statements filter through the agency and influence how everyone, from the receptionist to the treatment team chief, perceives and interacts with the family. The clinical social climate improves when professionals control their biases, and cognitively incorporate positive concepts about families and the right of families to participate in the treatment process. Individuals have a right to work with social workers and treatment facilities who believe that families

- deserve accurate, timely information about the condition, treatment, and prognoses of a family member;
- do not cause the family member's mental illness;
- can be trained or educated about their family member's illness;

- deserve deferential support, information, and expectations;
- can provide meaningful diagnostic and treatment information;
- can change behaviors to help reduce the ill family member's symptoms or increase the ill member's quality of life;
- if properly trained and supported, can provide the ill member with rehabilitative treatments and crisis interventions;
- do not need to live with the ill member to be involved and provide meaningful support and treatment;
- have the right to limit or refuse responsibility and health care for their mentally ill adult family member without being made to feel guilty or enduring hostility.

These beliefs underscore the social worker's responsibility for assessing and differentially working with families who desire a partnership with the treatment team. In addition, recognition is given to the fact that not all families believe that it is within their ill member's best interest to provide support and direct assistance. Some individuals who wish to withdraw their support will reconsider when assured that particularly bothersome problems can be resolved. The hospital, for example, may need to demonstrate that the client learned to smoke in a safe manner or no longer spends nights restlessly pacing and loudly responding to hallucinations before the ill person is discharged back to the family. Some families need the clinical personnel to resolve certain problems before they can help the ill person manage other symptoms and problems.

Involvement in training and routine work with the ill family member can be difficult for individuals because of the unavailability of such things as day care, transportation, and financial support. Health problems, work requirements, and other family obligations also create barriers for family training and participation with the treatment team. Whatever the issue, it is the social worker's job to create a safe environment that permits realistic problem-solving and does not unjustly obligate the family to work beyond their capacity and willingness to help and learn about the disorder. For numerous reasons, a few individuals simply do not have the energy or the ability to participate in the rehabilitation or actively support a family member with serious mental illness. Whether the family members are responding to real or imagined stressors, beliefs, or information, their right to withdraw support must be validated and understandingly accepted by the treatment team.

Most often, the social worker is responsible for bridging and ameliorating difficult communications and perceptions occurring between the family and the treatment team. Many times, families anger clinicians because they increase rather than relieve the treatment center's work and service obligations. Obviously, these are misplaced and anti-therapeutic emotions. Our job is to rehabilitate and assist the identified patient, not to penalize the family. Furthermore, by validating the family's decisions, a more meaningful partnership among the client, family, and treatment providers may eventually develop. Verbal confrontation almost never provides a therapeutic breakthrough when working with the seriously mentally ill client or the person's family.

Ethical and legal issues surrounding confidentiality can also hinder the flow of information to families. Clients who are paranoid, embarrassed, or angry may want little or no family involvement. These problems are resolved many times by patient education, compromise, and supportive treatments. Every social work treatment plan needs to include a goal and methods for helping the patient accept increasing levels of family involvement. For example, some patients will allow one specific family member to visit and communicate with the clinicians. Others insist that they be present for all formal and informal family sessions. An intermediary, such as a trusted friend or religious leader, may be accepted for serving as a link between the client, clinicians, and family. Perhaps more important, the treatment team must concretely demonstrate that informing and involving family members is almost always a vital part of the clinical treatment. A client's need for unrealistic confidentiality will often disappear as his or her health improves. It is important to address repeatedly, in differing ways, not only how the family can help, but also the importance of reconnecting with family. Additionally, the treatment team can symbolically model family values and problem-solving methods. That is, symptoms may more rapidly decrease if family involvement is normalized, rewarded, and expected by clinicians. Exposure and discussions with other clients who have resolved family conflicts and stress can also help unite individuals with their parents, siblings, and marital partners.

ASSESSING AND THINKING ABOUT FAMILY CULTURE

Assessing a family's historical and current culture is usually inappropriate until the individuals start to experience emotional relief, cognitive control, and a decrease in fear and anxiety. When in a state of crisis, families need immediate support and understanding, rather than a search for cultural identity. Nonetheless, even in periods of crisis, the social worker is responsible for practicing culturally safe methods and relating to the family in a manner that fits with its cultural background. Once treatment moves beyond emergency care, social-cultural beliefs and perceptions need to be completely explored. Cultural assessments are essential for all clients and families entering a mental health treatment program. Ecological and social learning theories remind us that culture is a continuously evolving process for all people (Kune-Karrer & Taylor, 1995).

Focusing cultural concerns only on minority clients is a modern form of stereotyping and an incorrect use of theory. We cannot assume that because people are members of a recognizable minority or are obviously middle-class majority citizens that we understand their beliefs and life experiences. More than in any other profession, it is social work's responsibility to understand and teach other treatment team members how the family as a unit and as individuals culturally perceive or experience the world.

Understanding how ethnic minority and majority citizens view society and mental health services is important, but it is not the essential cornerstone for performing a family cultural assessment. During periods of crisis and high anxiety, the worker may need to use group generalizations for establishing communication style and treatment tone. For example, understanding that Native Americans distrust promises and power stemming from business and government bureaucrats (Hill, 2006) or that Asian-Americans experience high degrees of shame when receiving mental health interventions (Lee, 1997) may provide important human links in an emergency room situation. However, one must quickly move from these generalities into the family's specific current and historical cultural perceptions. Social workers must be careful not to create new stereotypes by forcing individuals and families to fit into a specific global or cultural model. A model for developing questions to help families and individuals tell their cultural story has been outlined by Kune-Karrer & Taylor (1995). Their outline provides one pathway for exploring a family's cultural history, experiences, and perceptions.

As with any family, there is no single way to engage and support individuals who differ from you in culture, ethnicity, or race. Nonetheless, it is important early in the relationship-building phase to acknowledge these differences, and to learn from each other. The social worker should neither come across as the expert on family life within the client's culture, nor as a blank slate. That is, we help the family members to tell their personal story, rather than sounding as if we expect individuals from their cultural background to act, behave, and speak in a certain manner. Families form a unique separate culture within the boundaries of their majority community culture. If we do not recognize and acknowledge this, we will employ stereotypes that can injure individual family members. Within the first few meetings, it is important to learn how the family has experienced the mental health system. Reassurance, understanding, acceptance, and assistance must be immediately provided if harm, doubt, or hurt feelings have occurred from actual or perceived prejudice and oppression. Your perception and understanding of each individual member are never completely set, but rather are confirmed or changed as you learn about the family's social-cultural history, economic situation, micro-system structure, power and role assignments, beliefs and life experiences

(Kune-Karrer & Taylor, 1995). A planned semi-structured interview will assist one in developing a conversation and assessment with families from minority, racial, or ethnic communities. The family's personal story and cultural beliefs must quickly replace our limited and preconceived cultural knowledge. Seeing the world through the family's eyes is important in all social work interventions.

REFERENCES

Dumaine, M. L. (2003). Meta-analysis of interventions with co-occurring disorders of severe mental illness and substance abuse: Implications for social work practice. *Research on Social Work Practice 13*, 142–165.

Evavold, S. A. (2003). *Family Members of the Mentally Ill and Their Experiences with Mental Health Professionals*. Ph.D. dissertation, Virginia Polytechnic Institute and State University, Blacksburg, VA.

Franks, D. D. (1990). Economic contribution of families caring for persons with severe and persistant mental illness. *Administration and Policy in Mental Health and Mental Health Service Research, 18*(1), 9–18.

Goldman, H. (1982). Mental illness and family burden: A public health perspective. *Hospital and Community Psychiatry, 33*, 557–560.

Hill, D. L. (2006). Sense of belonging as connectedness, American Indian worldview, and mental health. *Achieves of Psychiatric Nursing, 20*, 210–216.

Holden, D. F., & Lewine, R. J. (1982). How families evaluate mental health professionals, resources, and effects of illness. *Schizophrenia Bulletin, 8*, 626–633.

Jensen, P. S., Penny, K., & Mrazek, D. A. (2006). *Toward a New Diagnostic System for Child Psychopathology*. New York: The Guilford Press.

Knapp, M., Mangalore, R., & Simon, J. (2004). The global costs of schizophrenia. *Schizophrenia Bulletin, 30*(2), 279–293.

Knight, E. B., & Ridgeway, L. E. (2008). The role of family treatment. In D. Reitman (Ed.), *Handbook of Psychological Assessment, Case Conceptualization and Treatment* (Vol. 2, pp. 126–158). Hoboken, NJ: John Wiley & Sons.

Kune-Karrer, B. M., & Taylor, E. H. (1995). Toward multiculturality: Implications for the pediatrician. *The Pediatric Clinics of North America: Family-Focused Pediatrics: Issues, Challenges, and Clinical Methods* (Vol. 42, pp. 31–46). Philadelphia: W. B. Saunders.

Lee, E. (1997). Overview: The assessment and treatment of Asian American families. In E. Lee (Ed.), *Working With Asian Americans: A Guide for Clinicians*. New York: Guilford Press.

Munger, R. L. (1998). *The Ecology of Troubled Children: Changing Children's Behavior by Changing the Places, Activities, and People in Their Lives*. Cambridge, MA: Brookline Books.

Richmond, M. E. (1917). *Social Diagnosis* New York: Russell Sage Foundation.

Taylor, E. H. (1995). Understanding and helping families with neurodevelopmental and neuro-psychiatric special needs. In W. L. Coleman & E. H. Taylor (Eds.), *The Pediatric Clinics of North America: Family-Focused Pediatrics: Issues, Challenges, and Clinical Methods* (Vol. 42, pp. 143–152). Philadelphia: W. B. Saunders.

Taylor, E. H. (2006a). *Atlas of Bipolar Disorders*. London: Taylor & Francis Group.

Taylor, E. H. (2006b). The weaknesses of the strengths model: Mental illness as a case in point. *Best Practices in Mental Health: An International Journal, 2*(1), 1–29.

Taylor, E. H., & Edwards, R. L. (1995). When community resources fail: Assisting the frightened or angry parent. In W. L. Coleman & E. H. Taylor (Eds.), *The Pediatric Clinics of North America: Family-Focused Pediatrics: Issues, Challenges, and Clinical Methods*. Philadelphia: W. B. Saunders.

Wyatt, R. J., Henter, I. D. S., Leary, M. C., & Taylor, E. H. (1995). An economic evaluation of schizophrenia, 1991. *Social Psychiatry and Psychiatric Epidemiology, 30*, 196–205.

/// 3 /// THE COMPREHENSIVE CONTINUOUS ASSESSMENT

Before starting an assessment, social workers need to develop an awareness of how they listen to and interpret client information. Over-learned theoretical constructs can create automatic thinking. When this occurs, we are no longer listening to what the client is saying, but rather are filtering information through learned dogma. That is, one is not effectively listening when more mental energy is expended interpreting the meaning of what the client is saying, rather than withholding judgment until the entire story is completed.

In order to clinically listen, social workers must know exactly how they define mental disorders. If we conceptualize mental disorders as related to unconscious conflicts, family dysfunctions, personal choices, or societal shaping, we will look for and find logical factors that support these beliefs. All helping theories and models will bias a clinician's perceptions and threaten an assessment's validity. In the past, clinicians were overly focused on internalized unconscious disturbances; bioecological social workers, on the other hand, risk illuminating human problems as brain illnesses, and minimizing the interactive and dynamic forces of environment, trauma, individual uniqueness, and macro policies.

A comprehensive social work assessment, however, does not explore a client's issues from a favored clinical behavioral, cognitive, bioecological, or psychodynamic theoretical perspective. Our general assessment goals are to document, in as unbiased a manner as possible, facts, beliefs, and assumptions that are cross-validated by others, as well as by clinical observations across ecological settings. At the end of an assessment, the social worker is to understand the client's reality, strengths, perceptions, and emotions. Using a theoretical framework for learning about a client will excessively dictate the type of questions asked and will possibly trigger false conclusions. A primary goal of the social work assessment is to differentiate and clarify sound, factual information elicited from and about the client from beliefs held by the client or others, which may or may not be factual, and assumptions made within and across the individual's social settings. The determination of whether information is fact, belief, or assumption is atheoretical and is determined by concrete evidence. It can be helpful to think of assessments as requiring a generally open approach that allows findings to support specific theoretical perspectives and sometimes multiple interpretations (Hallam, 2013).

Even though this textbook focuses heavily on neurobiological disorders, the purpose of a social work assessment is not the identification of causality. Research underscores that mental disorders are not simply the result of environmental or biological factors. There is growing agreement that mental illness arises from the brain's ongoing development, genetic interactions, ecological realities, and how the social context is differentially experienced or perceived (Jensen, Penny, & Mrazek, 2006). As a result, pinpointing causality is beyond the scope of a social worker's assessments. The following abbreviated case study illustrates how difficult it is to identify what causes a disorder, when it starts, and the role that environment plays.

WHAT HAPPENED? THEY BOTH LIVE IN THE SAME HOUSE

The Franklins are an upper middle-income family. Both parents are corporate executives in the United States and have university degrees. They have had a stable marriage for approximately 18 years and are the birth parents of two children. The family lives in a semi-rural area on several acres of land, which is only minutes away from a small city. Additionally, they have strong relationships with their extended family and numerous lifelong close friends who are within easy driving distance. The mother and father were 37 years old when the first child was born, and had been married for 11 years. An emergency C-section was required due to the mother having severe toxemia. This was her first full-term pregnancy, although she had suffered two previous miscarriages. The second daughter was born without complications after a full-term pregnancy. However, at birth she was diagnosed with hip dysplasia and spent her first 6 months in a harness or splint. Fortunately, with time and medical attention, the physical problem was completely resolved. The child has had no further medical problems. At the time of her birth, the parents were 39 years old and had been married for 13 years. After each child was born, the mother took a full year of maternity leave, and then went back to work 4 days per week. After she returned to work, the children were cared for in licensed in-home day cares that have an excellent reputation. This has proved to be a stable and positive situation. Since the day care started, the children have only changed day care homes once. They have been attending the current day care home (now on an after-school basis) for almost 6 years. These two daughters, who are now 9 and 11 years old, have lived in the same house since birth.

There is no history of abuse or neglect of the children from parents, extended family, or care providers. Neither parent has substance abuse or mental health problems. There is, however, some belief that Mr. Franklin's mother may have bipolar disorder, but there has never been a formal diagnosis, or a history of hospitalization. Both parents are in good physical health, and have a strong marital relationship.

The eldest child, Karen, has presented many challenges from almost the very beginning of infancy. The parents and aunt state that early on, Karen went beyond what is referred to as a "fussy" baby. She cried almost constantly and was very difficult to soothe. At 3 months of age, the baby had to be soothed by constantly walking with her and simultaneously rocking her in your arms. If this was not done, Karen would begin screaming. The parents would take turns driving with her because the motion of the vehicle comforted her. As she got older, the parents noticed a growing list of difficulties. Karen had strong reactions to certain textures against her skin. They went on a family holiday at the beach and discovered that she could not stand the feeling of sand against her skin. Additionally, certain kinds of clothing were also intolerable, in particular anything tight, and anything scratchy or synthetic. The mother learned very quickly that she had to buy her daughter very loose and light cotton clothing.

Karen also was unable to stand having her clothing even slightly damp, let alone wet. While these issues were difficult, the child and family were also facing more serious issues. Karen wet the bed until age 7 and had ever increasing tantrums. The more severe tantrums were described as total "meltdowns" in which the child appeared to lose complete control. These occurred at least weekly and included head banging. It was often a mystery as to what triggered the tantrum. However, it was clear that the smallest disappointment, which most children would hardly acknowledge, created an uncontrollable response from Karen. Sleeping was also a problem. Until the age of 7 she consistently woke up after falling asleep and often awoke screaming. On one occasion they found her in the bathroom, curled up beside the toilet, screaming, "Don't hit me! Don't hit me!" On another occasion they woke up in the middle of the night to find her standing by the end of their bed, naked, simply staring at them.

The child also has what might be termed "savant" characteristics. A child psychologist placed her in the 98th percentile for visual memory. Karen can recall a scene with incredible accuracy. This year, as Karen turned 11 years old, her behavior is getting much better. There are fewer meltdowns, and she no longer is bedwetting. Karen now sleeps through the night more often than not, and seldom awakes screaming. She started sporadically wearing blue jeans last year, and for several years has been able to go to the beach and play in the sand. However, while she is great with younger children (in her day home she is seen as a wonderful help), and generally gets along well with older children, Karen struggles with peers her own age. At her eighth birthday, no one showed up for her party. She also has developed learning problems and in particular has trouble reading. Physically she is of average height and slightly underweight. Her health is good to excellent, and she has no allergies.

From birth, the second child, Polly, has been very calm and easygoing. She has not demonstrated any of Karen's problems. Polly has no history of uncontrolled tantrums, and no difficulties with textures, sleeping, or bedwetting. She does very well in school and is especially good at reading. Polly has many friends her own age and is popular. At her sixth birthday, every girl she invited attended the party. Physically Polly is a bit on the short side and is of average weight. Her health is also good to excellent, with no allergies. She does, however, have a slight lisp.

There are several important assessment issues illustrated by the case study. First, even though we have developmental information, it remains uncertain as to when the current problems for an 11-year-old child started. Logically, we would point to the early infant soothing difficulties. The infant crying and sleeping difficulties may indicate that deep brain areas known as the limbic system were not receiving comforting environmental cues and were not forwarding calming messages to the developing frontal cortex. This, however, is at best an undocumented assumption. In reality, why and what caused the infant to express distress is unknown. Furthermore, we cannot even be certain that the early infant difficulties are directly linked to the toddler and older child problems. Similarities found in behavioral symptoms do not document a constant singular disorder. We simply know that problems have followed this youth from birth to present. As a result, we must be extremely careful in how the assessment information is interpreted to the family. Karen's family will want the assessment to provide concrete causation information, and to certify that they are not to blame for the difficulty. It can be helpful to families if the social worker explains that professional assessments cannot answer specifically what caused the child's problems. Parents additionally need to hear that if the professional community can neither predict nor identify causation, it follows that they could not possibly have adjusted their parenting style to better fit the child's clearly unknown needs.

This case underscores an important issue for social workers to consider. There is no doubt that this family has provided the best enriched and caring environment possible. Most likely the child is improving partly because of the consistent and loving home environment. Nonetheless, this does not mean that the home environment has created the best possible fit for the child. Unfortunately, our assessment can only estimate how to adjust and change the child's home social climate. How the child perceives her environment and what she is specifically responding to is most often unknown. Additionally, the social worker must keep in mind that as the brain develops, neuroprocessing, perceptions, interpretation of environmental cues, and reactions to ecological settings will change. It is therefore unrealistic to think that parents or professionals can accurately identify how to best manipulate the environment and respond to a child's internal thoughts and emotions. In the end, the process of adjusting the environment for children like Karen consists of experimenting and systematically discovering what works. Sadly, the experimentation is often left completely to the parents, and incorrect choices can result in the adults being labeled as bad parents.

Consider how easily one could mistakenly diagnose Karen with attachment disorder, or post-traumatic stress disorder. An attachment- or stress-related diagnosis would trigger accusations, possible protective service investigations, and a host of inappropriate interventions. When working in mental health, logical connections found in an assessment do not necessarily explain causation. The fact that behaviors look like an attachment or stress issue does not automatically rule out alternative explanations. As professional helpers, social workers are obligated not only to conduct comprehensive assessments, but additionally, to responsibly and correctly interpret the findings.

You may have noticed that Karen's behavior points to several diagnostic categories in addition to those mentioned. Autism spectrum disorder is one such possible category. However, it would be incorrect to suggest a diagnosis. The limited information provided simply alerts clinicians that a full assessment is required, and that the diagnosis is unknown. We may, however, in writing an assessment referral, request that the treatment team rule out neurodevelopmental, autism, attachment, and stress-related disorders. The term "rule out" simply means that we want the assessment to as completely as possible determine that the stated disorders are *not* causing the client's problems. In all cases, however, a social worker uses diagnostic labels only after a complete assessment is concluded. Only through a comprehensive investigation can one distinguish whether a client's difficulties relate more to problems-in-living, toxic environments, unique behaviors, or mental disorders. Once this is known, we can then work to determine pathways for resolving the problems.

THE ASSESSMENT PROCESS

There is growing evidence that structured manualized assessments provide far more diagnostic accuracy than free-style clinician interviews (Doss et al., 2008). This is because a comprehensive assessment gathers information from multiple sources.

Unfortunately, there are only limited structured assessments, and most require specialized training. Therefore, free-style interviews will remain a necessary skill for some time to come. When preparing to conduct an assessment, it can be helpful to prepare a list of questions organized by topics (Doss et al., 2008). This can help keep the free-style interview organized and can ensure that every important topic is covered. Developing questions for each of the topics illustrated in Figure 3.1 can aid in the construction of a comprehensive assessment plan. Additionally, a more complete outline that can serve as a guide for assessment development is provided in Appendix 1.

While gathering client data, the social worker must quickly separate facts from assumptions and opinions. Before reaching a conclusion, each bit of sorted information must be analyzed, first as an independent variable and then as a whole, or gestalt. It is important to determine whether single factors outweigh the combined information picture, or if the gestalt signals that isolated events and facts are irrelevant. The process

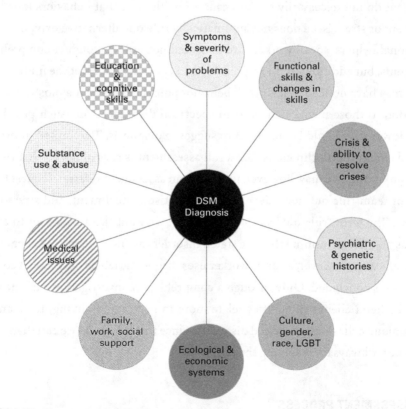

FIGURE 3.1 The Assessment Gestalt.

Each circle represents an area of inquiry that is independent, but the areas interact and together form the assessment gestalt. A complete assessment gestalt includes measurement and consideration of the client's strengths, deficits, and symptoms in each of the 10 assessment areas.

demands an attitude that is open to discovering whether a client's problems primarily relate to neurobiological, environmental, behavioral, medical, or developmental elements, or some combination thereof. Symptoms of mental disorder are often triggered by the interaction between brain development, learned behaviors, and environmental structures, rather than a single dynamic. That is, a client's problems most often consist of many interconnected components. Still, one factor or cluster often is primary and establishes the tone and direction for treatment planning. Thus a good assessment clarifies and documents which factors are primary, rather than secondary, contributing elements; primary influences most often require a higher treatment priority.

The reduction of the severity of first-order factors may automatically solve secondary problems or may provide the client with the internal resources and energy needed for self-care. However, the assessment may also indicate that the primary source of problems cannot be addressed, and only secondary elements can be treated. Addictions, for example, represent both neurobiological and environmental issues. When the neurobiology of addiction is primary, a client may need immediate medical detox treatment, followed by inpatient symptom management, group therapy, and psychoeducation. However, the assessment may indicate that the environment is more primary than the individual's biological addiction. In this case, the client may not need medical attention, but rather immediate support within the community, family education, employment, mentors, and help developing new friends who are drug-free. In some cases, though, the treatment of primary and secondary elements will not be effective unless provided at the same time. A client who has schizophrenia and lives where drug and alcohol use is common, for example, most likely requires simultaneous medication treatment for the neurobiological disorder and community interventions, as it is unlikely that the help in reducing his or her psychosis and illicit drug use will produce any change until he or she has moved into new supportive drug-free housing. In some clinical cases, the concerns are neurobiological, and safety must therefore be seen as equally primary; in many cases, if not most, an abused child must be quickly moved from the source of abuse and instantaneously treated for trauma and acute stress. This is equally true for a person with depression who has developed a plan for suicide. Furthermore, a small minority of individuals with neurobiological disorders become dangerous to others and need immediate hospitalization and community services. Through an assessment we consequently both identify and gather evidence for our primary focus for understanding a person's symptoms and planning treatment.

Major depressive episodes serve as another example of how a comprehensive assessment can direct our clinical thinking. This is primarily a neurobiological illness that may or may not be complicated by environmental factors. Even if the depression is interacting with environmental forces, our first or primary focus most often is the person's neurobiological symptoms. Through the assessment, we must ensure that the person is not at risk of taking his or her own life, and we must gather enough information for determining the appropriateness of medication and psychotherapy treatments. When neurobiological disorders such as depression are primary, the environment may

- help decrease severity of symptoms;
- increase severity of symptoms;
- neither decrease nor increase the severity of symptoms.

Consequently, the primary target for more severe neurobiological disorders is most often the illness first, followed by environmental treatment, though there are always exceptions. However, if one accepts that neuropsychiatric disorders are biological, and the assessment indicates a brain illness, then in most cases symptom treatment is primary. Still, as discussed in other chapters, the appropriate treatment must be differential and is not always medication related.

A successful assessment places the client and family at ease, and creates an atmosphere of reciprocal sharing and respect. The social worker is not conducting an interrogation, but rather is guiding participants in a systematic search for information that explains problematic symptoms, highlights significant strengths, and provides a foundation for treatment planning. We are working with clients, not suspects, so assessment questions should not induce fear or a feeling of being blamed. Family members often worry that they are the cause of the mental health problem, and clients can believe, incorrectly, that they are overstating their difficulties or should have enough will power to overcome personal problems. Unfortunately, it is easy to rapidly ask consecutive questions that are not placed in a supportive context, and that consequently leave clients to make their own inaccurate sense and meaning of the process. Clients and families deserve to know the clinician's logic and purpose for asking a series of questions, as well as how the questions fit into an evidence-based inquiry. Explaining one's professional theory, assumptions, and methods before stating assessment questions can alleviate worries for some clients. As a bioecological theorist, clinicians are encouraged to consider covering the following points before initiating the assessment:

1. Verbalize that you work from a point of view that families do not cause mental disorders, and that the problems expressed are real and painful.

2. If it is found that the identified problems stem from a disorder, then the disorder is an illness, much like any other physical illness, and can be systematically treated and helped.

3. One can have difficulties that look like a mental disorder, but are not in fact a mental illness.

4. The environment, whether home, school, or work, may or may not completely support the needs of any one person; that does not, however, signal that someone is doing something wrong or inappropriate.

5. As a clinical social worker, I help people by supporting their needs, suggesting available resources, providing education, and when appropriate engaging cognitive, behavioral, family, or other forms of psychotherapy.

6. An assessment is not simply me asking questions, and you answering; it is a conversation allowing me to hear your questions, listen to your thoughts, understand your point of view, and help you define the type of help that you want.

7. So, what if we start by exploring your questions or concerns? Perhaps you would like to ask questions about me, or share something about yourself.

Notice that the last statement slows the assessment process down and allows the participant a sense of control. We are always striving to make the assessment process reciprocal among clinician, family, child, school, and significant others. That is, the clinician is responsible for creating an environment that allows participants to freely state their information, concerns, beliefs, questions, and experiences. Ideally, the social worker joins with each person, including the client, in such an individualized and professional manner that the participants feel valued, and that they are treatment team members rather than simply information providers.

In order to accomplish this sense of community, the assessment must consist of a discussion, rather than being dominated by the clinician's questions or advice. Everyone must be given time to tell their story, experience the satisfaction of being heard, and know that personal concerns, beliefs, and insights are a helpful part of the assessment. Far too often within the assessment discussion, clinicians give advice rather than seek consultation from the participant. Parent enthusiasm, for example, will decrease if, after disclosing that their child will not obey, they are immediately instructed in how to use time-out and reward parenting methods. By the time parents have come to see a social worker, they have often tried all of the commonly recommend solutions. Therefore, unsolicited advice can make parents feel that they are being blamed for the child's problems or that they are uninformed parents. Negative emotions of this type are not the result of client resistance, but rather are feelings and self-thoughts inappropriately triggered by the social worker. This can be avoided simply, however, by asking questions such as, "What have you tried to correct the behavior?" or "What have you found that works, and what does not help?" and "How effective are methods like time-out and rewards with your child?" Often times, the clinician believes that a method such as time-out has failed because it is being applied incorrectly. However, the assessment in most cases is not the place for on the spot corrections. Remember, as a clinician you are trying to gain open and unguarded communications. An unexpected teaching session ends the discussion, diminishes the participant, establishes a power struggle, and limits the flow of information.

ECOLOGICAL ASSESSMENT

Historically, social work has taught that assessments always include an analysis of the environment. An ecological assessment emphasizes the incorporation of both the immediate environment and invisible power structures, such as macro policies, laws, and cultural expectations (Haight & Taylor, 2013). It is the bioecological perspective that even when symptoms stem from neurobiological disorders, a complete evaluation of every setting in which the client has participated is required. Social workers are responsible for helping team members, clients, and families understand which environmental elements are the most and least helpful for decreasing symptoms and improving quality of life. A detailed discussion of ecological systems is included in the Chapter 1.

Conducting an ecological assessment requires the acceptance of the following clinical assumptions:

- Observed behaviors must be understood within a social context.
- All social settings have their own personality, which influences the human participants to differing degrees.
- All interactions are reciprocal, but the power between two individuals, families, or groups is not necessarily equal.
- A lack of fit between an individual and a system can trigger behaviors and symptoms that mimic mental disorders.

The goal of an ecological assessment is to determine the degree that environments, cultural perceptions, beliefs, bio-social-cognitive interactions, and unique events account for an individual or group's behavior (Haight & Taylor, 2013; Munger, 1998). An example of an ecological assessment outline that can be modified for each client's situation is provided in Appendix 2.

To make ecological concepts useful, we attempt to understand observable behaviors in a manner that captures their meaning within a specific environmental context: the person does not simply cry, but cries at a certain rate, tone, and volume within a specified environment. An ecological assessment pays equal attention to the person's actions and the setting where the behavior is taking place. Furthermore, because interactions are reciprocal, it is assumed that behavior and emotion always vary as the environment changes. People do not have a single personality response. From an ecological perspective, the concept of personality must be operationalized both behaviorally and within a defined and prescribed environment. That is, we want to capture how the client behaves and reacts within the boundaries of an assessed and measured environmental setting. Perhaps we notice that the client makes more eye contact and verbal communications when in a certain room with a single individual, but moves to a specific corner when several people enter the room. A bioecological social worker would want to know if the selection of the corner was random, and if not, what it was about that part of the room that attracted the person's attention. From an ecological perspective, a person does not simply withdraw, but rather makes decisions based on reciprocal interactions, perceptions of power, and interpretation of the setting's rules and expectations. Additionally, it is assumed that behavior and personality adjustments will also occur as the power within a setting is shifted among participants. Therefore, an ecological assessment strives to discover not only how the client behaves, but what elements within and across settings create changes within the client's strengths and symptoms.

Expanding assessments of mental disorders and unhealthy behaviors to include evaluation and understanding of the client, family, and all ecological settings can greatly increase the possibilities for interventions (Munger, 1998). As detailed throughout this book, mental disorders are framed as neurobiological. The causes of the neurological abnormalities and the timing of their occurrence are less clear. Nonetheless, from a bioecological perspective, assessing and treating the environment are viewed as a mandatory part of comprehensive mental health intervention plan.

THIS IS ALL VERY HELPFUL, BUT HOW DO I CONDUCT AN ASSESSMENT?

Assessments are always planned and designed to comprehensively "rule out" as many alternative hypotheses for explaining symptoms as clinically possible. The social worker is responsible for ensuring that all possible explanations for a cluster of symptoms have not only been explored, but are examined to make certain that correct assumptions and diagnoses are being applied. Gathering information from multiple sources and clinical observations across client settings decreases the probability of accepting incorrect conclusions and diagnoses.

Return your thoughts to the case study above. How could you factually know that the parents are providing an enriched loving environment, have not abused the daughter, and continue to improve the child's home environmental fit? As the vignette is currently written, you are being asked as clinicians to accept assumptions or beliefs, rather than facts. To turn the information from suppositions to clinical facts, one needs to observe the family across settings. From multiple observations in differing settings one may learn, among other things, how

- the parents respond to the children in both less and highly structured environments;
- they communicate with the girls when tired or preoccupied;
- consistently the parental support is maintained in changing situations;
- adult anger with each other and the children is handled; and
- equal is the treatment and attachment among the parents and daughters.

Observations may also reveal whether the parents are overly concerned about and consequently attempt to prevent the daughters from talking privately with other adults. Sometimes parents are concerned about family secrets—including, but not limited to, abuse—and want to hear everything the child or children tell other adults. To control access with adults, a parent may attempt to always be with the child, may question the youth intensively about what was said, or may try to find out what was discussed while in conversation with the adult. When this occurs, the social worker has not turned an assumption into fact, but rather has found, and should document, support that additional assessment is required. These indicators could mean many different things, including socially learned habits, traditions brought forward from homes of origin, cultural adaptations, or protecting the child from labeling. Thus a major hazard in assessments is declaring assumptions to be facts and then jumping to a false diagnostic conclusion.

In addition to such observations, one may want to interview the child's medical doctor, schoolteachers, and extended family members, as well as review all possible psychiatric, psychological, health, and educational records. The social worker may also want to evaluate how the home is set up and whether the "meltdowns" occur in certain parts of the house, at specific time periods, or only when specific people are in the house. It would be helpful to know, for example, if moving the child to a bedroom nearer the parents or rearranging the furniture in the current bedroom help resolve the sleeping problem. Sometimes children sleep better if they go to bed with a transitional object. In order to turn assumptions into facts and help the Franklin family, we need to collect individual, family, institutional, and ecological data.

Assessments must be made to fit the requirements and concerns of clients. Nonetheless, as shown in Figure 3.2, there are general topics that can guide an assessment. To make an assessment functional, one must analyze the information and determine what the sum total of facts and assumptions mean. This is known as the case formulation, and when the overview of findings is given to the client or family, it is often called the client interpretive session. What is important to recognize is that the assessment flows from collected information, and the formulation comes directly from the assessment findings, which, in turn, serve as the foundation for developing the treatment plan.

To develop the assessment case formulation, we first look at the gathered data item by item and then as a whole. It is possible that one factor could outweigh the sum of the whole, though, in the experience of this clinician, this is a rare occurrence. However, a single piece of medical evidence may explain all, or most, psychiatric symptoms. Even elements such as grief reaction tend to require an understanding of the gestalt, rather than just knowing that someone close to the client has recently died. The case

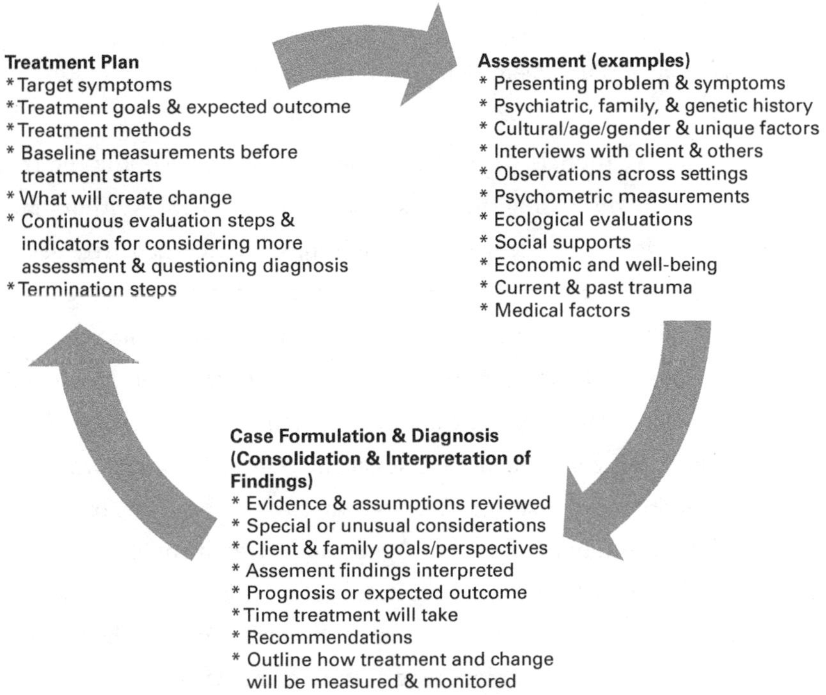

Treatment Plan
* Target symptoms
* Treatment goals & expected outcome
* Treatment methods
* Baseline measurements before treatment starts
* What will create change
* Continuous evaluation steps & indicators for considering more assessment & questioning diagnosis
* Termination steps

Assessment (examples)
* Presenting problem & symptoms
* Psychiatric, family, & genetic history
* Cultural/age/gender & unique factors
* Interviews with client & others
* Observations across settings
* Psychometric measurements
* Ecological evaluations
* Social supports
* Economic and well-being
* Current & past trauma
* Medical factors

Case Formulation & Diagnosis (Consolidation & Interpretation of Findings)
* Evidence & assumptions reviewed
* Special or unusual considerations
* Client & family goals/perspectives
* Assement findings interpreted
* Prognosis or expected outcome
* Time treatment will take
* Recommendations
* Outline how treatment and change will be measured & monitored

FIGURE 3.2 Assessment and Treatment Planning Concepts.

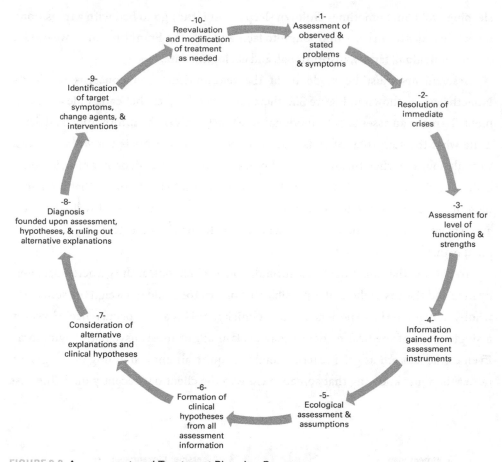

FIGURE 3.3 Assessment and Treatment Planning Process.

formulation provides a rationale or clinical perspective for developing the treatment plan and systematically discussing the assessment with the client. Without fail, every treatment plan is to reflect the evidence and assumptions documented in the assessment.

The assessment and formulation also provide a means for determining what in the treatment must come first. If a client is in crisis, then the treatment plan is to reflect an immediate intervention that addresses the crisis. This is illustrated in Figure 3.3, along with a logical flow of steps for completing different sections of the assessment. There is no set order for conducting a comprehensive assessment. Figure 3.3 simply reminds social workers that one section of an assessment flows from and through each of the other sections. Additionally, clinical hypotheses of diagnoses and treatment always stream from the total assessment, rather than a single section. When this concept of linkage is followed, it prepares the social worker for documenting how decisions have been made. Figure 3.4 demonstrates that assessment reports, treatment plans, and clinical notes are all informed by each other. A supervisor should be able to read any clinical progress note and find the bases for the session or decision in both the written assessment and treatment plan. If our progress notes do not reflect findings in the assessment, then we have either gone off course in our treatment or the client's situation has changed and a new assessment is required. The comprehensive assessment process is always ongoing and only ends when the final outcome evaluation is completed and the client has been discharged.

CONFRONTING CLINICAL BELIEFS TO IMPROVE ASSESSMENTS

Assessments are living investigations into the problems and successes of real people and constitute a professional privilege. Assessments often illicit more sensitive and confidential information about a person's history, mental status, intellect, behavior, beliefs, fears, hopes,

Integrated Summary

Linked to findings from assessment, treatment plan & all clinical notes

Assessments

Linked to all measurements symptoms, unique client factors, environmental & biological factors and diagnosis

Assessment Gestalt

How does interaction within & between assessment sections change or support the assessment as a whole

Clinical Notes

Directly linked to targeted symptoms, goals, methods, & evaluation

Plan

Targeted symptoms linked to diagnosis, goals linked to target symptoms, methods linked to goals & evaluation steps linked to outcome

Diagnosis

Based on the Assessement Gestalt how is the client's problem conceptually understood and what factors support or fail to support a diagnosis

FIGURE 3.4 Steps in Record Keeping Process.

Starting with the assessment, and continuing to the final integrative summary/termination note each clinical record informs, builds, and links with each other. Once treatment ends, the entire case record forms a gestalt providing a consolidative, factual, connected, comprehensive picture of the client, environmental factors, interventions and outcomes.

sadness, loneliness, joys, strengths, symptoms, social skills, and family-community than is known or volunteered to any other single individual. However, the result of this trust is an important responsibility for understanding one's own diagnostic beliefs, clinical skill set, and agency expectations and goals. Additionally, the mandate to assess also requires that we do not simply assign a diagnostic label and quickly abandon the client. That is, ethically we are expected to educate clients and families about the diagnosis and to assist them with finding and receiving both appropriate and wanted help. The client and family should never feel alone or forced into treatment that they do not understand or may not want. Consequently, ethical and accountable social workers must continuously learn and adapt new evidence into their client assessments. If your assessments are founded only on what you learn today, you can be assured that you will simply be fooling yourself and your clients tomorrow; the right to assess and diagnose clients thus carries a lifetime responsibility to continuously educate yourself about both your practice and your clients.

Both new and experienced mental health professionals, for many reasons, make assessment errors. Particular practices to beware of include echoing the ideas of individuals perceived as voices of authority and unknowingly accepting an agency's boundaries and theoretical perspectives. Copying techniques used by a favorite supervisor or expert, rather than developing individual methods of assessment, may reduce a social worker's concerns related to inexperience and limited self-assurance, but it can also produce a shallow assessment founded on rehearsed techniques rather than questions and responses that fit a specific client's needs and situation. As confidence and assessment skills develop over time, we err by trusting clinical knowledge and methods that have become part of a personal repertoire.

Experience and personal beliefs can stand in the way of social workers accepting even replicated findings or moving on from analytical tools whose use is otherwise considered outdated. For example, psychologists have continued to use the Rorschach and other projective instruments, even though they are consistently found to have little or no psychometric value. In a literature review, one author claimed that the following are reasons which explain this phenomenon, that is, why professionals continue to use assessment practices that contradict evidentiary support:

1. Faith in authority: the professors and field instructors must have known what they were doing.
2. Social proof and cognitive illusions: Can all those books, people at the conference, and my observations be wrong?
3. Clinical validation and testimonials: I have seen this work and I have heard clients testify that they had a valuable experience.

4. Anecdotal evidence and self-reinforcement: I and other clinicians have success-fully used these methods for years.

5. Powerful personal experiences and self-consistency: yes, this is anecdotal, but I had a client commit suicide when the method was not followed—besides, I don't see how I and all the others could have been wrong for all these years (Wood, Nezworski, Lilienfeld, & Garb, 2003).

Though the value of the Rorschach and other projective instruments is questioned, there are numerous scales and neuropsychological batteries that consistently help clinicians make informed diagnoses. Indeed, psychometrically sound rating scales and other instruments are readily available for social workers, and can offer added insights when conducting an assessment. Perhaps the most famous social work leader in the development of evidence-based measurement scales is Walter W. Hudson. He produced a number of self-rating scales that have proved over the years to be reliable and valid across numerous client populations (Taylor, 2005). These instruments can be reviewed on the web at http://www.walmyr.com/perscales.html.

When incorporating instruments into an assessment however, one should keep several issues in mind. First, an instrument's reliability and validity do not extend beyond the populations that were psychometrically studied. An instrument may have extremely strong measurement properties for one cultural or economic group, but no assessment value with other populations. Therefore, simply discovering that a scale has high reliability and validity does not ensure that it is safe and meaningful to use with your specific client. Moreover, most self-rating and short-form instruments are screening rather than assessment tools. A depression or suicide scale, for example, only tells the social worker if a client's score falls more in a group with a higher or lower probability of having depression or suicidal behaviors. The scale does not predict that the specific person has or does not have the qualities measured by the scale. There will be people in both the high and low probability groups who have depression or who will take their own lives. Unfortunately, the scales cannot identify the individuals who are in need of immediate help. Self-rating scales, however, are still very helpful tools. If a scale predicts that a client is in a high-risk group, we know that there is a greater need for a full assessment than if the person's score places him or her in a lower category. Measurement instruments also provide a means of tracking change while in treatment. The Hudson scale and many others are specifically designed for repeated use with a single client or family. As illustrated in Figures 3.3 and 3.4, every assessment requires a plan for continued outcome evaluation, and sound psychometric instruments provide a means for accomplishing this vital task.

Blindly accepting and following boundaries and opinions of agencies also represent a significant danger to accurate assessments, as the very agency we work for openly and covertly shapes and limits our perceptions, diagnostic beliefs, and assessment methods. Agencies are forced to develop procedures based on funding criteria and available resources. Even when agencies permit workers to expand boundaries and creatively explore unique assessment avenues, it is tempting for clinicians to remain concretely within the program's routine standard operating procedures. Furthermore, agencies can bias assessments covertly by seducing clinicians into a "group think" mentality. That is, critical and creative thinking becomes difficult when peers and supervisors as a group attempt to shape and guide our immediate thoughts. A major role for clinical supervisors is assuring that clients receive evidence-based assessments that are as accurate and as free as possible of individual and agency bias. Independent and creative thinking that differs from agency beliefs is extremely difficult, regardless of experience.

Even experienced clinicians from established agencies may be influenced by organizational practices to limit their diagnostic assessments. Research indicates that many mental health workers, before completing an assessment, determine a diagnosis and then search for confirming information while systematically ignoring factors that counter their intuition (Doss, Cook, & Mcleod, 2008). In addition, clinicians may mix information that neither correctly links together nor conforms to *DSM* criteria in order to fit their clients into a predetermined diagnostic schema (Angold & Fisher, 1999; Doss et al., 2008; Garb, 1998, 2005). Social workers become particularly vulnerable for making these mistakes when they are yielding to agency culture, professional peer pressure, or insisting on using a favorite theory. Often a program cultivates a clientele from a specific area or with similar problems and circumstances. This can result in diagnostic and severity levels based on how a person compares with the majority of clients served by the clinic. If we primarily see people with severe depression, then it becomes easy to minimize or overlook complaints presented by a person with mild depressive symptoms. Clients have a right to trust that social workers can articulate specifically why they are employing evidence-based practices, practice wisdom, agency mandates, or personal expectations. If our assessment does not reflect evidence-based information-gathering methods, we must more closely examine whether personal and agency bias is overly guiding the conclusions, diagnosis, and clinical decisions. Breaking from a learned and practiced assessment model requires overcoming our own automatic biased thinking, clinical habits, personal comfort zone, and inertia.

The first step in neutralizing personal and professional biases is recognizing that our training, beliefs, and doubts are both our strengths and our weaknesses. Before entering the mental health assessment arena, it is imperative to know how you define, understand, and hear the differences and similarities among (1) mental disorders, (2) behavior problems, (3) deviant behaviors, (4) unique unconventional behavior and personalities, (5) reduced mental capacity, (6) medically triggered mental problems, (7) substance problems, (8) developmental delays, and (9) decreased mental wellness not related to mental disorders. Furthermore, social workers, before assessing, must have an ability to articulate how a client's cultural history and practices will be assessed, understood, valued, and separated from pathological labeling.

The comprehensive social work assessment is not designed simply to identify or rule out mental disorders. In mental health cases, we continuously measure a person's symptoms, functional limitations, strengths, deficit, and recent changes in established skills. Additionally, social work assessments measure how ecological systems provide support, establish barriers to resources, or account for the client's problems. Therefore, upon completing an assessment, a clinician should be able to document (1) major symptoms that are not cultural artifacts, (2) whether symptoms arise more from neuro-biological factors or social learning, (3) outside circumstances creating stress or symptom behaviors, (4) functional skills and strengths, and (5) how the environment helps, hurts, or plays little or no role in the person's internal difficulties.

Assessment and diagnosis are more than a checklist of symptoms matched against *DSM* criteria. When done correctly, a diagnosis is the logical conclusion developed from a multidimensional assessment. Within the maze of a client's culture, symptoms, strengths, development, family, community, group, and ecological experiences is a story about life, struggle, victory, defeat, good, evil, and humanity. The story captured in the assessment process is always interesting, similar to other lives, yet fascinatingly unique. Encouraging clients to tell their story requires, among other things,

- planning before and after client contact;
- convincing professional knowledge (clients do not want an amateur diagnosis);
- having an organized assessment framework that provides clarity and is followed, understood, and accepted by the client;
- having a questioning and discussion method that frees clients to provide complete responses and not feel obligated or forced to respond;
- an ability to sense the need for silence and when to talk;
- asking answerable non-combative questions that address the client's problem, rather than random fact gathering; and
- providing empathy that helps client safely self-disclose.

Interventions can fail when assessments focus on the wrong issues or produce an incorrect diagnosis. Therefore, when an intervention is not successful, examine whether your assessment stood in the client's way of telling a complete story in the person's own voice. Performing an assessment is a position of power, authority, and prestige. Without care and awareness, we will overlook that our questions, tone, and body language are either helping or preventing clients from disclosing or withholding information. Furthermore, how questions are ordered, along with our non-verbal signals, can shape how clients emphasize and even specify their concerns.

Clients are dependent upon us for cuing them about what information we want. In most cases, they want to help the social worker make sense and meaning of their situation. Therefore, it is not unusual in an assessment for the person to follow the clinician's affect and spoken or non-verbal point of view. If early in the assessment it is signaled that a client's difficulties are believed to stem more from a hazardous environment than internal factors, or visa versa, the client may very well try to help the social worker prove the unspoken clinical assumption. A misplaced nod or anxious moving of one's food can miscue individuals being interviewed. A client, for example, interpreting that the social worker believes the person's environment is toxic, may increase blaming, over-emphasize emotions, or overstate ecological issues. The first step in a good assessment is allowing clients to tell their stories, rather than shaping them into your theoretical and psychological worldview. The art of assessment interviewing requires

- thinking critically and multidimensionally;
- questioning in an empathic non-judgmental manner;
- authenticating pain without endorsing the story;
- listening; and
- reaching a valid conclusion that directs treatment planning.

For some, it is uncomfortable to think about validating a client's pain, but not the person's story. In reality, these are two different functions. Whether an individual's pain stems from reality or misperception, internal hurt is immediately accepted as real and acknowledged, whereas the validity of the personal story can only occur after enough facts are collected and alternative perspectives are ruled out. It is through the assessment that clinicians determine if a client's beliefs and environmental perceptions are founded in reality, and allow one to rule whether a diagnosis is appropriate. Furthermore, the assessment singularly guides the diagnosis, while the assessment and diagnosis jointly direct which methods and intervention elements are included in the treatment plan. Knowing that a person has depression provides important treatment information, but fails to place the illness and person in context. Therefore, one must return to the assessment details to understand how to fit the treatment to the client.

This textbook hopefully offers insights into assessing, diagnosing, and treating mental illness. Unfortunately, however, like all models, it also biases your judgment and limits your creativity. Theories, models, and diagnostic frameworks are extremely important for understanding mental illness, but they also can trigger rigid and careless automatic thinking.

REFERENCES

Angold, A., & Fisher, P. W. (1999). Interviewer-based interviews. In D. Shaffer, C. P. Lucas, & J. E. Richters (Eds.), *Diagnostic Assessment in Child and Adolescent Psychopathology* (pp. 34–64). New York: Guilford Press.

Doss, A. J., Cook, K. T., & Mcleod, B. D. (2008). Diagnostic issues. In D. Reitman (Ed.), *Handbook of Psychological Assessment, Case Conceptualization and Treatment* (Vol. 2, pp. 25–52). Hoboken, NJ: John Wiley & Sons.

Garb, H. N. (1998). *Studying the Clinician: Judgment Research, and Psychological Assessment.* Washington, DC: American Psychological Association.

Garb, H. N. (2005). Clinical judgment and decision making. *Annual Review of Clinical Psychology, 1*(1), 67–89.

Haight, W. L., & Taylor, E. H. (2013). *Human Behavior for Social Work Practice: A Developmental-Ecological Framework for Social Work* (2nd ed.). Chicago: Lyceum Books.

Hallam, R. S. (2013). *Individual Case Formulation.* Boston: Elsevier.

Jensen, P. S., Penny, K., & Mrazek, D. A. (2006). *Toward a New Diagnostic System for Child Psychopathology: Moving Beyond the DSM.* New York: Guilford Press.

Munger, R. L. (1998). *The Ecology of Troubled Children: Changing Children's Behavior by Changing the Places, Activities, and People in Their Lives.* Cambridge, MA: Brookline Books.

Taylor, E. H. (2005). Using self-rating scales for assessing the severely mentally ill client: A clinical and psychometric perspective. *Journal of Human Behavior in the Social Environment, 11,* 23–40.

Wood, J. M., Nezworski, M. T., Lilienfeld, S. O., & Garb, H. N. (2003). *What's wrong with the Rorschach?* New York: Jossey-Bass.

APPENDIX 1: MENTAL HEALTH ASSESSMENT INTERVIEW OUTLINE

THE MENTAL HEALTH ASSESSMENT

A symphony of knowledge and art conducted by the clinician

THE PURPOSE OF AN ASSESSMENT

- Qualify and quantify a person's symptoms, problems, strengths, skills, and support systems.
- Identify biosocial treatment needs.
- Clarify mental health history of individual and family.
- Rule out alternative clinical diagnostic hypotheses.
- Determine need for specialized assessments.
- Develop a diagnosis that informs an evidence-based treatment plan.

IDENTIFYING INFORMATION

Who Is the Client

- Discover how the client perceives her or himself as a unique individual, family person, worker, peer, community member, member of a culture or group, and member of society (may want to ask the client, "How would you describe or introduce yourself?").
- Who is involved in the assessment?
- At what point in the client's history is this assessment being conducted?

REASON AND PURPOSE FOR ASSESSMENT

- Who wants the assessment and why
- Who does not want the assessment

PRESENTING PROBLEMS

- Client's view and what most concerns client
- Family and others' views and what most concerns family/others
- Clinician's first impressions, view, or hypotheses

DEFINE ALL CURRENT AND PAST SYMPTOMS

- "Define" how and when symptoms behaviorally occur.
- Explain symptom severity (How often do they occur? How do they disrupt client and/or family life? What behaviors and emotions are triggered, and how are the symptoms cognitively perceived?).
- Indicate whether identified by client, family, or clinician.
- Indicate if symptoms are accepted by the client, family, and clinician.
- What has person or family done to try to treat or stop the symptoms, and what did and did not work?

BIOLOGICAL, GENETIC, AND MEDICAL FACTORS

- Individual
  - Documented mental and physical health problems
  - Possible mental and physical health problems
  - Last full physical, eye exam, hearing exam
- Family (3 generations if info is available)
  - Documented mental and health genetic history (include type of treatment, severity, year or age of onset, results of treatment over time)
  - Possible mental and health genetic factors

PSYCHIATRIC TREATMENT (CURRENT AND HISTORICAL OVERVIEW)

- Problems recognized but never treated
- Outpatient treatment (what, when, where, how, reason for stopping, results)
- Inpatient treatment (what, when, where, how, reason for stopping, results)
- Non-traditional treatment for psychiatric symptoms (what, when, where, how, reason for stopping, results)
- Family and client's beliefs about past and current treatment
- How much did treatment help and what helped the most?
- Did any treatment cause the client or family problems?

PSYCHIATRIC TREATMENT (MEDICATION)

- History of past medication (what, when, where, how, reason for stopping, results)
- Current medications (provide following for past and present meds)
  - *Name of all current and past medications*

- *Amount prescribed*
- *When drug is/was taken*
- *Purpose of drug*
- *Who prescribed drug*
- *Client's compliance*
- *Problems caused by the medications (side effects, interpersonal, or work-related difficulties)*
- *How much do medications help?*
- *How much do current and past medications help?*
- *What side effects did past medications cause?*
- *Client and family's beliefs about the medications*
- *Vitamins, minerals, herbs, natural medications, homeopathic medications*
- *Food selections or omissions used as treatment*

MENTAL STATUS EXAM

- Physical appearance
- Cognition, intelligence, and memory
- Orientation to person, place, and time
- Affect, anxiety, and ability to tolerate stress
- Motor skills and nervous habits or reactions
- Ability to relate to others
- Social skills and social intelligence
- Social insight and understanding of problem

SUICIDALITY, SELF-HARM

- Current problems
- Past history
- What has previously helped, and what has previously increased self-harm?
- Family or significant other history of suicidality

HOMICIDALITY, HARM TO OTHERS, DESTRUCTION OF PROPERTY

- Current problems
- Past history

- What has previously helped, and what has previously increased the aggression?
- Family's/significant other's history of violence to others or property

DRUG AND SUBSTANCES USE

- Identify
  - What is used
  - Amount
  - When used and when not used
  - History
  - Who substance is used with
  - Level/severity (see scale below)

SUBSTANCE LEVEL/SEVERITY SCALE

- Use—substance such as alcohol used without negative consequences
- Misuse—substance used with negative consequences
- Abuse—continued use despite negative consequences
- Addiction—compulsive use regardless of negative consequences

CULTURAL ISSUES (NOTE: WE ALL HAVE A HISTORICAL AND CURRENT CULTURE)

- Person's historical culture
- Person's current culture
- Current and past cultural strengths
- Current and past cultural conflicts
- How does person identify self?
- Cultural issues requiring immediate attention
- Unique client/family/community circumstances

GENERAL ECOLOGICAL SYSTEMS AND SOCIAL CONSIDERATIONS

- Briefly list and explain
  - Family, marital, peer relationships/support/problems
  - Community and work/school successes and problems

- Economic factors contributing to current and past successes and problems
- Situational stressors not otherwise mentioned in report

IMPACT OF ECOLOGY ON FUNCTIONING

- Impaired functioning or increased symptoms within specific settings
  - What skills / behaviors measurably decrease?
  - What social duties or roles are expected of client in these settings?
  - With time, do symptoms change within these settings?
  - What is the climate of these settings?

IMPACT OF ECOLOGY ON FUNCTIONING

- Functions/behaviors/symptoms that improve within specific settings
  - What skills/behaviors measurably increase, and how much do they improve?
  - What social duties or roles are expected of client in these settings?
  - Does improvement last as long as person is in setting?
  - What is the climate of these settings?

IMPACT OF ECOLOGY ON FUNCTIONING

- Functions/skills/behaviors/that are not altered by illness (skills that remain healthy)
  - What skills/behaviors remain healthy?
  - What expectations or roles does client fulfill in settings where specific skills remain healthy?
  - What is the climate of these settings?
  - Are there settings where these healthy skills are decreased?

IMPACT OF ECOLOGY ON FUNCTIONING

- What setting or situation creates the most problems for the client?
  - Client's perspective
  - Family and others' perspective

- Clinician's observations (if client is observed in multiple settings)
- What settings or situations are the most supportive for the client?
  - Client's perspective
  - Family and others' perspective
  - Clinician's observations (if client is observed in multiple settings)

OTHER ECOLOGICAL FACTORS

- Identify any ecological, psychological, social, family, medical, or other stressors that have not been previously discussed and are impacting the client or family's current problems.
- Identify any ecological, psychological, social, family, medical or other stressors that **have been resolved** and no longer negatively impact the client or family's current problems.

PSYCHOMETRIC EVALUATIONS

- What instruments and measurements were used for this assessment?
- Are the instruments reliable and valid for **this client?**
- What were the major findings?
- Do the instrument's findings support conclusions and data from other assessment sources?
- What additional clinical steps are needed (or were taken) if instrument findings conflict with other assessment data?

INTEGRATIVE DIAGNOSTIC OVERVIEW AND JUSTIFICATION

- Suggest a *DSM-5* diagnosis for guiding treatment.
- Briefly explain which *DSM-5* criteria the client does and does not fit.
- Justify why you are disregarding criteria that the client does not fit.
- Outline which and how alternative diagnoses that match client symptoms were ruled out.
- What concerns do you have about the diagnosis?
- What specialized assessments do you recommend to better clarify the diagnosis or symptoms?

OUTLINE OF *DSM* CATEGORICAL DIAGNOSIS

- Axis I (Clinical disorders and other conditions that may warrant clinical attention)
- Axis II (Personality disorders and mental retardation)
- Axis III (Medical conditions)
- Axis IV (Psychosocial and environmental problems)
- Axis V (Global Assessment of Functioning Scale)

APPENDIX 2: ECOLOGICAL ASSESSMENT OUTLINE

Observed behaviors must be understood within a social context. The goal of an Ecological Assessment is to determine the degree to which environments, cultural perceptions and beliefs, bio-social-cognitive interactions, and unique events account for an individual or group's behavior.

Describe the environment and systems.

- Interacting settings and their climates
- Micro, meso, macro
- Subsystems and power distribution
- Historical versus current culture
- Rules and boundaries
- Expected roles and behaviors
- Goodness-of-fit as helpful and harmful
- Expectations of client and others
- Power relationships
- Attachment and loyalty issues of participants (hierarchical attachments)
- Environmental experience, perceptions, knowledge, and memories

Describe whether larger or more powerful systems or subsystems account for any of the observed behaviors.

- What was the **reciprocal impact** from interactions with the concrete environment, abstract environment, and key individuals in the system?
- What happened in the system historically, immediately before, and immediately after the observed behaviors?
- How does the setting's social climate impact the participants individually?
- What is the purpose or goal of the setting/system, and how does that fit with the client's goals and self-perceived purpose?
- What *cues* are given by the environment, participants, and client?
- How do the environment, interaction, and larger systems influence the participants' schema?

What role does time or point in time play in the behaviors?
- **Attending Focus**: Within each setting, what do people attend to or focus their attention on? What is the contextual point of attention within the setting?

- **Boundaries**: Are the setting's boundaries open, semi-permeable, solid, closed, or unidirectional?
- **Distance and Space**: How does space play a role among individuals in a setting?
- **Energy**: What types of energy and action are stimulated by the setting? Does the setting have rules about how personal energy will be used?
- **Linkage**: Among systems, systems and individuals, and individuals with other individuals within and outside of the current setting
- **Memory**: Social or environmental memory, memory response (reaction to environment shaped by past experiences—behavior occurs without thought—a different form or unconscious behavior)
- **Perceptions**: Perceptions of environment, interactions, communication, power, and self
- **Problem-Solving**: Social problem-solving, specific, general, targeted, and so on
- **Power Enforcement**: What happens if rules are followed, broken, or power is challenged?
- **Prediction**: Environmental prediction, expectation of stability within the environment
- **Reciprocal impact:** Created by interaction
- **Response to Change** (within and across settings): How do environmental and behavioral changes impact each person within the immediate setting, and what happens when a person transitions from one changed setting to another setting that has not changed?
- **Roles**: Assigned or ascribed, personal, perceived by group and individual
- **Rules**
- **Unique and Shared Environments**: What part of the environment impacts only an identified person or group, and what environmental impact is experienced by everyone sharing the setting?

4

SCHIZOPHRENIA

UNDERSTANDING SCHIZOPHRENIA

Overview

In the most global sense, schizophrenia is a neurobiological disorder that disrupts normal thought processes, reduces social skills and problem-solving, depletes motivation, exaggerates or minimizes emotions, and bends at least part of everyday reality into unreal perceptions, sensations, and beliefs. This leads many to associate this illness with hallucinations or delusions. However, describing the disorder as a disturbance of thought processes and an inability to separate reality from psychotic, unreal, and disoriented perceptions fails to capture the catastrophic nature of this illness. Furthermore, like most types of illnesses, the general descriptive symptoms affect individuals differently. That is, we can describe the disorder, but cannot specifically predict how it will impact the skills, emotions, perceptions, logical reasoning, and well-being of specific individuals. Even clients with severe symptoms will have neurological domains and competencies that are not disrupted by schizophrenia. Individuals with very mild symptoms may have mostly hidden problems that are compensated for by personal strengths and productive life activities. Nonetheless, schizophrenia is one of the most serious and most difficult to treat forms of mental illness, regardless of the level of severity. Even the best of treatments, helpful ecological systems, and time seldom result in complete recovery.

Still, an individual's ability to blend in socially is not always entirely impaired. Some individuals with schizophrenia mix completely or mostly unobtrusively from one social setting to another. Symptoms for these individuals can be observed only under certain situations or when we are invited to enter his or her private thoughts, anxieties, and perceptions. These are individuals who secretly live in a mysterious, sometimes frightening, internal world that can suddenly become void of routine pleasures, and that is controlled by recurring, unexplainable thoughts and beliefs. The only hints observed by outsiders are moments of social awkwardness and asociality, which are usually interpreted as aloofness or eccentricity, rather than as symptoms of a neurobiological illness. Few observers are aware that the person's energy and concentration are focused on maintaining contact with reality and the task at hand, rather than social cultural expectations. This can result in a constant quasi-social-withdrawal that hides symptoms and permits some individuals to quietly sidestep or limit labels and societal stigmatization. Unfortunately, many individuals with schizophrenia have neither the physical ability nor cognitive skills to hide their symptoms from the public's eye. The casual observer is tempted to separate from the individual with schizophrenia and to think in terms of labels rather than symptoms of a disability.

Thus, the client with schizophrenia is often described as having threatening body movements, poor motivation, odd behaviors, and a willful disregard for conventional hygiene, social customs, manners, and personal control. At best, the client is labeled "lovable, but different," and at worst, "crazy and dangerous." Furthermore, empathy is often overshadowed by beliefs and myths that have been passed across generations. It becomes tempting to distance oneself from physical, social, and emotional pain by earnestly declaring that the mentally ill person simply is not trying, receives secondary gains from the symptoms, does not want to improve, has inappropriately used the good will of others, and has made a psychological or existential choice to be dysfunctional. Negative public and family perceptions are obviously worrisome and dangerous to the health of individuals with schizophrenia. We know, for example, that there is a relationship between stress and increased hospitalizations for clients with schizophrenia (Taylor, 2006; Torrey, 2006). Therefore, it is paramount for social workers to learn how to effectively advise and educate families, community agencies, and neighborhoods about this disorder. Far too many view people with schizophrenia as distasteful, frightening, and dangerous.

In the past, textbooks and folklore painted the illness as hopeless and non-responsive to treatment. This is far from accurate. Some clients, as happens in any illness, are non-responsive to medical and social treatments. The majority of people with schizophrenia, however, receive major benefits from treatment and rehabilitation assistance. Currently, treatment can control major symptoms completely for some and partially for others. As a result, schizophrenia is conceptualized as responding to treatment, much like diabetes. We hope to end or dramatically reduce symptoms, but we cannot cure the disorder.

Levels of Severity

Moderate to severe schizophrenia has the ability to attack and change a person's behaviors, perceptions, cognitive abilities, emotions, neuromotor functions, and social skills. Additionally, the disorder inhibits one's ability to incorporate historical with new information, understand abstractions, and learn from life experiences. Many with this disorder find it impossible to maintain concentration throughout a short conversation, to reduce anxiety to a comfortable level, to read a single short newspaper column, or to watch a half-hour popular television program. No other psychiatric disorder so dramatically and for such an extended length of time alters an individual's existing core skills and characteristics. Because most clients develop in a normal trajectory until schizophrenia unexpectedly appears, the illness can trigger crisis, grief, sorrow, anger, and other emotions within the client and the family.

When severe schizophrenia strikes, it is as if the person everyone knew is gone, replaced by a similar body, yet different in physical appearance, and strangely different in behavior, skills, beliefs, and life perspectives. Family members often remark that severe schizophrenia is worse than losing a loved one by death, particularly given that most clients will never return to their pre-illness level of daily functioning and potential for future achievements. The ill person and family are reminded daily that schizophrenia is a thief that robs sanity and the intrinsic qualities that uniquely defined the very essence of an individual. It is important to underscore that many clients and most families understand and grieve the losses caused by this disorder. For many, this grief is at best tolerated and accepted as part of life, but never completely resolved. When understood from a client or family perspective, schizophrenia is far more complicated and devastating than what is briefly described in *DSM-IV*.

HISTORICAL OVERVIEW

Schizophrenia is one of the earliest described disorders experienced by humans. Troubling and mystifying, it exists globally across all nations, cultures, and socioeconomic conditions (Ho, Black, et al., 2003). Descriptions of schizophrenia have been found in early Egyptian papyrus records, 1400 B.C. Hindu writings, and Chinese medical texts appearing around 1000 B.C. (Korn, 2001). In 1400 B.C. the Greek writers described the very symptoms that we currently call schizophrenia. By the early fifth century B.C., Greek scholars had discarded theories attributing psychosis to demonic forces. Hippocrates and others taught that "madness" results from a brain dementia, which significantly differs from mania and melancholia (Simon, 1980). This definition reflects in part how the disorder is defined today.

Despite these early shifts in recognition, the Greeks had little success in treating schizophrenia. Interestingly, they did, however, develop alternative forms of treatment, such as interventions that employed music and swaying beds for treating agitated patients (Deutsch, 1949; Korn, 2001). By the second century, Greek medical writings advocated light and airy living facilities for the mentally ill, and for physicians to develop an interpersonal relationship with their clients. Additionally, Greek clinicians were taught that the social environment must be assessed before a patient could be fully understood, and that corporal punishments were not to be used for correcting mentally disordered individuals (Korn, 2001). But while the Greeks, and in fact the Romans, described symptoms of psychosis and mania, they never gave a concise definition of schizophrenia. There also is no evidence that there was any understanding that schizophrenia started in late adolescence and young adulthood, which research now proves to be the case (Torrey, 1980).

As the Greek enlightenment crumbled, agreement on how psychosis and severe mental illness are best defined, studied, and treated varied among scientists, religious leaders, and social-political philosophers. Theories attributing psychoses to demonic possession, divine punishment, psychological weakness, brain dysfunction, and other causes vied for public and academic credibility. Treatment often consisted of banishment, devil exorcism, isolation, confinement in jails and asylums, and sometimes torture and death, marking a regression from the understanding developed by the Greeks (Deutsch, 1949; Torrey, 1980; Korn, 2001).

Nonetheless, voices advocating biological explanations for schizophrenia were present almost every century, leading to a renaissance in medical perspectives in the 1800s. Emil Kraepelin, a German (1856–1926) psychiatrist and professor, drew attention to neurological explanations for schizophrenia. Kraepelin assigned the term *dementia praecox* specifically to the symptoms and course of illness that we now call schizophrenia (Torrey, 1980; Korn, 2001). Kraepelin, more than anyone, has had a lasting impact on how we think about and study schizophrenia. Some of his major contributions include (Torrey, 1980; Korn, 2001):

- developing a systematic diagnostic classification system for schizophrenia;
- defining schizophrenia or *dementia praecox* as a brain disorder;
- identifying that the onset of schizophrenia occurs at a relatively young age in previously mentally healthy individuals;
- observing that the disorder is often progressive and attacks both emotional and cognitive skills;
- demonstrating that the course of schizophrenia can range from mild to severe, but that most patients experience multiple relapses and a progressive deterioration of their mental skills;

- clarifying how the deteriorating process of schizophrenia differs from manic depressive episodes that generally have a better prognosis;

- arguing that while schizophrenia is seldom cured, and patients are seldom returned to their former level of functioning, symptoms can often be reduced and quality of life and skills improved; and

- discovering that about 13% of patients with schizophrenia have stable symptoms and do not appear to have a progressive deteriorating illness.

However, Kraepelin was incorrect in assuming that schizophrenia caused a progressive brain deterioration that left patients little hope for rehabilitation; we now know that treatment and symptom improvement is a realistic goal for most clients. Nonetheless, Kraepelin established important medical insights and illness criteria that became the foundation for modern research into schizophrenia.

Another twentieth-century leader who helped shape the modern perspective of schizophrenia was Eugene Bleuler (1857–1934), a Swiss psychiatrist. Bleuler was primarily responsible for changing the name of *dementia praecox* to schizophrenia. Perhaps his most important contribution was identifying cognitive deficits as the principal abnormality associated with schizophrenia. Bleuler was among the first to focus on and identify symptoms of disturbed thought as a key to diagnosing this disorder. For example, hallucinations and delusions were seen by Bleuler as important but secondary to the reduction of cognitive and problem-solving skills (Beng-Choon, Black, et al., 2003).

During and following World War II, neurobiological explanations for understanding schizophrenia, though not disappearing completely, substantially decreased in acceptance. Until the late 1980s, however, schizophrenia was believed by many influential Western mental health workers and educators to result from disordered family communication styles, unconscious conflicts triggered by mothers who gave and then withdrew affection, or an individual's choice to sink into a psychotic state. The famous Palo Alto Group led by Gregory Bateson devised the "double bind" communication theory to explain schizophrenia. The illness was thought to occur when parents gave conflicting messages over an extended time that had no satisfactory resolution (Bateson, Jackson, et al., 1956). As an example, a parent may lecture a child for failing to reciprocate or show positive feelings for the family, but also declare that the individual should not be so outwardly affectionate. In the end the child is rejected, belittled, or invalidated if affection is or is not demonstrated.

Psychodynamic clinicians used a number of mother-oriented models to explain the illness. One psychoanalytic concept framed schizophrenia as resulting from the "good breast, bad breast mother." It was conceptualized that at the beginning of infancy, a mother randomly switched between breast-feeding her baby with love, care, and attention, to feelings of anger, inattentiveness, and blame for demanding to be fed. As a result, the infant could never predict whether hunger cries would bring the good or bad breast, and in turn, the uncertainty created anxiety, social withdrawal, and for some, schizophrenia.

Others, such as Thomas Szasz, developed a social constructionist theory of schizophrenia. Szasz was a trained psychoanalyst who became dissatisfied with psychodynamic theory and fashioned a mental health philosophy based on personal choice and societal biases against certain behaviors. He taught that mental illness does not exist, and that schizophrenia is either a choice made by individuals to escape the realities of their world, or a label placed by society to control behaviors (Szasz, 1984). Each of these theories over time has been discredited by research, and has given way to more empirically based neurobiological models of schizophrenia

SYMPTOMS SEEN IN PSYCHOSIS

Schizophrenia causes one's brain to secretly distort, falsify, and change personal experiences, perceptions, and inner thoughts into a web of false realities. The adjective "secretly" implies that most individuals in the beginning, and some throughout the illness, are unaware that their ability to think, problem-solve, and understand complex abstract concepts is not only changing but also dramatically decreasing. Distortions become concretely authentic, and remain unchecked and unchallenged by alternative solutions, facts, logic, or physical proof of irrational thinking. As in all disorders, symptoms will cluster and differ from client to client, and are difficult to identify in their mildest state. These specific subtypes of schizophrenia are discussed later, though all variations of the illness create three common factors. In differing levels of severity clients, will have (1) misperceptions and a diminished orientation to reality, (2) observable reductions in social skills and abstract cognitive functioning, and (3) what has become known as negative, or type II, symptoms.

Positive, or type I, symptoms consist of elements that are most often associated with a thought disorder, such as hallucinations, delusions, disorganized thinking and speech, and unusual behaviors. These symptoms are generally found in the first two factors and result in a false sense of reality and reduced social and cognitive functioning. Negative, or type II, symptoms include symptoms such as loss of motivation, inability to experience pleasure, blunted affect, reduced concentration, and decreased personal hygiene. Additionally, between psychotic episodes almost all clients with schizophrenia will continue to have some negative symptoms that prevent them from completely returning to their pre-illness state of social functioning, whereas many clients, with proper treatment, experience no positive symptoms between psychotic episodes.

Before symptoms of schizophrenia are described in more detail, however, we need to remind ourselves that the term "psychosis" is a concept that involves clusters of symptoms. This term implies that a person is not oriented in some way to current environmental and cultural realities. Psychosis by definition means that the client previously understood the realities of cultural expectations, concepts of time and place (such as day, month, year, and location), and generally understood what is and is not culturally accepted as reality. In a state of psychosis, the person's ability to identify, interpret, and respond to concrete and abstract environmental events is diminished, and is at least partially replaced with false realities and beliefs. All or part of what one perceives or believes during episodes of psychosis is incongruent with reality as experienced by most people, and as previously accepted by the client.

Finally, we need to acknowledge that psychosis is not a diagnosis. One can have psychotic symptoms, as described in the following pages, without having schizophrenia. Psychosis can occur in major depressive episodes, bipolar disorders, borderline personality disorder, brief psychotic disorders, drug- or alcohol-induced psychosis, and numerous other medical conditions, as well as in schizophrenia. Diagnosis is further complicated by the fact that psychotic symptoms can look identical across all of these illnesses. This can make it difficult to determine a diagnosis immediately when a person experiences his or her first psychotic episode. Nonetheless, by understanding psychosis, correctly applying the criteria required for schizophrenia, and ruling out other possible explanations for diminished reality symptoms (see Figure 4.1), social workers can successfully assess and identify the illness of schizophrenia. Specifics for differentiating schizophrenia from other forms of psychoses are provided in the assessment section.

Diminished Reality

Schizophrenia reduces the client's ability to distinguish what is real and how to respond to environmental stimuli in a culturally acceptable manner. Hallucinations and delusions are among the most devastating and clear symptoms, but they are not the only examples of reality deficits. A client's inability to correctly perceive and interpret the environment may also appear in the form of altered behavior or emotions. Symptoms involving impaired reality are complicated, occur in different forms for different clients, and link to numerous other symptoms and bioecological factors. It is therefore paramount for social workers to have a solid understanding of schizophrenia as an illness,

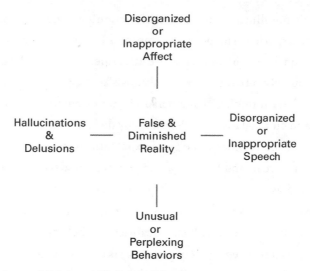

FIGURE 4.1 Symptoms of False and Diminished Reality.

Systems associated with false or diminished reality. The term "diminished reality" is used because clients often have varying degrees of false realities. A person may live in a mixed world of false, diminished, and factual perceptual realities.

and impaired reality as a neurobiological symptom, before attempting to address the deficits in treatment or family education.

Clients are experiencing a hallucination when their brain incorrectly signals or interprets and labels visual, auditory, olfactory, gustatory (taste), kinesthetic (false body or movement sensations), or tactile sensations that are not stimulated by valid environmental input (Strub & Wise, 1997). That is, the individual is seeing, hearing, smelling, or feeling something that is not actually occurring or caused by the immediate social or physical environments. Hallucinations are not forms of cognitive imagination, memories, hypnotic altered perceptions, or an effort to creatively redefine the social environment, though they do occur in people with schizophrenia across all cultures. However, the type and frequency, and the personal experience produced by hallucinations, appear to vary with a person's culture, life experiences, and background (Ndetei & Vadher, 1984).

Research indicates that the sensations are produced by the brain as if the event were actually taking place in the environment (Ho, Black, et al., 2003). Through the magic of modern brain imaging, neuroscientists have shown that brain sections known to control vision or hearing are activated and functioning during a hallucination much as they do when stimulated by environmental realities. One study showed that the auditory cortex during a hallucination competes for neurophysiological resources with environmental sounds (Hubl, Koenig, et al., 2007). Auditory hallucinations can cause the person to hear an undefined sound, a very clear understandable voice, or multiple sounds and clashing or conflicting arguing voices. It is not unusual for people with schizophrenia to hear voices that talk back, yell, scold, denigrate, or belittle them. Likewise, visual hallucinations range from sketchy undefined lines, dots, and patterns to clearly defined dimensional objects, people, or spirits. The important point for social workers to understand and to help others to understand is that within the brain of a schizophrenic person who is hallucinating, the sound, visual, or other phenomena are physiologically taking place. For the person who is hallucinating, a voice, sight, or other sensation is being activated in the brain and is occurring in real time. As a result, the client has little choice but to interpret the event as actually taking place.

Diagnostically, it is important to determine if the person senses that a visual or auditory sensation is believed to occur in the environment outside the head, or is taking place within the brain. In most cases, a true visual or auditory hallucination will be perceived by a client as happening outside him- or herself. Visual and hearing stimuli identified as being within the brain or mind are considered pseudohallucinations and do not qualify for diagnosing schizophrenia (Heilbrun, 1993; American Psychiatric Association, 2000). It should also be noted that it is not uncommon for people with no mental disorder to report hearing humming or other sounds within their head, or having visualizations upon going to sleep or awaking from sleep, and therefore these symptoms do not suggest schizophrenia either (American Psychiatric Association, 2000; Cummings & Mega, 2003). In addition, clients who report occasionally hearing their name called and finding no one around are not considered to be hallucinating. If one often hears his or her name called, or other very brief repetitive unexplained words or sounds, the person may be suffering from a medical illness such as a seizure or auditory disorder (Strub & Wise, 1997; Cummings & Mega, 2003). Shortly after the death of a loved one, it is not unusual for individuals to report awakening and seeing or hearing the deceased individual. This phenomenon usually discontinues as normal grieving comes to an end, and is not considered a hallucination, nor is it associated with schizophrenia (DeSpelder & Strickland, 2002; Cummings & Mega, 2003; Haight & Taylor, 2007).

Children may vividly report playing and communicating with an invisible friend, animal, or object. Imagination and visualizations of this nature are considered part of normal childhood development and are not part of the psychotic domain. However, there is some, but weak evidence that under stress, children are more likely than adults to experience hallucinations (Remschmidt, 2001; Cummings & Mega, 2003). Nonetheless, hallucinations in children independent from other required symptoms listed in *DSM-IV-TR* are not diagnosed as schizophrenia. Studies document that childhood schizophrenia onset closely resembles the criteria established for adult onset. This is especially true for older children and younger adolescents. However, children may not report or interpret hallucinations and delusions as intrusive or unusual (Asarnow & Karatekin, 1998). In addition, the onset of childhood schizophrenia may occur extremely gradually. This makes interviewing difficult. A child generally will not automatically report symptoms or cognitive concerns. Therefore, anything that the child is not directly asked has a high probability of not being reported. The children's lack of awareness that their internal experiences are unusual prevents them from providing a spontaneous report. Unfortunately, if the clinician is overly insistent, asks leading questions, or provides little structure or guidelines, a child who actually has no early onset symptoms will create answers that point toward a diagnosis. Children and adolescents often want to please the interviewer and will try to create information that they think the social worker wants to hear (Asarnow & Karatekin, 1998).

The brain has the ability to fool us in amazing ways, as similar experiences can be caused by a number of very different and unrelated disorders. Therefore, in order to help distinguish between these, one must not confuse illusions with visual hallucinations. An illusion is a misinterpretation and incorrect labeling of a real but ambiguous object observed in the immediate environment. For example, a child may interpret a shadow as a monster. Or a situation may arise like the following. A friend reported that her 89-year-old mother, who resided in a nursing home, consistently reported that every night a man came and got in bed with her. When questioned, the mother stated that the man did nothing to her, just got in bed, brushed her hair back with his hand, and disappeared before morning. The family thought their mother was having a recurring hallucination. However, to be certain that no one was assaulting the woman, her daughter one evening remained in the nursing home room overnight. Around midnight a male nurse entered the room, leaned over close to the mother's ear, and said in a caring, clear voice, "I have to give you your shot now." After administering the small needle injection, he brushed her hair back and left. The next morning the daughter asked, "Did the man come and get in your bed last night?" The mother reported, "Oh yes, you must have been sleeping."

The story dynamically illustrates why all suspected hallucinations must be completely assessed. A careless clinical interview could easily incorrectly record the illusion as a hallucination; diagnostically, a visual hallucination is not associated with any actual environmentally observed shape or form. However, all hallucinations take on cultural overtones. If one, for example, hears the voice of God, the voice will most often be in tones, decibels, words, and phrases that reflect the client's cultural and religious teachings. Once a person has schizophrenia, hallucinations can be triggered or increased by stressful situations. Stress, however, is not thought to be a primary cause or explanation of the illness (Taylor, 2006). This is not to say that stress cannot cause hallucinations. We know, for example, that sleep deprivation and mental torture can cause hallucinations. However, as discussed below, hallucinations stemming from known situations, chemicals, medical illnesses, or without other categorical symptoms are not related to schizophrenia. Hallucinations signal the possibility of schizophrenia, but do not within themselves provide a definitive diagnosis.

Auditory and visual hallucinations are much more common than olfactory, gustatory, kinesthetic, and tactile sensations. Auditory hallucinations are found in 28% to 72% and visual hallucinations occur in as many as 50% of individuals with schizophrenia (Strub & Wise, 1997; Cummings & Mega, 2003). While we know that auditory hallucinations are more frequently encountered than visual or other forms of hallucinations, the exact percent of occurrence has yet to be determined. Clients may experience a single type or combinations of different forms of hallucination. Furthermore, the severity, type, duration, experience, and time between episodes of hallucinations can change for people over time. Olfactory hallucinations cause the person to smell aromas in the environment that are not present, and sometimes occur along with gustatory hallucinations. This combination will be reported as having unpleasant tastes and odors, either simultaneously or independent of each other (Cummings & Mega, 2003; Ho, Black, et al., 2003). The smell of automobile tires or other rubber burning can be associated with schizophrenia, but is also found in people with certain types of neurological problems, rather than neuropsychiatric disorders.

Generally, olfactory, tactile, and gustatory hallucinations are rare in clients with schizophrenia. As a result, an immediate neurological consult is in order for a person who experiences these forms of hallucinations, even if there has been a recent medical examination (Asaad 1990; Cummings & Mega, 2003; Sadock & Sadock, 2007). Tactile hallucinations can present in any form of physical feelings on the skin or within any bodily organ. Most often, the sensation is unpleasant, such as burning, itching, or pain, but it can also be pleasant. All hallucinations are generally experienced as frightening, or at least annoying, and usually increase the client's anxiety. In rare cases, clients report enjoying the sensation created by their hallucinations. It is more common to find clients who derive no pleasure from hallucinating but rather have learned to live with and possibly accommodate these intrusive events.

During the assessment process, social workers need to determine if the hallucination is telling or ordering the client to perform some type of act of action or behavior, such as hurting someone or making a suicidal attempt. These are known as command hallucinations and can be extremely dangerous for the individual or others. It should be underscored, though, that most people with schizophrenia do not have command hallucinations, and never become violent. The client sometimes identifies the voice as coming from God, the devil, an angel, or a saint. In the rare cases where command hallucinations occur, a physical attack or suicide attempt can take place with little or no warning.

Violence can also occur if the hallucination changes how another individual is perceived. A brain that is ill from schizophrenia can make one believe that another person morphs into the form of someone or something evil. A young man well known by the treatment team struck his psychiatrist several times in the face without warning, knocking him to the ground. After the doctor fell to the ground, the patient severely kicked him in his ribs. An interview found that a hallucination had caused the client to see and believe that the psychiatrist was in the process of transforming from a human to a devil. In the client's mind, he was not striking his doctor, but rather the devil who was taking over the psychiatrist's body. In actuality, the client was very fond of the doctor and the entire treatment team. Previously the individual had never been violent, despite having a long history of schizophrenia. In 2008 a middle-aged man with schizophrenia was riding a Greyhound bus in Canada. Without making a sound or warning, he shockingly stabbed and decapitated a young person riding in the seat next to him. When arrested, he was puzzled why the other passengers and police did not see him as a hero. For him, it was unbelievable that the other passengers had not seen that the person beside him was a dangerous evil devil. It was later discovered that, along with the visual hallucination, the man also was experiencing auditory command hallucinations instructing him to decapitate the "devil" seated next to him.

Hearing the voice of God or seeing religious figures such as angels, the Virgin Mary, or prophets are common hallucinatory themes. Because religion is strongly woven into the nation's cultural fabric, reports of experiencing, seeing, or hearing spiritual beings must be carefully assessed (see Box 4.1). Religious people across the United States and the world who have no mental disorders often report holy visions, internal directions from God, signs sent by God that have specific meaning, divine healings and other miracles, the hand or force of God knocking them off their feet or causing convulsions, and verbal commands.

The social worker's job is to respect these personal experiences as real for the individual and beyond the proof of science unless concrete evidence of a hallucination triggered by mental illness is determined through a diagnostic assessment. We must always be vigilant of the fact that many cultures and religious groups believe in parapsychological phenomena. Therefore we do not accept, reject, or label as pathological such reported experiences without performing a complete and systematic assessment. Addressing the following items will help social workers document whether a client's

BOX 4.1

ASSESSING HALLUCINATIONS

1. What is the client experiencing (auditory, visual, smells, physical sensations, etc.)?
2. When did hallucination-like events first occur?
3. What is the client's history of hallucinations and how have they changed over time?
4. Can you rule out that the reported event is partly true, has a reasonable probability of being possible or an illusion, or has explanations other than a hallucination?
5. Does the client have any doubts about the hallucination (individuals with mild schizophrenia and clients who have received psychosocial-education may understand that the event is coming from their illness)?
6. Can the hallucination be contributed to medical illness or injuries, medications or drug interactions, substance abuse, or exposure to toxins, rather than schizophrenia?
7. How organized and specific are the details making up the hallucination?
8. How often do the hallucinations occur?
9. Do the hallucinations occur randomly, or do they seem to be triggered by certain settings or environments (in most cases, but not all, schizophrenia causes the hallucinations to occur randomly; however, they often increase as stress, anxiety, and other psychotic symptoms increase)?
10. How much anxiety does the client experience before, during, and after the hallucination?
11. What meaning, if any, does the client assign to the hallucination?
12. If auditory or visual, what is being heard or seen?
13. If auditory, is the sound coming from inside or outside the person's head (in most, but not all, schizophrenia cases the sound seems to occur outside the head, and often to the right or left of the person)
14. If auditory, can the person understand what is being said, who is making the comments, and how many voices are heard?
15. If auditory, is the voice commanding the person to harm self or others?
16. Does the client have any history of command hallucinations?
17. If auditory, is the voice (or voices) belittling, condemning, or in any way being derogatory to the client (voices that are critical of the client can increase the risk for suicide)?
18. If auditory, has the client, because of the voices, ever made a suicide attempt?
19. If visual, does the hallucination cause others to appear as evil, or as threatening individuals or objects?

20. If the hallucination causes others to appear as evil or threatening, how is the person currently reacting, and how have they historically reacted?
21. Does the hallucination cause the client to see others morph into an evil person or object?
22. If the hallucination causes others to morph into evil, how is the person currently reacting, and how have they historically reacted?
23. Have hallucinations ever been linked to attempts to hurt self or others?

religious visions or auditory sensations are hallucinations. When possible, determine from both the client and the person's family if any of the following factors have occurred:

1. Other symptoms of schizophrenia or psychosis are documented.
2. The person's social and cognitive functioning is substantially reduced from a documented previous skill level.
3. The religious vision or auditory sensation occurs randomly in numerous locations, situations, and time periods.
4. The religious vision or auditory sensation occurs when others are present, but no one else sees or hears what the client is experiencing.
5. The vision or auditory sensation is described as coming from outside the head rather than within one's mind, thoughts, feelings, or head.
6. Receiving holy visions or voices is generally not experienced or highly accepted by the person's religion, culture, or family.
7. The family or significant others are worried that the person's visions or auditory sensations are symptoms or a problem rather than a true religious experience.
8. The person has no doubts that the vision or voice is from God or directed by God.
9. The person not only interprets the vision or auditory sensation or other religious issues concretely, but is also concrete and unable to think abstractly when talking about non-religious issues.
10. The visual or auditory sensation is accompanied by increased anxiety.
11. The vision or voice is perceived as commanding the person to act as God's agent and to carry out judgments, punishments, destruction, or other acts that are dangerous to others or the individual.

A person with a hallucination may not meet all 11 of the above criteria, and religious individuals with no mental disorder may fit a few of the items. Nonetheless, clients who are having religiously oriented hallucinations will fulfill a majority of the assessment factors.

Clinicians are reminded, however, that individuals with schizophrenia may also have strong religious beliefs that are completely separate from their illness. Furthermore, their spirituality may neither reflect the majority culture's concept of religion, nor spring from their illness. For these individuals, the social worker is ethically and clinically obligated to separate the religious beliefs and behaviors from the person's schizophrenia symptoms. This requires understanding the teachings and common experiences of the religious group the client identifies with, and assessing whether the religious experiences have merged into the person's psychotic symptoms. Some clients have very separate symptoms that do not incorporate their strong religious beliefs. Other individuals become confused. Metaphoric and abstract religious concepts may sometimes overlap with their symptoms, while at other times they can cognitively separate religious conviction from their psychosis. For yet others, the two blend together into an inseparable overlay of behavior, making it impossible to determine religious beliefs from symptoms. In all cases, church leaders and families need to be reminded that schizophrenia causes people to think concretely, and to have difficulty concentrating and following sermons or long conversations. Furthermore, arguing or overly trying to persuade a person with schizophrenia to accept or reject religious doctrines can be counterproductive. Attempting to change the person's religious beliefs may cause obsessive thinking, may incorporate religious concepts into hallucinations or delusions, or may alienate relationships.

Delusional thinking is another way in which schizophrenia alters a person's perception of reality. In a psychotic state, the brain creates and acts upon concepts, ideas, perceptions, and information that are false, while simultaneously preventing one from accepting proof that indisputably refutes the incorrect beliefs and logic. We think of a delusion as a false belief built on incorrect logic that is impervious to alternative explanations (Jasper, 1968; American Psychiatric Association, 2000). The content of a delusion always consists of beliefs that largely are not founded on reality or that do not mirror contextual and logical thinking. Nonetheless, segments of a client's delusion can reflect elements of sound reasoning and reality.

Jasper (1968) is credited for setting the parameters that the *DSM-IV-TR* (2000) used for defining a delusion. A slightly different concept suggests that delusions consist of beliefs (1) that are mentally or perceptually protected in a manner that prevents them from being proven or disproven; (2) that others view as failing to match basic cultural expectations; (3) that do not explain past reality-oriented events or predict future events; (4) for which no testable evidence corroborating the delusional beliefs is presented; (5) that are attached to or that trigger strong emotions; (6) that are constantly supported with trivial and random events or occurrences that are deemed by the individual as significant (Leeser & O'Donohue, 1999).

Understanding delusions as protected beliefs that have intense emotional meaning and that are validated for the person by random occurrences that others see as unprovable can help social workers identify less obvious and well hidden delusions. We can easily identify that a client who believes that a computer chip was placed in his head so the police can monitor his thoughts is delusional and suffers from diminished reality. Assessing whether beliefs are delusional that are linked partially to reality or even urban legends requires more skill and precision. Is a person who claims that the grocery store's scanner and automatic gasoline pumps are programmed to overcharge every third customer delusional, overly suspicious of technology and large corporations, or simply susceptible to believing urban myths? Using criteria outlined by Leeser and O'Donohue or the assessment outline suggested by this text can help clinicians determine whether a client is delusional or simply more suspicious than most individuals.

The six steps proposed by Leeser and O'Donohue, as well as this textbook's more extensive assessment, reflect the idea that a delusion consists of several cognitive processing steps. Once the brain encodes a delusional belief, schizophrenia (or other mental difficulties) causes the individual to become anxious and obsessed with the idea that the belief is real. The belief's intensity and accompanied anxiety cause the person to be overly watchful for indicators or signs that the feared event is occurring. This is known by neuropsychologists as being hypervigilant. It is somewhat like being alone in a house, experiencing increased anxiety, and then hearing noises that previously had gone unnoticed. Immediately after identifying something that validates the delusional belief, the person shifts into a state of hypovigilance. The client had been watching every environmental nuance, certain that evidence supporting the belief would appear; after identifying what in his mind is "proof," the client then stops watching and scrutinizing the surrounding environment.

Often the states of hyper- and hypovigilance are coupled with increased anxiety, making problem-solving, questioning, and testing or validating the observation impossible. If a person, as an example, believes that foreign agents are following him, the person will be hypervigilant, watching for suspicious-looking people. Once the brain sends a false message that danger is following behind, the person experiences increased anxiety, and simply wants to flee. In the mind of the delusional person, there is neither the time nor need to question and test the reality of the observation. Delusions occur in part because the brain loses its ability to accurately evaluate cues occurring in the environment and develop an accurate mental gestalt for interpreting environmental contingencies and events (Robbins, 2004). Like hallucinations, delusions are found in numerous psychiatric, neurological, and toxic-metabolic disorders (Cummings & Mega, 2003).

Delusions can take on numerous forms, including paranoia; persecution; grandiosity; somatic pains and illnesses; nihilistic beliefs that either the self, parts of self, or the world does not exist; beliefs that certain bodily organs have disappeared; sexual beliefs about one's self and others; and religious concerns. Grandiosity can focus on ideas of greatness and self-importance, special powers, perceptions of personal wealth, beauty or talent, having powerful friends, or even being a current or historical figure such as Hitler. A sexual delusion may cause the client to believe that a certain person, or group, is a prostitute, rapist, or pedophile. Others may think that a partner is cheating or committing adultery. Clients may also be deluded into thinking that everyone knows their sexual activities, or that people are signaling and desiring to have sex with them, or even that their sexual habits, such as masturbation, have caused them to have physical or psychiatric illnesses. Religious delusions can range from feeling that one has committed an unforgivable sin or is the antichrist, to unshakable beliefs of being anointed by God and chosen for fulfilling prophecy or an important task. A nihilistic delusion occurs when clients believe they are dying, have already died, or that they, others, or the world no longer exists.

Delusions may also take on the form of thought broadcasting, withdrawal, or insertion. The brain can make people believe that their silent internal thoughts are being sent to others in the same manner that television broadcasts pictures and sound. Other clients develop a fear that their thoughts and skills are literally being drained away, perhaps robbed or stolen by a known or unknown person or force. Still others believe that their thoughts are being controlled or inserted by objects such as radios, televisions, phones, and so on. A variation is when clients believe that an object such as a radio is broadcasting information about them, or giving them special instructions. Additionally, one can experience a combination of delusional concepts. As an example, it is not unusual for themes of grandiosity and religiosity, or sexual concerns and paranoia, to coexist. Clients with somatic delusions may simultaneously have nihilistic beliefs about the nonexistence of other life forms or the world. However, a belief solely focused on the disappearance of a specific body part or organ is generally considered nihilistic rather than a somatic delusion.

Nested within most delusions are obsessions, compulsions, and preoccupations (Scheiber, 2003). These elements can help us assess the severity and structure of delusional themes or whether the stories are in fact delusions at all. One must listen carefully and ask probing questions to identify whether a client's story is delusional, a misunderstanding of events, or a reality that is unfamiliar to you and other clinicians, such as alternate worldviews, experiences, or learned perceptions. Additionally, it is not unusual for delusions to reflect cultural relevance and to sound plausible, rather than bizarre and improbable. This text, as an example, has been written at a time when the Western world has extreme worries about terrorist attacks. The extensive news coverage and government actions currently cause many people to be suspicious and some to incorporate actual events into their delusional system. Knowing that these world circumstances are real, it is a challenge to assess a client who states that the FBI thinks that he is part of a terrorist cell and that the government has tapped his phones and e-mail accounts and is watching his actions. He is certain of this, he claims, because he has traveled in the Middle East, has friends in Iran, and regularly phones and e-mails acquaintances who live in several Middle Eastern and European countries. The client also assures you that these are long-term friends met during his freshman year in college. Without a systematic assessment, you will not be able to accurately judge whether this individual is delusional, overly concerned and anxious because of current events rather than delusional, or squarely facing reality.

To evaluate whether beliefs and thoughts are delusional, the social work clinician at a minimum will need to (1) authenticate whether a client's thought processes are based in reality, distortions of reality, or qualify as a delusion; (2) determine the severity and structure of the delusion; and (3) determine whether the client or others are placed in risk for harm because of the delusion. The social worker's responsibility is not only to identify unusual thinking, but more importantly, to assess whether the person's thought content is simply unique, different, or delusional.

An important part of assessing delusions is measuring how often repetitive thoughts that are unfounded in reality force their way into the awareness of the client. The reoccurring thoughts are most often accompanied by high anxiety, and increase other symptoms such as restlessness, hallucinations, and compulsive behaviors. Compulsions are ritualistic behaviors that the person feels must be performed. Schizophrenia makes it impossible for most clients to identify that repetitive thoughts and actions violate cultural norms and are irrational, as opposed to clients with obsessive-compulsive disorder, who usually know that obsessive thoughts and compulsive behaviors are abnormal. This is a problem, because obsessive thoughts can be dangerous. Rituals linked to thoughts of low self-worth, as an example, can trigger suicidal or self-harming behaviors. In addition, obtrusive reoccurring thoughts can preoccupy a client and further decrease the person's concentration skills. As concentration is depleted, the probability for accidental injuries to self and others increases. It is not unusual to see a client with schizophrenia focusing on obsessive thoughts and carelessly stepping in front of traffic, unaware of the danger.

Scheiber (2003) reminds us that clients with schizophrenia gain no enjoyment from compulsive behaviors, but may feel momentary relief from tension and stress by performing ritualistic acts. Delusions also can additionally cause a high level of preoccupation for extended periods. Clients with schizophrenia often lose themselves within their own thoughts. They become so preoccupied with internal cognitions and emotions that time and other ecological realities cannot be captured and processed. In the mildest form, a person may simply appear inattentive, distant, or forgetful. Severe preoccupation results in interpersonal withdrawal, limited and incomplete communications, and an inability for tracking and understanding minute by minute realities. Clients thought to be in a state of preoccupation always need to be assessed for suicidal and homicidal thoughts. Box 4.2 outlines the steps for authenticating and assessing the severity of a delusion.

The first six assessment items in Box 4.2 authenticate whether a client is experiencing a delusion. Item 6 asks if the individual has any doubts about the reality and appropriateness of his or her thought process. A client who doubts the validity of his or her own story may be having distorted thoughts caused by an illusion or other environmental events, or the person may simply have a milder form of schizophrenia or delusion symptoms. Delusions caused by schizophrenia most often occur randomly and are not closely related to specific settings or environments. However, environmental factors may generally increase or trigger the delusions for some clients. This is particularly true when the illogical thought processes are linked to instruments such as radios or take on a highly specialized theme (Cummings & Mega, 2003). A delusion, as an example, focused on jealousy or suspicion that a lover is having an affair may be triggered by the presence or absence of that individual. Item 5 attempts to clarify such diagnostic dilemmas, though this is not always successful.

Items 7 through 15 are designed to help clinicians determine the severity and structure of the delusion. This concept of structure refers to the theme, complexity, and specificity, ecological boundaries and rules, roles and behavior expectations, included and excluded participants, and anxiety created by the delusion. Families and treatment teams cannot easily improve a client's environmental fit, interventions, and acceptance without understanding the pervasiveness and severity of delusions and other symptoms. These assessment items also help social workers better understand how a delusion relates to a client's other symptoms. Knowing if delusions are preceded, accompanied, or followed by hallucinations, social withdrawal, high anxiety, or repetitive thoughts and behaviors can help direct treatment planning. Additionally, it is important to understand exactly how much distress delusions and other symptoms cause clients and their families.

BOX 4.2

AUTHENTICATING AND ASSESSING THE SEVERITY OF DELUSIONS

1. Describe client's belief system that does not appear to reflect reality or the person's culture.
2. When did delusional events first occur?
3. What is the client's history of delusions, and how have they changed over time?
4. What factors in the client's story fail to match cultural reality?
5. Can you rule out that the story is partly true, has a reasonable probability of being possible, or an illusion, or explanations other than delusional thinking?
6. Does the client have any doubts about the delusional beliefs?
7. Are there any specific times of day, locations, or other ecological factors that appear to trigger or play a role in the delusion?
8. If the client is delusional, can the disordered thoughts be contributed to medical illness or injuries, medications or drug interactions, substance abuse, or exposure to toxins, rather than a mental disorder?
9. How organized and specific are the details making up the beliefs?
10. What is the specific focus of the delusion, for example, grandiosity, paranoia, persecutory, sexuality, religiosity, nihilistic?
11. How often does the delusion occur?
12. How often do obsessive thoughts occur, and what are they?
13. Are compulsive behaviors linked to the delusion or obsessions?
14. Does the client have compulsive behaviors, when do they occur, and do they place the client or others in danger?
15. What level of severity is the client's anxiety before, during, and after delusional thoughts?
16. How often is the client preoccupied or lost in his or her thoughts?
17. Does the client have observable psychotic symptoms other than delusions?
18. Is the person preoccupied or obsessed with thoughts of suicide, self-harm, property destruction, homicide, or other forms of harm to others?

Item 18 of the assessment addresses the issues of suicide, homicide, and destruction of property. The importance of always including this item when assessing delusions cannot be overstated. Severely ill clients will sometimes lay out exactly how they plan to handle the fears or other emotions created by a delusion. Therefore, they may clearly state, if asked, plans to take their own or someone else's life. Yet others, from either past experience or insight, understand that affirming suicidal or homicidal thoughts can trigger a mandatory hospitalization. These clients tragically will hide their thoughts and accompanying anxiety. As a result, the clinician must pull together a gestalt from available information that projects the client's probability for risky behaviors. Sadly, as outlined in other sections of this book, the risk for danger is more heavily weighted if the delusion has previously been associated with harm to self or others.

Diminished Reality Manifested by Behavior, Emotions, or Speech

In addition to hallucinations and delusions, schizophrenia can cause individuals to behave, speak, or show emotions in ways that are viewed as inappropriate within the person's own culture. These clusters of symptoms are often referred to by clinicians as forms of mental disorganization. However, they represent not only illogical and unorganized thinking, but also an inability to connect with reality. If individuals with psychoses were able to test and interpret reality, they would understand, even if they disagreed, why others perceived them as eccentric at best, and at worst, frightening. Schizophrenia not only makes it difficult to see one's behavior through the eyes of others, but also to recall and use previously learned culturally accepted social solutions. Behaviors, emotions, and speech that are incongruent with reality or that defy conventional wisdom and rules also reflect the person's incapacity for abstract thinking, and decreased social judgment and social problem-solving skills. Individuals with schizophrenia may concretely know what they are doing, but not understand the purpose, or have the ability to prevent, control, or change their actions. Additionally, this illness depletes one's capability for cognitively interpreting and explaining internal experiences and personal behaviors. Like hallucinations and delusions, these are symptoms of an illness produced by abnormal brain functions that are beyond the client's control. Schizophrenia does not allow one to simply self-will a culturally correct social reality, nor does it permit individuals to recognize and understand their culturally inappropriate emotions, speech, beliefs, or behaviors.

Unusual behaviors are manifested in many individualistic ways. Characteristically, the behavior appears not to be goal oriented or understandable within the person's cultural experience. One may, among many possibilities, wear winter clothing in the heat of summer, dress overly casually or formally, insist on always wearing a particular item, or wear odd combinations or loud and clashing colors. Other clients will show diminished reality and disorganized behavior by making inappropriate gestures or sitting and standing in unusual postures. Morrison tells about treating a client who had spent such a long time lying rigid that he could no longer walk or feed himself because his ankles and wrists had become physically immobilized (Morrison, 2007). This resembles a form of highly disorganized motor behavior known as catatonia. Catatonic clients have abnormalities in their postures, muscle tone, motor control, and speech. These symptoms appear behaviorally as mutism, echolalia, palilalia, echopraxia, stupor, automatic obedience, or negativism. The person's loss of motor control can cause partial or complete immobility. Additionally, catatonic clients can experience extended periods of either uncontrolled hyper- or hypoactivity (Cummings & Mega, 2003). The symptoms and terms characterizing the abnormal motor features of catatonia are provided in Box 4.3.

BOX 4.3

MOTOR FEATURES OF THE CATATONIC SYNDROME

ABNORMALITIES OF POSTURE
- Catalepsy (tendency of maintenance of postures for long periods)
- Psychological pillow (patients retrain their head in an elevated position as if lying on a pillow)
- Persistent abnormal posture (flexed, lordotic, twisted, tilted, awkward)

ABNORMAL SPONTANEOUS MOVEMENT
- Limb stereotypies (movement that is not goal directed and is carried out in a uniform way)
- Handling (patient touches and handles everything within reach)
- Intertwining (patient continually intertwines fingers or grasps clothes or kneads cloth)
- Abnormal trunk movements (such as rocking)
- Grimacing and facial movements (including Schnauzkrampf [form of grimacing], consisting of marked wrinkling of the nose with pouting of the lips)

ABNORMALITIES OF TONE AND MOTOR COMPLIANCE
- Waxy flexibility (patient allows posturing similar to bending a warmed candle)
  - Gegenhalten (opposition movement in which patient resists passive movements of the body to precisely the same degree as the pressure exerted by examiner)
  - Automatic obedience (patient carries out every command given in an automatic manner)
  - Mitgehen (patient moves body in response to light pressure by examiner)
  - Mitmachen (patient allows passive movement of the body made by examiner but returns limb to resting position when examiner releases the patient)
  - Ambitendency (intermittent cooperation and withdrawal of cooperation)
  - Echopraxia (tendency to echo movements of the examiner)

- Negativism (active lack of cooperation and defiance of attempts to influence behavior)

ABNORMALITIES OF SPEECH
- Mutism (absence or severe reduction of speech)
- Echolalia (repeating what the examiner says)
- Palilalia (repeating what the patient says)
- Perseveration (repetition of single words or phrases)
- Verbigeration (senseless incomprehensible sounds that are frequently repeated)
- Speech-prompt catatonia (patient answers with intelligible words that are the first thing that comes to mind)

ABNORMALITIES OF AROUSAL
- Hyperactivity (catatonic excitement)
- Hypoactivity (catatonic stupor)

Source: Reprinted with permission from Cummings, Jeffrey L. and Mega, Michael S. (2003) Neuropsychiatry and Behavioral Neuroscience. New York: Oxford University Press Page 302 Table 20.1 Motor Features of the Catatonic Syndrome.

A client who is in a catatonic stupor remains conscious but has a marked reduction or total loss of spontaneous movement and speech. In contrast, catatonic excitement consists of abrupt, rapid uncontrolled impulsive and combative behavior (Cummings & Mega, 2003). Clinicians and family must be sensitive to the fact that a mute person in an uncomfortable, possibly harmful posture is not going to complain or ask for help. Furthermore, the combative or hyperactive client cannot be commanded to control his motor impulses. Whether the client is in a hypoactive or hyperactive state, someone other than the ill individual must quickly make a decision to seek emergency help and expert treatment. This normally means calling 911 for an emergency medical service ambulance, and hospitalizing the person on a psychiatric unit. Catatonia is not unique to schizophrenia, but rather is found in numerous psychiatric and medical disorders, including bipolar disorders, mania, and major depression.

Another form of abnormal behavior is found in individuals who make religious signs, such as crosses, or obscene gestures for no known purpose or goal. The sign of the cross, as an example, appears to be made either randomly or obsessively rather than as an expression of faith at culturally appropriate times. Schizophrenia may cause others to curse angrily, or give "the finger" to people who are simply passing by and have done nothing to them. Yet other clients will direct growls and strange faces to unknown people, objects, animals, or even open spaces. Other clients, because of their decrease in social judgment, may openly have sex or masturbate in public places, or proposition strangers passing by for sex. Unfortunately, unacceptable sexual behaviors can result in police encounters and incarceration rather than community mental health treatment.

Disordered and inappropriate speech not only illustrates diminished reality and confusion, but can also stimulate illogical behaviors. When I worked at St. Elizabeth's Hospital in Washington, D.C., a middle-aged man with schizophrenia would see me walking across campus with one of our female social workers. He would run close behind, shouting over and over, "man you got yourself a pretty one, help me get one like her." Any explanation denying a romantic relationship was met with statements of doubt and sexual innuendos and inappropriate self-touching. Over time we learned that his following, questioning, off-colored remarks and behavior aggressively increased as we attempted to reshape his perceptions, cognitions, and verbal responses. His disordered speech, along with our ineffective interventions, interacted and triggered additional behavioral symptoms. If we made no direct response to his comments, but rather engaged the person about other topics, such as the flowers or weather, his inappropriate sexual talk either completely stopped or greatly diminished, demonstrating the importance of recognizing how to appropriately respond to such public encounters. One can imagine how the combination of behavior and inappropriate speech would alarm laypeople in the community and families who have no knowledge of mental illness, making it difficult for them to process and thus respond in the most effective manner.

Schizophrenia can also cause speech to be partially or completely unorganized or inappropriate. Communications can be so impaired, jumbled, and unorganized that the person's meaning and intent cannot be deciphered. This is referred to as "word salad" and occurs along with severely tangential thinking. The client is experiencing derailed thoughts that are replaced by ideas only loosely associated with the original concept. As a result, either words within a sentence or group of sentences have little meaning for those who are listening (Cummings & Mega, 2003). Word salad communications are difficult to interpret. Furthermore, it is unclear whether the words actually have a specific or global meaning to the client. It is also possible that what is communicated in the first part of an extended statement is no longer valid, or a point of focus, for the client toward the end of the extended statement. This can be a source of stress for the client, family, and individuals in the community who must communicate with the client. In the most severe state, clients with schizophrenia communicate in shouts of profanity, grunts, snorts, barks, and other animal sounds. These are usually involuntary verbalizations called "coprolalia" and are more often seen in Gilles de la Tourette syndrome, but they also occur in a small number of clients with schizophrenia (Cummings & Mega, 2003).

The way a person writes can also suggest diminished reality and an inability to organize. Because schizophrenia limits clients' ability to concentrate, incorporate complex concepts, organize material, and use socially acceptable reasoning, their writing may lack coherent meaning, structure, and focus. Writing or verbal communications that are tangential or unresponsive, that fail to link obvious points, or that seem overly confusing or empty of content indicate that the person may need to be screened for psychosis.

A good clinical screening for speech organization is a systematic process designed to indicate if a complete mental health assessment is in order. The professional clinician is responsible for concretely ruling on whether verbal and written problems stem from a psychotic mind or represent cultural artifacts, education and experience deficits, insufficient communication skills, reduced motivation, temporary problems, anxiety, drug reaction, or an ongoing medical problem. For example, screening for psychotic verbal content includes asking questions that clarify whether the symptoms represent a state of confusion or difficulties that are not associated with schizophrenia and psychosis. This can be done in part by determining if the client can shift from one topic to another, or becomes lost within topics. The clinical social worker may also, in a kind but direct manner, tell the client that she or he does not understand what the person is saying. People without psychosis usually make attempts to clarify their meaning, while schizophrenia often sends the client being asked to clarify a confusing conversation into higher levels of anxiety and increased disorganization.

The final form of diminished reality is inappropriate or unusual emotions. Individuals with schizophrenia and other disorders may have emotions that are incongruent with events occurring in the environment. The environmental context may call for speaking softly and expressing empathy, but the client talks in a booming voice, makes jokes, and laughs. In some cases, the client will have a very limited emotional repertoire. These individuals will use one or two emotional responses, at the same level of passion, for every situation. It becomes predictable, for example, that upon hearing important or trivial information the person will either loudly weep or laugh. Other clients may respond to every inquiry as if they are angry. It is also not unusual to find individuals with severe schizophrenia who maintain a fixed sad or upset look, but refuse to speak, regardless of where they are or what is happening. In all of these situations, the person's brain is having difficulty organizing and selecting emotional responses that correctly match environmental expectations. A summary of diminished reality is provided in Box 4.4.

The following is an example of how faulty written communications can signal possible signs of diminished reality. Dr. Richard Arum, a professor at New York University,

BOX 4.4
SUMMARY OF DIMINISHED REALITY

DIMINISHED REALITY CLINICAL FACTS

1. The term refers to a reduced ability to know, interpret, and understand or learn from experience or information which stimuli are and are not real.
2. To qualify as diminished reality, one must have previously been able to separate reality from false beliefs, incorrect perceptions, and other stimuli that do not match culturally taught and accepted realities.
3. Learned cultural expectations largely determine or guide a person's understanding and experience of reality.
4. Diminished reality must be assessed or measured by comparing a person's cultural training with his or her current perceptions of reality, rather than simply determining whether one's perspective agrees with the prevailing majority culture.
5. Diminished reality occurs in numerous mental and medical disorders, not just schizophrenia.
6. A person who has psychotic symptoms does not necessarily have schizophrenia, but a person with schizophrenia will at some point have experienced psychosis.
7. Symptoms of diminished reality include hallucinations, delusions, unusual or disorganized behaviors, speech, and writing, and emotions.
8. The presentation of diminished reality symptoms greatly varies from client to client.
9. Few clients have all of the symptoms that indicate diminished reality.
10. Clients are not required to have hallucinations or delusions to suffer from diminished reality.
11. A client may experience mild, moderate, or severe lost of reality.
12. The first line of treatment for diminished reality is most often neuroleptic medication.

and I were interviewed about the May 2007 Virginia Tech shootings on Voice of America. Shortly after the broadcast, the e-mail reproduced below, addressed to Dr. Arum and copied to my e-mail account, was received. The message is copied verbatim. Notice not only the wording but also the lack of spacing, and how sentences run together.

Mr. Arum,

It's more simple than you present (see Virginia Tech below). More certainly needs to be investigated regarding these shootings and others. There is no need to go through twisted explanation for these "modern phenomena" of school shootings which defy the traditional behaviors of mentally disturbed humans. Read on below from a summary I gave in response to an inquiry. Virginia Tech, like other events such as Colombine (see below), the Port Arthur Australia and Dunblane leave much more to the eye of the less naive of society. Port Arthur, for example was an event which led up to draconian anti-firearm legislation (Virginia Tech as well). Speaking of Port Arthur, policemen are speaking up about the inordinate number of intelligence officers present in the Broad Arrow Cafe, oh, what's this? Australian Intelligence Officer (ASIS) Nightingale said what to the gunman?

"Mr Nightingale stood up when the shooting started and called out *'No no not here'*, he was then shot, a single shot to the neck area" (Court Document page 83). The time lapse between the fourth and fifth shots is 0.60of a second. Firstly a person cannot utter the words spoken by Anthony Nightingale in that short period of time. Secondly, it takes more than 0.6of a second to turn 180 degrees and then fire a shot.

I have the interview with the retired Australian policeman and his investigation as well as the massacre at Dunblane Scotland (I won't get into that gunman's background and his connections to child porn rings for the elite and politicians...), I will send them to you if you desire. In both of these cases, there is unusual stone walling by the government to inquiries by independent investigators. There are MANY more anomalies [sic] which are too many to cover here.

In [sic] interesting thing happened in Austin Texas in 1966 with that infamous shooting: *"About 20 minutes into the attack, civilians started to arrive with deer rifles. They helped police return fire."* ** Why were law enforcement held back at VT? Here's what happened in Austin in 1966: *"Pistol in hand, Officer Martinez made his way up the Tower.

The elevator let him out on the 27th floor, where Officer Jerry Day and a citizen named Alan Crum had arrived minutes earlier." *http://www.news8austin.com/content/news_8 explores/ut_tower_shooting/?ArID=16723 9&SecID=552

VIRGINIA TECH

Regarding *Virginia Tech*, Bill Zabel did an interview with the Grassy Knoll last month and it was fascinating to hear. Like how the classroom doors were chained from the outside, the standdown by law enforcement, the late announcement of the shooting as it had been going on, and on another show comments were made about how such Manchurians have lost time when investigating their histories as they are under "psychiatric" care... apparently, Tim McVeigh was being "treated" by the premiere MKULTRA CIA doctor prior to the OKC bombing. Another intriguing aspect of this is the sheepish behaviour of the SWAT types at the Virg. Tech campus. Perhaps we should have sent some Iraq vets (or perhaps, better yet Israeli commandos) to raid the classroom. For christ's sake, have even law enforcement become feminized along with the rest of the US male population? If they can storm an airliner, they can do something like this without standing back as young students are being slaughtered. Come on now. They knew that it was probably one guy, maybe two if the profiler didn't know his history and that's assuming law enforcement wasn't held back for other political reasons (more on the COINCIDENTAL...ahem...pending gun legislation for the Virginia House below).

Zabel is writing a book about Colombine and it is interesting to hear about the 100+ bombs and dozens of 55 gallon drum fuel bombs and sophisticated mercury switch propane bombs found in the cafetria as well as many pipe bombs. Zabel sent me 3 gigs of FOIAs on Colombine and I have yet to sift through them. Witnesses described numerous adult "perps" seen carrying guns and explosives during the event. Zabel lives near the area and has received leaks about this from local police and feds.

About Virginia, Tech, normally psycho killers do the deed, then collapse off the adrenaline and surrender or shoot themselves. They don't shoot people, then re-emerge two hours later and methodically continue to kill people. Zabel also stated that in the Virginia Tech killings, the perp had peered into several classrooms and methodically scanned the students' faces and continued to the next classrooms as if looking for particular people.

Most disturbing of all, is the Virginia state hand gun laws were undergoing review by the state legislature and the law makers were favouring more gun rights for the citizenry (as if gun rights are there for the legislature to screw around with). You will remember that right after OKC bombing, the Omnibus Anti-terror bill was passed within a month. Same goes for the Patriot Act. This is an old playbook and VERY easy to discern. Many people are getting very suspicious, including victims' families. Frankly, this won't be able to go on for much longer because too many are getting wise to it.

SEE ALSO: CIA control of the media OPERATION MOCKINGBIRD http://deliberatecoincidences.blogspot.com/2007/03/operation-mockingbird-central.html.

It is impossible and inappropriate to surmise whether the person has a mental disorder. Nonetheless, the writing offers important signs that justify an assessment for mental health problems. Note the possible delusions of both paranoia and grandiosity. The individual is certain of a conspiracy and indicates that he or she has solutions to the problem. Next notice the structure of the message. There is almost no introduction to the topic or writer. Overall, the message is largely understandable, but is nevertheless disorganized and difficult to follow. It jumps from school violence in the United States to an incident in Australia, back to the United States, and sandwiches in accusations about CIA conspiracies. The writer seems to take it for granted that we know about the "Port Arthur Australia and Dunblane" incidents. Additionally, one is asked to take at face value the writer's statement that "[t]here is no need to go through twisted explanation for these 'modern phenomena' of school shootings which defy the traditional behaviours of mentally disturbed humans. Read on below from a summary I gave in response to an inquiry."

Statements made in this vein signal, but do not completely document, grandiosity. The writer believes very strongly that he or she has insights that most of us lack. We cannot overlook, however, the possibility that this is simply a person who is a poor writer and who has a strong belief that the CIA is working against the American nation it is supposed to protect. If there are no other neurobiological symptoms, the person could benefit from help with expressing him- or herself in writing, but needs no mental health intervention. As social workers we must always remember that a person can have faulty beliefs without having a mental disorder. However, only a complete mental health assessment will identify if the person needs help for delusions and other symptoms of diminished reality. You may correctly ask if it is ethical to question a person's mental status without concrete evidence of a major disorder. Certainly a single e-mail does not constitute evidence for or against a disorder. Nonetheless, one can also argue that it is unjust to have learned about the signs of mental instability and pain, but fail to use that information in the service of others.

A person always has the right to refuse to participate in a screening or assessment, and the topic must be approached with honesty and concern. We are ethically obligated to ensure that the person knows that you are a clinician, and that you have concerns about his or her mental health. An individual, even if the person has a psychosis, has a right to know that the social worker is not simply chatting, but rather is assessing for mental health difficulties. Additionally, we are ethically bound to inform the person that participation is not required. Reassure clients that we never know by looking at one item, such as an e-mail, whether professional help is needed, but that the writing (or other indicator) raises questions that an assessment can clarify. If, however, the person refuses and does not want to participate, break off the confrontation by saying, "That is your perfect right, and I completely respect it. If you change your mind, or find that you are worried, call me, here is my card."

A brief screening for disorganization of verbal, written, or emotional skills may include some or all of the steps outlined for assessing delusions and hallucinations, questions to discover or rule out other symptoms of diminished reality, and an attempt to determine if the person's social, work, or educational skills have deteriorated. Many times, clients are unable to assess or unwilling to report decreased skills. In these cases, collaboration and insights are needed from people who are close to the individual. While doing the screening, keep in mind that we are only determining whether a complete assessment is warranted. A screening neither tells us that a person has a disorder, nor indicates the specific disorder that the individual may have. For example, the lack of organization, structure, and topic of the e-mail above is similar to writing that is routinely seen from people with schizophrenia, bipolar disorders, delusional disorder, learning disorders, and no mental disorder.

NEGATIVE SYMPTOMS

Researchers think of positive symptoms, which we have called diminished reality and addressed above, as exaggerations of normal neurobehavioral functions, and negative symptoms as a loss or reduction of normal functions (Andreasen, 2001). The term "negative symptom" generally applies to behaviors that fall within these global categories:

1. *Alogia* (can be part of anhedonia, defined below), a decrease in spontaneous speaking or a pronounced poverty in the content of speech;
2. *Avolition,* or the reduction of skills, motivation, and drive for establishing, or completing goals;
3. *Anhedonia,* or the loss of one's ability to experience pleasure from situations and events that previously were rewarding;
4. *Attentional or concentration impairment,* which decreases ability for planning, following step-by-step instructions or schedules, quickly focusing on appropriate stimuli, or maintaining attention over time; and
5. *Blunted affect,* which may appear as an almost frozen blank or other facial expression, slowed body movement, poor eye contact, few gestures while talking, and slowed speech containing few inflections or changes in tone (Andreasen, 2001; Ho, Black, et al., 2003).

It has been known since the 1980s that schizophrenia indicators cluster into the two separate categories of positive and negative symptoms (Crow, 1980; Andreasen, 1982). Research has further found that the primary negative symptoms are not caused as a side effect of medications (Kelley, van Kammen, et al., 1999; Ko, Jung, et al., 2007). Research also supports the idea that negative symptoms do not necessarily increase or decrease as symptoms of diminished reality or positive symptoms change, whereas hallucinations can directly increase or decrease a client's delusions (American Psychiatric Association, 2000; Ho, Black, et al., 2003). Newer studies using factor analysis have found that schizophrenia is actually a three-factor illness consisting of negative, psychotic, and disorganized symptoms (American Psychiatric Association, 2000; Buchanan & Carpenter, 2001; Breier, 2004). This supports the idea that negative symptoms are influenced by different neurophysiology or neurochemistry than positive psychotic symptoms. Additionally, neuroimaging studies have demonstrated an association between greater number or more pronounced structural brain abnormalities and more severe negative symptoms (Cummings & Mega, 2003). Figure 4.2 illustrates how positive and negative symptoms, reduced social functioning, and an inability to regain pre-illness skills dynamically interact and create a gestalt of increasing and decreasing symptoms. While we can academically divided symptoms into subcategories, they are in reality part of a complex neurosystem that impacts and often changes the entire person.

Untrained clinicians, families, and people in the community are tempted to label individuals with schizophrenia as lacking motivation. They observe clients wandering aimlessly, not caring whether their clothing and body are clean, failing to complete task after task, and seldom attempting anything new or different. This, however, is not laziness or willfully defiant behavior, but rather the product of negative symptoms. The brain is failing to generate an ability to concentrate and produce the energy

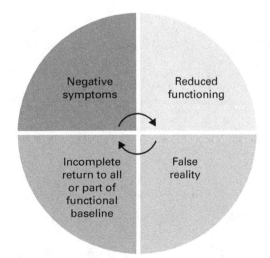

FIGURE 4.2 Elements of Schizophrenia.

These elements largely define schizophrenia. During periods of psychotic remission, "false reality" symptoms may disappear. However, to some extent, the other three elements often remain, even after psychosis has lifted.

and organizational skills required for planning, task completion, goal perception, and motivational drive (Graybiel, 1997; Andreasen, 2001; Hugdahl, Bjørn, et al., 2004; Mohanty, Herrington, et al., 2005; Benes, 2007).

THE BIOLOGY OF SCHIZOPHRENIA

Genetics and Environment

Over the past 20 years, a great deal has been learned about what schizophrenia is, and how it affects individuals and families, though we have yet to identify what actually causes this illness, or when it actually begins. There is strong evidence that many, but not all, cases are related to genetic factors. Identical twins, adoption, and family history studies present convincing evidence that a large number of cases are explained by genetic factors (Torrey, Bowler, et al., 1994). There is an 8%–12% chance that if one dizygotic (not identical) twin develops schizophrenia, the other twin will also become ill. This is approximately the same probability for non-twin siblings when one has schizophrenia. The concordance rate (both twins becoming ill) jumps to between 42% and 50% for monozygotic twins who share identical genes (Torrey, Bowler, et al., 1994; First & Tasman, 2004). Family and twin genetic studies (Gottesman, 1991; Owen, O'Dovovan, et al., 2002) indicate that individuals have the following risk for developing schizophrenia when the ill family member is a

> first cousin = 2%
> uncle or aunt = 2%
> nephew or niece = 4%
> grandchild = 5%
> half sibling = 6%
> parent = 6%
> sibling = 9%
> child = 13%
> fraternal twin = 17%
> identical twin = 48%.

Clearly, genes do not alone explain the onset of schizophrenia. There is a growing consensus that rather than a single gene, schizophrenia requires multiple genetic factors and environmental influences to develop (Tsuang, Stone, et al., 2007).

Conceptualizing environment, however, as a partial or interacting influence for triggering schizophrenia is highly complicated. Simple conceptualizations of bad parenting, ineffective communications, or inappropriate behavioral reinforcement as environmental causes for schizophrenia have been disproven and removed from scientific consideration (Taylor, 2006). There is a possibility, however, that for some, schizophrenia is triggered by a combination of genes that interact with (1) prenatal neuroviruses; (2) obstetric problems such as maternal preeclampsia, or hypoxia and reduced oxygen; or (3) substance abuse by the client at specific sensitive developmental periods (Razahan, O'Daly, et al., 2007). This gene-environment interaction theory has been supported by findings that individuals with schizophrenia who experienced fetal hypoxia tend to have more structural brain abnormalities than their siblings and study controls (Cannon, van Erp, et al., 2002). Presently, however, we must keep in mind that the entire field of gene-environmental interaction relating to mental disorders is a relatively new area of study, filled with more questions than answers.

Some researchers believe that genes are not always involved directly with the onset of schizophrenia. A large but incomplete body of research suggests that neuroviruses during the second trimester of pregnancy and birth trauma alone can result in schizophrenia (Torrey, Bowler, et al., 1994; Torrey, Taylor, et al., 1994). There is replicated evidence that schizophrenia rates increase for individuals conceived during influenza epidemics (Torrey, Bowler, et al., 1994; First & Tasman, 2004). Furthermore, in a study of twins discordant for schizophrenia, there were minor findings suggesting that the ill twin, but not the well twin, may have had a neurovirus during the second trimester of the pregnancy (Torrey, Bowler, et al., 1994). Some believe that neuroviruses alone can cause schizophrenia, while others believe that research findings point to an interaction between a genetic predisposition and second trimester viral infections (Torrey, Bowler, et al., 1994; Tsuang, Stone, et al., 2007). Overall, the evidence supporting the virus theories with or without gene interaction remains rather weak and in need of more definitive studies (First & Tasman, 2004).

The relationship between substance abuse and schizophrenia is controversial, and requires additional investigation. Epidemiologists have documented that alcohol and other drug use is known to increase prior to observable schizophrenia symptoms, and as a group the illness starts at a younger age for those with a history of using substances (Razahan, O'Daly, et al., 2007). Obviously, only a fraction of people using substances develop schizophrenia. Exactly how genes and addictive substances are linked to schizophrenia is not clear, and the evidence is based on limited studies of association that cannot establish causation. As an example, one study established that methamphetamine users who developed schizophrenia had a significantly higher number of family members with the schizophrenia, and more childhood traits for mental disorders than methamphetamine users who remained free of schizophrenia (Chen & Murray, 2004; Razahan, O'Daly, et al., 2007). Studies of this type cannot determine whether the individuals would have remained schizophrenia-free had they not used an addictive substance. Additionally, these clients may have become involved with substances as a means of self-medicating for their still hidden schizophrenia. Prior to observable symptoms, some clients start having minor undefined cognitive or affective problems, and knowingly or unknowingly gravitate to alcohol or other substances for relief. In other cases, mild undiagnosed schizophrenia can blunt a person's judgment without causing a complete psychotic episode. This can result in clients appearing in control of their decision-making skills, but highly vulnerable to peer suggestions and street drug dealers.

Brain Structure and Development

Research has steadily documented that schizophrenia is a neurodevelopmental disorder. There is little debate that the symptoms and disabilities seen in this illness strongly relate to structural and functional changes in the brain (Andreasen, 2001; Cummings & Mega, 2003; First & Tasman, 2006). We are not certain when neurological alterations first take place, and to what degree major brain structures and activities show abnormalities before the first concrete schizophrenia symptoms are observed. There is some evidence that structural modifications may start before a person is born. The largest study of twins discordant (one with and one without) for schizophrenia found that brain changes for the ill twin may have started while in the mother's womb. Disruptions, possibly from genetic problems, neuroviruses, toxins, or other aberrations, are thought to cause an abnormal migration of cells needed for programming the development of the brain (Wright, Gill, et al., 1993; Torrey, Bowler, et al., 1994; Cannon, van Erp, et al., 2002; Lewis & Levitt, 2002; Camargo, Collura, et al., 2007).

Difficulties of this type may further alter how neurons are pruned during the child's first 2 years of life and possibly later during adolescence (Torrey, Taylor, et al., 1994; Cannon, van Erp, et al., 2002). Animal studies indicate that between adolescence and young adulthood the frontal cortex continues to evolve, build linkages, and prune neurons (Juraska & Markham, 2007). Additionally, brain mapping using high-resolution magnetic resonance imaging (MRI) has shown that young adolescents with early onset schizophrenia have lost brain gray matter in an accelerated manner compared to normal study controls (Thompson, Vidal, et al., 2001). This supports the hypothesis that early onset schizophrenia may be a neurodegenerative disorder. The findings, however, do not determine if structural brain abnormalities increase with additional episodes. There is also beginning evidence that the brain's global gray matter in adults may decrease after a client's first episode of schizophrenia (Cahn, Pol, et al., 2002).

Findings of this type have already changed treatment protocols. Because there is a reasonable chance that psychotic episodes injure the brain's structures and functions, it is generally believed that medication treatment should start at the first symptoms of schizophrenia (First & Tasman, 2006; Tsuang, Stone, et al., 2007). However, both the early onset and adult findings need to be replicated using larger samples. Currently it appears more probable that adult onset schizophrenia follows a path of abnormal neurodevelopment rather than degeneration (Zipursky, 2006). In other words, schizophrenia occurring in late adolescence or adulthood associates more with a process of atypical development rather than a process involving cell death, but additional research is needed to confirm whether early or adult schizophrenia kills brain cells and if damage follows each episode.

Abnormalities in both brain structures and functioning have been well documented in schizophrenia research. Areas from deep within the brain to the outer surface have been found to differ from matched controls that had no history of mental disorders. Neuroanatomical structures known to deviate in client groups with schizophrenia are the limbic system, ventricles, cortex, temporal lobe, striatum, and the brain's gray and white matter (First & Tasman, 2004; Taylor, 2006). Note how the above sentence states that the structures are "... known to deviate in client groups with schizophrenia." The importance of this statement is that neuroscience shows that brain abnormalities and deviations do not occur or appear identically in everyone who has schizophrenia. We also know that there are almost no clients who have all of the structural and functional deviations discussed in this chapter. As a group, however, many of the identified brain structural abnormalities are more often observed in people with schizophrenia than in people with no history of the illness. This is an important psychoeducational point for clients and their families. It is helpful for clients to know that having an MRI that finds few or no deficits in areas normally associated with schizophrenia does not necessarily invalidate their diagnosis. We also need to keep in mind that a client's brain may have changed, but not to the degree seen in other people with schizophrenia.

Individual clients seldom have pre- and post-schizophrenia onset brain MRIs that could identify minor structural changes. This was illustrated by Torrey et al.'s (1994) discordant twins study. The researchers found a number of ill subjects who had ventricles that both measured and appeared normal. However, when compared to the well identical twins, it was discovered that the ill twins' ventricles were larger. This finding gains importance considering that there were no differences in ventricle size for sets of related sibling twin serving as controls (Torrey, Bowler, et al., 1994). The study demonstrates that a client's structural brain can appear normal even though in actuality small undetectable changes have occurred. Unfortunately, most of us do not have a genetically identical twin who can be used for neurodevelopmental comparisons. Presently there simply is no acceptable standard that defines optimal sizes or shapes for brain sections. Therefore, in most cases it is not beneficial from a diagnostic perspective for clients to have an MRI.

Without a single standard against which to judge within a group, we can only determine whether there are significant differences in brain areas between groups of individuals with and without mental disorders. Nonetheless, documentation of brain abnormalities in schizophrenia should be thought of as real rather than hypothetical. This chapter can only present a fraction of the neurophysiological findings that have been discovered and in many cases replicated by researchers. The brain's hippocampus and amygdala, which are part of what is known as the limbic system, are often decreased in size or have irregular shapes in clients with schizophrenia. The limbic system as a whole, but in particular these two structures, plays a major role in forming and controlling emotions, environmental sensory perceptions, partially processing and passing on contextual-abstract environmental information, and helping interpret experiences by comparing present to past experiential events—all of which are abilities that can be greatly affected by this disease (Bogerts, 1997).

Other areas of the limbic system that have been found by MRI studies to be abnormal include the parahippocampal gyrus, anterior cingulate, and entorhinal cortex (First & Tasman, 2004). Technically the hippocampus, and entorhinal cortex are part of the parahippocampal gyrus, and sometimes as a group are referred to as mesiotemporal structures (First & Tasman, 2004). There also appears to be a decrease in the size of the superior temporal gyrus, and shrinkage (atrophy) of the prefrontal cortex (Torrey, Bowler, et al., 1994; Ho, Black, et al., 2003; First & Tasman, 2004). Together these brain areas control much of human behavior and emotion, and influence how schizophrenia symptoms are manifested within a social-environmental context. However, we have not advanced to the point where brain structures can be used for diagnosing schizophrenia, predicting the severity of episodes, or predicting the probability for rehabilitation and recovery.

One of the major advances in mental health research has been the ability for neuroscientists to study how the living brain functions. In clients with schizophrenia, we have learned that in almost all cases the frontal cortex fails to function as robustly and fast as seen in people with no history of the illness (Torrey, Bowler, et al., 1994). The frontal cortex along with the frontal lobe is responsible for forming decisions requiring abstract reasoning, producing good judgment that fits the environmental context, and generally guiding social functioning. When people with schizophrenia are resting and not trying to problem-solve, their frontal cortex and frontal lobe function in a similar manner to what is seen in the normal control subjects. However, upon receiving a task requiring frontal cortex or frontal lobe functioning, the rate of glucose metabolism decreases in the clients with schizophrenia and sharply increases in the normal controls (Torrey, Bowler, et al., 1994; Taylor, 2006). As the frontal cortex and lobe slow, one's ability to reason, make decisions, and employ what we think of as common sense becomes less accurate and logical.

This partially explains why a client with schizophrenia may appear to grasp the steps for resolving a routine social situation during a treatment session, but then experience increased symptoms and failure when actually facing the practiced situation in daily life. Imagine, as an example, that you are at a fast food restaurant and order more food than you have money for, and you are alone and without a credit card. You would most likely feel anxious, perhaps embarrassed, and have an increased heartbeat as the unexpected price was announced. Your frontal cortex, however, would swing into action, directing you to cancel the fries and switch from a large to a small drink. If, however, you had schizophrenia, you would not only experience anxiety but simultaneously a sudden uncontrollable drop in the neurological functions required for comprehending the social situation, problem-solving, and making quick sound decisions. As this occurs the person may argue, freeze, speak loudly, flee, bargain, become confused, or, if paranoid, make unreasonable accusations. Therefore, a clinician working with the client would want to help the fast food staff and family understand that the individual was faced with having to perform abstract social problem-solving, mathematical computations, and extremely fast reasoning while the very part of the brain responsible for performing these tasks was dramatically failing to properly function. A brain ill from schizophrenia simply has difficulty dealing with unexpected circumstances and making quick, clear, and socially acceptable decisions.

It has long been known that schizophrenia reduces cognitive skills, and one's ability to concentrate or attend to a task from start to completion (Bleuler, 1924; First & Tasman, 2006). However, thanks to newer imaging methods, science is explaining why this happens. Using functional magnetic resonance imaging (fMRI), researchers have demonstrated that key areas of the brain responsible for cognition and attention have abnormally low rates of activation. Specifically, decreased metabolism was found occurring in the dorsolateral prefrontal cortex, nucleus accumbens, and other ventral limbic areas, while simultaneously unusually high levels of glucose metabolism were occurring in the hippocampus and amygdala (Mohanty, Herrington, et al., 2005). The amygdala is responsible for signaling emotional responses and, along with the nucleus accumbens and other limbic areas, helping to integrate cognitive signals. The hippocampus monitors, stores, and in a limited manner, in coordination with the amygdala, interprets immediate events taking place in the environment. As a result, an internal neurobiological conflict is repeated over and over in the brain of a person with schizophrenia. That is, the neurological tools designed for producing and processing cognitive functions operate overly slow (frontal cortex), while brain sections responsible for producing emotions (amygdala) and deciding which environmental factors should be attended to (hippocampus) are either over- or under-activated.

This can result in increased or decreased emotions; affect and behaviors that fail to fit the environmental context; poorly formed cognitive responses; and attention that jumps from issue to issue and seems disconnected from reality. Additionally, it is known that brain areas responsible for mental state attributions, or the ability to mentally create and use abstract constructs, are less active in clients with schizophrenia (Russell, Rubia, et al., 2000; Paradiso, Andreasen, et al., 2003; Hugdahl, Bjørn, et al., 2004).

It has also been proven that clients with schizophrenia who have severe negative symptoms show metabolic functioning that significantly differs from individuals with schizophrenia who have predominantly positive symptoms. These differences consisted of lower glucose metabolism in the right temporal lobe and ventral prefrontal cortices, and higher rates of activation in the cerebellar cortex and lower cerebella nuclei (Potkin, Alva, et al., 2002). Together, modern brain studies explain why clients with schizophrenia experience decreased information-processing skills, have difficulty interpreting abstractions, and often become either overly emotional or socially disengaged. They also help explain unusual body movement, bizarre repetitive or obsessive behaviors, and activities such as long periods of back-and-forth pacing.

In addition to being shaped by brain structures and functioning, schizophrenia symptoms are also influenced by the brain's chemistry. What has become known as the dopamine hypothesis is often used for explaining psychotic episodes. Dopamine is one of many chemical neurotransmitters responsible for sending encoded messages from one neuron to another. Extremely simplified, the hypothesis proposes that psychosis occurs when the brain manufactures more dopamine than its receptors can process or handle. There is no doubt that dopamine plays an important role in the production of most positive symptoms. Many of the antipsychotic or neuroleptic medications work by blocking brain receptors and rendering them unable to receive dopamine. Once a person is on a therapeutic dose of the correct neuroleptic medication, hallucinations, paranoia, affective inappropriateness, and other positive symptoms most often subside.

While this demonstrates that dopamine is a key agent in producing and controlling symptoms, it does not provide an adequate explanation for causation. Dopamine alone is a complex neurotransmitter requiring five different subtypes of receptors located differentially throughout the brain. Along with dopamine, science has showed that schizophrenia is associated with abnormalities in numerous other neurotransmitters and receptors. Currently, in addition to dopamine, researchers are focused on serotonin, norepinephrine, glutamate, and peptides. There remains much to be learned about brain chemistry. Our knowledge, however, has advanced from single focused explanations to an understanding that schizophrenia involves interactions among multiple neurotransmitters, genetic predispositions and changes, abnormal brain structures and glucose metabolism, and ecological factors.

EPIDEMIOLOGY AND COURSE OF ILLNESS

Clients and families want to know from their social worker whether the person with schizophrenia will get well, or at least significantly improve. This is a difficult question to answer because the illness is extremely heterogeneous across client populations and can have varying effects over time. The question is also difficult to answer because studies on the course of illness have design flaws, and researchers for many years were biased by incorrect assumptions. Kraepelin (1912), for example, believed that schizophrenia was progressive and akin to dementia. As a result, recovery, remission, or even significant improvement was not expected. This was an overly pessimistic view that continues to influence some clinicians and families, despite evidence to the contrary.

Despite being a devastating illness, schizophrenia is nonetheless treatable, and hope for remission can be held for large numbers of clients. Longitudinal studies that followed clients for 20 or more years report that by the end of the observation period between 40% and 66% of the individuals were either symptom-free or experiencing only mild psychiatric problems (Breier, 2004). One of the most famous projects, known as the Vermont Longitudinal Study, started in the 1950s and followed 118 institutionalized patients with schizophrenia for 32 years. The clients' psychiatric conditions greatly varied as the study ended. At the final follow-up, 82% were no longer hospitalized, 81% were meeting their own basic self-care needs, and 68% had only mild or no positive symptoms. Additionally, social functioning was rated as "good" for 60% of the patients (Harding, Brooks, et al., 1987). After reviewing the literature, Torrey (2007) found that when all people with schizophrenia symptoms are included in studies for any period of time, the recovery rate is about 25%, but this figure drops when the study narrowly defines the illness and includes only individuals who continuously have symptoms for 6 or more months. Also, it should be noted that the probability for full recovery and complete return to premorbid functioning for all clients who fully meet *DSM-IV-TR* criteria for schizophrenia is extremely low. The literature does indicate, however, that as time passes there is a 10% increase in the number of clients who have improved symptoms. Unfortunately, moving to improved, more stable health can take between 10 and 30 years for many clients (American Psychiatric Association, 2000).

Overall, the newer epidemiological findings prove Kraepelin's progressive dementia assumption for schizophrenia to be incorrect. With time, many clients experience less severe symptoms and fewer psychotic episodes. As a result, it is difficult to conclude what role, if any, modern medications and early treatment play in the natural course of the disorder. There is some evidence that people who have a complete recovery usually have had no more than two psychotic episodes, and are symptom-free within 2 years after illness onset (Torrey, 2006). Characteristics indicating that a client may have such milder symptoms and a good prognosis include

1. An acute onset of illness after adolescence or early adulthood;
2. Female;
3. Married;
4. Positive history for premorbid social, cognitive, and work functioning;
5. Short duration of psychotic symptoms;
6. Observable affective symptoms;
7. Strong support systems; and
8. No family history of schizophrenia (Ho, Black, et al., 2003; Sadock & Sadock, 2007).

Conversely, studies across nationalities and cultures indicate that people with schizophrenia are at a higher risk for severe symptoms and poor response to treatment if they

- are socially isolated;
- have lengthy psychotic episodes;
- have psychiatric problems and treatment before the onset of psychosis;
- are unmarried prior to onset;
- had childhood or adolescent behavioral problems (World Health Organization, 1973, 1979).

Keep in mind that even when a person has one or more of the World Health Organization risk factors, it is not possible to predict what the individual's course of illness will be over time.

Early Onset

Epidemiologists have documented that onset mostly occurs in the late teen and early adult years of life; however, larger clinics annually see a number of early and mid-age adolescents who fully meet *DSM-IV-TR* criteria for schizophrenia. This is significant because developing schizophrenia as a child or young adolescent reduces the probability for recovery and increases the chance for relapse and increased illness severity. Additionally, individuals with early onset are reported to have poorer responses to treatment by medication. Only between 13% and 26% of early onset cases are thought to have good outcomes (Carlson, Naz, et al., 2005). "Very early onset schizophrenia" refers to schizophrenia whose symptoms present before a child reaches the age of 13. "Early onset" refers to youths who become ill between the ages of 13 and 15. Generally, however, adult onset is thought to start around the age of 17, though some researchers use the term "adolescent onset" to refer to youths who develop schizophrenia between the ages of 13 and 19.

It is rare to see children below the age of 10 diagnosed with schizophrenia, and many researchers question whether the *DSM-IV-TR* criteria are accurate for assessing very early onset schizophrenia (Remschmidt, 2001). The youngest known child to be diagnosed with schizophrenia in the current psychiatric literature was 3 years old, followed by a number of cases in which a 5-year-old was given the diagnosis (Gillberg, 2001). Between 1.6 and 1.9 in 100,000 children are thought to develop schizophrenia before their thirteenth birthday (Gillberg, 2001). The numbers, however, increase dramatically during the teen years. Between 0.23% and 1.34% of adolescents in the general public will experience the onset of schizophrenia before reaching adulthood (Gillberg, 2001). Under the age of 6 years old, children seldom have highly structured delusions, and hallucinations can be difficult to assess. Therefore, very young children under 6 years of age are better served if given a preliminary diagnosis, or if their diagnosis is deferred for an extended period of time before schizophrenia is concretely assessed (Gillberg, 2001). It should be remembered, however, that most research supports the idea that neither delusions nor hallucinations are part of normal child development (Volkmar, 2001). Children and young adolescents who have schizophrenia may show more negative than positive symptoms. As the youth reaches mid- to older adolescence, however, type I, or positive, symptoms become more dominant. In late adolescence and early adulthood, clinicians can expect to see high levels of both positive and negative symptoms (Remschmidt, 2001).

Children who are developing schizophrenia often have a history of neuromotor and sensorimotor deficits. When examined closely, most children with schizophrenia have or have had either minor or major developmental delays. Early onset schizophrenia is often preceded by difficulties in concentration, school performance, socialization, or emotional or adjustment problems (Torrey, Taylor, et al., 1994; Walker, Kestler, et al., 2005). About 50% of children with schizophrenia were described as being withdrawn, shy, introverted, sensitive, and anxious prior to onset (Remschmidt, 2001). Additionally, it is not unusual to learn that similar problems existed during the childhood of some individuals who develop schizophrenia in early adulthood (Torrey, Taylor, et al., 1994).

While early developmental difficulties are associated with schizophrenia, they do not predict that a person will develop the disorder. Therefore, early developmental difficulties do not within themselves justify assessing children for schizophrenia. Furthermore, social workers would be misinterpreting research data and incorrectly alarming parents to suggest that developmental problems predict or increase the risk for schizophrenia. Presently all early risk factors are overly broad, overlap with developmental delays, and do not provide enough specificity to permit early detection or preventive treatment of schizophrenia (Hollis, 2001).

Worldwide Rates of Incidence

In respect to rates of incidence, studies show that approximately 24 million people worldwide have schizophrenia. Slightly less than 50% of those who have this disorder receive treatment, and 90% of the untreated reside in developing countries (World Health Organization, 2007). Studies by the World Health Organization (WHO) document that schizophrenia is found internationally and across all cultures (World Health Organization, 1973, 1979). The WHO studies are older, but remain important because they used identical criteria worldwide for estimating the number of cases existing within industrialized, emerging, and impoverished nations. The researchers found that the incidence of schizophrenia per 1,000 people ranges from a low of approximately 0.15 in Demark to a high of 0.42 in India (World Health Organization, 1973, 1979). Stated another way, 15 to 42 people out of every 100,000 worldwide develop schizophrenia.

Currently between 2 and 3 million Americans have or will have schizophrenia (NIMH, 1990). Even with improved treatment methods, approximately 50% of all psychiatric inpatient hospital beds in the United States are used for patients with schizophrenia (Sadock & Sadock, 2007). Furthermore, 16% of all individuals in this country receiving psychiatric treatment have schizophrenia (Sadock & Sadock 2007). According to the Epidemiologic Catchment Area (ECA) research, the lifetime prevalence rate in the United States is about 1% (Regier, Myers, et al., 1984; Robins, Helzer, et al., 1984; Robins & Regier, 1991). The ECA studies sponsored by the National

Institute of Mental Health have become the primary data source for prevalence rates of mental disorders in the United States. Unfortunately, because of cost and other factors, the study has never been repeated.

Gender and Rates of Incidence

There has long been a belief that schizophrenia is equally distributed between males and females. Newer studies, however, indicate that this is incorrect, demonstrating instead that significantly more males than females develop the illness. Meta-analysis, for example, of epidemiological findings in the United States report a male to female risk ratio of 1.4 (Aleman, Kahn, et al., 2003). The ratio also varies across cultures, as a study found that twice as many men as women in West Ireland develop schizophrenia (First & Tasman 2004). As a result, additional studies are now needed to confirm if more males than females have schizophrenia. What we do know, however, is that males have an earlier illness onset, more severe symptoms, and are less helped by neuroleptic medications than women (Ho, Black, et al., 2003; First & Tasman, 2006). First episodes often occur in late adolescence for males and early twenties for women, and generally, onset is 3.5 to 6 years earlier for men than women (First & Tasman, 2004).

Ethnicity and Rates of Incidence

Based on ECA findings, there are no significant differences in the number of Caucasians and African-Americans who become ill with schizophrenia (Robins & Regier, 1991). Reports of higher prevalence in African-American communities most likely reflect differences in patterns of seeking psychiatric help within racial and ethnic groups, and past biases within diagnoses, treatment, and commitment proceedings (Adebimpe, 1994). Socioeconomic findings also likely contributed to overestimates of the number of African-Americans having schizophrenia. For many years, poverty and urbanization appeared to be risk factors for schizophrenia, and studies continuously found higher rates of schizophrenia in poor inner-city communities, such as those inhabited by African-Americans at the time. Newer studies, however, have demonstrated that bias skewed earlier findings, and that schizophrenia caused people to drift into lower social-economic conditions, rather than poverty causing or creating a risk for schizophrenia (Murphy, 2007).

Some communities within the United States and other countries may also have higher levels of schizophrenia because of previous social drift, causing a concentration of people who genetically pass the illness from one generation to the next. Additionally, poorer medical and prenatal care may result in higher rates of neuroviruses during pregnancy, and delivery problems during the birth process. Explanations of this type, however, must be seen as hypotheses to be proven and not epidemiological facts.

THE SOCIAL AND ECONOMIC EFFECTS OF SCHIZOPHRENIA

While living in a lower social-economic community may not increase the risk for schizophrenia, the illness does create economic, social, and emotional burdens for clients and their families. Healthcare for clients with schizophrenia is estimated annually to cost between $19 and $22.7 billion, and other costs resulting from the illness, such as lost productivity, housing, transportation, suicide attempts, and added homemaking expenses, cost Americans an additional $32.4 to $46 billion (Wyatt, Henter, et al., 1995; Wu, Birnbaum, et al., 2005). Approximately $7 billion per year is spent by families caring for loved ones with schizophrenia, and between 25% and 42% of clients live with their parents or other relatives (Wyatt, Henter, et al., 1995). One researcher estimates that approximately 550,000 adults with schizophrenia reside with family members (Torrey, 2006). Between 60% and 70% of individuals with this disorder will never marry (First & Tasman, 2006).

It is helpful for social workers to understand that having schizophrenia seldom removes the desire or the remorse of being unable to fulfill personal, family, and cultural expectations. Clients reflect on what would or may have been if their life had not been altered by schizophrenia. This was graphically driven home when a young adult client, preparing to go to a sibling's wedding, stated, "I'm older than my brother, he has a college degree and is getting married. If I did not have schizophrenia, I would have an engineering degree, and maybe my brother would be attending my wedding—will I ever be normal enough to be a husband and father—I know I will never become an engineer." The following week he made a serious suicide attempt, barely escaping death.

Suicide is highly associated with schizophrenia, and the risk increases if a client

- is a young male at beginning stage of illness;
- is depressed;
- is known to have a history of prior suicidal attempts;
- is living mostly in isolation;
- is facing a personal loss;
- expresses hopelessness;
- is agitated; or

- is chronically ill and has experienced numerous relapses and rehospitalizations (Siris, 2001; First & Tasman, 2006; Sadock & Sadock, 2007).

Between 5% and 15% of people with schizophrenia will succeed in taking their life, and between 20% and 50% will attempt suicide (Siris, 2001; First & Tasman, 2006; Torrey, 2006). Within the general public, about 1% of deaths are by suicide (Siris, 2001; First & Tasman, 2004).

DIAGNOSIS AND CATEGORICAL *DSM-IV-TR* ASSESSMENT OF SCHIZOPHRENIA

A major task throughout a categorical or *DSM-IV-TR* assessment is determining whether or not the symptoms are better explained by ecological factors or illnesses other than schizophrenia. We must always remain aware that a person can be psychotic without having schizophrenia. Both the principles of social justice and the unquestionable right for clients to expect an accurate assessment demand that every alternative explanation be ruled out before a diagnosis of schizophrenia is given.

Diagnosing schizophrenia independently or in isolation is extremely hazardous for the client. Before reaching a final diagnostic decision, the social worker needs input and specialized assessments documenting that the psychotic symptoms are not better explained by depression, bipolar disorders, trauma, substance abuse, interactions from prescribed or over-the-counter medications, environmental toxins, consumption of poisons, or medical illness. In addition to requesting specialized assessments, social workers need to explore the client's symptoms, strengths, and support across major ecological systems before offering a diagnostic label. This ideally requires not only interviews with the family, friends, employers or teachers, and other treatment specialists, but also visits to and observations of the client's interactions within and across all home and community settings. Observational assessments allow one to determine whether symptoms remain the same, increase, or decrease within each environmental setting. Our goal is to discover whether certain settings as a whole or elements within settings are more toxic for the client. This is accomplished by analyzing the observational data for commonalities that appear to have positive and negative effects on the client across different settings. This information is then used to inform treatment planning and psychosocial-education sessions.

Complete physical, hearing, and eye exams, as well as an exhaustive medical history, are also needed in order to ensure that the psychotic symptoms are not resulting from unknown health problems. A neuropsychological examination is always in order when psychiatric problems decrease a person's cognitive and social functioning. Individuals who have documented head trauma occurring at any time prior to the onset of psychotic symptoms become candidates for both a neurological and a neuropsychological examination. The neurologist may be able to determine if past head trauma explains, complicates, or does not account for the psychotic symptoms. A neuropsychological assessment will help define specific cognitive and memory deficits and strengths. Together, these investigations can help shape treatment, rehabilitation, and educational recommendations.

An important indicator of schizophrenia is the failure to completely regain previous social or cognitive skills once the psychotic episode ends. Even with proper treatment and medications, most people with this illness do not return to their previous functional baseline in areas like problem-solving, abstract thinking, concentration, socialization, personal hygiene, and planning skills. Some clients will maintain deficits in all of these domains, while others will regain full skills in some areas, but not in others. Furthermore, how much improvement is gained across functional domains greatly varies from client to client, and from episode to episode. A client may have more or less skill reductions after an episode than he or she experienced following previous periods of psychosis, or the person's negative symptoms may improve or decrease as time between episodes lengthens. This is equally true for positive symptoms. For some individuals, medications will completely remove their positive symptoms. However, even with sound drug treatment, many clients experience less severe but near constant positive symptoms, while still others have positive symptoms that come and go at varying levels of severity. Therefore, it is helpful for clinicians to track and rate severity and changes that occur for each negative and positive symptom experienced by a client.

Measurements of this type are taken during and after each psychotic episode. Changes in negative and positive symptoms can help inform treatment planning and the employment of preventive interventions. If, for example, we know from previous assessments that a specific increase in symptom severity signals a need for hospitalization, the treatment team can initiate emergency steps and try to prevent the person from experiencing another inpatient admission. Furthermore, as one recovers and has less severe symptoms, the treatment team can experiment and alter treatment by adding additional self-care and productivity responsibilities. The term "experiment" is used because there is no way to predict if added responsibilities will be helpful or will trigger more frequent symptoms. Anytime that treatment and self-care changes are imposed, a social worker is obligated to intensively follow and evaluate the client. Both negative and positive shifts in symptoms and behaviors require immediate attention. An increase in symptoms signals the need to quickly reduce stress and have a psychiatrist assess the person's medications. Decreased symptoms and improved behaviors, however, can be praised, built upon, and incorporated into rehabilitation planning.

Consistently measuring symptoms will help treatment teams and families to decrease their control and appropriately empower a client as improvement occurs and to increase or change interventions as symptoms increase. Symptoms sometimes respond to changes in the environment. Therefore, as positive or negative symptoms increase, it is appropriate for social workers to reassess the client's major social settings. However, as detailed earlier in this chapter, both positive and negative symptoms may increase when no ecological changes have occurred and little environmental stress exists. Without conducting an ecological assessment, the role, if any, played by environmental settings in a client's increased symptoms cannot be determined.

The keys for diagnosing whether a person has schizophrenia are illustrated in Figure 4.3. These items provide a visual framework to help clinicians recall primary domains and problems that must be included in a schizophrenia assessment. People with schizophrenia will have significant problems in many, but seldom all, of the domains represented by the keys. In almost all cases, schizophrenia causes a diminished reality, negative symptoms, reduced functioning, and a permanent or long-term loss of abstract problem solving, and social skills. Research has consistently found that there are three distinct symptom domains that relate to schizophrenia. These include

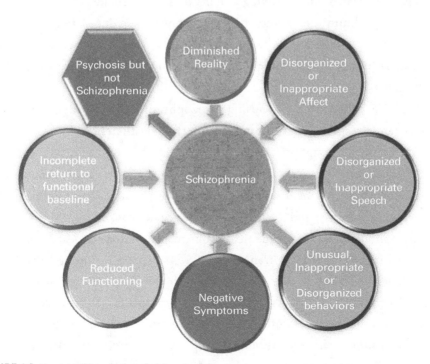

FIGURE 4.3 Keys to Diagnosing Schizophrenia.

(1) hallucinations, delusions, and paranoia; (2) thought disorder and bizarre behaviors; and (3) negative symptoms (Tamminga, 1997; Ho, Black, et al., 2003). The first domain is nested in the key illustration labeled "diminished reality," while the second domain is represented by the three separate keys of affect, speech, and behavior. In addition to negative symptoms, the illustrated keys add reduced functioning, and the fact that most clients do not return in all areas of functional skills to their pre-illness baseline. In some ways, reduced functioning during an episode and failure to return in all or some skills to a previous baseline after episodes are directly related to negative symptoms. We know that negative symptoms continue after positive symptoms have subsided (Buchanan & Carpenter, 2001; Ho, Black, et al., 2003). It is reasonable, therefore, to hypothesize that an interaction among reduced concentration, abstraction, planning, and other skills associated with negative symptoms compound and further reduce the client's social, educational, and work competence.

The illustrated keys provide a good point for organizing and starting both a *DSM* categorical and functional diagnostic assessment interview. The exception to this rule is when the client or family have specific concerns that need immediate attention, or when the symptoms obviously suggest an alternative disorder. As stated throughout this book, with few exceptions we start clinical assessments by addressing the primary concerns of the client and family. Nonetheless, when schizophrenia is to be ruled out, we spend a great deal of time clarifying whether persistent problems exist in the symptom domains of diminished reality, negative symptoms, reduced functioning, and incomplete return to baselines between episodes. All of the keys, however, are important and are required for diagnosing schizophrenia and identifying the disorder's specific subtypes.

DSM-IV-TR criteria for diagnosing schizophrenia are provided in Box 4.5. The clinician is responsible for documenting that (1) the client has at least two measurable positive symptoms; (2) symptoms have been observable for at least 1 month; (3) client has had a reduction in at least one area of social, occupational, or educational skills; (4) measurable signs of mental problems are documented for a minimum of 6 months; and (5) the symptoms are not caused by a disorder other than schizophrenia or another medical problem. In addition to establishing the criteria for diagnosing schizophrenia, Box 4.5 also specifies important diagnostic exceptions and clarifications. For example, the length of time that symptoms must persist to fulfill criteria "A" (Characteristic symptoms) is reduced when the symptoms have been successfully treated. Successful treatment also reduces the time that delusions or hallucinations must be present for clients with a pervasive developmental disorder to also receive a diagnosis of schizophrenia. Once an

BOX 4.5
DSM-IV-TR DIAGNOSTIC CRITERIA FOR SCHIZOPHRENIA

A. *Characteristic symptoms*: Two (or more) of the following, each present for significant portion of time during a 1-month period (or less if successfully treated):
   1. Delusions
   2. Hallucinations
   3. Disorganized speech (e.g., frequent derailment or incoherence)
   4. Grossly disorganized or catatonic behavior
   5. Negative symptoms, that is, affective flattening, alogia, or avolition.
   Note: Only one Criterion A symptom is required if delusions are bizarre or hallucinations consist of a voice keeping up a running commentary on the person's behavior or thoughts, or two or more voices conversing with each other.

B. *Social/occupational dysfunction*: For a significant portion of the time since the onset of the disturbance, one or more major areas of functioning such as work, interpersonal relations, or self-care are markedly below the level achieved prior to the onset (or when the onset is in childhood or adolescence, failure to achieve expected level of interpersonal, academic, or occupational achievement).

C. *Duration*: Continuous signs of the disturbance persist for at least 6 months. This 6-month period must include at least 1 month of symptoms (or less if successfully treated) that meet Criterion A (i.e., active-phase symptoms) and may include periods of prodromal or residual symptoms. During these prodromal or residual periods, the signs of the disturbance may be manifested by only negative symptoms or two or more symptoms listed in Criterion A present in an attenuated form (e.g., odd beliefs, unusual perceptual experiences).

D. *Schizoaffective and mood disorder exclusion*: Schizoaffective disorder and mood disorder with psychotic features have been ruled out because either (1) no major depressive, manic, or mixed episodes have occurred concurrently with the active-phase symptoms; or (2) if mood episodes have occurred during active-phase symptoms, their total duration has been brief relative to the duration of the active and residual periods.

E. *Substance/general medical condition exclusion*: The disturbance is not due to the direct physiological effects of a substance (e.g., a drug of abuse, a medication) or a general medical condition.

F. *Relationship to a pervasive developmental disorder*: If there is a history of autistic disorder or another pervasive developmental disorder, the additional diagnosis of schizophrenia is made only if prominent delusions or

> hallucinations are also present for at least a month (or less if successfully treated).
>
> *Classification of longitudinal course* (can be applied only after at least 1 year has elapsed since the initial onset of active-phase symptoms):
>
> **Episodic With Interepisode-Residual Symptoms** (episodes are defined by the reemergence of prominent psychotic symptoms); *also specify if*: **With Prominent Negative Symptoms**
>
> **Episodic With No Interepisode Residual Symptoms**
>
> **Continuous** (prominent psychotic symptoms are present throughout the period of observation); *also specify if*: **With Prominent Negative Symptoms**
>
> **Single Episode In Partial Remission**; *also specify if*: **With Prominent Negative Symptoms**
>
> **Single Episode In Full Remission**
>
> **Other or Unspecified Pattern**
>
> ---
>
> *Source: Reprinted with permission from the* Diagnostic and Statistical Manual of Mental Disorders, Fourth Edition, Text Revision *(Copyright 2000). American Psychiatric Association.*

individual has had schizophrenia for a year, clinicians can also use the "classification of longitudinal course" (see Box 4.5). This added element quickly identifies whether the illness has been persistent, intermittent, partially in remission of some symptoms, or was a single episode with all symptoms in remission. However, one cannot help but notice that time specifications appear to be somewhat arbitrary. The *DSM* authors made decisions of this type based on a consensus by expert panels. There also are no guidelines regarding how many days symptoms that are successfully treated must last to be classified as schizophrenia. While this is also true for section "C" (Duration) the purpose is clearer, even if subjective. Requiring a 6-month period of ongoing observable disturbance assures that clinicians will not make quick diagnoses, and allows time for specialized assessment referrals and community observations. The *DSM-5*, published in mid-2013, made a few minor changes to the criteria for diagnosing schizophrenia and schizoaffective disorders (American Psychiatric Association, 2013a, 2013b). An overview of the *DSM* changes are provided in Box 4.6.

After diagnosing schizophrenia, the social worker can also determine which *DSM-IV-TR* subtype best classifies the person's symptoms. *DSM-5* has discontinued the official classification of schizophrenia subtypes (American Psychiatric Association, 2013a). However, it can be helpful to understand how clinicians for a number of years have grouped the psychotic symptoms. Schizophrenia presents with a cluster of symptoms that are subcategorized as (1) catatonic, (2) paranoid, (3) disorganized, (4) undifferentiated, or (5) residual. Unfortunately, symptoms seldom cluster neatly into a single subtype, and clients may have problems that meet more than a single subcategory. When this occurs, the following rules establish which designation is to be assigned:

BOX 4.6

DSM-5 DIAGNOSTIC CRITERIA DIFFERING FROM *DSM-IV-TR* FOR SCHIZOPHRENIA

- The definition of schizophrenia remains much the same in *DSM-IV-TR* and *DSM-5*.
- *DSM-5* no longer states (as did *DSM-IV-TR*) that only one characteristic symptom (criterion A) is required if the client has bizarre delusions or hears voices that make commentaries about the person's behavior, or has hallucinations of two or more voices conversing with each other. The new criteria for diagnosing schizophrenia require a person to experience two or more of the following specific symptoms: delusions; hallucinations; disorganized speech; grossly disorganized or catatonic behavior; or negative symptoms. Research has indicated poor reliability among clinicians in identifying and defining bizarre delusions or distinguishing content of audio hallucinations.
- The *DSM-IV-TR* schizophrenia subtypes have been dropped. Identifying clients as having paranoid, disorganized, catatonic, undifferentiated, or residual schizophrenia has not been productive for treatment or research.
- A diagnosis of schizoaffective disorder requires the same criteria found in *DSM-IV-TR*. However, *DSM-5* requires that the client meet all requirements for a major mood disorder concurrently while demonstrating symptoms identified for diagnosing schizophrenia. *DSM-IV-TR* had simply required that a person meet the criteria for schizophrenia and at some point experience a major mood disorder. The new criteria requires at least a 2-week period of psychotic features with no significant mood disorders. This helps identify that the client has schizophrenia. However, after the schizophrenia criterion is met, a major mood disorder must be present for most of the illness.

Source: The above information is paraphrased from the DSM-5 *and a web report (American Psychiatric Association 2013a, 2013b)*

1. Before being assigned a subtype, the client should clearly meet the criteria required for the diagnosis of schizophrenia.

2. Catatonic subtype is assigned regardless of other types of symptoms that are present when catatonic symptoms are central, or are causing the primary disability.

3. If catatonia is not present, but the client has disorganized speech and behavior, and flat or inappropriate affect, use the disorganized subtype.

4. When the client has no catatonia, and does not meet requirements for disorganized schizophrenia, but does have a recurring preoccupation with delusions, or has recurrent hallucinations, assign the subtype of paranoid schizophrenia.

5. If a person does not clearly meet the criteria for catatonic, disorganized, or paranoid, we use the undifferentiated subtype.

6. The residual subtype is assigned when a client's symptoms no longer qualify as indicators for diminished reality, but do continue to cause milder problems, such as unusual ideas or beliefs, or improved, but still measurable, negative symptoms (American Psychiatric Association, 2000; Barlow & Durand, 2005).

After reading the brief subtype descriptions, notice now many of the definitions are rather general, and that the diagnostic criteria most often consist of only one or two symptoms. The brevity and general nature of the subtypes suggest that researchers and clinicians have not yet identified definitive schizophrenia subtypes. This is further evident and supported by the fact that there are no differential medications or therapy treatments shown by research to be more effective in treating specific subtypes (Cummings & Mega, 2003; Lehman, Lieberman, et al., 2006). Additionally, over time a client's cluster of symptoms may change and require assignment of a different subtype. As the fields of neuroimaging and chemistry grow, these categories will be replaced with subtypes founded on neurological findings rather than observational data. Nonetheless, the former *DSM* subtypes can help clinicians more logically select the symptoms that are to be immediately targeted for treatment and ongoing evaluation. The concept also helps organize information presented in psychoeducation classes.

The **catatonic subtype** is distinguished by extended periods of rigid fixed body positions, uncharacteristic and spontaneous hyper movements, abnormal communication patterns, or arousal that is either hyper- or hypoactive (Cummings & Mega, 2003). To meet *DSM* criteria, a client's principal problems must stem from any two of the following five symptoms:

1. Trance-like state known as catalepsy, causing stupor or muscles to have a waxy flexibility (limbs, as an example, will remain as placed by client or others for extended periods);

2. Spontaneous hyper body movements that cannot be accounted for by environmental influences;

3. Even though client has no motive for resisting the person, completely fails to respond to all instructions (known as negativism) or responds with an extremely rigid posture when others attempt to move the individual, or remains completely silent when addressed by others and when alone (mutism);

4. Purposefully makes unusual stereotyped movements, such as maintaining self in uncomfortable or bizarre postures for an extended period, repeated stereotyped movements, prominent idiosyncratic movements, or frozen facial expression of grimacing;

5. Constantly repeats exact words or phrases stated by others (echolalia) or performs the same body movements of others (echopraxia) (American Psychiatric Association, 2000).

The symptoms of catatonia are listed and explained in Box 4.7. This subtype of schizophrenia is generally thought of as a psychotic state involving abnormal motor

---

BOX 4.7

DSM-IV-TR DIAGNOSTIC CRITERIA FOR 295.20 CATATONIC TYPE

A type of schizophrenia in which the clinical picture is dominated by at least two of the following:

1. Motoric immobility as evidenced by catalepsy (including waxy flexibility) or stupor;

2. Excessive motor activity (that is apparently purposeless and not influenced by external stimuli);

3. Extreme negativism (an apparently motiveless resistance to all instructions or maintenance of a rigid posture against attempts to be moved) or mutism;

4. Peculiarities of voluntary movement as evidenced by posturing (voluntary assumption of inappropriate or bizarre postures), stereotyped movements, prominent mannerisms, or prominent grimacing;

5. Echolalia or echopraxia.

Source: Reprinted with permission from the Diagnostic and Statistical Manual of Mental Disorders, Fourth Edition, Text Revision *(Copyright 2000). American Psychiatric Association.*

responses. The symptoms can range from mild to extremely severe. They are always considered involuntary symptoms that are out of the individual's control. The client, for example, will echo someone's words, mimic movements, or remain locked in a rigid posture, not to be defiant, but because the person's brain will not discover and allow other more appropriate behaviors.

Tracking and constantly evaluating whether catatonic symptoms are increasing is an important clinical task. In a moderate or severe state, clients can accidently injure themselves by remaining rigid for an extended period of time, or crashing into things or falling while in a state of extreme motor excitement. Keeping the catatonic person safe requires close clinical observation, referral to a psychiatrist for a medication and physical review, family education and support, and often hospitalization.

Paranoid schizophrenia is highlighted by clients who have moderate to severe delusions, hallucinations, or both (see Box 4.8). However, to qualify for having paranoid schizophrenia, the *DSM* requires only that a person has one or more delusions, or often experiences auditory hallucinations. Additionally, the *DSM* authors clarify that not only do the delusions or hallucinations have to be prominent, but in order for a client to be diagnosed with paranoid schizophrenia, the person cannot have disorganized speech or behavior, catatonic symptoms, or flat or inappropriate affect (American Psychiatric Association, 2000). More than in any other subtype, individuals with this form of schizophrenia often have relatively intact cognitive and affective skills (American Psychiatric Association, 2000; Ho, Black, et al., 2003). In particular, clients with this subtype of schizophrenia remain highly verbal, and are better able to organize their affect and behavior (Morrison, 2007). This can help clients hide their symptoms and verbally defend their misperceptions, delusional beliefs, and other weakened sense of reality. Some people, however, with paranoid schizophrenia demonstrate a marked decrease in

---

BOX 4.8

DSM-IV-TR DIAGNOSTIC CRITERIA FOR 295.30 PARANOID TYPE

A type of schizophrenia in which the following criteria are met:
  A. Preoccupation with one or more delusions or frequent auditory hallucinations.
  B. None of the following is prominent: disorganized speech, disorganized or catatonic behavior, or flat or inappropriate affect.

Source: Reprinted with permission from the Diagnostic and Statistical Manual of Mental Disorders, Fourth Edition, Text Revision *(Copyright 2000). American Psychiatric Association.*

verbal communications and functional skills. When one worries about delusional events or experience, maintaining previous social and work skills becomes very difficult.

As the term "paranoid" implies, delusions often focus on perceptions and beliefs of being targeted for persecution. However, the subcategory is somewhat misnamed and over-inclusive. Clients with grandiosity and delusional illnesses and pain (somatization), as well as those with delusions incorporating jealousy and religiosity, are included in this subtype of schizophrenia. Delusions with a jealous or religious theme do not necessarily stir fears and beliefs of self-persecution (American Psychiatric Association, 2000; Morrison, 2007).

Delusions often cluster around a single theme, such as being pursued by an intelligence agency, but some clients experience several delusional themes that are completely independent of each other. In addition to the symptoms outlined above, delusional beliefs can also take on any of the following cognitive forms:

- Sin—thoughts and emotions that one has committed unforgivable or particularly evil sins against God;
- Guilt—unfounded feelings of guilt—client believes that he is being punished or deserves to be punished for his past actions or crimes toward a certain person or group;
- Ideas of reference—belief that certain people or items such as phones, radios, and televisions are sending messages to or about the individual—client may believe that a TV advertisement or program, for example, has a message and information directed specifically to him or is talking about him—client may also believe that the way objects are arranged, when mail arrives, the appearance of certain numbers, or other environmental events are messages referencing him;
- Delusions of control—refers to the belief that an individual, group, or force is controlling the individual's thoughts or actions—may involve the idea that a computer chip or other device has been implanted in his body to control how the person thinks and behaves;
- Thought insertion—a type of delusion of control in which the client believes that others can place thoughts into his head;
- Thought withdrawal—a form of delusion of control in which the client believes that his own personal thoughts are being taken away by a person, group, or force;
- Thought broadcasting—a form of delusion of control causing the client to believe that his thoughts can be heard by others—a client may believe that his thoughts are so loud that people can hear all of his thoughts, or the client may indicate that

a transmitter was placed in his head and is broadcasting his thoughts to the general public or to a specific person, group, or force;

- Somatic—a belief that one has an illness such as cancer, or that a headache, for example, is occurring because his brain is decaying;
- Imposter—a belief that a family member or other significant person has been replaced by a "look-alike" imposter;
- Love—the client expresses certainty that a person, who may or may not know the client, has strong romantic feelings for him—the focus of delusional love is often placed on a person with higher social status or a public figure such as a performer or politician;
- Nihilism—beliefs that one has died or never lived, or no longer exists;
- Mood—a sense and belief that people, places, or events have changed, causing unfamiliarity or a feeling of suspicion or danger—often seen at the onset of schizophrenia;
- Poverty—the client is economically sound, but sincerely believes that he is either poor or will soon experience poverty.

In schizophrenia the most common delusions are themes of persecution, reference, and grandiosity (Maher & Spitzer, 1993; Ho, Black, et al., 2003; Mueser & Gingerich, 2006). Delusions focused on sin and guilt are seen more in psychotic depression than schizophrenia. Additional assessments should be done to assure that a client does not have a mood disorder, rather than schizophrenia, when delusions of sin or guilt are discovered (Tsuang, Faraone, et al., 1999). Furthermore, it is considered a delusion of persecution when people believe they are falsely accused of sins, crimes, or other actions they did not commit. Delusions of sin or guilt are represented as behaviors that were performed by the client and therefore are deserving of punishment. Self-punishment for delusional sin and guilt can range from beliefs that one's soul is doomed to hell to self-mutilation.

Disorganized schizophrenia attacks the client's ability to be in command of speech content, and to perform behaviors that meet cultural expectations; and it can kindle flat or inappropriate affect (see Box 4.9). Even hallucinations and delusions appear to be disorganized experiences, rather than a coherent understood event. The meaning and content of a hallucination or delusion does not seem to form a complete mental gestalt that can be communicated. The opposite is generally true for paranoid schizophrenia (First & Tasman, 2004). Clients with disorganized schizophrenia verbally move from one topic to another with no transitions, or nest within the same sentence two or more disconnected ideas. This, along with the loss of insight, makes it difficult to determine if a client understands assessment questions, and what the individual's reply represents. That is, one cannot easily identify if the person correctly received the question,

---

BOX 4.9

DSM-IV-TR DIAGNOSTIC CRITERIA FOR 295.10 DISORGANIZED TYPE

A type of schizophrenia in which the following criteria are met:

  A. All of the following are prominent:
   1. Disorganized speech
   2. Disorganized behavior
   3. Flat or inappropriate affect
  B. The criteria are not met for catatonic type.

Source: Reprinted with permission from the Diagnostic and Statistical Manual of Mental Disorders, Fourth Edition, Text Revision *(Copyright 2000). American Psychiatric Association.*

---

has a clear logical answer in mind but cannot verbalize the thought, or if the person is experiencing both cognitive slippage and jumbled or meaningless verbalizations. The idea that schizophrenia can cause cognitive deficits and an inability to transition from one idea to another while communicating was first introduced by Bleuler in the early 1900s, and later refined by psychologists in the 1960s (Bleuler, 1924; Meehl, 1962, 1989). In his 1908 textbook (translated into English in 1924), Bleuler declared that disorganized thinking, including speech, was the most important symptom or indicator of schizophrenia.

It is almost impossible to hold an ongoing conversation with a person who has disorganized schizophrenia. Verbal and written communications are distorted by the individual's poverty of speech, poverty of content of speech, incomplete cognition and thoughts, incorrect or incomplete subject content, derailment, and tangentiality (Andreasen, 1979, 2001; Ho, Black, et al., 2003). Poverty of speech implies that the quantity of words and sentences are limited, and answers to questions have little or no elaboration. In more severe cases, the client may use monosyllabic words or simply remain silent. In contrast, a person having poverty of content of speech (sometimes called "empty speech") will express an adequate amount of speech, but because of vagueness, obscure or cumbersome phraseology, or meaningless repetition, communicates only limited information.

Poverty of speech and poverty of content of speech can cause a client's communications to range from disjointed but understandable to illogical. However, the two symptoms do not automatically mean that the person's speech is completely incoherent. The following is an example of how a person having poverty of content of speech may answer a social worker asking, "Was your room overly warm last night?"

The night was long. The room is down the hall, I'm not sure how many doors down. The room is by the heater, well not right by the heater, well actually the heater is in the hallway, but real near my room, it is really hot next to the heater. The heater is really hot. Last night I did not sleep.

The client's statement fails to answer the question, rambles, communicates limited information, and is vague. We cannot know for certain if the reference to the room down the hall means the client's room or a different location. One thought immediately follows another, but none communicates a single point of view. We can follow the flow of ideas; however, the loosely linked concepts fail to tell a cohesive story. Each of the client's thoughts appears to be almost independent of the previous idea, and instantly is derailed by the next loosely linked idea. A person who has poverty of speech, on the other hand, may answer the question of whether the room was overly warm with silence or with simple statements such as "yes," or "don't know."

Derailment, sometimes called loosening of association, refers to a sudden shift in a client's focus and verbal direction for no known reason. When a person's thinking is derailed, the person loses sight of what he or she was attempting to communicate, and with no explanation or transition moves to a completely different thought and communication goal. The two or more differing concepts are pushed together as if they presented a single idea (Sadock & Sadock, 2007).

In contrast to this is the symptom of blocking, which is also seen in disorganized schizophrenia. Blocking takes place when one stops speaking before completing a thought because the idea or notion suddenly slipped out of consciousness. When thought content is blocked, clients briefly stop talking and cannot recall what they were going to say, or what they had just been talking about. Other terms that are synonymous with blocking include "thought deprivation" and "increased thought latency" (Ho, Black, et al., 2003; Sadock & Sadock, 2007). The following is an example of blocking: "In the middle ages knights were——I'm sorry, what were we talking about?"

Unlike derailment and poverty of content of speech, the symptom of blocking does not cause diverse thoughts to collide into a disjointed series of concepts. When clients have symptoms of blocking, their speech will suddenly stop before the communication is completed. This occurs because the concept, idea, or point the person wanted to make is lost from the immediate working memory. Thoughts and known information slip away before the initiated mental or verbal process can be completed. Most often, clients with schizophrenia are aware when recall is blocked, but are less conscious of poverty of content and derailment symptoms.

Disorganized schizophrenia can also be characterized by flat or inappropriate affect, and unusual behavior. People are considered to have flat affect when they fail to make or change expressions over a reasonable period of time. One may, for example, never smile, frown, appear surprised, or show delight or unhappiness throughout an entire assessment or conversation, but rather remain in a frozen empty facial expression with an almost vacant or distant look in their eyes. Other clients with this subtype of illness will have periods of affective responses that do not match the environmental situation or cultural expectations. They may laugh, cry, or become animated at inappropriate times. Furthermore, some clients will not only laugh or cry at the wrong times, but their responses may take on unusual qualities, such as being overly loud, continuing for an extended time, or having an abnormal sound. For yet others, the illness is highlighted by peculiar behaviors, such as wearing winter clothing in warm weather or insisting on always dressing in strange-appearing clothing. The disorganized subtype also includes hoarding, repetitive and compulsive gestures or other actions, and grimacing. Every subcategory of schizophrenia, but especially disorganized schizophrenia, can elicit behaviors that mirror obsessive-compulsive symptoms. When this occurs, clinicians must assess whether the client has obsessive compulsive disorder (OCD) along with schizophrenia, or if the disorganized schizophrenia symptoms simply have some of the features seen in OCD (Sadock & Sadock, 2007).

The symptoms seen in disorganized schizophrenia also often overlap into other subtypes. This is particularly true when the client is having a severe psychotic episode. The category does help clinicians better communicate a client's cluster of symptoms, and signals that until the episode ends, cognitive and group process-oriented therapies will not be productive. Furthermore, people with this cluster of symptoms tend to have more social problems, an earlier age of onset, poor prognosis, and neuropsychological test scores that indicate more severe brain deficits (American Psychiatric Association, 2000; First & Tasman, 2004).

We must, however, keep in mind that none of the subtype symptoms is necessarily, in and of itself, evidence of schizophrenia. Disorganized thinking that mimics schizophrenia is also found in clients experiencing manic and major depressive episodes. Additionally, delusions and hallucinations can occur in all disorders that cause psychosis, dementia, or Parkinson's disease (Ho, Black, et al., 2003).

The undifferentiated schizophrenia subtype was created as a diagnostic label for clients who meet all of the criteria for schizophrenia, but do not easily fit into any of the other subcategories (see Box 4.10). Clients who fall into this category have at least two of the following symptoms: delusions, hallucinations, disorganized speech, disorganized

---

BOX 4.10

DSM-IV-TR DIAGNOSTIC CRITERIA FOR 295.90 UNDIFFERENTIATED TYPE

A type of schizophrenia in which symptoms that meet Criterion A are present, but the criteria are not met for the paranoid, disorganized, or catatonic type.

Source: Reprinted with permission from the Diagnostic and Statistical Manual of Mental Disorders, Fourth Edition, Text Revision *(Copyright 2000). American Psychiatric Association.*

BOX 4.11

DSM-IV-TR DIAGNOSTIC CRITERIA FOR 295.60 RESIDUAL TYPE

A type of schizophrenia in which the following criteria are met:
   A. Absence of prominent delusions, hallucinations, disorganized speech, and grossly disorganized or catatonic behavior.
   B. There is continuing evidence of the disturbance, as indicated by the presence of negative symptoms or two or more symptoms listed in Criterion A for schizophrenia, present in an attenuated from (e.g., odd beliefs, unusual perceptual experiences).

Source: Reprinted with permission from the Diagnostic and Statistical Manual of Mental Disorders, Fourth Edition, Text Revision *(Copyright 2000). American Psychiatric Association.*

---

or catatonic behavior, and negative symptoms. Their symptoms, however, do not satisfy the requirements needed for paranoid, disorganized, or catatonic subtypes of schizophrenia. The *DSM-IV-TR* describes the undifferentiated subtype as a "residual" category distinguished by active symptoms (American Psychiatric Association, 2000). This means that clients continue to have positive and negative symptoms, but the symptoms fail to have the prominence, frequency, or clarity of problems found in the other subtypes. Because symptoms overlap among subtypes and occur in disorders other than schizophrenia, social workers are advised to always employ evidence-based assessments, observe the client over time, and receive professional supervision and consultation before making a diagnosis of schizophrenia.

Residual schizophrenia is assigned as a subtype when clients have had at least one episode of schizophrenia, but presently there are no active psychotic or positive symptoms (see Box 4.11). Undifferentiated subtype represents people who have residual positive and negative symptoms that can be observed and measured. In other words, the person continues to have at a minimum a low grade of schizophrenia. Clients move into the residual schizophrenia category when they have inactive positive symptoms and the psychosis has cleared. People in this subgroup, however, most often continue to experience negative symptoms and manifest remnants of previous symptoms. While the psychotic episode is gone, they may continue to have very concrete thinking and difficulty concentrating or following directions. Clients with residual schizophrenia are generally able to hold jobs, participate in family activities, and even existentially make sense and meaning of their situation. Nonetheless, they seldom fully return to their original social, cognitive, or work functional baseline, and may continue to exhibit odd behaviors, have unusual ideas, or experience fragments of past delusions or hallucinations (First & Tasman, 2006). While it is cannot be predicted how long a person will remain free of psychotic symptoms, the residual state offers the best hope for making improvements in a client's social, environmental, and family situation. The freedom from positive symptoms allows space for clients and social workers to experiment with environmental enhancements, job training and placement, advanced psychoeducation, social relationship building, and cognitive behavioral therapies.

TREATMENT

Successful treatment of schizophrenia largely depends on correctly completing the *DSM* categorical diagnosis as well as a comprehensive functional and ecological assessment. We want to know how the client's functioning within environmental settings validates the categorical diagnosis. A functional and ecological assessment requires tracking the client's level of symptom severity and ability to meet cultural expectations, goals, roles, and production requirements within the family, work or education, recreation, peer groups, and other community settings over time. In addition to quantifying and describing strengths and deficits across environments, we also want to measure the amount of effort used to complete required tasks within each setting. That is, estimate how hard the person must work or concentrate, compared to pre-illness rates, to complete a task or reach his or her current level of functioning. In most cases these estimates can only be made after interviewing the client, family, and significant community informants. The idea is to identify a specific task and have informants describe how quickly, completely, accurately, and timely the person now performs the activity compared to his or her performance before the onset of illness. Effort and concentration used by the client to complete a task now and prior to onset can loosely be estimated by asking the informants to rate each on a 10-point scale, with 0 representing no effort or concentration and 10 representing the most effort of concentration a person could reach.

After assessing that a person has schizophrenia, a social worker inherits several important responsibilities. Keep in mind that schizophrenia is often considered the most difficult and complicated of the mental disorders to treat (First & Tasman, 2004). Therefore, individuals with limited experience are advised to refer clients with schizophrenia and other psychotic illnesses to more skilled clinicians, or to seek close supervision throughout the treatment process. One of the most important early treatment tasks is assuring the client and family that while schizophrenia is not considered curable, it is absolutely treatable. There is a temptation to either focus on the devastating symptoms of the illness or optimistically overstate the miracles of modern treatment. While it is wrong to believe and communicate that schizophrenia is a doomsday diagnosis, it is equally unethical to offer vulnerable clients and families false hope. As E. Fuller Torrey points out, one must be careful not to speak in a manner that tells clients they are not trying if recovery is elusive (Torrey, 2006).

Social workers are also reminded that providing realistic hope and timely information about treatment advances is not only for clients and families experiencing their first psychotic episode. Schizophrenia symptoms often change, intensify, or return after seeming to have disappeared or greatly improved. No matter how many episodes and setbacks a person has experienced, changes and recurrence of symptoms is disheartening and anxiety provoking. Empathetically validating the client and family's fears, grief, and disappointment, along with reviewing treatment options and advancements, can help renew strength and hope. For many, because of schizophrenia's evolving and changing nature, information sharing, educational updating, and reassurance are periodically required. A brief list of evidence-based interventions for treating schizophrenia is provided in Box 4.12.

Without question, the first and most important treatment for schizophrenia is appropriate neuropsychiatric medication given in a therapeutic dose, and correctly taken by the client. The family of drugs used is frequently referred to as antipsychotics, but the more accurate term is "neuroleptic medications." In the past, social workers had little or no responsibility for the medication treatment of people with schizophrenia. Today that has changed, and our profession plays a major role in helping clients receive, understand, and comply with drug therapy. It is important to stress, however, that we never prescribe or recommend medications. That is the responsibility of the medical professions.

As part of the treatment team, however, social work clinicians are expected to educate and sometimes re-educate clients and families about the benefits and side effects of drug therapies. In addition to emphasizing the importance of medications and specific side effects, families and clients need to know how long it takes for medications to work and what symptoms the drugs often do not improve. For example, all of the neuroleptic

---

BOX 4.12

**OUTLINE OF EVIDENCE-BASED PRACTICE INTERVENTIONS FOR
TREATING SCHIZOPHRENIA**

Treatment of schizophrenia requires a multi-system-treatment approach:
- Medications (key to treating all psychotic episodes);
- Psychosocial education for client;
- Psychosocial education for all family members;
- Concrete support for client;
- Concrete support for family;
- Problem-solving for family;
- Social-skills training for client;
- Assertive community case management;
- Advocacy and education for community/work/school and client's friends/ extended family;
- Cognitive therapy/training for coping with hallucinations and life problems;
- Behavioral interventions for decreasing behaviors that cause problems for client or others.

---

medications are more effective at stopping or decreasing positive symptoms than negative symptoms. Individuals also need to know that for a small number of people with this illness, medications either offer little relief, or create intolerable side effects, causing the prescribed drug to be discontinued. Additionally, social workers can play an important role in helping monitor their clients' cognitive, physical, and emotional reactions to medication. Knowing whether a client's work habits, interpersonal skills, and emotional stability change is important information for helping a psychiatrist determine if medications or dosage levels need adjusting. The good news is that medications do work for most clients and can be psychically and emotionally tolerated. While there is no question that medications are the first line of defense for schizophrenia, newer studies, however, are questioning the practice of keeping patients on antipsychotic drugs for an extended period- of-time. Research on the efficacy of antipsychotic medication treatment for 10 or more years has resulted in mixed findings (Harrow & Jobe, 2013). More and better controlled studies are required before recommendations and long-term treatment protocols can be developed. Nonetheless, there is enough evidence to hypothesize that some patients will have improved treatment outcomes by not receiving antipsychotic medications for an extended period of time. Unfortunately, we currently neither have enough replicated studies nor the ability to predict which clients with schizophrenia are best served by shorter medication treatments.

All clients on neuroleptic medications must constantly receive monitoring for drug-induced movement disorders known as tartive dyscanesia. The primary obligation for detecting movement disorders falls on the attending psychiatrist. Unfortunately, medical doctors have far fewer appointments with clients than do social workers. Early detection of changes in a client's ability to control his or her body and facial movements can prevent a temporary disorder caused by medication from becoming a permanent disfiguring and debilitating problem. Therefore, social workers may want to get instructions and supervision on using measurement instruments, such as the Abnormal Involuntary Movement Scale (AIMS), for monitoring changes in a client's motor skills and muscle control (Munetz & Benjamin, 1988). It is beyond the scope of this text to provide specific information on movement disorders; however, examples of abnormal movements in schizophrenia can be found on the Internet. A training video for using the AIMS is available on YouTube (http://www.youtube.com/watch?v = nCfUsIPaLCs).

Social workers are often responsible for developing plans and methods that help clients comply or take their medications as prescribed. It can be tempting for a client to double a dose if the medication had earlier been forgotten. Clients may also believe that it would be helpful to increase their dosage as symptoms worsen, and decrease or skip medications when symptoms improve. Furthermore, family members, friends, and religious leaders, out of concern, beliefs, and desire to help, sometimes suggest modifications in the prescribed drug treatment without consulting the client's medical doctor. Therefore it is imperative for the client and all significant people who may influence medication compliance to receive information about the importance of taking drugs exactly as prescribed by the psychiatrist. Particularly during and immediately after early psychotic episodes, clients both forget and purposefully stop taking their medications. This can occur because of poor concentration and memory, concerns about medication side effects, delusions that the treatment drugs are actually poison or have been given for mind control, or a belief that the medications are not needed. Additionally, clients may stop taking their medications believing that the drugs are not working, that the symptoms either have dissipated or can be controlled through religious meditation, or other methods. In some cases the illness prevents individuals from understanding and accepting that they have a mental disorder. Schizophrenia can cause a small but significant group of clients to perceive themselves as having no illness, and to see their behaviors and thought processes as normal. These individuals are extremely difficult to treat, and often reject any form of assistance.

When working with a client about medication compliance, try to address the core concerns as concretely as possible, and with only a few short sentences. Often it is helpful to enlist help from family members and community or religious leaders. I have successfully talked clients into remaining on medications by having key family members ask the individual to take the drugs for them, so the family will not worry. At other times it has been helpful to have a religious figure respected by the client sanction the medication treatment.

Another group of clients can better comply with medications when placed on a well-designed behavioral rewards program. Rewards can be particularly important when prescribed medications are accompanied by difficult physical side effects. When developing a behavioral program, use only positive reinforcements or rewards. There is to be no punishment for not taking a dose of medication, other than not getting the agreed-upon reward. Additionally, when clients are first starting on medications, as well as during and immediately after active psychotic episodes, rewards need to be given instantly after the medication is taken. Once the person understands the benefits of the medication treatment and is used to the regimen, a point system that earns larger, more costly, or more meaningful rewards can be instituted.

While psychotic episodes render some clients unable to monitor their medications, others are able to administer their own drugs. Obviously we want to allow individuals the right and dignity of controlling their medications whenever possible. There are, however, clients who, even when they are not in a psychotic state, require supervision and reminders to take their medication. Unfortunately, there is no assessment that can be done, other than trial and error, to determine which clients are most likely to succeed in self-supervision of their medications.

Treating Hallucinations

As described earlier in this chapter, hallucinations are created by the brain, and are experienced as an actual event. Think about how strongly you would refute someone who argued that the pages you claim to be reading have no words. You know there are words, because you see them. Convincing you to change your perception of the page would be quite impossible. After all, you know what you see. For the same reason, clients cannot be talked out of hallucinations. Why should a person give in, and claim to not see or hear something they actually experience? Trying to talk a person out of his or her hallucination only creates stress, arguments, anger, decreased relationships, and often increased symptoms. The first step in successfully treating hallucinations is always medications. Neuroleptic drugs will completely stop hallucinations for some clients and decrease them in others. There are, however, people who receive no measureable improvement in their hallucinations from medications.

When medications remove or partially decrease hallucinations, a systematic form of cognitive therapy can be used to help the person cope and in some cases decrease their attention or focus on the perceived sensations. The treatment method primarily requires acknowledging that the person is having the reported event of hearing, seeing, feeling, or smelling something that is not observed by others. Follow this with an educational statement confirming that the sensation is coming from a brain illness called schizophrenia. A brief statement such as, "I understand you are hearing a voice, I believe you, however the voice is coming from an illness you have called schizophrenia." If the client will allow, one can elaborate on the statement by explaining that schizophrenia is a brain illness and medications can make the voices go away or reduce how often they occur. Immediately after validating that the stated sensation does occur because of a treatable disease, refocus the conversation to another topic. We do not want to process the actual events or details of a hallucination. Discussing the details of a hallucination often increases the client's anxiety and integrates hallucination perceptions into concrete cognitive symbols and reinforced memory. The final step is reassurance. Hallucinations can be frightening, therefore it is helpful to concretely state that (1) you understand that hearing voices (or other sensations) can be frightening and can make a person anxious; (2) you and the treatment staff are going to keep the person safe; and (3) medications over time often help do away with the sensation. When a client insists on talking about a hallucination and will not permit the focus to be altered, minimize your responses, reinforce that the sensations are created by an illness, and quickly but politely end the conversation. Case managers are often used to teach cognitive methods for responding to hallucinations to family members, employers, teachers, clergy, and other community people involved with the client.

Virtually every client with schizophrenia requires some form of case management, along with family support. Far too often, families are expected to pilot the person with schizophrenia through a maze of medical, social, and community treatment resources with little or no assistance. Linkage to concrete services and client education for productively using the provided assistance is the role of trained case managers, and a job often assigned to the social worker. Effective case management requires finding resources that the client is prescribed, services that will help the client and family but are not necessarily requested by the treatment team or client, and assistance specifically requested by the client or family.

An important element of case management is listening to the family and offering each member specific help and psychosocial education. Families often know exactly what will work with the ill person, services the client will reject, and the services that are vitally needed. The expertise and experience of families can save case managers from failure and unnecessary or unproductive work. Schizophrenia, however, also creates many anxieties, concerns, financial stresses, frustrations, anger, and emotional grief throughout a family. Therefore, case managers have to engage families at a level, emotion, and perspective that each member can accept. That is, one not only learns to technically address family questions and concerns, but also how to employ differential language, symbols, stories, and examples that more dynamically and meaningfully connect with the family. Case managers are constantly providing clients, families, educators, and community workers with support, training, and psychosocial education. After services are identified, a case manager is expected to assure that the client and family understand the purpose for the service, rules or expectations when using the service, any personal costs or requirements, and exactly how to use the service. In addition, clients and families find it helpful to know exactly how much assistance they will receive, how much using the service will help them, and any negative factors or experiences the service may trigger. Research has documented that case management increases client and family clinical satisfaction, helps reduce family burden, and decreases the long-term cost of care (Ziguras & Stuart, 2000; Rapp & Goesha, 2004). The treatment of schizophrenia can be thought of as a coordinated dance among medication, case management, support, skills training and education, rehabilitation for returning to work or school, and cognitive interventions. Each must be applied at the right time and in the correct amount.

Among individual treatment methods, social skills training appears to be the most helpful, while psychoanalytic and other insight-oriented therapies offer little or no rehabilitative help. Moreover, there is evidence that psychodynamic insight therapy is not only ineffective, but is harmful for some clients with schizophrenia (Herz & Marder, 2002; Torrey, 2006; Bentley, Boyd, et al., 2007). An example of cognitive treatment was presented in the section focused on hallucinations. The following is an overview of two different supportive and skills-building methods. One method is designed to psychiatrically stabilize clients and develop medication compliance, while the other focuses on building community and relationships, along with increasing personal empowerment and self-determination.

Hogarty, a social worker and pioneer in the study of schizophrenia, developed an intervention called personal therapy (PT). This was among the first schizophrenia treatments developed from empirical research findings and outcome evaluations. PT is a manualized, three-phase supportive program tailored to address individual psychiatric treatment needs, reduce social stress, increase internal coping, and improve social and vocational skills. Because this is a long-term treatment program, it is most often nested in large psychiatric facilities. PT has a primary goal of helping clients reach and maintain medication compliance, along with increasing individualized skills. Additionally, specific family training and education steps are included, as well as psychological support and concrete services for the identified client. Hogarty developed the model largely on findings from neuroscience, cognitive information-processing studies, and social intelligence theories (Hogarty, 2002). Effectiveness research on PT has found mixed results. Initial studies indicate that risk for relapse improves only for clients living with families. However, all individuals participating in PT appear to make gains in their social functioning (Hogarty, Greenwald, et al., 1997; Hogarty, Kornblith, et al. 1997; Bentley, Boyd, et al., 2007). The method provides a logical treatment framework that can be employed by skilled social workers. However, further evaluation research is called for before the methods can be adopted for a wide range of clients.

The clubhouse movement is an excellent example of programs that combine supportive, educational, and rehabilitative services. Over the years the model has evolved into numerous variations. Nonetheless, they all have a central theme of empowering the client. In differing ways, clubhouses develop an accepting positive environment that highlights strong interpersonal connections, enhances social and work skills, and assists with problem-solving and decision-making. In many clubhouse organizations the person can drop in and leave as wanted. More important, however, the person is not treated or perceived as a patient, client, or case, but rather as an individual with personal desires, goals, needs, and skills. The program's goal is to move away from the medical-clinical treatment models and help individuals rediscover their self-worth, skills, and methods of personal empowerment (Jackson, 2001). Most clubhouse programs strongly support a client's need for medications, and understand schizophrenia as a neurobiological disorder. Their purpose, however, is to allow clinical treatment facilities to address symptoms and pathology while the clubhouse creates an environment of community and self-determination.

This is not to say that clubhouses do not provide meaningful interventions. They most often try to create positive change and growth by employing support, ongoing relationships, modeling, environmental stability, and education. These methods help individuals better relate and interact with the immediate environment, discover and use a safe niche in society, improve family relationships, and adapt to environmental demands. The treatment also involves actively incorporating the person into the management of the clubhouse. Club members elect committees, sit on advisory boards, make key rules and decisions, share tasks and responsibilities, and provide peer education and support. Through a process of support and shared responsibilities, the members experience renewed acceptance and discover areas of personal empowerment and

self-determination (Jackson, 2001). Additionally many clubhouses include an emphasis on job training, continuing education, and re-entry into the workforce. These programs systematically help individuals gain part-time employment and increase their
knowledge though worksite tours and volunteer experiences at nonprofit organizations
(Flexer & Solomon, 1993; Jackson, 2001).

A major part of treatment planning is providing support and education to the client's family. Every family member needs to understand, at a minimum, the following
information:

- that the family did not cause the illness;
- a clear definition of schizophrenia, along with examples of major symptoms;
- an overview of how we know schizophrenia is a neurobiological disorder;
- the importance of medications and how they are administered;
- the possible side effects of medication;
- when to call for help and go to the emergency room;
- what to tell friends, neighbors, and employers;
- how to deal with grief, anger, and other emotions;
- where one can get help;
- how to address specific symptoms at home, work, or school;
- the importance of getting rest;
- the finances of schizophrenia; and
- that there is hope.

Additionally, families need help with decision-making and problem-solving. This
is an ongoing task that for many is best addressed within family support groups.
Schizophrenia triggers many feelings and thoughts that can cause grief, blaming,
grandiosity, and false hope. Figure 4.4 illustrates some of the emotions and ideas
that families experience. These can occur randomly, or follow an anniversary, such as
the ill member's birthday, or a change in symptoms. Re-entering an inpatient service
can cause each family member to experience feelings of defeat, fear, or even anger.
Almost every family at some point develops a sense of false hope or miracle searching. It can simply seem logical for people living with schizophrenia every day of their
life, that there must be a better, faster, or more complete cure. When this happens, the
family is vulnerable to being defrauded and taken advantage of by professional con
artists and salespeople.

To help families examine their emotions and problem-solving methods, a system
was developed using the Family Reaction Diagram (Figure 4.4). Families meet in a

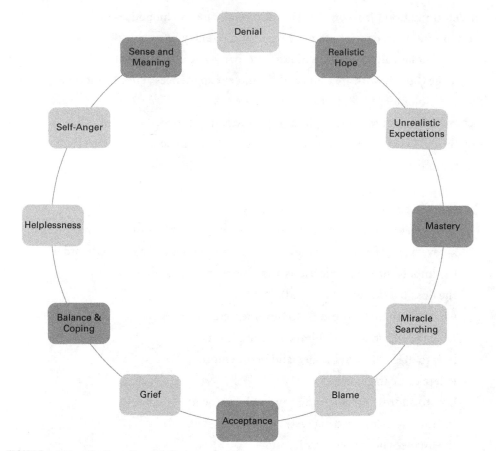

FIGURE 4.4 Family Reaction Diagram.
Family members may shift from one emotion and cognitive perspective almost randomly, or as symptoms change for the family member with schizophrenia.

group composed of individuals who have varying experience and time in dealing with an ill person. Each participant is taught how to personally identify the emotions, methods, and perspectives illustrated by the Family Reaction Diagram. As individuals discuss events and decisions, they are encouraged to determine which label on the Family Reaction Diagram fits their decisions, thoughts, or responses. When a negative emotion or method was used, the group provides support and assurance. It is extremely helpful for families to hear that others have made similar missteps. Most often, individuals leave with new ideas for handling difficult issues, and a better understanding of themselves. Helping families gain information, reassurance, and problem-solving skills is a major purpose for the group. However, an equally important goal is to help members make sense and meaning of their situation and to discover hope. When leading this type of group, one finds that members constantly shift their emotions and thought perspectives. A person who has mastered working with the illness on one evening will arrive to another meeting grieving, searching for a miracle, or using one of the other negative problem-solving methods. When this occurs, the leader should ensure that the group provides support and positive reflections, rather than blaming the person for regressing from a more positive perspective.

REFERENCES

Adebimpe, V. R. (1994). Race, racism, and epidemiological surveys. *Hospital and Community Psychiatry, 45*, 27–31.

Aleman, A., Kahn, R. S., et al. (2003). Sex differences in the risk of schizophrenia: Evidence from meta-analysis. *Archives of General Psychiatry, 60*(6), 565–571.

American Psychiatric Association. (2000). *Diagnostic and Statistical Manual of Mental Disorders, Text Revised* (4th ed.). Washington, DC: American Psychiatric Association.

American Psychiatric Association. (2013a). *Diagnostic and Statistical Manual of Mental Disorders* (5th ed.). Arlington, VA: American Psychiatric Association.

American Psychiatric Association. (2013b). Highlights of changes from DSM-IV-TR to DSM-5. Retrieved August 2013 from http://www.dsm5.org/Documents/changes%20from%20dsm-iv-tr%20to%20 dsm-5.pdf.

Andreasen, N. C. (1979). Thought, language, and communication disorders, I: Clinical assessment, definition of terms, and evaluation of their reliability. *Archives of General Psychiatry, 36*, 1315–1321.

Andreasen, N. C. (1982). Negative symptoms in schizophrenia: Definition and reliability. *Archives of General Psychiatry, 39*, 784–788.

Andreasen, N. C. (2001). *Brave New Brain: Conquering Mental Illness in the Era of the Genome.* New York: Oxford University Press.

Asaad, G. (1990). *Hallucinations in Clinical Psychiatry.* New York: Brunner/Mazel.

Asarnow, R., & Karatekin, C. (1998). Childhood-onset schizophrenia. In E. Coffey & R. A. Brumback (Eds.), *Textbook of Pediatric Neuropsychiatry* (pp. 617–646). Washington, DC: American Psychiatric Press.

Barlow, D. H., & Durand, M. V. (2005). *Abnormal Psychology: An Integrative Approach.* Belmont, CA: Thomson Wadsworth.

Bateson, G., Jackson, D. D., et al. (1956). Toward a theory of schizophrenia. *Behavioral Science, 1*, 251–254.

Benes, F. M. (2007). Corticolimbic circuitry and psychopathology. In D. Coch, G. Dawson & K. W. Fischer (Eds.), *Human Behavior, Learning, and the Developing Brain: Atypical Development* (pp. 331–361). New York: Guilford Press.

Beng-Choon, H., Black, D. W., et al. (2003). Schizophrenia and Other Psychotic Disorders. In R. E. Hales & S. C. Yudofsky (Eds.), *The American Psychiatric Publishing Textbook of Clinical Psychiatry* (pp. 379–438). Washington, DC: American Psychiatric Publishing.

Bentley, K. J., Boyd, S. A., et al. (2007). Schizophrenia. In B. A. Thyer & J. S. Wodarski (Eds.), *Social Work in Mental Health: An Evidence-Based Approach* (pp. 251–285). Hoboken, NJ: John Wiley & Sons.

Bleuler, E. (1924). *Textbook of Psychiatry* (A. A. Brill, Trans.). New York: Macmillan.

Bogerts, B. (1997). The temporolimbic system theory of positive schizophrenia symptoms. *Schizophrenia Bulletin, 23*(3), 423–435.

Breier, A. (2004). Diagnostic classification of the psychoses: Historical context and implications for neurobiology. In D. S. Charney & E. J. Nestler (Eds.), *Neurobiology of Mental Illness* (pp. 237–262). New York: Oxford University Press.

Buchanan, R. W., & Carpenter, W. T. J. (2001). Evaluating negative symptom treatment efficacy. In R. S. E. Keefe and J. P. McEvoy (Eds.), *Negative Symptom and Cognitive Deficit Treatment Response in Schizophrenia* (pp. 1–18). Washington, DC: American Psychiatric Press.

Cahn, W., Pol, H. E. H., et al. (2002). Brain volume changes in first-episode schizophrenia: A 1-year follow-up study. *Archives of General Psychiatry, 59*, 1002–1010.

Camargo, L. M., Collura, V., et al. (2007). Disrupted in Schizophrenia 1 Interactome: Evidence for the close connectivity of risk genes and a potential synaptic basis for schizophrenia. *Molecular Psychiatry, 12*(1), 74–86.

Cannon, T. D., van Erp, T. G. M., et al. (2002). Fetal hypoxia and structural brain abnormalities in schizophrenia patients, their siblings, and controls. *Archives of General Psychiatry, 59*, 35–41.

Carlson, G. A., Naz, B., et al. (2005). The phenomenology and assessment of adolescent-onset psychosis. In R. L. Findling & S. C. Schulz (Eds.), *Juvenile-Onset Schizophrenia* (pp. 1–38) Baltimore: Johns Hopkins University Press.

Chen, C. K., & R. M. Murray (2004). How does drug abuse interact with familial and developmental factors in the etiology of schizophrenia? In M. S. Keshavan, J. L. Kennedy, & R. M. Murray (Eds.), *Neurodevelopment and Schizophrenia* (pp. 248–272). Cambridge, UK: Cambridge University Press.

Crow, T. J. (1980). Molecular pathology of schizophrenia: More than one disease process? *British Medical Journal, 280*, 66–68.

Cummings, J. L., & Mega, M. S. (2003). *Neuropsychiatry and Behavioral Neuroscience.* Oxford: Oxford University Press.

DeSpelder, L. A., & Strickland, A. L. (2002). *The Last Dance: Encountering Death and Dying.* Boston: McGraw Hill.

Deutsch, A. (1949). *The Mentally Ill In America.* New York: Columbia University Press.

First, M. B., & Tasman, A. (2004). Schizophrenia and other psychotic disorders. In M. B. First & A. Tasman (Eds.), *DSM-IV-TR Mental Disorders Diagnosis, Etiology and Treatment* (pp. 639–735). West Sussex, UK: John Wiley & Sons.

First, M. B., & Tasman, A. (2006). *Clinical Guide to the Diagnosis and Treatment of Mental Disorders.* West Sussex, UK: John Wiley & Sons.

Flexer, R. W., & Solomon, P. L. (1993). *Psychiatric Rehabilitation in Practice.* Boston: Andover Medical Publisher.

Gillberg, C. (2001). Epidemiology of early onset schizophrenia. In H. Remschmidt (Ed.), *Schizophrenia in Children and Adolescents* (pp. 43–58). Cambridge, UK: Cambridge University Press.

Gottesman, I. I. (1991). *Schizophrenia Genesis: The Origins of Madness.* New York: Freeman.

Graybiel, A. M. (1997). The basal ganglia and cognitive pattern. *Schizophrenia Bulletin, 23*(3), 459–469.

Haight, W. L., & Taylor, E. H. (2007). *Human Behavior for Social Work Practice: A Developmental-Ecological Framework.* Chicago: Lyceum Books.

Harding, C. M., Brooks, G. S., et al. (1987). The Vermont longitudinal study of persons with severe mental illness. II. Long-term outcome of subjects who retrospectively met DSM-III criteria for schizophrenia. *American Journal of Psychiatry, 144*, 727–735.

Harrow, M. & Jobe, T. H. (2013). Does long-term treatment of schizophrenia with antipsychotic medication facilitate recovery? *Schizophrenia Bulletin, 39*(5), 962–965.

Heilbrun, A. B. (1993). Hallucinations. In C. G. Costello (Ed.), *Symptoms of Schizophrenia* (pp. 56–91). New York: John Wiley & Sons.

Herz, M. I., & Marder, S. R. (2002). *Schizophrenia Comprehensive Treatment and Management.* Philadelphia: Lippincott Williams & Wilkins.

Ho, B.-C., Black, D. W., et al. (2003). Schizophrenia and other psychotic disorders. In R. E. Hales and S. C. Yudofsky (Eds.), *The American Psychiatric Publishing Textbook of Clinical Psychiatry* (pp. 379–438). Washington, DC: American Psychiatric Publishing.

Hogarty, G. E. (2002). *Personal Therapy for Schizophrenia and Related Disorders: A Guide To Individualized Treatment.* New York: Guilford Press.

Hogarty, G. E., Greenwald, D., et al. (1997). Three-year trials of personal therapy among schizophrenic patients living with or independent of family. Part II. Effects on adjustment of patients. *American Journal of Psychiatry, 154*, 1514–1524.

Hogarty, G. E., Kornblith, S. J., et al. (1997). Three year trails of personal therapy among schizophrenic patients living with or independent of family: Part I. Description of study and effects on relapse rate. *American Journal of Psychiatry, 154*, 1504–1513.

Hollis, C. (2001). Diagnosis and differential diagnosis. In H. Remschmidt (Ed.), *Schizophrenia in Children and Adolescents* (pp. 82–118). Cambridge, UK: Cambridge University Press.

Hubl, D., Koenig, T., et al. (2007). Competition for neural resources: How hallucinations make themselves heard. *British Journal of Psychiatry, 190*, 57–62.

Hugdahl, K., Bjørn, R. R., et al. (2004). Brain activation measured with fMRI during a mental arithmetic task in schizophrenia and major depression. *American Journal of Psychiatry, 161*(2), 286–293.

Jackson, R. L. (2001). *The Clubhouse Model: Empowering Applications of Theory to Generalist Practice.* Belmont, CA: Wadsworth/Thomson Learning.

Jasper, K. (1968). *General Psychopathology.* Chicago: University of Chicago Press.

Juraska, J., & Markham, J. (2007, March 13). The brain loses neurons during adolescence. *EurekAlert.* http://www.eurekalert.org/pub_releases/2007-03/uoia-pcl031307.php.

Kelley, M. E., van Kammen, D. P., et al. (1999). Empirical validation of primary negative symptoms: Independence from effects of medication and psychosis. *American Journal of Psychiatry, 156*, 406–411.

Ko, Y.-H., S.-W. Jung, et al. (2007). Association between serum testosterone levels and the severity of negative symptoms in male patients with chronic schizophrenia. *Psychoneuroendocrinology, 32*(4), 385–391.

Korn, M. L. (2001). Historical roots of schizophrenia. *Medscape.* Retreived June 27, 2014, from http://www.medscape.org/viewarticle/418882,1–17.

Kraepelin E. *Lectures on Clinical Psychiatry* [1904]. Third English Edition, Johnston T, ed. New York, NY: William Wood and Company; 1912.

Leeser, J., & O'Donohue, W. (1999). What is a Delusion? Epistemological Dimensions. *Journal of Abnormal Psychology, 108*(4), 687–694.

Lehman, A. F., Lieberman, J. A., et al. (2006). Practice guidelines for the treatment of patients with schizophrenia. In J. S. McIntyre & S. C. Charles (Eds.), *American Psychiatric Association Practice Guidelines for the Treatment of Psychiatric Disorders: Compendium* (2nd ed., pp. 565–746). Arlington, VA: American Psychiatric Association.

Lewis, D. A., & Levitt, P. (2002). Schizophrenia as a disorder of neurodevelopment. *Annual Review of Neuroscience, 25*, 409–432.

Maher, B. A., & Spitzer, M. (1993). Delusions. In C. G. Costello (Ed.), *Symptoms of Schizophrenia* (pp. 92–120). New York: John Wiley & Sons.

Meehl, P. E. (1962). Schizotaxia, schizotypy, schizophrenia. *American Psychologist, 17*, 827–838.

Meehl, P. E. (1989). Schizotaxia revisited. *Archives of General Psychiatry, 46*, 935–944.

Mohanty, A., Herrington, J. D., et al. (2005). Neural mechanisms of affective interference in schizotypy." *Journal of Abnormal Psychology, 114*(1), 16–27.

Morrison, J. (2007). *Diagnosis Made Easy: Principles and Techniques for Mental Health Clinicians.* New York: Guilford Press.

Mueser, K. T., & Gingerich, S. (2006). *The Complete Guide to Schizophrenia.* New York: Guilford Press.

Munetz, M. R., & Benjamin, S. (1988). How to examine patients using the Abnormal Involuntary Movement Scale. *Hospital and Community Psychiatry, 39*, 1172–1177.

Murphy, J. M. (2007). Social environment and psychiatric disorders. In M. T. Tsuang, W. S. Stone, & M. J. Lyons (Eds.), *Recognition and Prevention of Major Mental and Substance Use Disorders* (pp. 53–74). Washington, DC: American Psychiatric Publishing.

Ndetei, D. M., & Vadher, A. (1984). A comparative cross-cultural study of the frequencies of hallucinations in schizophrenia. *Acta Psychiatrica Scandinavica, 70*, 545–549.

NIMH. (1990). *Schizophrenia: Questions and Answers.* D. Shore (Ed.). Rockville, MD: National Institute of Mental Health, Schizophrenia Research Branch (pp. 1–19).

Owen, M. J., O'Dovovan, M. C., et al. (2002). Schizophrenia. In P. McGuffin, M. J. Owen, & I. I. Gottesman (Eds.), *Psychiatric Genetics and Genomics* (pp. 247–266). Oxford, UK: Oxford University Press.

Paradiso, S., Andreasen, N. C., et al. (2003). Emotions in unmedicated patients with schizophrenia during evaluation with positron emission tomography. *American Journal of Psychiatry, 160*(10), 1775–1783.

Potkin, S. G., Alva, G., et al. (2002). A PET study of the pathophysiology of negative symptoms in schizophrenia. *The American Journal of Psychiatry, 159*, 227-237.

Rapp, C. A., & Goesha, R. J. (2004). The principles of effective case management of mental health services. *Psychiatric Rehabilitation Journal, 27*(4), 319–333.

Razahan, A., G. O'Daly, O., et al. (2007). Environmental determinants of psychosis. In M. T. Tsuang, W. S. Stone, & M. J. Lyons (Eds.), *Recognition and Prevention of Major Mental and Substance Disorders* (pp. 21–74). Washington, DC: American Psychiatric Publishing.

Regier, D. A., Myers, J. K., et al. (1984). The NIMH epidemiologic area program. Historical context, major objectives, and study population characteristics. *Archives of General Psychiatry, 41*(10), 934–941.

Remschmidt, H. (2001). Definition and classification. In H. Remschmidt (Ed.), *Schizophrenia in Children and Adolescents* (pp. 24–42). Cambridge, UK: Cambridge University Press.

Robbins, T. W. (2004). Animal models of the psychoses. In D. S. Charney & E. J. Nestler (Eds.), *Neurobiology of Mental Illness* (pp. 263–286). Oxford, UK: Oxford University Press.

Robins, L. N., Helzer, J. E., et al. (1984). Lifetime prevalence of specific psychiatric disorders in three communities 1980 to 1982. *Archives of General Psychiatry, 41*(10), 949–958.

Robins, L. N., & Regier, D. A. (1991). *Psychiatric Disorders in America: The Epidemiologic Catchment Area Study.* New York: Free Press.

Russell, T. A., Rubia, K., et al. (2000). Exploring the social brain in schizophrenia: Left prefrontal underactivation during mental state attribution. *American Journal of Psychiatry, 157*, 2040–2042.

Sadock, B. J., & Sadock, V. A. (2007). *Synopsis of Psychiatry Behavioral Science/Clinical Psychiatry.* Philadelphia: Lippincott Williams & Wilkins.

Scheiber, S. C. (2003). The psychiatric interview, psychiatric history, and mental status examination. In R. E. Hales and S. C. Yudofsky (Eds.), *The American Psychiatric Publishing Textbook of Clinical Psychiatry* (pp. 155–187). Washington, DC: American Psychiatric Publishing.

Simon, B. (1980). *Mind and Madness in Ancient Greece: The Classical Roots of Modern Psychiatry.* Ithaca, NY: Cornell University Press.

Siris, S. G. (2001). Suicide and schizophrenia. *Journal of Psychopharmacology, 15*(2), 127–135.

Strub, R. L., & Wise, M. G. (1997). Differential diagnosis in neuropsychiatric disorders. In S. C. Yudofsky and R. E. Hales (Eds.), *The American Psychiatric Press Textbook of Neuropsychiatry* (pp. 331–346). Washington, DC: American Psychiatric Press.

Szasz, T. S. (1984). *The Myth of Mental Illness: Foundations of a Theory of Personal Conduct* (rev. ed.). New York: Harper Perennial.

Tamminga, C. A. (1997). Neuropsychiatric aspects of schizophrenia. In S. C. Yudofsky and R. E. Hales (Eds.), *The American Psychiatric Press Textbook of Neuropsychiatry* (pp. 855–882). Washington, DC: American Psychiatric Press.

Taylor, E. H. (2006). *Atlas of Bipolar Disorders.* London: Taylor and Francis.

Taylor, E. H. (2006). The weakness of the strengths model: Mental health as a case in point. *Best Practice in Mental Health: An International Journal, 2*(1), 1–29.

Thompson, P. M., Vidal, C., et al. (2001). Mapping adolescent brain change reveals dynamic wave of accelerated gray matter loss in very early-onset schizophrenia. *Proceedings of the National Academy of Sciences of the United States of America, 98*(20), 11650–11655.

Torrey, E. F. (1980). *Schizophrenia and Civilization.* New York: Jason Aronson.

Torrey, E. F. (2006). *Surviving Schizophrenia: A Manual For Families, Patients, and Providers.* New York: Harper Collins.

Torrey, E. F., Bowler, A. E., et al. (1994). *Schizophrenia and Manic-Depressive Disorder: The Biological Roots of Mental Illness as Revealed by the Landmark Study of Identical Twins.* New York: Basic Books.

Torrey, E. F., Taylor, E. H., et al. (1994). Prenatal origin of schizophrenia in a subgroup of discordant monozygotic twins. *Schizophrenia Bulletin, 20,* 423–432.

Tsuang, M. T., Faraone, S. V., et al. (1999). Schizophrenia and other psychotic disorders. In A. M. Nicholi (Ed.), *The Harvard Guide to Psychiatry* (pp. 240–280). Cambridge, MA: The Belknap Press of Harvard University Press.

Tsuang, M. T., Stone, W. S., et al. (2007). Toward prevention of schizophrenia. In M. T. Tsuang, W. S. Stone, & M. J. Lyons (Eds.), *Recognition and Prevention of Major Mental and Substance Use Disorders.* Washington, DC: American Psychiatric Publishing.

Volkmar, F. R. (2001). Childhood schizophrenia: Developmental aspects. In H. Remschmidt (Ed.), *Schizophrenia in Children and Adolescents* (pp. 60–81). Cambridge, UK: Cambridge University Press.

Walker, E. F., Kestler, L. P., et al. (2005). Development during childhood and adolescence: The manifestations of impending schizophrenia. In R. L. Findling & S. C. Schulz (Eds.), *Juvenile-Onset Schizophrenia* (pp. 174–198). Baltimore, MD: The Johns Hopkins University Press.

World Health Organization (1973). *Report of the International Pilot Study of Schizophrenia,* Vol. 1. Geneva: World Health Organization.

World Health Organization (1979). *Schizophrenia: An International Follow-up Study.* New York: John Wiley & Sons.

World Health Organization (2007). *Schizophrenia.* Retrieved August 16, 2007, from http://www.who.int/mental_health/management/schizophrenia/en/.

Wright, P., Gill, M., et al. (1993). Schizophrenia: Genetics and the maternal immune response to viral infection. *American Journal of Medical Genetics, 48*(1), 40–46.

Wu, E. Q., Birnbaum, H. G., et al. (2005). The economic burden of schizophrenia in the United States in 2002. *Journal of Clinical Psychiatry, 66*(9), 1122–1129.

Wyatt, R. J., Henter, I., et al. (1995). An economic evaluation of schizophrenia—1991. *Social Psychiatry and Psychiatric Epidemiology, 30*(5), 196–205.

Ziguras, S. J., & Stuart, G. W. (2000). A meta-analysis of the effectiveness of mental health case management over 20 years. *Psychiatric Services, 51,* 1410–1421.

Zipursky, R. (2006). *The Biological Underpinning of First Episode Schizophrenia.* Second Biennial Schizophrenia Treatment: Bridging Science to Clinical Care, Minneapolis, Minnesota, International Congress on Schizophrenia Research, Department of Psychiatry, University of Minnesota.

5

MAJOR DEPRESSIVE AND DYSTHYMIC DISORDERS

Introduction and Comparison Between *DSM-IV-TR* and *DSM-5*

Depression is classified by *DSM-IV* as a mood disorder that, diagnostically, includes major depressive disorder (MMD), bipolar disorders, dysthymic disorder, and cyclothymic disorder. This chapter addresses the first of these, major depressive and dysthymic disorders. Bipolar and cyclothymic disorders will be discussed in the following chapter. In addition, the diagnoses of mood disorders due to general medical conditions and substance-induced mood disorders are also part of the mood category. These two disorders will be briefly discussed in this chapter's assessment section. The fact that multiple illnesses and substance abuse can alter our mood signals why every generation finds these disorders difficult to define, explain, and treat. *DSM-5* made no significant changes to the steps and criteria required for assessing and diagnosing the above illnesses. Dysthymia received a name change, and is referred to as persistent depressive disorder.

The new manual (*DSM-5*) did add a diagnosis of disruptive mood dysregulation disorder (DMDD) and premenstrual dysphoric disorder. DMDD is used for children up to 18 years of age who experience chronic irritability and frequent and extreme behavior control problems (American Psychiatric Association, 2013). A discussion of this disorder is included in Chapter 9, which provides an overview of child and adolescent mental disorders. Premenstrual dysphoric disorder is diagnosed when frequent mood changes, dysphoria (feeling unpleasant, unhappy, dejected, dissatisfied, etc.), and anxiety occur repeatedly during the cycle's premenstrual phase, and dissipates at the start or shortly after the start of menses (American Psychiatric Association, 2013). One, however, does not assign this disorder unless specific *DSM-5* criteria and symptom clusters have been reported for most menstrual cycles over the past 12 months. There are a number of concerns with the premenstrual diagnosis. Placing the symptoms as a mental disorder has great potential for stigmatizing women. Additionally, the criteria are overly general, extremely common, easily met, and may result in unneeded pharmacological and psychotherapy interventions (Haight & Taylor, 2013; Paris, 2013). Social workers may want to delay using this diagnosis with clients until additional evidence documents the need, reliability, and validity of the disorder.

HISTORICAL OVERVIEW

Throughout recorded time, depression has been discussed by everyone from scientists and writers to everyday people, including descriptions of the affliction as well as theories regarding the cause and treatment of the disorder. For example, the biblical description of King Saul, the first Israelite monarch, includes symptoms of major depression, mania, and psychosis; we will revisit King Saul in Chapter 6 on bipolar disorders. Early Greek and Roman physicians believed depression or melancholy to be caused by black bile entering a person's blood. Treatment consisted of systematically bleeding the person and releasing the bile (Gelenberg et al., 2010; Glas, 2003). While it is hard to understand the Grecian logic, it is interesting that in the fifth century B.C., mood disorders were seen as a medical problem; biological explanations for depression, as with the other mental disorders, were largely over looked or minimized during the Middle Ages. Interest in depression relating to the central nervous system did not appear until the mid- to late eighteenth century (Gelenberg et al., 2010). In North America and Europe, the popularity of Freudian theory during the era around World War II once again slowed the search for and explanation of how depression links to brain functioning (Gelenberg et al., 2010). While there are numerous psychodynamic theories about depression, most still reflect, in some form, Freud's belief that depression is caused by the super ego harboring unconscious hostility or anger, targeted at a damaged relationship. This over-focus on environmental and psychological forces for explaining depression has diminished as our understanding of neuroscience has expanded, but it has not completely disappeared (Glas, 2003). The invention of brain imaging techniques has ushered in a modern era of understanding depression from a biological and bioecological perspective.

Additionally, history demonstrates that depression has impacted the lives of people from all walks of life. An Internet search for famous people with depression produces a long list of historical figures and current newsmakers. During an episode of depression, Amy Tan's grandmother committed suicide, and the Chinese American writer reports that both she and her mother have battled depression as well. Entertainers, artists, and leaders thought to have dealt with depression at some point in their life include Sting (Gordon Sumner), Elton John, Billy Joel, Sheryl Crow, Tammy Wynette, Robbie Williams, Alanis Morissette, John Denver, Cole Porter, Beethoven, Irving Berlin, Princess Diana, Abraham Lincoln, Tipper Gore, Menachem Begin, Theodore Roosevelt, Winston Churchill, and Richard Nixon (see http://www. depression-help-resource.com/articles/famous-depressed-people.htm and http://www. naminh.org/action-famous-people.php).

UNDERSTANDING DEPRESSION

The emotions and behaviors associated with depression are well known. You can probably list a number of indicators for depression without reading this chapter. One can argue, however, that our familiarity with the concept of depression can be problematic for clinicians, families, clients, and society—that is, personal experiences can cause one to incorrectly define depression and to expect individuals to work, think, or reason their way out of depression, and can limit empathy for people suffering with depression. We have all been sad, felt motivation and caring drain away, had our appetite disappear, and worried through an endless, sleepless night. Yet, as painful as these events may have been, they neither define nor experientially assure an accurate or complete understanding of major depression. If we equate all despair, grief, anguish, disappointment, and devastation with depression, rather than the uneven flow of normal existence, we diminish the seriousness of mood illnesses and risk misdiagnosing and inappropriately treating depressed clients.

This limited or incorrect understanding of depression can take root when one's personal experiences become the principal source used to define a mood-related disorder. Confusion is also caused by imprecise psychiatric terms and antidepressant advertising that oversimplifies diagnostic criteria and symptom clusters. Researchers, for example, are far less sure than most textbooks, clinicians, and individuals about how to define "sadness." Among other things, they see depression and grief as at best related to, but different from, sadness. Grief is more related to loss, combinations of emotions, and specific cultural rituals than is sadness, while depression is associated with an ongoing illness that prevents or blocks most positive cognitions and emotions for weeks and months. Psychological studies suggest that sadness is an emotion related to an unpleasant event, resulting from an unachieved but wanted goal (Bar-Zisowitz, 2000; Camras & Allison, 1989; Ellsworth & Smith, 1988; Shaver, Schwartz, Kirson, & O'Connor,

1987). Perhaps more important, sadness is simply described as a state of emotion that is the opposite of pleasure (Bar-Zisowitz, 2000). This is an important point because while depression incorporates elements of sadness, it is not simply the opposite of pleasure or happiness. Sadness, anger, and guilt all provide individuals with flexibility and the means to respond to changing environmental events. Common emotions can be thought of as adaptive elements that allow us to change, adjust, and respond to the realities occurring in our world (Bar-Zisowitz, 2000; Tomkins, 1962). In this sense, emotions are most often temporary, whether serving as a protective or a troublesome life element. Depression, as will be demonstrated throughout this chapter, is never a normal adaptive response, has little flexibility, is always destructive rather than protective, and is never temporary.

Accurate understanding of depression is further complicated by the fact that no single set of symptoms universally affects individuals in an identical manner. Each person may experience symptoms that are different from yet similar to the symptoms of others with the same diagnosis. This is because depression is a very individualized disorder that differentially attacks the client's neurological, physical, perceptional, and emotional systems. As such, mood disorders in general, and depression specifically, can be conceptualized as neurobiological illnesses that relentlessly assault the entire body and mind repeatedly for such a long, painful, time that the very essence of one's being, motivation, and soul is defeated. Sadly, a sizable minority of people never fully recover from the numbing and torment of depression. Fortunately, however, as documented later in the chapter, many clients with proper treatment return to a vigorous state of health.

DEPRESSION: MORE THAN SADNESS

While depression is a whole body experience, client problems often appear in the affective-emotional-cognitive-behavioral symptom domains listed in Figure 5.1. Clients will dynamically know how to describe exactly how many symptoms impair their lives or create internal pain. However, some symptoms leave the person with an awareness of the presence of difficulty, but without specific words to describe the experience. Other symptoms are clearly noticeable to observers, but are outside the client's consciousness; yet other symptoms are hidden from both the person's awareness and the knowledge of onlookers. Therefore, neither the therapist, family, nor client is ever fully aware of the problems, pain, disadvantages, and neurobiological changes created by depression.

Saying that clients are not fully aware of how depression is affecting and negatively impacting their lives may sound somewhat condescending; every client is painfully aware of many, perhaps even most, of their difficulties, reduced skills, and symptoms.

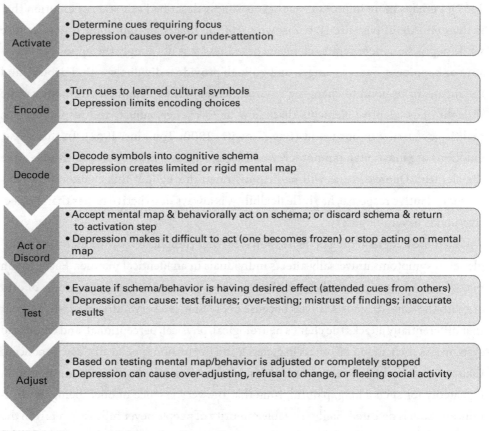

Activate
- Determine cues requiring focus
- Depression causes over-or under-attention

Encode
- Turn cues to learned cultural symbols
- Depression limits encoding choices

Decode
- Decode symbols into cognitive schema
- Depression creates limited or rigid mental map

Act or Discord
- Accept mental map & behaviorally act on schema; or discard schema & return to activation step
- Depression makes it difficult to act (one becomes frozen) or stop acting on mental map

Test
- Evauate if schema/behavior is having desired effect (attended cues from others)
- Depression can cause: test failures; over-testing; mistrust of findings; inaccurate results

Adjust
- Based on testing mental map/behavior is adjusted or completely stopped
- Depression can cause over-adjusting, refusal to change, or fleeing social activity

FIGURE 5.1 Assessing Information Processing.

However, depression decreases a person's ability to self-observe, self-reflect, and to know when to self-correct. As a result, clients are not always fully aware of how their behaviors are perceived by others, how abstract and fast-moving situations are not adequately comprehended, or that their problem-solving is taking into account only part of the available information. Some clients, especially at the start of an episode, are totally unaware that depressive symptoms are present and that their behavior is changing. For these individuals, selected family members and social workers who have a relationship with the client must gently point out the depression indicators and guide the person to treatment.

Symptom identification and guidance are effective if a high level of trust and confidence has been developed with the person prior to the onset of a new episode. Clients suffering from chronic depression often feel more secure knowing that a trusted non-judgmental person stands ready to alert them as the first signs of symptoms appear. Additionally, therapists and family members can help by simply acknowledging that they cannot begin to know the pain and internal feelings that the person is experiencing. Sincere statements of this type validate the person's emotional pain and help strengthen interpersonal relationships. If, however, a social worker cannot truthfully say something empathetically, it is best to remain silent. Insincerity can drive clients away from treatment and deeper into their thoughts of hopelessness.

EPIDEMIOLOGY AND CAUSE OF MAJOR DEPRESSION

While depression is rightfully known as a neurobiological illness, it is unclear how an episode develops and is triggered (Gelenberg et al., 2010). There is some evidence that stressful life events may be a primary force for some, but for others the primary factor is biology (Young, Rygh, Weinberger, & Beck, 2008). Stress can cause the brain to experience long-term functional and structural changes, though it is uncertain how much stress and at what point of development it must be experienced for neurological changes to occur. For example, it has been demonstrated that rat pups removed from their mother have neuroendocrine abnormalities, but this problem is not necessarily permanent. These problems will improve with antidepressant medication treatment or social attention from a caring adult rat (Gelenberg et al., 2010). Animal studies of stress and depression, however, present some special problems. As pointed out by Dunlop and Nihalani (2006), the frontal cortex of a rat's brain is underdeveloped, making it difficult to directly compare rat to human child reactions. They also point out that early life stress in children has not created uniform or even predictable changes.

There is also a growing belief by researchers that stressful life events are more associated with the onset of depression, rather than with ensuing episodes (Glas, 2003; Young et al., 2008). Additionally, we seldom know when a client's depression actually started, making it more difficult to determine the cause. For example, abnormal brain activity, causing a very slow, mild onset of illness that the person is not yet aware of, may trigger social and self-perceptions that do not fully reflect environmental realities; this is further discussed below. It is also reasonable, however, to hypothesize that some, but not all, depression is triggered more from ecological than biological factors. What is clear, however, is that once a person experiences depression, future episodes appear to be more associated with neurobiological abnormalities.

One way of thinking about environmental versus biological causation is to compare depression to other health problems. Some people can prevent or recover from a heart attack through specific diet and exercise. Yet other people with a long history of healthy diets and regular exercise and no history of tobacco use or other environmental risk factors not only develop heart issues, but are unable to overcome them. In the first example, the heart changed or had potential for change and protection because of biology responding to environmental factors. The second is an example of biology being primary and environment offering little explanation for illness or protection from death. In both cases, regardless of what triggered the first episode, physical changes in the heart would be seen as the primary cause of future problems.

As mentioned, the task of identifying the actual point of onset is extremely complicated. Major depression for some individuals starts suddenly and without warning. Others, however, experience a prodromal period consisting of increased anxiety and mild depressive symptoms. Prodromal symptoms may last from weeks to months before converting to a major depressive episode (American Psychiatric Association, 2000; Megna & Simionescu, 2006). Therefore, it would take either advanced training or unusual insight for a person to clearly identify and label the start of very mild depressive symptoms. After all, periods of feeling a little down, tired, less motivated, and slightly more "nervous" than usual have been experienced by most of us. As described in this chapter, depressive episodes decrease a person's social, work, cognitive, and interpersonal functional skills. Fortunately, once an episode ends, most people, regardless of the type of depression, return to their pre-illness level of functioning. Up to 20% of individuals with major depression, however, are treatment-refractory and do not completely return to their previous skill level (Young et al., 2008). Additionally, many of these clients either slip into a dysthymic disorder, or almost continuously have several low-grade symptoms.

Major depression has a lifetime prevalence rate of approximately 5%–17% or an average of 11%–12% across studies, whereas dysthymic disorder, at any given time, is experienced by 3%–6% of North America's population. However, the combined rate for all disorders in the unipolar depressive spectrum (major depressive episode, dysthymic disorder, minor depressive disorder, and recurrent brief depressive disorder) increases the lifetime depression prevalence rate in North America to 20%–25% (Sadock & Sadock, 2007). There are no gender differences in childhood onset depression, yet within adults, twice as many women develop some form of depression. The lifetime prevalence rate for major depression is approximately 20% for women but only 10% for adult men (Baldwin & Birtwhistle, 2002). Some studies also suggest that women as a group have more severe symptoms and a more difficult course of illness (Baldwin & Birtwhistle, 2002; Megna & Simionescu, 2006; Sadock & Sadock, 2007). Science has yet to provide an explanation for why gender differences exist. The bioecological perspective hypothesizes that an interaction among female body chemistry, mothering or other caregiving responsibilities, and the lack of total societal equality increases a women's risk and vulnerability for depression. There is also the possibility that men simply do not report or receive help for mood disorders. However, this concept is suspect when one considers that the gender gap for major depression remains about the same across countries and cultures (Sadock & Sadock, 2007).

DOMAINS AND BEHAVIORS ALTERED BY DEPRESSION

Communication with clients and families about depression is further complicated by the arbitrary manner in which symptoms appear. As therapists, we seldom identify all of a client's symptoms. Problems are expressed differently, with inconsistent emphases and changing levels of severities from person to person and from culture to culture. Moreover, clients vary greatly in their ability to explain what is being internally experienced. The focus of one person may simply be expressed as a feeling of constant fatigue, while another person describes in detail his experience of physical pains, inability to sleep, and hopelessness. This can be confusing for practitioners and family members. A clearer and more specific picture of how depression is affecting a client, however, is gained by thinking in terms of symptom behavioral clusters and neurodomains. This is a simple intuitive method of grouping and surveying symptoms and problems that fall into the six functional areas overviewed below.

The Emotional-Affective Domain

Some of the most common problems seen in depression are changes in how individuals emotionally involve themselves with others and physically or verbally express their feelings and thoughts. Depressive symptoms originating from the emotional-affective domain often result in clients distancing themselves from their families and friends. Changes in this domain are found in most people with moderate to severe depression. What the client perceives as causing his or her decreased socialization, however, varies across the population and must be individually assessed. Social drifting while depressed may occur from feelings of fatigue, emotional or physical pain, hopelessness, memory difficulties, slowed information processing, fear of embarrassment, anxiety, or internal agitation. For some, social-emotional disengagement occurs simply because activities that had been pleasurable or important no longer hold meaning. Not only has the interest in routine life requirements diminished, but additionally the ability to automatically engage in social and work obligations in an energetic and culturally appropriate manner becomes extremely difficult.

The emotional-affective domain is a cluster of symptoms that subvert a client's (1) emotional involvement, (2) expressive affect or tone, and (3) spontaneous, mindful emotional control, or sustained mood. Throughout each day, countless split-second decisions must be made concerning how emotionally involved to become with individuals, ideas, and events. Most people have a rich repertoire of verbal and non-verbal methods for signaling emotional involvement. Consider the strong feelings, mood changes, and signs of involvement that may occur in discovering that your favorite social work professor was racist. On the other hand, consider the wave of emotions and energetic involvement that occurs when it is found that, rather than being racist, the professor is a master teacher who has just sent your emotions on a roller-coaster experiential learning ride. At that minute of discovery, you may not know whether you are delighted or angry at the theatrics. However, there is no doubt that you were, and perhaps remain, emotionally involved.

A depressed person going through this same experience may experience either a rocket ride or a trip on a slow, boring ride. That is to say, depression can cause one to either become overly emotionally involved, rocketing into an escalating emotional response, or seemingly lack the energy to care. Stereotypically, we often picture depression as producing a lack of personal connections and low affective responses. Nonetheless, the same illness that limits one's involvement can also cause agitation, concern, and emotional energy that are beyond the reality or context of the situation.

When in a state of depression, modulating and sustaining appropriate emotional involvement within changing ecological and work circumstances is at best difficult and at worst impossible. Most people, when not depressed, shift their involvement to match the ecological context almost without thought. Countless times a day, we must become more or less emotionally involved with life events. In a meeting, for example, an individual who has missed several previous sessions may cognitively choose to decrease her advice giving, withhold oppositional language, and become more supportive. Once the meeting ends, an attempt may be made to explain the missed meetings and to assure others that future sessions will be wholeheartedly supported. Even though this is accomplished almost automatically, having been learned from cultural experiences and expectations, it requires increased energy and a rush of frontal cortex problem-solving and judgment-formation neurobiological activity that is problematic for those suffering from depression.

In addition to our emotional involvement, we also communicate internal feelings and mood through visible expressive affect or mood tone. Generally, a person's mood tone shifts almost automatically to match the social context across a spectrum of pleasure, displeasure, delight, sadness, agreement, and anger to accommodate ever-changing social transactions. Expressive affect or emotional tone consists of both our internal feelings and our behavioral responses to these feelings. They are produced by quick mental instructions, attitudes, perceptions, interpretations, ideas, social interactions, life events, memories, and our general state of mind (Ayd, 1995). When participating in a boring conversation one may, nonetheless, present body language suggesting interest, attention, and a positive mood. When not depressed, individuals often control both their expressions of internal feelings and the mental framing of the immediate environment—that is, one may be bored with a conversation, but happy nonetheless to be included in it. Furthermore, when we are not depressed, our internal mood experience changes with the flow of events. Sadness, for example, may dissipate upon seeing a close and supportive friend.

The impact that depression has on one's experience and expression of emotion is both varied and far-reaching. Depression makes it difficult to match one's expressive visible affect with the immediate environment. Therefore, if depression triggers environmentally inappropriate sadness or anger, it is difficult for clients to quickly identify that their internal emotions do not match the immediate ecological context. If this lack of fit is recognized, and it is instantly understood that feeling sad is not congruent with the situation, depression can further prevent one from controlling the sadness and expressing the appropriate feelings for the social circumstances. Additionally, a depressed client may be unaware that it is self-defeating to fail to modulate internal emotions and express publicly acceptable feeling tones. Other clients comprehend that their affect is not in sync with the situation, but have no energy to make corrections or have lost the ability to mask internal feelings and present socially acceptable affect.

Depression also removes or limits a client's affective expression and tone flexibility. Deficits in one's expressive skills can cause unresponsiveness, limited or inappropriate verbal and behavioral responses, limited or inappropriate facial expressions, unexplained body-muscle tension, flat communication tones, or unexplained anger. Such inappropriate expressive affect is often triggered when a person's internal emotions and perceptions are rigid and become thoroughly incompatible with social and cultural expectations (Rothschild, 1999). Depression, however, may also cause intense emotions that fluctuate rapidly in an unpredictable manner, though these changing short-lived expressive feelings and tones are more often seen in depressed children and adult clients with bipolar mood disorders, borderline disorder, and early stages of schizophrenia (Campbell, 2004; Rudolph & Lambert, 2007; Woo & Keatinge, 2008).

Feelings and affective expressions formally become a "mood" once the tone is sustained for an extended period of time (Ayd, 1995; Campbell, 2004); a key factor in depression is that a self-defeating mood is sustained at the cost of health and spontaneity and interferes at points where mindfully controlled mood shifts need to occur, such as in family situations. Parents who do not suffer from depression, even under stress, often maintain a pleasant, caring, and interacting presence with their children. For the sake of their children, they subordinate one set of feelings to another. They are mindfully able to move from self-focused affect to a family-centered mood. A complete mood repertoire available to a non-depressed person provides a means for mindfully controlling responses that need to be subordinated to a disciplined sustained emotional attitude while still allowing for spontaneous feelings to override such control when appropriate. However, these mental behaviours are almost impossible for clients dealing with a major depressive episode. It is equally hard for these individuals to spontaneously experience and maintain a level of joy. Events and activities that normally produce joy may at best spike momentary gratification, but the relief will soon be defeated and replaced by the dominant depressed mood. This is sometimes referred to as anhedonia or emotional blunting.

Problems affecting how one is emotionally involved, expresses feelings, or the ability to mindfully control and sustain a mood that adequately fits with the environment suggest the need for a comprehensive mental health assessment that rules out major depressive episodes. However, the emotional-affective domain is only one cluster of symptoms experienced when depressed. When depressed, however, whether one's moods are frozen, limited, or unpredictable, they dictate the person's (1) emotional involvement with others; (2) communication and expression of feelings and perceptions; and (3) sustained negative affective experience. As social workers, it is important to understand that this occurs without intent and is not within the client's control.

The Physical Domain

For many, major depression creates not only emotional pain, but also numerous physical, eating-related, and sleep-disruption problems. For example, complaints of headaches, constipation, diarrhea, and multiple or continuous viral colds and flu commonly accompany depressive episodes. Additionally, depressed clients often report either no appetite or constant consumption of food and beverages. The body seems to either find no food appealing or gravitates obsessively to a need to eat. The overeating seldom has little to do with hunger and becomes both a learned and biological response. As we increase our eating, and shorten the time between snacks, our body physically demands either more food, or a continuation of the amplified intake schedule. We also cognitively and emotionally learn bite by bite to momentarily block pain, anxiety, boredom, and confusion with almost automatic obsessive eating. Along with physical pain and eating problems, many depressed people also express either an inability to sleep or are constantly oversleeping and are unable to get out of bed in the morning.

Physical difficulties and changes in eating and sleeping patterns are generally freely reported by a client or the person's family, but disruptions and abnormalities in the depressed client's motor skills, body-muscle tension, and coordination are often less obvious to the client and are easily overlooked by social work assessments. Motor skills are orchestrated by the brain's basal ganglia. This brain section does not actually move your muscles, but rather serves as the conductor or organizer. When you close a door, for example, the basal ganglia calculate the speed, force, direction, and motion needed for completing the task. If depression interferes with the brain's ability to estimate the force or even direction, the door will be slammed or not completely closed.

Over time, this inability to control one's motion becomes aggravating for family members. A client whom the author treated opened her car door in a forceful quick manner that always loudly crashed into her husband's beloved truck when both vehicles were parked in their garage. In therapy sessions the client was described convincingly as angry by family members, who told stories of her punishing others by slamming doors and banging her car door into the truck. Even though the client denied being angry, she was unable to explain the behaviors, and her expressive affect looked angry. As a result, misplaced anger became the primary focus and therapy theme for several meetings. While the husband felt supported and vindicated, the intervention was nonetheless a failure. The client maintained that even though the banging-slamming behaviors were increasing, she had no unresolved anger. One evening, to change topics and lighten the room's environment, a soft sponge ball was introduced and tossed from one family member to another. Almost by accident, it was observed that the client was overly clumsy in catching and throwing the sponge ball. When asked if this was normal, her husband quickly responded, "No, she was never great, but usually not this off target." Now we had new information and a revised clinical hypothesis to work with. The conversation shifted away from anger and how depression can disrupt coordination and motor skills. This psychoeducation freed the husband to voluntarily offer to park his truck in a spot that was safely out of the wife's range. This created a major positive shift in the therapy. Rather than insisting that his wife change, the husband became a creative force within the therapy and provided a supportive and workable solution. As the wife started recovering, she automatically regained motor control and her angry expressive affect dissolved.

Along with affecting motor skills and coordination, depression is also capable of causing tension in part or all of the body's muscles. When this occurs, a client may show stress in the face, extend the neck in a forward, backward, or upward manner, hunch the shoulders, or stiffen one or both legs. The tension may also change how the person walks, sits, stands, positions the mouth, or squints their eyes. Still, as social workers, we never assume that a client's physical problems, sleeping and eating difficulties, or motor-related abnormalities are simply byproducts of a major depression. Rather than relating to depression, the symptoms may be signaling a major physical disorder, such as a brain tumor, requiring specialized medical treatment. It is unethical for a social worker or any non-medical doctor to treat depression without ruling out whether any depressive symptom, but especially physical, eating, sleeping, or motor complaints, stem from a hidden medical rather than neurobiological psychiatric disorder. Additionally, it is not predictable whether depression will attack one, multiple, or none of a client's motor skills, coordination, and muscle tension. Furthermore, the impact will be different and unique for each person.

The Information-Processing Domain

To some extent, this is almost always altered when depression is experienced. How our brain receives information and decides to either act on or discard the input is a science unto itself. This is part of our inherited and learned cognitive functions. However, information processing provides important insights into the understanding of depression and therefore is treated for illustration purposes as a separate neurodomain. In reality, it is one of the many cognitive and social cognitive tasks that our brain performs countless times each day. There are numerous theories, and even a cursory review of the existing research findings is beyond the scope of this textbook. Reviewing the basic cognitive steps involved in processing social ecological information can, however, help us better understand depression. As a simplistic model, we can think of information processing as consisting of the following steps:

1. Perceiving and alerting to social cues;
2. Encoding these cues into meaningful symbols;
3. Decoding the symbols into cognitive schema;
4. Acting on the cognitive schema;
5. Testing the schema;
6. Adjusting the schema or moving on.

Our brain must be alerted to and must attend to environmental social cues before information is recognized and managed.

Alerting and Attending

Ecological settings provide countless cues, all bidding for our attention. Consider the confusion we would face if our brain soaked up and attempted to process every sound, movement, color, texture, smell, conversation, contextual shifts, and abstract meta-communication filling a given environmental setting. Likewise, having no neuro input would equally create a chaotic and overwhelming situation. Fortunately, the brain, working with radar-like precision, guides one's focus to stimuli of immediate interest while simultaneously filtering unneeded, unrelated, unwanted, and unimportant social cues. When depressed, however, a client is often unable to navigate this balance, becoming either hyper- or hypo-attentive to environmental cues.

Hyper-attention occurs if the brain directs one to attend to as many signals as possible (more than average). As a result of this, the individual may fail to grasp complex issues, may link topics that are only tangentially related, and may have long pauses between responses. If a person is weighing every possible cue and nuance, processing is slowed and the working memory circuits become overloaded. As this working memory fails, clients may suddenly appear as if they do not know what they were talking about, lost in their thoughts, "rattled," withholding information, or unable to make a commitment.

Conversely, cues and social stimulations are significantly blocked from conscious awareness when depression causes hypo-attention. Clients in this situation may seem to look through you and be unable to connect with any conversations or environmental stimuli. Attending to a single thread of information requires their maximum energy, and multitasking is almost impossible. During periods of hypo-attention, individuals are often accused of not caring, carelessness, preoccupation and spacing-out, being mentally slow, and being unable or unwilling to follow through and dependably complete simple tasks. Family members and supervisors frequently become frustrated, develop false beliefs, and make unfounded declarations. If one does not understand that depression can block mental awareness, it is understandable that depressed individuals are thought to not want to pay attention, lack motivation, and choose to be forgetful. The ease with which hypo-attentive behaviors can be misinterpreted underscores the importance of family and community education about these issues.

Encoding

Once selected cues activate one's attention, the brain must transform the stimuli into meaningful symbols representing specific personal meaning. How facial expressions, tones, words, and objects are assigned meaning is a process that is largely an artifact of culture. For example, furniture with a flat surface and four legs designed for placing items on its horizontal top is assigned the symbol of "table." As we advance in age, the symbol of table is further defined into specific types, such as dining, coffee, or work-table. Repeated cultural observations, cognitive practice, behavioral responses, and personal experiences link social cues to specific neurologically coded symbols stored in the brain's memory banks. When working appropriately, encoded symbols accurately represent the cultural meaning of events occurring within the environment and guide our verbal and non-verbal responses.

For most people, depression alters not only the number of social stimuli focused upon (the alerting stage described above) but additionally how these cues are encoded into symbols. A peer's supportive statement, said with emphasis, can sound unimportant or ingenuous to one depressed person, while another individual, equally depressed, encodes the accentuated declaration as a symbol of indignation, unfriendliness, or a lack of sympathy. Yet a third depressed person may interpret the same statement in an overly positive manner as evidence of romantic love or a verbal contract of support never intended by the peer. Predicting which social cues will alert a client and how the stimuli will be encoded is impossible. The process varies from person to person. For some clients, the encoding process is somewhat random, while others rigidly decode symbols and create and follow a constant repeated and predictable behavior theme.

An important assessment step, therefore, is determining which cues capture a client's attention, and how they are encoded. Assessing cognitive attention, focus, and encoding helps the clinician better understand what clients internally experience within their environmental and interpersonal exchanges. Additionally, psychoeducation is measurably improved and interventions are more creatively managed when social workers are able to explain how cues are omitted or focused upon and encoded into culturally learned symbols.

Decoding Into Schema

After cues are encoded into symbols, they are either discarded or decoded into a cognitive schema. Decoded symbols interact with memory elements such as learned knowledge, past experiences, emotional tones, predictions, and perceptual expectations about the immediate events. Together, these elements create a neuro-organizing framework or mental map known as a cognitive schema or action plan (Breedlove, Rosenzweig, & Watson, 2007). In most social situations, our mental maps need to be flexible and able to automatically shift as the environmental context changes. Numerous subtopics and off-topic issues, for example, may be mixed with a conversation focused on planning an important work project. The mind must map a plan for accomplishing the work goals, yet nimbly shift and respond to innuendos, jokes, gossip, incorrect facts, and perhaps an invitation for dinner nested in the primary focus and purpose of the meeting.

These neurological accommodations for social contextual changes are relatively easy until depression alters the brain. Once depressed, clients often develop rigid, concrete schematic responses, and find the tracking of changing topics difficult. Rigid mental maps can make others, including family members, feel that the depressed individual does not want to cooperate or discounts all ideas except her own. As conversations become more abstract and require rapid processing, depressed clients may form only partial mental maps and appear preoccupied or unable to comprehend complex ideas and topics. Tracking numerous shifts in a conversation requires using mental energy that is not available when one is depressed. As social engagement becomes tiring, frustration and anxiety increase, causing stressed facial and voice tones. Additionally, clients may respond with agitation and anger when social situations are fast moving or tense. In some cases, clients form a completely sound mental map, but their energy or emotional state does not allow them to behaviorally act on the cognitive information. Family members, supervisors, and peers frequently perceive this non-response as being negative in nature. Depression also generates instant, unprocessed neuroemotional responses. Emotional and anxiety-charged neurochemical messages bypass the brain's network of checks and balances. As a result, our limbic system, or neuroemotion center, circumvents the frontal cortex's judgment-screening filters, and produces verbal or behavioral responses that do not match social interpersonal requirements (Kraly, 2006).

The other response to encoded symbols is recognition that they are not necessary, or fail to fit the immediate environmental context and are therefore quickly stopped from becoming a cognitive response. During depression, however, symbols with little meaning or only a tangential relationship to reality may trigger ruminating symptoms. When this occurs, the client is obsessed with a single or series of incomplete ideas that will not stop running through the person's conscious mind. While ruminating thoughts and behaviors resemble symptoms seen in obsessive-compulsive disorder (OCD), they are actually a component of the client's major depressive episode. Nonetheless, when symptoms indicative of another possible disorder are documented, the added or alternative diagnosis must be ruled out. A client can suffer simultaneously from multiple neurobiological disorders (Cassano, Rossi, & Pini, 2003). Individuals with OCD often go without a diagnosis for years before receiving appropriate professional treatment (Sadock & Sadock, 2007). Obsessive symptoms caused by depression, however, do differ from OCD in several ways. Depressed clients generally view recurring unstoppable thoughts as reality, whereas individuals with OCD recognize that obsessive thinking is a creation of the mind and does not reflect a legitimate perspective (Woo & Keatinge, 2008). Furthermore, depressive ruminations are experienced as painful insights that others largely misunderstand, while the symptoms trigger embarrassment and secretly endured internal pain for those with OCD (Cassano et al., 2003).

Testing and Adjusting Schema

With the exception of casual situations, individuals are seldom satisfied with the mental map guiding their interactional behaviors and communications. Consider how often the tones and content of a conversation shift. We are constantly testing our schema by watching facial and verbal tones from others. As individual and group reactions are automatically calculated, we alter the schema or completely extinguish the existing map and adopt a new behavioral approach. Unfortunately, depression depletes our ability to test and nimbly change cognitive and behavioral directions. If we cannot test how our behavior is being received by and is affecting others, demonstrating empathy or joining with individuals and groups is much more difficult. Assessing where and how such social information processing is failing will help verify or rule out the diagnosis of major depressive episode. Additionally, understanding how a person cognitively forms mental maps provides specific directions for formulating family education and client interventions. The diagram in Figure 5.1 outlines the key factors used for assessing how information is processed.

Memory, Information Processing, and Depression

Associated with successful information processing is the ability to recall dependably, with minimum energy, simple or complex items from memory. Depression can diminish almost every form of memory, but among the forms that, perhaps, most disadvantage clients with depression is disruption of short-term, long-term, and working memory. Short-term memory is largely contained in the brain section know as the hippocampus. It is the job of the hippocampus to capture information from the environment and hold it for immediate use, movement to long-term memory, or simple deletion. If you hear a telephone number and immediately recall the digits, the short-term memory is activated. With practice, the brain's chemically coded number then moves from the hippocampus to long-term memory. Because depression disrupts both attention and short-term memory, both of which are required for such a process, it can be difficult to tell if the inability to capture and hold information is more an issue of attention and concentration deficits or short-term memory problems. With some clients, even immediate practice fails to hold the information in short-term memory or to move it forward to long-term memory. Because of the combination of attention and hippocampus dysfunctions, it is not unusual to observe short-term memory difficulties in depressed clients.

Some clients, especially when their depression is severe, also experience "holes" in their long-term memory; that is, some factors remain easy to recall, while other well-practiced information cannot be accessed. The client or family may report that the individual is suddenly forgetting well-known routines or information. Combined difficulties with both long-term memory and the brain's basal ganglia, which are responsible for orchestrating movement, may result in clients hitting the wrong buttons on familiar equipment, or completely blocking operational procedures. Families may misread this as the person simply wanting others to operate the equipment or to perform a boring task. In aged clients, long-term memory loss can cause clinicians to overlook depression and to give a diagnosis of dementia too readily.

Depression also almost always alters the person's working memory. As we communicate and perform tasks, the brain pulls pertinent information from memory, assesses the environmental context, and guides us in completing the discussion or task. One of the reasons you can systematically give an oral presentation, moving logically from one interrelated point to another, is because your working memory is correctly functioning. It is as if you have an invisible teleprompter scrolling the information through your mind. If, however, the teleprompter fails, it suddenly appears to others that you either do not know the information or have not completely learned the subject. This is a very familiar experience for depressed clients. One cannot keep discussing factual information or even casual conversations when the brain stems the flow of learned and experienced knowledge. When working memory fails, the client may also experience a rush of anxiety. The loss of memory in the midst of a discussion, combined with sudden anxiety, may trigger additional symptoms. The resulting behavior is unique for each person, though observers may see the person become agitated or even angry. Others may declare the topic of discussion unimportant, or imply that everyone knows where the topic was going. Additionally, clients may quickly make an excuse and flee, while less intimidated clients may simply announce, "I lost my train of thought," and move to another topic. When the process is slowed, and clients are helped to over-ride their anxiety, they can often regain their working memory and continue the discussion or task. Obviously, this becomes more difficult as the depression's severity increases.

Depression may also create problems in a client's verbal and social memory domains. Verbal skills are largely dependent on memory. Through practice, education, and experience, we learn to use the correct word or phrase that matches the social situation. When depressed, the correct word or phrase needed to respond to a social exchange can disappear from the mind. This is known as "blocking." Clients may report that they become absent-minded in the middle of a sentence. When blocking occurs, a person's train or flow of thoughts is disrupted before the idea being expressed is completed. It is not unusual for a depressed person who is blocking to stop talking, remain silent for seconds or minutes, and then state that he or she does not recall either what he or she was saying or meant to say. We can only be certain that blocking is taking place when clients openly state that they lost their train of thought, or offer this as a reason upon questioning by the observer. Without client validation, we may incorrectly label the observed behavior. Depression, for example, can also disrupt one's ability to retrieve words. One may fall silent in the middle of a sentence if a word or expression that is well known and often used suddenly cannot be called up from the mind's memory bank. Word retrieval problems and blocking can behaviorally look identical. Clinically they are differentiated by helping the client to verbalize and validate what he or she is experiencing.

The Cognitive Domain

The cognitive domain is always functionally reduced by depression. The most common symptoms within this domain are obsessive thinking, reduced concentration, decreased ability to form and interpret abstract concepts, increased concrete thinking, complete or inaccurate social perceptions and judgment, and reduced trust in people and organizations. Clients may present with a single or multiple cognitive problems (Kraly, 2006). As with other symptoms of depression, the individual's awareness of the difficulty can vary from recognition and worry to being unaware and unable to acknowledge the cognitive deficits. Depression can trigger constantly replayed obsessive thoughts, unspoken and long-running mental dialogues and debates, as well as stress and anxiety. Each of these symptoms derails the client's ability to focus and track extended or complex issues. Additionally, depression can cause the brain simply to shut down efforts to concentrate. When this occurs, clients have difficulty explaining their lack of focus and may talk about feeling empty, uninterested, or careless in a very negative sense. Additionally, they often have a frozen appearance and reduced motor skills. That is, movements, such as walking, may be slowed or less coordinated, while their face remains fixed in a single expression.

Social intelligence, the ability to make contextually accurate social-emotional decisions and behaviors in a timely appropriate manner, becomes dulled, slowed, and inexact during a depressive episode (Taylor, 1990; Taylor & Cadet, 1989). Responding to social situations, including casual conversations, requires correctly perceiving verbal, non-verbal, and environmental cues, processing the information, and making a reasoned response. These mental actions must be done quickly and require interpreting incomplete and abstract information. Think back to a conversation you just had. How much complete concrete information was available for forming your response? Most likely you made quick decisions that made logical connections and linked incomplete vague cues into logical patterns. Consider the difficulty of performing these same routine operations if your brain overlooks and misperceives key social cues, slows or becomes frozen, is confused by rapid abstractions, and cannot form a meaningful mental picture from the received incomplete information. Imagine the frustration that can occur from having to forcibly make your mind attend to social interactions that previously would have been tracked without difficulty. Furthermore, when the client's responses are received by others as awkward and disconnected, the depressive symptoms may intensify, causing the person to withdrawal, become emotional, anxious, or agitated, or demonstrate inappropriate behaviors.

For some, depression distorts their cognitive processing, causing an overriding feeling of suspicion and paranoid thinking. Clients may report that almost everyone is against them, or they may obsess about a person or certain people no longer loving, befriending, or valuing them. Family members, work supervisors and specific teachers are often the focus of the incorrect perceptions and mistaken obsessive beliefs. This is a form of paranoia that seems similar to, yet significantly differs from, psychotic paranoia. In both disorders the client obsesses, has an unshakable belief, and is vigilant, fearing that he or she will be taken advantage of or hurt. However, paranoia in the non-psychotic depressed client is almost never bizarre and is readily noticeable to causal observers. That is, depression confines the distrust to a particular person or group, and is basically reality based. Psychosis creates a complete break with reality and plants ideas that are at most only loosely connected to the person's actual life experiences. The psychotic client, for example, may believe that because he knows a person from the Middle East the FBI has identified him as a terrorist and is trying to arrest him. Depression causes individuals to focus on responses perceived as derogatory and overly interpret verbal and non-verbal messages as speaking against them. This hypersensitivity instigates ongoing obsessive beliefs that they are disliked or targeted by a supervisor. These beliefs are at times, but not always, anchored partially in reality. Depression does cause family, friends, and employers to distance themselves from the client, and it can trigger behaviors that can result in the loss of jobs, marriages, and friends. When this occurs, the client is not paranoid, but is reporting a sad and painful truth. However, paranoia as a symptom of depression creates a magnification of real or perceived adverse events that in actuality are not as desperate as they seem to the individual. Some clients perseverate about their paranoid thoughts for long periods of time, privately or with select individuals, while others only think about or discuss the issue when they are reminded of or in the presence of the distrusted person or organization. Furthermore, depression can also trigger distrust and negative beliefs that reflect a distorted or incomplete reality. In a severe state of depression, a person may declare that her boss hates her and is going to fire her because he looked down at the floor when they passed in the hall. Upon investigation, you may discover that the boss has no recollection of the event and harbors no ill feelings against the client.

In all cases of major depression, the cognitive domain's scope of problem-solving skills is narrowed, limiting one's ability to develop alternative solutions for resolving personal, interpersonal, and environmental problems. Additionally, while severely depressed, clients find it impossible to accept alternative solutions presented by their therapist, family, and friends. Their ability for critical thinking, questioning, testing options, evaluating outcomes, and reflecting largely disappears. It is as if all possible alternative solutions are contained in a mental box that has shrunk or has no entrance and exit holes. As a result, only one or two possible solutions can be cognitively accessed by the client. Furthermore, the mental solutions box is fortified to keep outside information from penetrating and the single solution trapped within from escaping. Figure 5.2 illustrates the depressed blocked brain and the more open nondepressed brain. The drawing also underscores that even when we are in a healthy mental state there are facts and abstractions that our neurosystem simply cannot consider and process. Unlike depression, our limitation for flexable and open processing of information represents an interaction between learned cultural-social factors and neurobiological development.

As a social worker, it is important to remember that when depressed clients agree with you about alternative solutions, they are not necessarily accepting the proposed options as realistic and meaningful for them. The client may verbally concur as you suggest that the situation is not bleak and that each of the suggested solutions is workable. However, the person's mind may, unfortunately, be yelling, "Get out of here! This social worker may be nice but does not understand that these ideas may work for others, but will never work for me!" This can be tragic if the client feels totally hopeless, and the only answer in the person's mind box is suicide. However, inflexible and limited cognitive

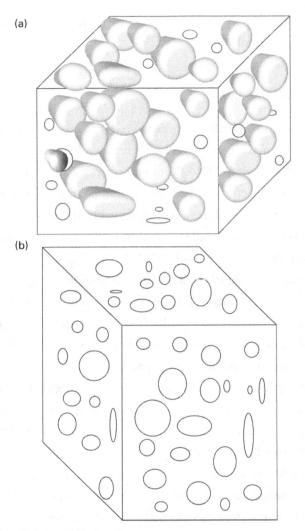

FIGURE 5.2 Problem-Solving Skills in a Box.

A. The Depressed brain preventing the flow and processing of multiple sources of information and development of alternative solutions. **B**. The nondepressed brain with limited flexibility, but much more ability to accept information and develop alternative solutions than the depressed brain.

solutions can trigger not only suicide, but also other drastic responses: self-injury or self-inflected punishment; unexpected divorces and questionable marriages; inappropriate compliance to the will or desires of others; child abandonment; child neglect or abuse; abandonment of employment or school; physical and verbal combat; entrance into cults and questionable organizations; selection of inappropriate friends; legal or cultural infractions, and in rare cases, homicide. When the mind believes that there is truly only one solution, individuals become destructive to themselves and others. Therefore, one indicator of whether a client requires hospitalization is the content of that person's obsessive beliefs and his or her ability to develop alternative solutions for resolving the perceived problem.

THE BRAIN AND DEPRESSION

Brain imaging studies indicate that depression relates to changes in certain structures of the brain and abnormal functioning of major limbic and frontal brain areas (Baldwin & Birtwhistle, 2002; Taylor, 2006). Depressive symptoms result from the interaction of numerous brain sections and neurotransmitters that fail to work as genetically designed and culturally trained. However, depression-driven behavior almost always includes either overly slow or rapid metabolism in the amygdala, frontal cortex, and memory centers (Baldwin & Birtwhistle, 2002; Stahl, 2001).

The amygdala is the principal brain section responsible for regulating emotion and, as such, hyper- or hypo-activity of this region of the brain partially determines how mood is expressed and the degree to which individuals become emotionally involved in events around them. When slowed, a client may have dulled affect. A person who is highly sensitive without depression and is prone to cry rather easily may report that since developing depression she no longer can cry, even when others find events to be unusually sad and emotional. In contrast, clients with a rapid, overactive emotional center will be highly reactive and may cry or express intense changes of mood for reasons that cannot be explained by the individual or others. In addition to emotions, the amygdala is responsible for assisting with tasks requiring rapid learning and the immediate linking of environmental cues to appropriate emotional responses. Neurotransmitters travel across nuclei connecting the amygdala with the hypothalamus, hippocampus, neocortex, and thalamus. This small almond-shaped subsection of the limbic system, found deep in the brain, communicates with the middle (thalamus) and front brain (cortex) regions responsible for coordinating, processing, and making mental decisions. For social workers, this is important information for understanding and educating clients and their families. Among other things, it explains why a depressed person is often slow to learn from events that are quickly incorporated by others, and responds emotionally in an odd manner.

The hippocampus is also part of the limbic system, and works with the amygdala. Virtually all new memories start and are temporarily stored in this region of the brain. Short-term memory, along with what is known as episodic or declarative memory, is largely influenced by the hippocampus. Declarative memory allows us to associate specific environmental cues with learned information. It is our personal memory of time, space, place, along with concepts and rules that are generally interconnected with environmental signals. Additionally, episodic memory is part of our working memory system. Depression disrupts or distorts hippocampal short-term memory production, storage, and declarative memory. In coordination with the amygdala, environmental cues are mediated and even rearrange into short-term memory images. In healthy individuals this can create productive imagination and perceptions that cause spontaneous, culturally appropriate emotions. Unfortunately, for depressed clients the interaction can mislabel environmental stimuli, create frightening imaginations, and link verbal and non-verbal cues with perceptions that generate emotional distress. Additionally, deficits in concentration compound the memory and environmental association difficulties created by hippocampal dysfunction. Imagine how not being able to capture information into short-term memory, experiencing decreased working memory accuracy, and inappropriately labeling or associating environmental cues would increase your anxiety and trigger misstatements, upset feelings, and social withdrawal. These neurobiologically induced problems are experienced by depressed clients over and over for days, weeks, and months.

Near the center of our brain is an egg-shaped area known as the thalamus. This neurological site provides a gateway for emotions, environmental perceptions, and other sensory data headed for the cerebral cortex to become conscious decisions and internal thoughts. The thalamus, however, is far more than a simple relay station. It is the brain's most prominent routing and switching station. Most sensory and motor messages are received by the thalamus, partially interpreted into meaningful mental actions, and sent to the exact cerebral cortex section for final processing. Depression can disrupt the normal data input and output progression, causing changes in conscious awareness, attention, alertness, language monitoring skills, and translation of emotions. When these elements are altered, clients can, among other things, have difficulty tracking environmental cues, correctly analyzing information, and linking their thoughts with correct and meaningful words. Additionally, because the thalamus receives and integrates all sensory information, with the exception of smell, it plays a major role in understanding body boundaries and body image. We often see clients standing overly close or far from others. When this is not culturally learned and has developed with the depression, one can clinically hypothesize that the thalamus is not correctly relaying and preprocessing body boundary information. Furthermore, depressed clients often perceive their body image incorrectly. Our job as social workers is to measure whether the sensory perceptions, boundaries, and body image beliefs have developed from the depression or represent unique elements of the individual that are not associated with a mood disorder. Understanding that the thalamus helps to shape self-perceptions and how we integrate environmental events, process emotions, and even connect thoughts and language explains why factual information alone is seldom helpful for the depressed client. Their central information routing system is malfunctioning and cannot link the sensory concepts to the correct part of the cerebral cortex.

Our brain has a wonderful system for identifying conditions and situations where errors are likely to occur, and helping us to cognitively shift our mental perspective and prevent or minimize difficulties: the cingulate gyrus. It is the primary brain area that guides cognitive flexibility, changes in attention and focus, and allows one to accept appropriate changes in the environment. As part of the limbic system, the cingulate gyrus is linked to the emotional system. More important, however, it helps the mind follow and accept or reject ideas and alternative options. Without a functioning cingulate gyrus, we are less cooperative and have difficulty letting go of questionable ideas. When depression impacts this brain area, clients can demonstrate ongoing obsessive thoughts and compulsive behaviors, concrete unchangeable ideas, and agitation, which in some cases can shift into verbal or physical aggression. As the cingulate gyrus causes inflexible thinking, clients may be thought to be uncooperative, highly opinionated, and negative about any proposition. Families often complain that the depressed member responds with a "no" to every request, and argues about almost everything. Attention and information, therefore, need to be quickly provided to each family member. Consistent, ongoing negativity can damage relationships, end partnerships, and for some can become traumatizing.

While sensory input is largely preprocessed by the thalamus, our motor movements are orchestrated by the brain's basal ganglia. Our muscles and nervous system must work in harmony as a team. The basal ganglia are responsible for planning, sequencing, and the overall integration of motor activity. Depression can decrease these skills and cause the person to appear less coordinated, to walk or hold shoulders and head in a tense or unique and unnatural manner, or have jerky unexplained movements. Additionally, because the basal ganglia have links with major limbic system areas (thalamus, ventral striatum, and orbitofrontal cortex) they are also involved in the formation of cognitive thoughts, emotions, and language. Furthermore, reduced motivation and determination for reaching goals are partially related to the basal ganglia. Consequently, abnormal neurochemical responses in this brain region can create or complicate numerous motor, affective, cognitive, and verbal expression skills. Identifying indicators of basal ganglia dysfunction can help social workers assess the presence and severity of depression, and establish behavioral and physical markers for measuring improvement and regressive changes in clients receiving mental health treatments. Understanding the role of this brain region also prepares clinicians for helping families and clients understand how depression neurologically interferes with motivation and human drive.

Families, peers, and sometimes helping professionals believe that depressed individuals choose to not accomplish routine tasks and do not want to get better. This type of negative labeling frequently disappears once observers understand that the brain's motivation-producing instrument is producing incorrect chemical messages that the client cannot willfully correct.

One brain area that depression always impacts is the frontal cortex. This part of the brain is used to organize behavioral actions, develop cognitive plans, monitor and help shift behavior to fit changing environmental situations, guide decision-making, and assure that our actions fit within a cultural and moral context. The frontal cortex is sometimes referred to as the brain's executor because it is responsible for judgment, concentration, and general decision-making. It also serves as the final filter before neurochemical messages from other brain sections are processed and consciously acted upon, modified, or discarded. Depressive episodes slow frontal cortex metabolism, causing these functions to be flawed or more difficult to perform (Baldwin & Birtwhistle, 2002; Breedlove et al., 2007; Taylor, 2006). When a depressed client, for example, abruptly seeks a divorce for superficial reasons, numerous brain sections interact to trigger obsessive, inflexible, and concrete limited thinking. However, depression triggers irrational decisions partly because the frontal cortex fails to examine the worthiness of the cognitive plans, the validity of emotions, and the consequences of behaviors. We depend on our frontal cortex to use experiential learning, learned cultural rules, social expectations, and practical judgment to temper behaviors and decisions.

There is evidence that dysfunction in the orbitofrontal cortex during depressive episodes is related to suicide (Kraly, 2006). When a suicide attempt or death from suicide occurs, it is important for families to understand that the actions were caused by abnormalities in the brain that altered the person's judgment, and ability to realistically foresee alternative solutions. A depressed person does not choose suicide. The idea of death spontaneously floods the person's mind, automatically expanding until it eliminates all thoughts of hope, logic, or alternative solution. Social workers may find it helpful to frame suicide for families and clients as a take-over of the mind by abnormal neurochemical messages that rob the person of choices, insight, and futuristic thinking. For some clients, suicide planning and thoughts comprise a long torturous process. The decrease in frontal cortex functioning prevents individuals from challenging their logic and considering alternative solutions. Sadly, they are self-satisfied that death is the only available resource and answer. For other depressed clients, however, there is almost no process. The brain becomes overwhelmed with a flooding command or inserted obsession and compulsion demanding death. One client, after a serious suicide attempt, explained that he had spent no time planning to kill himself. Nonetheless, while standing on a train platform, he experienced his mind spontaneously instructing and demanding him to take his life. He reported feeling that his mind had taken over, blocking all thoughts other than suicide and forcing or propelling his perilous behavior. We can clinically hypothesize that the person's frontal cortex was unable to screen, employ previously learned experiential knowledge, interpret the situation and consequences, or filter the sudden abnormal impulse.

In addition to its association with changes in brain structures, depression is also influenced by and associated with the neurotransmitters serotonin, norepinephrine, and dopamine (Stahl, 2001). Neurotransmitters are chemically encoded messages or signals that are relayed from one neuron to another. Serotonin, because of drug company advertisement, has perhaps become almost a household name. While it strongly influences mood, emotion, anger, aggression, and even eating and sleeping, serotonin is not always the primary neurotransmitter associated with depression. Some clients' depression is more strongly associated with dopamine. This neurochemical is responsible for helping us appropriately experience a since of reward and motivation. Obviously, this is an important issue in understanding and treating depression. We can now provide answers for families regarding why a client finds nothing pleasurable or rewarding, and has no motivation to move forward. Neuroscientists have shown, though, that cocaine, heroin, alcohol, and nicotine increase dopamine in the sections of the brain responsible for pleasure. Additionally, dopamine provides signals for guiding and controlling voluntary movements (Gazzaniga & Heatherton, 2009). It is not unusual to see slowed movement and sometimes what appears as aimless wandering in depression. The aimlessness may, however, have more to do with preoccupation, rumination, and reduced concentration. The slow or hyper-arousal, decreased or increased alertness to environmental cues, and eating behavior changes commonly contributed to depression are largely triggered by norepinephrine. It should be noted, however, that it is an oversimplification to claim that depression is caused by one or even all three of the neurochemicals. Furthermore, it is not clear whether changes in the brain's structure, metabolism, and chemical functioning cause depression or are the result of depressive episodes.

DIAGNOSING MAJOR DEPRESSIVE EPISODES

To receive a diagnosis of major depressive episode, clients must fulfill specific *DSM-IV* criteria and not have symptoms that are explained by an alternative disorder, medical problems, substance abuse, or other causes such as grief. The *DSM* criteria for screening and assessing depression are provided in Box 5.1.

BOX 5.1

DSM-IV-TR CRITERIA FOR MAJOR DEPRESSIVE DISORDERS

CRITERIA FOR MAJOR DEPRESSIVE EPISODE

A. Five (or more) of the following symptoms have been present during the same 2-week period and represent a change from previous functioning; at least one of the symptoms is either (1) depressed mood or (2) loss of interest or pleasure. **Note:** Do not include symptoms that are clearly due to a general medical condition, or mood-incongruent delusions or hallucinations.

   1. Depressed mood most of the day, nearly every day, as indicated by either subjective report (e.g., feels sad or empty) or observation made by others (e.g., appears tearful). **Note:** In children and adolescents, can be irritable mood.

   2. Markedly diminished interest or pleasure in all, or almost all, activities most of the day, nearly every day (as indicated by either subjective account or observation made by others);

   3. Significant weight loss when not dieting or weight gain (e.g., a change of more than 5% of body weight in a month), or decrease or increase in appetite nearly every day. **Note:** In children, consider failure to make expected weight gains.

   4. Insomnia or hypersomnia nearly every day;

   5. Psychomotor agitation or retardation nearly every day (observable by others, not merely subjective feelings of restlessness or being slowed down);

   6. Fatigue or loss of energy nearly every day;

   7. Feelings of worthlessness or excessive or inappropriate guilt (which may be delusional) nearly every day (not merely self-reproach or guilt about being sick);

   8. Diminished ability to think or concentrate, or indecisiveness, nearly every day (either by subjective account or as observed by others);

   9. Recurrent thoughts of death (not just fear of dying), recurrent suicidal ideation without a specific plan, or a suicide attempt or a specific plan for committing suicide.

B. The symptoms do not meet criteria for a mixed episode

C. The symptoms cause clinically significant distress or impairment in social, occupational, or other important areas of functioning.

D. The symptoms are not due to the direct physiological effects of a substance (e.g., a drug of abuse, a medication) or a general medical condition (e.g., hypothyroidism).

E. The symptoms are not better accounted for by bereavement, i.e., after the loss of a loved one, the symptoms persist for longer than 2 months or are characterized by marked functional impairment, morbid preoccupation with worthlessness, suicidal ideation, psychotic symptoms, or psychomotor retardation.

DIAGNOSTIC CRITERIA FOR 296.2X MAJOR DEPRESSIVE DISORDER, SINGLE EPISODE

A. Presence of a single major depressive episode.
B. The major depressive episode is not better accounted for by schizoaffective disorder and is not superimposed on schizophrenia, schizophreniform disorder, delusional disorder, or psychotic disorder not otherwise specified.
C. There has never been a manic episode, a mixed episode, or a hypomanic episode. **Note:** This exclusion does not apply if all of the manic-like, mixed-like, or hypomanic-like episodes are substance or treatment induced or are due to the direct physiological effects of a general medical condition.

If the full criteria are currently met for a major depressive episode, *specify* its current clinical status and/or features:

Mild, moderate, severe without psychotic features/severe with psychotic features
Chronic
With catatonic features
With melancholic features
With atypical features
With postpartum onset

If the full criteria are not currently met for a major depressive episode, *specify* the current clinical status of the major depressive disorder or features of the most recent episode:

In partial remission, in full remission
Chronic
With catatonic features
With melancholic features
With atypical features
With postpartum onset

DIAGNOSTIC CRITERIA FOR 296.3X MAJOR DEPRESSIVE DISORDER, RECURRENT

A. Presence of two or more major depressive episodes.

    Note: To be considered separate episodes, there must be an interval of at least 2 consecutive months in which criteria are not met for a major depressive episode.

B. The major depressive episode is not better accounted for by schizoaffective disorder and are not superimposed on schizophrenia, schizophreniform disorder, delusional disorder, or psychotic disorder not otherwise specified.

C. There has never been a manic episode, a mixed episode, or a hypomanic episode. **Note:** This exclusion does not apply if all of the manic-like, mixed-like, or hypomanic-like episodes are substance or treatment induced or are due to the direct physiological effects of a general medical condition.

If the full criteria are currently met for a major depressive episode, *specify* its current clinical status and/or features:

Mild, moderate, severe without psychotic features/severe with psychotic features

Chronic

With catatonic features

With melancholic features

With atypical features

With postpartum onset

If the full criteria are not currently met for a major depressive episode, *specify* the current clinical status of the major depressive disorder or features of the most recent episode:

In partial remission, in full remission

Chronic

With catatonic features

With melancholic features

With atypical features

With postpartum onset

Specify:

Longitudinal course specifiers (with and without interepisode recovery)

With seasonal pattern

Source: Reprinted with permission from the Diagnostic and Statistical Manual of Mental Disorders, Fourth Edition, Text Revision (Copyright 2000). American Psychiatric Association. (Note that internal cross-references have been removed from the reprinted text.)

To qualify as *DSM-IV* criteria for major depression (Box 5.1), at least five specified symptoms must have been present for 2 or more weeks. One of the five symptoms
must be either a depressed mood or a decrease in the person's interest in activities or
ability to experience pleasure (American Psychiatric Association, 2000). Each qualify-
ing symptom is to be documented as either new or more intensely experienced than
before the depression started. Furthermore, the identified symptoms must have been
experienced across most environmental settings almost daily for a majority of awak-
ened hours (American Psychiatric Association, 2000). We generally anticipate that
all or most symptoms will occur most awake hours of each day (American Psychiatric
Association, 2000). Additionally, for a diagnosis of major depression, clients should
report that accomplishing routine activities constantly requires more energy, or that
their competency at social activities, educational studies, work obligations, or other
important life tasks has measurably decreased (American Psychiatric Association,
2000). Clients with major depression often also report that no activity is pleasurable
(American Psychiatric Association, 2000). Some clients, instead of using the term
"pleasurable," or similar expressions, will state that nothing in their lives has any
meaning. Box 5.2 provides examples of questions one can ask for assessing depression.
However, this is not a comprehensive list, but rather a beginning diagnostic framework.

BOX 5.2
EXAMPLE OF DEPRESSION ASSESSMENT QUESTIONS

This list represents the type of questions to consider when assessing for depression. This is only a representative list, and the questions have not been rank-ordered.
Social workers will want to select only appropriate questions and order them in a
logical sequence. Each clinician will also need to develop additional items that specifically fit the client being assessed. However, each of the major topics most likely
will need to be explored.

PHYSICAL EXAM AND PHYSICAL HISTORY
- When did you last have a physical exam?
- Are you currently taking medications for any physical problems?
- Has your doctor ever suggested that any medications or physical
  problems that you have could cause depression, feelings of sadness, or
  anxiety?
- Have you ever been hospitalized for a physical illness?
- How would you describe your physical health?
- What physical problems have you had in the past?

SYMPTOM SURVEY

- Describe or explain what is worrying or concerning you (review symptoms).
- Over the past weeks, what has changed or become more difficult for you to do?
- Are you less interested in events or activities that in the past held your attention?
- Do you find it difficult to participate in activities that you previously performed with either little effort or with enthusiasm?
- How has your mood changed? Can you give me an example?
- How have your emotions changed? Can you give me an example?
- How have your energy levels changed? Can you give me an example?
- When did these symptoms start? (You may need to ask when each individual symptom started; however, some clients can address the start of symptoms as a group. Asking "when did symptoms start?" also allows the social worker to see how the client handles a global question.)
- Are the problems becoming more severe, remaining about the same, or becoming less worrisome?

PSYCHIATRIC HISTORY

- Were you treated as a child for any problems? (If yes, gain age, problem, treatment method, length of treatment, and outcome.)
- Have you ever been treated or seen someone for depression? (If yes, gain age, problem, treatment method, length of treatment, and outcome.)
- Have you ever been treated or seen someone for another problem? (Note that we do not ask if the client has seen a mental health professional—the person may have seen a different professional or a non-professional.)
- Have you ever been hospitalized for depression or other mental health problems? (If yes, gain specifics of hospitalization.)
- Have you ever been treated with medications (if yes discover when, type and name of medications, dosage, length of time on medications, side effects experienced, and benefits gained from the medications)?
- Have there been times, at any point in your life, when you had concerns or worries that you may be depressed or have a mental health problem?
- How have the symptoms/problems affected your
  - Family and marital/partner life?
  - Parenting?
  - Work, employment, or schooling?
  - Friendships and community social life?
  - Problem-solving skills?
  - Concentration and thinking?
  - Memory?

- Health?
- Coordination?

FAMILY PSYCHIATRIC HISTORY

- Within your family, is there a history or the possibility that anyone in the past two or three generations had
  - Depression?
  - Bipolar disorder?
  - Mania?
  - Anxiety?
  - Schizophrenia or other similar problems?
  - Addiction to alcohol or drugs?
- Has anyone in your family been hospitalized for a mental health problem? (If yes, for any treatment method determine reason, diagnoses, interventions, length of treatment, and outcome.)
- Has anyone in your family been treated with medications for a mental health problem?
- Has anyone in your family received outpatient treatment for a mental health problem?

PERCEPTION OF ILLNESS

- How have these problems affected your personal and family finances?
- What do you think is happening to you?
- What do people in your life think is happening?
- How do you define depression?
- How do the significant people in your life define depression?

SUICIDE, SELF-HARM, AND HOMICIDE

- Have you had any thoughts about taking your own life? (survey for past and present thoughts)
- Have you ever made an attempt to kill yourself?
- Are you afraid that you may take your life?
- Has anyone in your family attempted to take their life? (If yes, did they succeed, how, any idea why, how close were you to the person, what are your thoughts about the person's actions?)
- Have any of your friends taken their life or tried to take their life? (If yes, did they succeed, how, any idea why, how close were you to the person, what are your thoughts about the person's actions?)
- Have you in the past or currently thought about physically hurting yourself in any way?
- Have you in the past or currently thought about physically hurting others?
- Have you ever attempted to physically hurt or kill someone?
- Why do you think I am asking you about suicide and homicide?

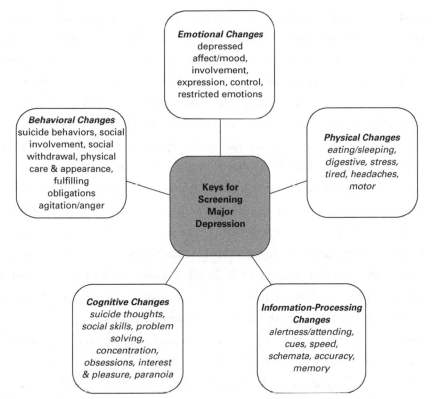

FIGURE 5.3 Keys for Screening and Diagnosing Major Depression.

Keep in mind that if a client has ever had a manic or hypomanic episode, unipolar major depression is automatically ruled out (American Psychiatric Association, 2000). Manic and hypomanic episodes signal clinicians to assess for a bipolar mood disorder rather than major or dysthymic depression. The diagram in Figure 5.3 provides a visual way of thinking about and organizing the primary criteria for diagnosing depression.

EARLY ONSET

It is rare for very young children to be found with depression. Nonetheless, major depression has been documented in children as young as 3 years of age (Luby, Si, Belden, Tandon, & Spitznagel, 2009). A study of 1,758 children between the ages of 5 months and 5 years of age found that 264 or 15% of the participants had a high rate of depressive and anxiety symptoms. Additionally, the children had a higher probability of having a mother with depression than participants without depressive symptoms. Difficult temperament at 5 months of age was a major indicator of future depression (Côté et al., 2009). Major depression in adults is generally associated with a classic depressed or sad mood, whereas depression in children may trigger either a depressed or irritable mood. When children are depressed, we may see a decrease in their interest and energy for playing, socializing, and completing schoolwork (Côté et al., 2009)—that is, the symptoms mimic adult depression. Some depressed children, however, become agitated, angry, and even aggressive, rather than demonstrating sadness and reduced energy. These children and young adolescents quickly become upset, argue intensely over minor issues, defy authority, or display verbal or physical aggression against others. A depressed child who normally does not curse may increasingly yell profanities at parents, authority figures, or peers (Naparstek, 2005; Rudolph & Lambert, 2007; Shamoo & Patros, 1997). Within children and young adolescents, depression is best understood as a continuum of symptoms. Mild, almost unnotice-able symptoms may continue to impair a child's functioning and emotional responses after more severe problems subside (Rudolph & Lambert, 2007). Social workers, therefore, are encouraged to continue periodic functional and symptom assessments for an extended time after a youth's major symptoms have abated.

To this end, there are numerous depression and suicide screening instruments available that will help the social worker track changes in symptoms, functioning, and suicidal thoughts. They also provide a concrete picture of client severity and progress for the treatment team and depressed person. The Generalized Depression Scale developed by Walter Hudson has been found to have an acceptable level of psychometric reliability and validity across many ethnic and age groups (Hudson, 1982). There is also growing use of the Patient Health Questionnaire 9 (PHQ-9) for screening adolescent depression. This instrument is free and can also be used with adults, though it does appear to be more sensitive to adolescent symptoms than adult indicators (Kroenke, Spitzer, & Williams, 2001). While the PHQ-9 is more sensitive with teens than adults, social workers need to be aware that the instrument also has a high rate of false-positive findings (Kroenke et al., 2001); that is, the instrument may score an adolescent as in need of a full assessment for depression when in reality the person is not depressed. In very young children residing in foster care, the Ages and Stages Questionnaire-Social Emotional (ASQ-SE) may have qualities for improving the rate of correct identification of mood and social adjustment problems (Jee et al., 2010). More replicated studies are required before the ASQ-SE can be fully endorsed. It is noteworthy, also, that among foster children different assessment tools may be needed and, indeed, all screening instruments have psychometric problems. No one scale can track symptoms, functioning, and suicidal thinking. Therefore, the social worker must determine with the client how many different scales and questions can be routinely tolerated. When a person is depressed, concentrating to complete surveys is not only difficult, but may also serve as evidence that recovery is impossible. Until one becomes experienced in assessing and treating depression, supervision in the use and selection of clinical instruments is highly recommended.

TREATMENT OF MAJOR DEPRESSION

From start to finish, when treating any form of depression, the social worker must be directly and indirectly assessing for signs of suicidal intentions. Without treatment, the risk for suicide or destruction of family, work, and peer relations greatly increases. Most likely, physical and social risks increase for some because of both biological factors and ecological stressors, including the interaction of brain abnormalities with environmental concerns, which results in the experience of a sense of helplessness and hopelessness. It has long been known that the serotonin metabolite 5-hydroxyindolecetic acid (5HIAA) is significantly reduced in depressed individuals who attempt suicide (Megna & Simionescu, 2006). However, the number of people with major depression who actually take their own life differs across studies. Some studies have very wide inclusion criteria, while other researchers require absolute evidence that the suicide was directly related to depression (Dunlop & Nihalani, 2006). While numbers across studies vary, we do know that 70% of people committing suicide have a history of depression (Stahl, 2001). The specific role that depression played in suicide is less certain. Nonetheless, estimates that approximately 15% of people with major depression will end their life by suicide are not unrealistic (Dunlop & Nihalani, 2006; Glas, 2003; Trentani, Kuipers, Ter Horst, & Boer, 2003). The items listed below provide a clinical starting point for thinking about a plan for treating major depression. When beginning with a client who has been assessed as having depression, mentally consider these points:

- Major depression is a serious mental disorder, but includes a continuum of symptoms and mental pain ranging from very mild to extremely severe.
- Even in mild clinical cases suicide thoughts and behaviors are very possible.
- Every clinical case of depression has similarities and dissimilarities to others, but always impacts each client uniquely.
- Assess and treat each client as a complex and unique individual, rather than just as someone suffering from depression.
- Depression is episodical, and when untreated, a major depressive episode may last between 6 and 12 months, and for some up to 24 months (Stahl, 2001; Woo & Keatinge, 2008).

- Only about 5%–10% of untreated clients experience an episode beyond 2 years (Stahl, 2001).
- Depression is treatable, and a client's symptoms are expected to go into complete remission (Stahl, 2001; Woo & Keatinge, 2008).
- While treatable, relapse is highly possible, with 50% experiencing relapse after one episode, 70% when two episodes have occurred, and 90% when a client has experienced three episodes (Stahl, 2001).
- Depression can affect the entire family, and a complete treatment plan always includes education, support, and, when needed, short-term treatment for family members.

How depression is treated largely depends on illness severity, desires and beliefs of the client, existing client support, and availability of mental health professionals. Dysthymia and mild cases of major depression are often treated with supportive and environmental interventions, while clients suffering from moderate to severe major depressive episodes tend to receive psychotherapy and medications. Whether symptoms are mild, moderate, or severe, social workers are strongly encouraged to assist depressed clients in arranging for a complete medical physical early in the treatment process. We are ethically obligated to rule out all possible medical and medication explanations for the client's depressive symptoms, regardless of their severity level. Generally, medical clearance should be given before clients invest in time-consuming and costly psychotherapy and counseling sessions.

In addition to receiving a medical consultation, part of all evidence-based depression treatment is patient and family education. Effective education is tailored to the client's needs, life situation, family involvement, and illness severity. Preplanned and published protocols become more realistic when they are modified to address specific client concerns and needs. Therefore, no matter how much one factually knows about depression, preparation time is required to identify when, how, and what information can be tolerated and used by the client and family. Education is a planned intervention requiring skill, judgment, and professional artistry. The need for individualizing depression education makes providing a standard unified framework difficult. A few broad topics and strategies, however, that can be built upon in most educational sessions include

- defining depression;
- linking the client's depression symptoms and behavior to the disorder;
- assurance that depression is an illness, not a sign of psychological weakness or manipulation;

- identifying how depression is different from sadness, grief, and other environmentally triggered emotions;
- assurance that depression is treatable and people return to their normal life, work, and activities;
- treatment choices and what research indicates are the best practice methods;
- the need for and scope of treatment to include support, psychotherapy, and possibly medication;
- the positive and negative factors surrounding each form of treatment;
- facts and concerns about suicide and depression;
- indicators of suicidal thought and what to do if thoughts of suicide occur;
- a reminder that depression may get worse before improving;
- how to get help during periods of increased symptoms;
- specific methods to help clients and family cope during a depressive episode.

Education starts during the assessment, but most often is intensified during the first few sessions, and is continued as needed throughout the treatment. However, one cannot have a strict order for the treatment steps. In the first sessions, an important goal is to provide some relief from the most pressing symptoms (Young et al., 2008). For clients with severe depression, for example, the early stages of therapy may contain a minimal education. Family education can precede individual technical information as long as the client agrees and signs a release of information form. When one is severely depressed, learning the causation of depression and what is chemically happening in the brain can have a low priority.

Regardless of the severity level, all depression treatment planning must include systematic screening for suicidal thoughts. This is most often accomplished with a combination of short scales and semi-structured interviews. Clinicians sometimes feel embarrassed for the client and try to indirectly question about suicidal intent. Making statements such as, "you would not try to take your life," or "you have too much to live for to take your life," signals to clients that you are not prepared to hear their real thoughts. One must be practiced and prepared to look clients' in the eye and in a firm but caring voice directly ask, "Have you had any thoughts of killing yourself?" An important part of prevention is training family members to recognize suicidal indicators and providing them with concrete steps to get immediate help. Families are often embarrassed to call hot lines and emergency rooms. When possible, help families and clients gain more self-confidence by taking them to meet suicide prevention call-in personnel and emergency room information workers. Simply hearing workers state that they want calls even when the family is not sure it is an emergency provides a sense of permission and a personalized link with the helping organizations.

Once depression reaches a mid-moderate to severe level, clients need both therapeutic and concrete support. Therapeutic support consists of varying forms of verbal assurance, advice, guidance, and counseling. It may also include a review of the client's strengths and referrals for spiritual counseling and ceremonies. In its most elementary form, therapeutic support simply provides an experience of acceptance and the echo of hope. This is an abstract form of support that is appropriate for all severity levels of depression.

Concrete support refers to the use of tangible goods and services for treating depression or other major disorders. This intervention is most often employed for clients at mid-moderate or severe levels of depression. In special cases where there are economic, transportation, child care, or other specific needs, the intervention is also used with clients suffering from very mild to lower-moderate depression. When clients reach the mid-moderate or higher levels of depression, they often find doing certain tasks at home and work impossible. When faced with this situation, a person not only needs abstract support in the form of reassurance and validation, but additionally the burdensome task needs to be concretely removed from his or her responsibility and concern. For some clients, this requires the social worker to identify family members who are willing to assist the person for an extended time. Unfortunately, families are not always available, and social workers must advocate for limited and highly regulated community resources to fill the gap. Moderate to severely depressed clients may also need the social worker to explain their illness to employers or teachers and negotiate a reduced workload.

There continues to be a belief held by some families and mental health professionals that providing concrete services is not part of direct treatment, and may cause the client to develop learned helplessness or dependency. This textbook, however, argues that from a neuroscientific point of view, depression diminishes brain functioning and reduces the person's functional skills. As these losses increase or do not improve, depressed clients perceive themselves as failing at tasks they normally accomplished with ease, and hopelessness is reinforced. Ecologically negative experiences interact with neurological dysfunctions and can create a sense of defeat and doom. Furthermore, the bioecological interactions and increased hopelessness can trigger suicidal thinking and planning. Additionally, clients may not want to reduce their obligation out of fear that the action represents giving up or may appear as weakness to others. A therapy technique developed by the author helps individuals accept temporarily delaying activities that their brain and body simply cannot perform. As clients describe frustration with failing at work, school, or social tasks, they are directed through the following imaging exercise.

Imagine that all the skills and information you have ever learned are in a keepsake box in a special place in your brain. The box has windows that automatically open when specific information is needed. That is, different types of information must go out assigned portholes. Try to imagine the keepsake box. Can you describe what it looks like in your mind's eye? If the client describes an image of a box, state "Wonderful, good, that is your skills keepsake box." When the person cannot visualize the box, simply state, "That is OK; many people cannot get an image, even people who are not depressed. How do you think a memory keepsake box would look?" That is a good description; keep your description in mind. What depression does is place a lock on many of the windows and prevents the assigned knowledge and skills from leaving and becoming usable. All of your knowledge is still in your brain, but locked away by depression. Visualize the keepsake box with most windows locked, and only a few able to open. Can you see the locked windows? Are any windows open? If the client answers yes, ask the person to identify a skill or personal strength that depression has not taken away and assign it to an unlocked window. If the person claims that no windows are open, gently suggest strengths that remain mostly or partly available. For some clients with very severe depression, the strength to name is simply that they are remaining in treatment or continuing to care about a child or family. After the open skills or strengths windows are identified, have the client once again imagine the keepsake box. Instruct the person to see the many closed windows and the very few open windows. Once the visualization or verbal description (if the client cannot visualize) is locked in by the individual, make an interpretation and suggestion. State in a confident voice, when skills are locked in a closed box we simply cannot use them or call them into action. We are wasting energy and developing stress that works against our recovery. Because your keepsake box is mostly closed, you need permission not to feel obligated to do jobs and tasks that are locked away. Would you name for me the most important skills that are out of your reach, that are locked in your keepsake box? Provide validation by simply stating "good," or "I agree," as the client names tasks that are impossible or difficult to do. If the person is unable to name any task, the social worker may identify items that appear difficult for the person. One may state, for example, "I recall how hard it is for you to take care of your child and prepare meals. Perhaps one or both of these windows are locked." After the client either independently names or is assisted to name locked windows, give an additional validation. Next, ask the client to keep the keepsake box in the mind's eye, and verbally give him- or herself permission to not use the skills or do the tasks that are locked away. Once agreement is reached, ask the person to once again name the items that will temporarily not be done. Remind the individual that as the depression lifts, the windows will open and all previous knowledge and skills will return. For clients who have a less severe illness, the clinician can role-rehearse them in stating how they will know when it is time to restart doing the activities. As a final part of the exercise, ask clients to do one more favor for you, and visualize their keepsake box with all of the windows open. After the image of the open keepsake box with open windows has either been visualized or described in words, tell the client that you know this is not how it is now, but you also know that the windows will open. However, to help open the windows, you must first give yourself permission to do less. An alternative and shorter version is to have clients visualize all of their knowledge in a metal box that reduces in size. The person is directed to see the box become smaller and smaller. When the shrinking box is visualized or verbally described, tell the person to keep in mind that one can only do what the mind-box can hold. "Since depression has currently made your box rather small, we need to limit a few activities." The social worker next helps the client identify tasks that are stressful, reaching an agreement to stop doing these activities until the mind-box once again expands. After agreeing to suspend the most difficult activities, reassurance is given that the depression will lift and the mind-box will expand. The exercise ends with clients visualizing the mind-box expanding. The intervention can be repeated and modified as the person improves or deteriorates. With an improved mood, the person visualizes either more windows opening or the brain-box increasing, and the return of familiar skills, tasks, and responsibilities. As symptoms worsen, portholes are closing or the box is shrinking, and stressful client obligations are reduced. Concrete support given to a person with moderate to severe depression provides space for other therapies to work. Additionally, it is arguable that the client cannot learn helplessness if the concrete support is artfully and therapeutically removed as the depression moves to a milder state.

Included in evidence-based treatment for some depressed clients is a combination of exercise, diet, vitamins/minerals, and medication. While for many people these are effective interventions, social workers never recommend, prescribe, authorize, or supervise client use of any medication, herbal/vitamin, exercise, or diet treatment. Certain herbs/vitamins and food restrictions or combinations can interact with prescription medications, allergies, and other health problems, causing further significant issues. Exercise needs to be cleared by a medical doctor for even healthy individuals, and can be fatal if a client has a cardiovascular condition, diagnosed or undiagnosed. We are not licensed or qualified to prescribe antidepressants or other medications. This includes over-the-counter drugs. We always refer the client to a physician for medication, prescriptions, and advice. Learning general information about antidepressants is relatively easy. Determining the correct medication and starting dosage, however, is complex, and requires years of training, practice, and supervision. The complexity of prescribing is illustrated by a long-time friend who had an unexpected neurobiological reaction to an antidepressant prescribed by a very capable medical doctor. The person was suffering from mild to low-moderate depression. After trying to deal with the symptoms through non-medical means, I was asked to refer the individual to a psychiatrist for medication treatment. The doctor prescribed a traditional low dose tricyclic medication. Prescriptions from this family of drugs have been used successfully for years. Unfortunately for my friend, it increased the depression symptoms. Upon returning to the doctor, a newer selective serotonin reuptake inhibitor (SSRI) antidepressant was prescribed. The new drug within a short time span caused severe, disabling symptoms and triggered suicidal thoughts. The SSRI caused what is known as serotonin syndrome. This is a serious medical condition that can end in a coma and death. The problem is rare, but occurs when an overabundance of serotonin is produced in the brain (Taylor, 2006). Further medical inquiries discovered that my friend's depression had little or nothing to do with serotonin. When placed on bupropion, a norepinephrine and dopamine reuptake blocker, the major depressive episode was brought under control and ended. While this is an extreme example, it nonetheless illustrates the dangers of incorrect prescriptions and why social workers neither prescribe nor recommend medications. Social workers do, however, have an important role in antidepressant medication treatment.

All clinical care providers have an ethical responsibility to inform clients about each of the evidence-based treatment pathways, and social workers are expected to help guide client decision-making by providing accurate information and clarifying choices. Research, for example, indicates that exercise, diet, and certain herbs are effective for mild to low-moderate depression. More robust moderate and severe depression respond best, or at least more quickly, to a combination of medications, psychotherapy, and support (American Psychiatric Association Steering Committee on Practice Guidelines, 2006; Baldwin & Birtwhistle, 2002; Gelenberg et al., 2010; Stahl, 2001; Taylor, 2006). Therefore, a social work treatment plan for treating a mild depression with psychotherapy is logical and is supported by research and expert panels (Gelenberg et al., 2010). Ethically, however, the client should also be informed of all alternatives, including antidepressant treatment. Before taking an antidepressant, though, every client needs to understand that the side effects of medication start almost immediately, while the treatment benefits are not experienced for 2 to 6 weeks (Stahl, 2001). Additionally, social workers often help clients know when a medication re-evaluation is needed, assist in monitoring side effects, and evaluate whether the treatment is reducing symptoms.

Because major depressive episodes can range from very mild to extremely severe, different intervention protocols are required to differentially treat clients. The four treatment outlines that follow are based on a review of current research and literature

(American Psychiatric Association Steering Committee on Practice Guidelines, 2006; Baldwin & Birtwhistle, 2002; Gelenberg et al., 2010; Megna & Simionescu, 2006; Stahl, 2001). They are provided as guidelines, but should not be seen as prescriptive. There are clients with very mild depression who have no response to treatment until medications are introduced, and clients with severe depression who receive very little help from medications. Additionally, the outlines are not to be seen as steps or stages of treatment. How the treatments are managed is dependent on clients' needs and the knowledge and artistry of the social worker. Furthermore, we seldom employ all of the possible treatments with a single client. Even clients with very mild depression would find being asked to suddenly modify their complete lifestyle rather overwhelming. However, as stated above, a medical referral, education about depression, and ongoing suicidal assessments and screenings are part of all depression treatment, regardless of the client's severity level.

EVIDENCE-BASED TREATMENTS FOR DIFFERING SEVERITIES OF DEPRESSION

Treating *Very* Mild Depression

- Medical care/exam
- Education
- Ongoing suicide assessment
- Diet
- Exercise
- Social involvement (assess for healthy involvement)
- Social adventure
- Change in schedule
- Rest
- Supplements (only if MD approved)
  - Omega-3 fatty acids
  - Sam-e
  - St. John's wort
- Stop all alcohol or other substances
- Brief cognitive therapy if above does not work or with above

Treating Higher-Mild to Lower-Moderate Depression

- Physical exam
- Ongoing suicide assessment
- Education
- Supportive therapy for client
- Cognitive-behavioral psychotherapy
- Repeat of methods used for very mild depression
- Hypnosis for reframing, relaxing, and recalling of non-depressed, happier times
- Support for client and family
- Referral for medications if above is not working

Treating Mid-Moderate to Severe Depression

- Physical exam
- Ongoing suicide assessment
- Education at level and speed client can use
- Referral for medications
- Supportive therapy for client
- Concrete support for client
- Cognitive therapy as starting point when depression is moderate
- Behavioral therapy when depression is severe
- Methods used for very mild depression to degree client can respond
- Client and family support
- Physical exam

Treating Very Severe Depression

- Physical exam
- Immediate referral for medications
- Immediate referral and assessment for inpatient treatment
- Ongoing suicide assessment
- Education in very slow small steps
- Supportive therapy for client
- Concrete support for client (such as transportation, house cleaning, child care, etc.)
- High level of family concrete support and problem-solving

- Behavioral therapy
- Cognitive therapy following behavioural treatment as depression improves
- Slow increase of social activity

As a clinician, the author has found that people with severe and sometimes high-moderate depression find responding to cognitive interventions overly difficult and discouraging. To overcome this and to prevent the client from dropping out of therapy, consider starting with appropriate behavioral tasks and introducing cognitive methods as the depression improves. The importance, however, of having the behavioral task match the level of illness severity and the client's personality cannot be overstated. Going to a movie is not a good treatment task for someone who is so depressed that simply getting out of bed seems impossible.

DYSTHYMIA

Dysthymic disorder is a low-grade depressed mood that can last with little relief for up to two years (American Psychiatric Association, 2000; Sadock & Sadock, 2007). Most cases are thought to start in late childhood and early adolescence (Paris, 2013). This is a chronic disorder; clients with dysthymic disorder often report that they have struggled with mood-related problems throughout their life (American Psychiatric Association, 2013; Sadock & Sadock, 2007). There is no gender difference for developing this disorder in childhood. Like major depression, however, more women than men develop dysthymia. Lifetime prevalence for adult women is 4.1% versus 2.2% for men (American Psychiatric Association, 2013). Woo and Keatinge (2008) reports that 75%–90% of individuals with dysthymia will at some point in adulthood have a major depressive episode.

Therapists have long known that dysthymic disorder often co-occurs with many clinical *DSM* Axis I and personality disorders (Sadock & Sadock, 2007; Woo & Keatinge, 2008). Additionally, depression can morph from a major depressive episode to a dysthymic disorder and back into a major depression. One mood disorder is superimposed on top of the other. This is known as "double depression," and leaves clients without full recovery or an opportunity to completely return to their pre-illness level of functioning. Studies indicate that approximately 25% of adults diagnosed with major depression have a history of dysthymia. Approximately 42%–75% of children and adolescents with a dysthymic disorder will develop major depression (Woo & Keatinge, 2008). In both youths and adults, double depression often starts with dysthymia and evolves into a major depressive episode (American Psychiatric Association, 2013; Sadock & Sadock, 2007; Woo & Keatinge, 2008).

Social workers, however, need to use caution when diagnosing dysthymia as a comorbid disorder. Depressed mood symptoms can overlap and stem from disorders other than depression. That is, illnesses such as borderline personality, schizotypal, anxiety, attention problems, and learning disorders can trigger mood-related symptoms that are part of the primary disorder, rather than symptoms of a co-occurring dysthymic disorder. The fact that dysthymia is often a comorbid disorder is not in question. Nevertheless, casual screenings with brief depression scales or global interviews, along with assessment inexperience, can cement an incorrect diagnosis that remains over time with the client and complicates treatment.

Diagnosing dysthymic disorder is similar to the steps used for identifying major depression. Clinically, individuals with dysthymia tend to describe feeling inadequate, socially withdrawn, guilty or concerned about past events, less interested than others in pleasurable events, irritable, and to experience decreased productivity (American Psychiatric Association, 2000). Because the disorder is chronic and impairs functional and social skills, the person's quality of life and ability to reach personal goals and potential skills are diminished. The disorder does differ from major depression in that clients tend to report fewer problems with sleeping, changes in eating habits or weight, and psychomotor difficulties (American Psychiatric Association, 2000, 2013; Sadock & Sadock, 2007; Woo & Keatinge, 2008). It has been this clinician's experience that adults with dysthymia manage to hide their illness for extended periods of time and generally make their way through school or work, and family obligations. To do this, however, requires a great deal of energy, resulting in a constant feeling of fatigue, irritability, and a general lack of fulfillment. To fully meet *DSM-IV* criteria, the person must have a depressed mood for most of each day. There can be days when the symptoms lift, but to qualify as dysthymia a depressed mood has to occur more often than symptom relief. Additionally, symptoms must persist for 2 or more years. The illness is ruled out if clients have suffered a manic, mixed, or hypomanic episode, or if a major depressive episode occurs within the first 2 years of reported symptoms (American Psychiatric Association, 2000). The complete *DSM-IV-TR* criteria outline is provided in Box 5.3.

POSTPARTUM DEPRESSION

Postpartum depression occurs in women within the first 12 months of delivering a baby. Up to 15% of women experience this disorder (American Psychiatric Association, 2013; Taylor, 2006; Woo & Keatinge, 2008). This rather high rate is most likely influenced by women going into labor and delivering while already suffering from an undiagnosed mood disorder. Moreover, having had a previous mood disorder, psychosis,

BOX 5.3

DSM-IV-TR DIAGNOSTIC CRITERIA FOR 300.4 DYSTHYMIC DISORDER

A. Depressed mood for most of the day, for more days than not, as indicated either by subjective account or observation by others, for at least 2 years.
   Note: In children and adolescents, mood can be irritable and duration must be least 1 year.

B. Presence, while depressed, of two (or more) of the following:
   1. Poor appetite or overeating;
   2. Insomnia or hypersomnia;
   3. Insomnia Low energy or fatigue;
   4. Insomnia Low self-esteem;
   5. Insomnia Poor concentration or difficulty making decisions;
   6. Insomnia Feelings of hopelessness.

C. During the 2-year period (1 year for children or adolescents) of the disturbance, the person has never been without the symptoms in Criteria A and B for more than 2 months at a time.

D. No major depressive episode has been present during the first 2 years of the disturbance (1 year for children and adolescents); i.e., the disturbance is not better accounted for by chronic major depressive disorder, or major depressive disorder, in partial remission.
   Note: There may have been a previous major depressive episode provided there was a full remission (no significant signs or symptoms for 2 months) before development of the dysthymic disorder. In addition, after the initial 2 years (1 year in children or adolescents) of dysthymic disorder, there may be superimposed episodes of major depressive disorder, in which case both diagnoses may be given when the criteria are met for a major depressive episode.

E. There has never been a manic episode, a mixed episode, or a hypomanic episode, and criteria have never been met for cyclothymic disorder.

F. The disturbance does not occur exclusively during the course of a chronic psychotic disorder, such as schizophrenia or delusional disorder.

G. The symptoms are not due to the direct physiological effects of a substance (e.g., a drug of abuse, a medication) or a general medical condition (e.g., hypothyroidism).

H. The symptoms cause clinically significant distress or impairment in social, occupational, or other important areas of functioning.

Specify if:
   Early onset: if onset is before age 21 years
   Late onset: if onset is age 21 years or older
Specify (for most recent 2 years of dysthymic disorder):
   With atypical features

or postpartum depression with another child increases the mother's risk with each delivery. One major study found that women with a history of bipolar disorder have a 67%–82% probability of experiencing postpartum depression (Haight & Taylor, 2013; Woo & Keatinge, 2008). The stress and hormonal changes, along with social pressures, may trigger previously low, nearly unnoticed depression. Postpartum depression is significantly different from what is commonly called the "baby blues" (see Box 5.4).

After delivery, mothers often report feeling "blue" and go through periods of crying and self-doubt. Fortunately, the baby blues, as opposed to postpartum depression, last only a few days and disappear with reassurance and usually without professional help.

Interestingly, *DSM-IV-TR* contains a diagnostic specifier in the mood section called "Postpartum Onset," but offers no diagnostic criteria for the disorder. A literature review additionally found that very few quality pharmacologic treatment studies have been conducted. This caused the authors to conclude that the lack of replicated research precluded making any strong evidence-based recommendations (Ng, Hirata, Yeung, Haller, & Finley, 2010). It is noteworthy that one study found that DHA fish oil offered no benefits for postpartum depression. However, social workers must keep

---

BOX 5.4

SYMPTOMS OF BABY BLUES

- Symptoms occur almost immediately after giving birth.
- Symptoms do not occur with every birth.
- Having not had the baby blues with a previous delivery does not signal that the symptoms will not appear when giving birth in the future.
- Having symptoms with one delivery does not predict that baby blues symptoms will appear in future births.
- Baby blues last between a few days and a few weeks, and spontaneously disappear.
- Major symptoms include
  - Fatigue;
  - Anxiety;
  - Irritability;
  - Crying (often for reasons the mother cannot explain);
  - Worry over mothering skills, ability to balance home, child care, work, and relationship responsibilities;
  - Inability to fall asleep;
  - Appetite fluctuations and sudden weight gain and loss.

Source: Reprinted with permission from Taylor, Edward H. (2006). Atlas of Bipolar Disorders. London: Taylor & Francis Group.

in mind that this is a single study and may later prove not to be valid (Makrides et al., 2010).

There is some evidence that the depression may stem from abnormal functioning of the brain's left dorsomedial prefrontal cortex. In mothers with postpartum depression, this area of the brain has been found to be less active than in healthy mothers (Moses-Kolko et al., 2010). However, the cause and complete neuromechanisms driving postpartum depression are not known. Onset is often 1 to 3 months after delivery, but may occur anytime in the first year (Taylor, 2006). Symptoms reflect those found in all depression and generally last 4 to 6 months (Woo & Keatinge, 2008). During a postpartum depression, it is not uncommon for mothers to believe that the child is suffering, is physically ill, is not cared for properly, deserves a better mother, or is doomed to live in a hurtful world (Taylor, 2006). In some cases, the mother determines that she is not worthy for parenting or does not want the baby. In an earlier publication, this author identified diagnostic indicators that may signal the onset of postpartum depression (Taylor, 2006). In addition to screening for routine signs of depression, such as changes in eating and sleeping, hopelessness, loss of enjoyment, physical complaints, suicidal thoughts, irritability, and feeling empty, social workers are encouraged to assess for postpartum depression if it is reported that the mother

- has concerns about mothering and care for the child;
- fears that she will injure the baby;
- obsesses about finances, religious beliefs, world events;
- shows decreased or little interest in the baby;
- receives no internal satisfaction from caring for the child;
- becomes upset when the child cannot be satisfied or does not sleep;
- expresses guilt for bringing a child into the world;
- finds decision-making difficult;
- describes the baby as sick, suffering, or underweight when medical experts see no problems with the child;
- has significant decreases in social or work skills.

Box 5.5 provides an outline of assessment and education steps that can systematically be taken before and after delivery to better identify and treat postpartum depression.

Because social stigma drives individuals away from seeking mental health, a specific education plan for educating mothers, fathers, and extended family members can be extremely helpful. Culture teaches that motherhood is not only an

BOX 5.5
AN OUTLINE FOR PREVENTING TRAGEDY

A planned program can prevent postpartum depression and postpartum psychosis from escalating into irreversible tragedy. A comprehensive program starts during the mother's pregnancy and continues after the child is born. The proposed recommendations include services to mothers and their families in both the pre-delivery and post-delivery periods. Culturally competent education, assessment, support, and treatment when needed can substantially reduce the risks of postpartum depression. While the outline is idealistic, the steps have been developed through interviews by the author with women and family members who have experienced the hardships of postpartum depression and the return of bipolar illness following delivery. Clinics and community organizations may want to consider altering and building on the broad steps outlined below.

PRE-DELIVERY PHASE: PREVENTION DURING PREGNANCY

1. Mother, father, and extended adult family members require education about postpartum depression:
   a. What it is and why it is a biological illness;
   b. Why postpartum depression is not a sign of weakness or a character flaw;
   c. The importance and effectiveness of psychiatric treatment;
   d. How to identify onset or risk indicators;
   e. When and how to seek professional help.
2. Every mother is screened at each trimester of pregnancy for depression, using a brief semi-structured interview and self-rating scales.
3. The mother's psychiatric history is gained using questionnaires and semi-structured interviews:
   a. The interview and questionnaire must be structured to identify all previously treated and untreated psychiatric disorders.
   b. Special attention and skill are needed for identifying untreated and previously undiagnosed dysthymia, cyclothymia, and hypomania.
   c. Mothers who may have had cyclothymia or hypomania should not be given an antidepressant as a monotherapy.
4. A genetic history for the mother's family is conducted using questionnaires and interviews:
   a. When possible, identify diagnosed mental disorders and indicators of undiagnosed disorders for the past two or more generations.
   b. Ask questions that help to identify undiagnosed addictions, alcohol abuse, all major mood disorders, schizoaffective disorder, major anxiety disorders, and psychosis across family members and generations.

POST-DELIVERY PHASE: PREVENTION AFTER DELIVERY

1. A packet and video are to be sent home with the family after birth reminding them that the baby blues are normal, and explaining how to identify signs of depression, the importance of support, and how and when to obtain professional help.
2. Depression screening is to be carried out by health professionals 3 weeks after the baby is delivered, and thereafter every 3–4 months during the first year.
3. Mother and family education and consulting should be available upon request.
4. Planned contact by mail, e-mail, or phone provides support and gives family permission to discuss concerns.
5. The mother is provided with depression self-rating scales and encouraged to track her mood and discuss ratings during phone conferences; she is encouraged to do self-ratings at weeks 3, 6, 8, and every 4–6 months thereafter for the first year.

The outline represents an idealized process that most clinics, because of limited resources, could not completely replicate. Medical insurance seldom covers this much personalized education, assessment, and follow-up. The steps nonetheless are presented to underscore two important points. First, education for postpartum depression, as for all disorders, must always include the family. Fathers, partners, and grandparents need to understand depression and know how and when to provide support. Furthermore, mothers in a state of depression cannot be expected to defy their family or culture and independently seek help. Strength and advocacy for using professional mental health resources must come from the family, not from within the mother. Finally, an idealized program is suggested to illustrate that prevention of postpartum depression and postpartum psychosis is possible, but will not materialize until a mandate, resources, and education are provided by governments, professional mental-health associations, businesses, and educational institutions.

Source: Reprinted with permission from Taylor, Edward H. (2006). Atlas of Bipolar Disorders. *London: Taylor & Francis Group.*

honor, but a joy. As a result, a mother who is developing postpartum depression may not recognize the symptoms, and may feel that something is morally wrong with her for not enjoying having a baby. When one experiences self-blame, guilt, and thoughts that break social rules, seeking help becomes difficult. However, social workers can help break the stigma by offering family and parent education about the disorder, and by routinely assessing new mothers for signs of postpartum depression.

DEPRESSION NOT OTHERWISE SPECIFIED

Social workers will have clients who do not fit neatly into a *DSM-IV-TR* depression category, yet there is little doubt that the individuals are suffering from a depressive mood. These individuals are given the diagnosis of depression disorder not otherwise specified (DDNOS). A person not fully meeting criteria does not signal

---

BOX 5.6

DSM-IV-TR CRITERIA FOR 311 DEPRESSIVE DISORDER NOT OTHERWISE SPECIFIED

The Depressive Disorder Not Otherwise Specified category includes disorders with depressive features that do not meet the criteria for major depressive disorder, dysthymic disorder, adjustment disorder with depressed mood, or adjustment disorder with mixed anxiety and depressed mood. Sometimes depressive symptoms can present as part of an anxiety disorder not otherwise specified. Examples of depressive disorder not otherwise specified include

1. Premenstrual dysphoric disorder: in most menstrual cycles during the past year, symptoms (e.g., markedly depressed mood, marked anxiety, marked affective lability, decreased interest in activities) regularly occurred during the last week of the luteal phase (and remitted within a few days of the onset of menses). These symptoms must be severe enough to markedly interfere with work, school, or usual activities and be entirely absent for at least 1 week postmenses.

2. Minor depressive disorder: episodes of at least 2 weeks of depressive symptoms but with fewer than the five items required for major depressive disorder.

3. Recurrent brief depressive disorder: depressive episodes lasting from 2 days up to 2 weeks, occurring at least once a month for 12 months (not associated with the menstrual cycle).

4. Postpsychotic depressive disorder of schizophrenia: a major depressive episode that occurs during the residual phase of schizophrenia.

5. A major depressive episode superimposed on delusional disorder, psychotic disorder not otherwise specified, or the active phase of schizophrenia.

6. Situations in which the clinician has concluded that a depressive disorder is present but is unable to determine whether it is primary, due to a general medical condition, or substance induced.

Source: Reprinted with permission from the Diagnostic and Statistical Manual of Mental Disorders, Fourth Edition, Text Revision *(Copyright 2000). American Psychiatric Association. (Note that internal cross-references have been removed from the reprinted text.)*

that the client is exaggerating or not fully disclosing. Box 5.6 provides the *DSM-IV* criteria for determining if a client's symptoms meet the criteria for a DDNOS diagnosis.

The disorder is treated in the same way that clinicians work with major depression. Once again, the level of illness severity determines the type of psychosocial intervention employed and whether medications are immediately required. The assessment and treatment plan for a client with DDNOS will always include complete and ongoing checks for suicidal thinking and behavior. Because the full criteria for depression have not been met, social workers are encouraged to periodically reassess the client's condition and diagnostic symptoms. In many cases, new problems appear over time and either clarify the depressive state or signal the need to consider a different diagnosis and treatment plan.

REFERENCES

American Psychiatric Association. (2000). *Diagnostic and Statistical Manual of Mental Disorders* (4th ed., text rev.). Washington, DC: American Psychiatric Association.

American Psychiatric Association. (2013). *Diagnostic and Statistical Manual of Mental Disorders* (5th ed.). Arlington, VA: American Psychiatric Association.

American Psychiatric Association Steering Committee on Practice Guidelines. (2006). *Practice Guidelines for the Treatment of Psychiatric Disorders Compendium*. Arlington, VA: American Psychiatric Association.

Ayd, F. J. (1995). *Lexicon of Psychiatry, Neurology, and the Neurosciences*. Baltimore, MD: Williams & Wilkins.

Baldwin, D. S., & Birtwhistle, J. (2002). *An Atlas of Depression*. London: Parthenon Publishing.

Bar-Zisowitz, C. (2000). "Sadness"—Is there such a thing? In M. Lewus & J. M. Haviland-Jones (Eds.), *Handbook of Emotions* (2nd ed., pp. 623–636). New York: Guilford Press.

Breedlove, M. S., Rosenzweig, M. R., & Watson, N. V. (2007). *Biological Psychology: An Introduction to Behavioral, Cognitive, and Clinical Neuroscience* (5th ed.). Sunderland, MA: Sinauer Associates.

Campbell, R. J. (2004). *Psychiatric Dictionary* (8th ed.). Oxford, UK: Oxford University Press.

Camras, L. A., & Allison, K. (1989). Children's and adults' beliefs about emotion elicitation. *Motivation and Emotion, 13*(1), 53–70.

Cassano, G. B., Rossi, N. B., & Pini, S. (2003). Comorbidity of depression and anxiety. In S. Kasper, J. A. den Boer, & J. M. Ad Sitsen (Eds.), *Handbook of Depression and Anxiety* (2nd ed., pp. 69–90). New York: Marcel Dekker.

Côté, S. M., Boivin, M., Liu, X., Nagin, D. S., Zoccolillo, M., & Tremblay, R. E. (2009). Depression and anxiety symptoms: Onset, developmental course and risk factors during early childhood. *The Journal of Child Psychology and Psychiatry, 50*(10), 1201–1208.

Dunlop, B. W., & Nihalani, N. (2006). Substrates of sadness: The pathophysiology of depression. In T. L. Schwartz & T. J. Peterson (Eds.), *Depression Treatment Strategies and Management* (pp. 9–40). London: Taylor and Francis.

Ellsworth, P. C., & Smith, C. A. (1988). From appraisal to emotion: Differences among unpleasant feelings. *Motivation and Emotion, 12*(3), 271–302.

Gazzaniga, M. S., & Heatherton, T. F. (2009). *Psychological Science* (3rd ed.). New York: W. W. Norton.

Gelenberg, A. J., Freeman, M. P., Markowitz, J. C., Rosenbaum, J. F., Thase, M. E., Trivedi, M. H., & Van Rhoads, R. S. (2010). Practice guidelines for the treatment of patients with major depressive disorder, third edition. *Supplement to The American Journal of Psychiatry, 167*(10), 1–118.

Glas, G. (2003). A conceptual history of anxiety and depression. In S. Kasper, J. A. den Boer, & J. M. Ad Sitsen (Eds.), *Handbook of Depression and Anxiety* (2nd ed., pp. 1–47). New York: Marcel Dekker.

Haight, W., & Taylor, E. H. (2013). *Human Behavior for Social Work Practice: A Developmental-Ecological Framework* (2nd ed.). Chicago: Lyceum Books.

Hudson, W. W. (1982). *The Clinical Measurement Package: A Field Manual.* Tallahassee, FL: WALMYR Publishing.

Jee, S. H., Conn, A.-M., Szilagyi, P. G., Blumkin, A., Baldwin, C. D., & Szilagyi, M. A. (2010). Identification of social-emotional problems among young children in foster care. *Journal of Child Psychology and Psychiatry, 51*(12), 1351–1358.

Kraly, F. S. (2006). *Brain Science and Psychological Disorders: Therapy, Psychotropic Drugs, and the Brain.* New York: W. W. Norton.

Kroenke, K., Spitzer, R. L., & Williams, J. B. (2001). The PHQ-9: Validity of a brief depression severity measure. *Journal of General Internal Medicine, 16*(9), 606–613.

Luby, J. L., Si, X., Belden, A. C., Tandon, M., & Spitznagel, E. (2009). Preschool depression: Homotypic continuity and course over 24 months. *Archives of General Psychiatry, 66*(8), 897–905.

Makrides, M., Gibson, R. A., McPhee, A. J., Yelland, L., Quinlivan, J., & Ryan, P. (2010). Effect of DHA supplementation during pregnancy on maternal depression and neurodevelopment of young children: A randomized controlled trial. *Journal of the American Medical Association, 304*(15), 1675–1683.

Megna, J. L., & Simionescu, M. (2006). Epidemiology, symptomatology, and diagnosis. In T. L. Schwartz & T. J. Peterson (Eds.), *Depression Treatment Strategies and Management* (pp. 1–8). London: Taylor and Francis.

Moses-Kolko, E. L., Perlman, S. B., Wisner, K. L., James, J., Saul, A. T., & Phillips, M. L. (2010). Abnormally reduced dorsomedial prefrontal cortical activity and effective connectivity with amygdala in response to negative emotional faces in postpartum depression. *American Journal of Psychiatry, 167*, 1373–1380.

Naparstek, N. (2005). *Is Your Child Depressed?* New York: McGraw-Hill.

Ng, R. C., Hirata, C. K., Yeung, W., Haller, E., & Finley, P. R. (2010). Pharmacologic treatment for postpartum depression: A systematic review. *Pharmacotherapy, 30*(9), 928–941.

Paris, J. (2013). *The Intelligent Clinician's Guide to DSM-5.* New York: Oxford University Press.

Rothschild, A. J. (1999). Mood disorders. In A. M. Nicholi (Ed.), *The Harvard Guide to Psychiatry* (3rd ed., pp. 281–307). Cambridge, MA: The Belknap Press of Harvard University Press.

Rudolph, K. D., & Lambert, S. F. (2007). Child and adolescent depression. In E. J. Mash & R. A. Barkley (Eds.), *Assessment of Childhood Disorders.* New York: Guilford Press.

Sadock, B. J., & Sadock, V. A. (2007). *Synopsis of Psychiatry* (10th ed.). Philadelphia: Wolters Kluwer/Lippincott Williams & Wilkins.

Shamoo, T. K., & Patros, P. G. (1997). *Helping Your Child Cope With Depression and Suicidal Thoughts.* San Francisco: Jossey-Bass.

Shaver, P., Schwartz, J., Kirson, D., & O'Connor, C. (1987). Emotion knowledge: Further exploration of a prototype approach. *Journal of Personality and Social Psychology, 52*(6), 1060–1086.

Stahl, S. M. (2001). *Essential Psychopharmacology of Depression and Bipolar Disorder.* Cambridge, UK: Cambridge University Press.

Taylor, E. H. (1990). The assessment of social intelligence. *Psychotherapy, 27*, 445–457.

Taylor, E. H. (2006). *Atlas of Bipolar Disorders.* London: Taylor and Francis Group.

Taylor, E. H., & Cadet, J. L. (1989). Social intelligence, a neurological system? *Psychological Reports, 64*, 423–444.

Tomkins, S. A. (1962). *Affect, Imagery, and Consciousness,* Vol. 1, *The Positive Affect.* New York: Springer.

Trentani, A., Kuipers, S., Ter Horst, G. J., & Boer, D. (2003). Intracellular signaling transduction dysregulation in depression and possible future targets for antidepressant therapy: Beyond the serotonin hypothesis In S. Kasper, J. A. den Boer, & J. M. Ad Sitsen (Eds.), *Handbook of Depression and Anxiety* (2nd ed., pp. 349–386). New York: Marcel Dekker.

Woo, S. M., & Keatinge, C. (2008). *Diagnosis and Treatment of Mental Disorders Across the Life Span.* Hoboken, NJ: John Wiley & Sons.

Young, J. E., Rygh, J. L., Weinberger, A. D., & Beck, A. T. (2008). Cognitive therapy for depression. In D. H. Barlow (Ed.), *Clinical Handbook of Psychological Disorders* (4th ed., pp. 250–305). New York: Guilford Press.

6

BIPOLAR DISORDERS

HISTORICAL OVERVIEW

Throughout history, scholars have described the symptoms and behaviors caused by bipolar disorders. Ancient Greek, Persian, and biblical writers recorded and attempted to explain the complexities of what became known in more modern times as manic-depressive illness, and later as bipolar disorder (Torrey & Knable, 2002). King Saul, mentioned in Chapter 5, may have had manic episodes. Aristotle described both depression and mania. Previously, mania was believed to be caused by black bile becoming overheated, causing madness, passion, cleverness, and talkativeness (Pies, 2007). In the second century A.D., Areteus wrote about patients who, in a state of euphoria, danced throughout the night, publicly talked and acted overly self-confident, then for no apparent reason shifted into a state of sorrow and despair (Deutsch, 1949; Post & Leverich, 2008).

In the fourth century B.C., Greek physicians, led by Hippocrates, were perhaps the first to hypothesize that symptoms we now call bipolar disorder represented a neurological illness highlighted by uncontrollable shifts in mood (Deutsch, 1949; Post & Leverich, 2008). These early Greek scholars further taught that mental illness is caused by natural rather than spiritual forces, and identified the brain as the major organ responsible for sanity and intellectual processes (Goodwin & Jamison, 2007; Post & Leverich, 2008). They also attempted to classify major neurological disorders, and developed crude medical treatments for mental disorders (Deutsch, 1949; Taylor, 2006).

The Greek and Romans recognized mania and depression as manifesting from brain abnormalities, but viewed them as two distinct and separate illnesses (Goodwin & Jamison, 2007). Unfortunately, Egyptian, Greek, Roman, European, and early American histories indicate that the neurobiological hypothesis for bipolar disorder gave way to assumptions of demonic possession, witchcraft, sinfulness, and other dehumanizing concepts (Deutsch, 1949; Taylor, 2006). Nonetheless, traces of scientific and medical inquiries into bipolar disorders periodically appear throughout history (Deutsch, 1949; Goodwin & Jamison, 2007).

One of the first to identify the link between mania and melancholia or depression was Theophile Bonet. In 1686 Bonet described patients who cycle between high and low moods as having "manico-melancolicus" (Pies, 2007) During the mid-1800s, French researchers Jean-Pierre Falret and Jules Gabriel François Baillarger each independently observed that patients having manic and depressive episodes were not experiencing two different disorders, but rather two different presentations of the same illness (Goodwin & Jamison, 2007; Pies, 2007). Falret described the disorder as "circular insanity" and listed the symptoms much as they appear in today's medical books and journals (Goodwin & Jamison, 2007; Pies, 2007). He also (remarkably) hypothesized that the illness was hereditary and believed that through research a medication would be found for effectively treating the symptoms (Goodwin & Jamison, 2007). The German psychiatrist Emil Kraepelin, building on Falret and Baillarger's work, in the late 1800s and early 1900s developed the definitive description and classification for manic-depressive illness that largely stands to this day (Goodwin & Jamison, 2007). Kraepelin is credited with sensitizing past mood studies, clearly documenting that mania and depression are different symptoms of the same disorder, and with being the first researcher to assert that all mood disorders are neurologically related (Deutsch, 1949; Goodwin & Jamison, 2007; Pies, 2007).

Kraepelin's basic concepts were challenged and widened by Eugen Bleuler in 1924. For Bleuler, mental disorders could not be classified, as Kraepelin claimed, into two major categories. Kraepelin believed that all mental illnesses fall into two basic but separate groups. An illness was classified either as causing periodic recurring symptoms, such as manic-depression, or as a disorder characterized by ongoing neurological deterioration, such as schizophrenia (Goodwin & Jamison, 2007). In his later work, however, Kraepelin did clarify that it was impossible to neatly place everyone with mental illness into these two categories, and that one cannot always discriminate among major disorders (Goodwin & Jamison, 2007). Bleuler argued that manic-depressive illness and *dementia praecox* (schizophrenia) were not separate classifications but rather a continuum. How a person was diagnosed and placed on the spectrum depended on the number of symptoms of schizophrenia that were found (Goodwin & Jamison, 2007). More important, Bleuler broadened the manic-depression classification by identifying a number of subcategories and introducing the term "affective illness" (Goodwin & Jamison, 2007). Between the early 1920s and mid-1980s criteria independently developed by Kraepelin and Bleuler shaped most of the world's psychiatric diagnostic systems (Goodwin & Jamison, 2007). It is also noteworthy that Kraepelin was a leader in pointing out that stress may be a trigger for initiating a bipolar episode (Goodwin & Jamison, 2007).

Between 1930 and 1940, mental health treatment providers largely abandoned the assumption that manic-depression and most other disorders, including schizophrenia and autism, developed from neurobiological abnormalities. Following World War II and until the early 1980s, mental health theory and treatment were mostly guided by psychoanalytic concepts proposed by Freud and his followers (Taylor, 2006). While psychoanalytic theory agreed that biological components played a role in affective disorders, practitioners insisted that early child-parent or other environmental conflicts usually explained the onset and recurrence of manic-depressive episodes. As a result, it was thought that manic-depressive symptoms would resolve if individuals gained insight into their unconscious anger or other hidden emotional conflicts. Even though psychoanalysis and other forms of psychotherapy offered little help for most patients with severe manic-depressive problems, talk therapies nonetheless became the treatment of choice for decades. This preference continued for a number of years, even after the introduction of lithium, the first drug found to successfully treat manic episodes (Deutsch, 1949; Taylor, 2006).

John F. J. Cade, a doctor in the Mental Hygiene Department of Victoria, Australia, was dedicated to the belief that manic-depression was a biological, not unconscious, psychological disorder. In the 1940s he was attempting to discover how urine toxicity levels from patients with various mental disorders differed. Cade wanted to inject guinea pigs with various concentrations of uric acid. However, uric acid is insoluble in water and difficult to inject. To resolve this problem, Cade mixed uric acid with lithium. To Cade's surprise, guinea pigs injected with the lithium solution had less toxicity in their urine. The scientist next injected the animals with lithium carbonate and observed that the animals remained conscious but less active and responsive to their environment. Based on these finding, Cade administered a lithium salt preparation to several highly agitated manic patients. Each of the patients had a remarkable reduction in symptoms. After Cade had successfully treated 10 additional patients with the solution, European doctors started to quickly accept lithium as an important advancement in treating bipolar disorders. Because of safety concerns documented by cases of hypertension and deaths resulting from a consumer salt substitute containing lithium, the drug was not approved for use in the United States until 1970 (Taylor, 2006).

DEFINING THE ILLNESS

Bipolar illness belongs to a spectrum of neurobiological diseases. The terms "manic-depressive" and "bipolar disorders" are often used interchangeably in popular and scientific literature and refer to an interrelated group of illnesses rather than a single disorder. The popular press and public speakers often use "manic-depression" and "bipolar I disorder" as synonyms for a single illness. This is understandable in that bipolar I disorder is one of the most severe forms of the illness (Goodwin & Jamison, 2007; Post & Leverich, 2008; Taylor, 2002).

Bipolar illness can be confusing to the public as well as clinicians. A client's symptoms can shift in severity, quantity, and focus within and between episodes. An episode of depression or mania can end within a day, or last considerably longer than a month. Furthermore, clients can be accused of having chosen not to control their symptoms, as functioning can return to a normal state between episodes (Taylor, 2006). The majority of people with a bipolar disorder revert to their baseline social and cognitive functioning once a depressive or manic episode is over (Goodwin & Jamison, 2007; Post & Leverich, 2008). Additionally, family and peers find it difficult to apprehend how the client's depression or mania differs in depth of feeling from the sadness, grief, and excitement they have experienced. We all have periods when emotions take over and we seem to not be ourselves. For most of us, however, control, judgment, and social skills are regained, and we quickly reconstitute and fit into the environment. Families, employers, and clients themselves question why individuals with bipolar illness do not simply learn to take responsibility for their emotions and behavior.

One method for helping address this concern is explaining that bipolar illness is more than emotional turmoil and degrees of sadness or excitement. Most people can better appreciate bipolar disorder as a true illness once it is framed as more than just emotional experiences. It is much easier to be empathetic and accept help if one understands that this is a neurobiological disorder that chemically blocks and prevents individuals from controlling their thoughts, identifying alternative problem-solving, and assessing their own thoughts and behaviours. Furthermore, because individuals cannot evaluate the reality and value of their thoughts, or contrast personal behavior with societal and cultural norms, self-harm becomes a realistic treatment concern (Goodwin & Jamison, 2007; Taylor, 2006). The client's self-analytic skills and judgment have been neurochemically locked away. Some families and peers are helped when they are metaphorically reminded that children and adolescents take chances because they lack life experiences, and cannot foresee and prevent danger. Though bipolar illness does not transform one back to childhood, the disorder does temporarily prevent clients from using experiential learning for decision-making, accepting that alternatives to depressed or manic thoughts exist, and fully understanding the impact and consequences of their behavior (Taylor, 2006). Just as cardiovascular disease alters the heart's rhythm, bipolar disorders change how clients perceive, experience, and cognitively understand their surroundings (Taylor, 2006).

These illnesses, along with other symptoms, alters the brain's functioning, and prevents individuals in varying degrees from wilfully regulating their mood (Goodwin & Jamison, 2007; Taylor, 2006). Like all physiological and emotional problems, bipolar disorders can range in severity from mild to extremely disabling. People with bipolar disorders often report having moods and feelings that take control of their behaviors, motivations, thoughts, perceptions, and ultimately their lives. In a major depressive episode, feelings such as sadness, hopelessness, mental pain, and fatigue are amplified far beyond the normal human experience (Post & Leverich, 2008; Taylor, 2002). Depression can create a pervasive and relentless sense of gloom, inadequacies, ruminations, guilt, and feelings of worthlessness that the person is unable to dispel with logic, past experiences, or personal will. Mania swings an individual from an upward feeling of well-being, past exuberance, through a state of unexplained euphoria, and finally into a chaotic state of racing incomprehensible disconnected thoughts (Taylor, 2002, 2006). Depressive and manic episodes are more than magnifications of everyday moods. They have the ability to decrease and control a person's cognitive information-processing speed and accuracy, word retrieval, memory, motor speed and skills, concentration, abstract thinking and problem-solving skills, and how the social world is perceived.

Most authorities believe that bipolar I and II and cyclothymic disorders represent differing types, symptoms, and severities of bipolar disorders. Schizoaffective disorder is also seen as part of the bipolar spectrum by some experts (Goodwin & Jamison, 2007; Taylor, 2002, 2006). Clients with schizoaffective disorders not only meet the *DSM* criteria for schizophrenia, but also have depressive or manic episodes. The affective symptoms can occur simultaneously with psychosis or when the client with schizophrenia is free of psychotic thinking (Taylor, 2002, 2006). The possible relationship between schizoaffective and bipolar disorders becomes clearer if one considers that these individual illnesses may be part of a spectrum of disorders relating to psychosis.

Bipolar I disorder is a severe form of manic-depressive illness and always includes the occurrence of at least one manic or mixed episode (American Psychiatric Association, 2000). Most individuals who have bipolar I disorder will at some point experience a major depressive episode, even though this is not a required criterion for the diagnosis. The illness can start with an episode of either mania or depression, and when the acute problems are severe, hospitalization may be required. Episodes do not necessarily alternate between depression and mania. It is not uncommon for a client to have a series of identical episodes without experiencing the opposite pole. Symptoms vary from client to client but may include psychotic episodes, extreme manic behavior, immobilizing depression, or suicidal thoughts. Not every episode of depression or mania spins into psychosis or suicide attempts. The social worker, however, needs to be aware that these are very real possibilities. When a person who has never had a history of mental health problems presents with depression, it is difficult to predict if the illness will turn into a bipolar disorder. Box 6.1 provides steps that can be taken to increase the accuracy of predicting whether a client with depression may actually have a bipolar illness.

Bipolar II is diagnosed if the person has one or more major depressive and hypomanic episodes, but no history of manic or mixed episodes (American Psychiatric Association, 2000). However, bipolar II is not simply a milder form of bipolar I illness. Both neurobiological illnesses can result in loss of employment, interpersonal relationship difficulties, decreased quality of life, and suicide (Taylor, 2006). Epidemiology research indicates that more women than men experience bipolar II, while bipolar I illness is equal across both genders (Kessler et al., 1994; Narrow et al., 2002). In about 60%–70% of cases, hypomania occurs immediately before or after a major depressive episode (American Psychiatric Association, 2000). Bipolar II diagnosis is not given if the person has at any time had a manic or mixed episode (mixed episode will be described later in this chapter). Furthermore, if a patient is experiencing a hypomanic episode, but previously has had a manic or mixed episode, the patient would be diagnosed with bipolar I rather than bipolar II disorder (American Psychiatric Association, 2000). Mania and hypomania differ only by degrees of severity.

Cyclothymia is the mildest yet most persistent form of bipolar illness. Onset most often occurs in late adolescence or early adulthood. Lifetime prevalence for the disorder is between 0.4% and 1% (American Psychiatric Association, 2000; Dubovsky, Davies, & Dubovsky, 2003). Diagnostically, cyclothymia has elements of hypomania and depression. Interestingly, however, the symptoms never meet the full criteria to be considered a hypomanic or major depressive episode (Taylor, 2002, 2006). Individuals with this disorder shift between elevated symptoms, such as inflated self-esteem, spurts of energy, or grandiose thinking, and mild indicators of depression. However, while the symptoms are noticeable by others, they remain less pronounced than those found in hypomanic or depressive episodes. The symptoms consistently fail to meet *DSM* criteria for an episode because there are too few symptoms, the severity of the symptoms are overly mild, or the symptoms fail to meet diagnostic time requirements (American Psychiatric Association, 2000; Dubovsky et al., 2003; Taylor, 2006).

In reality, people with cyclothymia do not experience episodes. The mild symptoms almost never leave the person. As a result, cyclothymia becomes a way of life (Dubovsky et al., 2003; Taylor, 2006). A key for diagnosing the disorder is that in a 2-year period the patient cannot have a symptom-free interval lasting more than

BOX 6.1

ASSESSING FOR BIPOLAR DEPRESSION WHEN CLIENT HAS NO PREVIOUS MENTAL HEALTH HISTORY

IMPROVING THE INITIAL MEDICATION ASSESSMENT

Identifying bipolar depression that precedes manic symptoms is extremely difficult, requiring active participation from the patient, family, and physician. The following are suggestions to promote improved communications and facilitate medication decisions.

IT IS HELPFUL IF PATIENTS EXPERIENCING THE ONSET OF DEPRESSION

- allow family or significant others to participate in the assessment and freely provide information and interpretations of the person's current and historical behaviors;
- attempt, prior to the assessment, to discover if any first-, second-, or third-generation family members had mental illness;
- identify whether, for the past three generations, any family members were not said to be mentally ill as such but were constantly noted for being "odd," different, shy, "hyper," or behaviorally strange (the lack of mental health resources and the stigma of mental disorders have prevented many from receiving needed assistance);
- understand that diagnosing and assessing require a doctor or therapist to evaluate how a person's behaviors, emotions, and social functioning have or have not changed within multiple community, family, and work settings;
- know that the first episodes of bipolar depression can occur even though there are no current or historical indicators of vulnerability for bipolar disorders;
- understand that early indicators of bipolar vulnerabilities do not necessarily mean that the depression will become a bipolar disorder;
- even though feeling tired and perhaps agitated from depression, attempt to concentrate, participate in the assessment, and recall examples of past and current behaviors.

IT IS HELPFUL IF THE DIAGNOSING PHYSICIAN OR THERAPIST

- talks with and listens closely to the patient's concerns, self-descriptors, what is and is not emphasized, and hints about issues that are difficult for the individual to talk about;
- attempts to help the patient discover and verbalize forgotten, overlooked life experiences that may seem unimportant to the person;
- discusses and gains the family's or significant others' perspectives of the patient's strengths, symptoms, illness history, copying style, support

systems, life situation and problems, willingness and ability to follow treatment recommendations correctly, and use of substances and over-the-counter medications;

- discovers what the family knows about depression, mania, and bipolar disorders, what they are experiencing in the way of hardships, fears, and other concerns, what they have as concrete support systems, and what they need immediately in order to care for themselves and the patient;
- develops a process that weaves education and assessment questions into an understandable gestalt and mutual discussion;
- overcomes the patient's concentration difficulties by providing information and asking questions in shorter but connected cognitive chains;
- slows the assessment process and helps the patient to understand better and recall possible hypomanic behaviors;
- looks for cross-family agreement of past and current hypomanic behaviors;
- attempts to inform and inquires about hypomanic symptoms in a manner that does not predispose responses from the patient or family;
- receives consultation when a patient has an unusual history or complicated symptoms, or the mental health professional has only limited experience in diagnosing bipolar depression.

Source: Reprinted with permission from Taylor, E. H. (2006). Atlas of Bipolar Disorders. *London: Taylor & Francis Group.*

2 months (American Psychiatric Association, 2000; Taylor, 2006) Additionally, while the client is experiencing cyclothymia, there can be no occurrences of major depression, mania, or mixed episodes (American Psychiatric Association, 2000). After receiving a diagnosis of cyclothymia, it is important for clients and families to know that there is a risk of the symptoms evolving into a more serious disorder. The exact probability is unknown; however, it is thought that between 15% and 50% of clients with this disorder advance to a diagnosis of bipolar I or bipolar II (Dubovsky et al., 2003; Taylor, 2006). Furthermore, not receiving treatment appears to increase the risk for developing a more severe lifetime disorder. Individuals with this disorder find that particularly during periods of depression it becomes difficult, but possible, to maintain their normal activities. When hypomania occurs, the person experiences an increase in activity and at least a slight decrease in judgment and problem-solving skills. Irritability may occur in both the hypomanic and depressed states (Taylor, 2006). Most individuals with cyclothymia appear fully functional, maintain their employment, and never seek professional help. What is not seen is their internal turmoil, decreased problem-solving skills, and the amount of energy required to complete required daily work tasks.

Schizoaffective disorder represents the other end of the spectrum. It is an extremely severe form of illness that incorporates symptoms found in both manic-depressive illness and schizophrenia. Schizoaffective disorder can produce a state of persistent psychosis, along with episodes of mania and depression (American Psychiatric Association, 2000; Taylor, 2002). Normally, the psychotic symptoms continue after the mood episodes dissipate. Some individuals appear to have a schizo-manic condition, while others have more symptoms of schizophrenia and depression. The fact that mood-stabilizing medications help people with schizoaffective illness, but generally are not helpful for patients with schizophrenia, argues for classifying the illness as part of the bipolar spectrum (Dubovsky et al., 2003; Taylor, 2002).

EPIDEMIOLOGY AND CAUSE

Bipolar disorders usually start in late adolescence and young adulthood. These illnesses however, can appear anytime between age 5 and 50, and in rare cases beyond the age of 50. Research indicates that between 25% and 30% of the people who develop a bipolar disorder as adults had one or more related symptoms before their sixth birthday (Goodwin & Jamison, 2007). The more severe forms of bipolar illness (bipolar I) are considered to be rare in prepubescent children. Only about 0.6% of adolescents are thought to have a bipolar I diagnoses, but estimates of teens with bipolar II disorder have reached as high as 10% (Goodwin & Jamison, 2007; Lewinsohn, Seeley, & Klein, 2003; National Institute of Mental Health, 2001; Post & Leverich, 2008).

Estimates of the number of people with a bipolar disorder vary. This occurs in part because of diagnostic difficulties and the fact that many people who have mild symptoms either do not seek or do not receive professional attention. At any given time, about 8% of America's population is at risk for developing a mood disorder. Most studies estimate that between 1% and 2.5% of the US population has a bipolar disorder (Kessler et al., 1994; Narrow, Rae, Robins, & Regier, 2002). A representative number of studies estimate that the prevalence of bipolar disorders is 3%–6.5% of the US population (Narrow et al., 2002). Unlike unipolar depression, bipolar disorders are found equally in females and males. Between 5% and 20% of adult cases that are first diagnosed as unipolar depression will over time receive a re-evaluated diagnosis of bipolar disorder (Goodwin & Jamison, 2007; Post & Leverich, 2008).

Science has gained a large amount of information about bipolar disorders, but has been unable to identify specifically how the illness starts. There are most likely several causes for this syndrome of disorders. Studies of families, twins, and adoptions suggest that most cases of bipolar disorder are genetically inherited. If one has a first-degree relative with bipolar illness, the probability of developing the disorder is 6 to 10 times greater than for individuals with no family history of bipolar illness (Nurnberger & Foroud, 2000; Smoller & Finn, 2003). There is a 15%–30% probability that a person born to one parent with bipolar I disorder will develop the illness. However, the likelihood increases to 50%–75% if both parents have bipolar I disorder (McGuffin, Rijsdijk, Sham, Katz, & Cardno, 2003). Furthermore, if a child in a family has a bipolar I disorder, there is a 15%–25% chance that a sibling will also develop the illness in youth or adulthood (McGuffin et al., 2003). There is only a limited amount of information from adoption studies on bipolar disorders. The available data documents that children adopted as infants from biological parents with a major mood disorder remain at an increased risk for developing bipolar disorders (Goodwin & Jamison, 2007; Smoller & Finn, 2003).

The link between genetics and bipolar disorders has also been established through the study of twins. Monozygotic twins show a concordance rate for bipolar I disorder of 62%–79%, while the concordance rate for bipolar I disorder in dizygotic twins drops to 22% (Smoller & Finn, 2003). Family research strongly suggests that individuals with relatives who have bipolar illness have an increased risk for both bipolar and unipolar disorders. While having relatives with unipolar disorders creates a greater risk for unipolar illnesses, it does not markedly increase the risk for bipolar disorders (Smoller & Finn, 2003). There is, however, growing evidence that bipolar and unipolar depression are genetically related and that these illnesses may represent two different points on a common illness spectrum (McGuffin et al., 2003). Genetics appear to be the major explanation for the onset of bipolar illness; however, there is growing evidence that the disorders may also occur from utero neuroviruses that attack the fetus's forming brain. Though the viral theory has been applied mostly to schizophrenia, new evidence indicates a fourfold increase in the risk of developing bipolar disorder in adulthood when a mother is exposed to influenza during pregnancy (Parboosing, Bao, Schaefer, & Brown, 2013). Findings of this type need to be replicated before they are accepted as more than an important working hypothesis, but this study does underscore that neuroviruses and immunologic abnormalities may play an important role in explaining how some neurobiological disorders, including bipolar and schizophrenia disorders, form.

DIAGNOSTIC CONSIDERATIONS AND UNDERSTANDING THE MAJOR SYMPTOMS OF BIPOLAR DISORDERS

The type of bipolar disorder a person has is largely determined by identifying the severity, number, and duration of manic and depressive symptoms a person has or is experiencing. Bipolar I disorder, according to *DSM-IV-TR*, for example, is diagnosed when a client has had at least one manic or mixed episode that was not induced by medications, substance abuse, toxins, or a general medical conditions (American Psychiatric Association, 2000). It is assumed that at some point the person having a manic episode will also develop a major depression. The criteria for major depressive episodes are provided in Chapter 5. Very few changes were made to the diagnostic criteria for bipolar disorders, manic or hypomanic episodes, or major depression in *DSM-5*. Box 6.2 outlines the primary changes in *DSM-5* relating to bipolar disorders.

Diagnosing bipolar disorders is complicated by the fact that many symptoms for unipolar depression and bipolar illness overlap. For example, agitation and insomnia can occur in both the depressed and the manic state. Hypersomnia and psychomotor retardation, however, are observed more in bipolar than unipolar depression (Post & Leverich, 2008; Taylor, 2006). Another problem in diagnosing bipolar disorders is that the *DSM* criteria have no indicators designating the dividing lines among

---

BOX 6.2

DSM-5 DIAGNOSTIC CRITERIA DIFFERING FROM *DSM-IV-TR* FOR BIPOLAR DISORDERS

- Primary criteria for diagnosing Bipolar I have not changed.
- The first requirement (criterion A) for manic and hypomanic episodes emphasizes changes in activity, energy, and mood. Criterion A in *DSM-IV-TR* focused more on changes in mood, while *DSM-5* requires changes in mood and goal-oriented activity or energy that last for at least a week.
- The diagnosis of bipolar I with mixed episodes has been removed. Mixed episodes required clients to experience mania and depression simultaneously. The designation has been replaced with a new specifier (bipolar I or bipolar II with mixed features). The specifier can be used with bipolar I or II diagnoses when features of mania or hypomania accompany major depressive episodes, or features of depression appear during a manic or hypomanic episode. The specifier does not require the person to fully meet the criteria for mania, hypomania, or depression, but rather to demonstrate some of the required diagnostic elements.
- A specifier for "anxious distress" can now be added to a bipolar diagnosis when symptoms of anxiety are reported, and the anxiousness appears to be separate from the bipolar criteria.

Source: The above information is paraphrased from the DSM-5 *and a web report (American Psychiatric Association 2013a 2013b).*

mild, moderate, and severe depression. Exactly where hypomania becomes mania, or higher levels of mild depression turn into moderate depression, is unknown. This is a major flaw in the *DSM* diagnostic system. Clinicians are forced to rely on personal experience for estimating severity levels, rather than on defined measurable evidence. Key symptoms to consider when assessing bipolar disorders are graphically provided in Figure 6.1, while Box 6.3 provides the specific *DSM-IV-TR* diagnostic criteria for bipolar I.

Mania is one of the most dangerous of the abnormal mood states, but fortunately it is not present in all forms of bipolar disorder. Mania or manic behavior found in bipolar I illness produces extreme and dramatic symptoms that can endanger the person's social and economic well-being, and can cause the individual to take life-threatening risks (see Box 6.4). The early stages of mania are often experienced as pleasant and uplifting. The person feels energetic, creative, and highly spirited and capable. In the beginning of a manic episode, individuals are filled with a pleasant mood, ambitious thoughts, and self-confidence. They see great promise in their relationships, personal talents, skills, careers, and future. Goals are clearer, tasks seem less difficult, and life

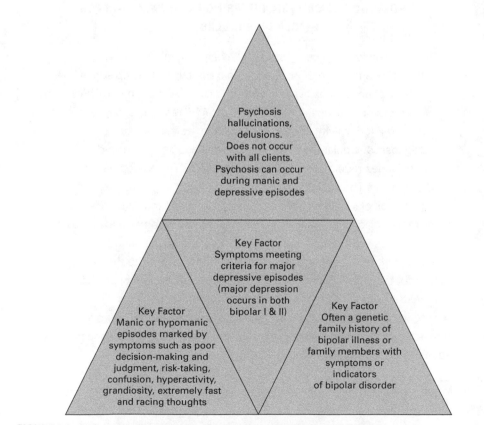

FIGURE 6.1 Global Keys to Assessing Bipolar Disorders (Bipolar I & II).

DSM-IV-TR DIAGNOSTIC CRITERIA FOR BIPOLAR DISORDERS

DIAGNOSTIC CRITERIA FOR 296.0X BIPOLAR I DISORDER, SINGLE MANIC EPISODE

A. Presence of only one manic episode and no past major depressive episodes.

  Note: Recurrence is defined as either a change in polarity from depression or an interval of at least 2 months without manic symptoms.

B. The manic episode is not better accounted for by schizoaffective disorder and is not superimposed on schizophrenia, schizophreniform disorder, delusional disorder, or psychotic disorder not otherwise specified.

Specify if:

  Mixed: if symptoms meet criteria for a mixed episode

If the full criteria are currently met for a manic, mixed, or major depressive episode, *specify* its current clinical status and/or features:

  Mild, moderate, severe without psychotic features/severe with psychotic features

  With catatonic features

  With postpartum onset

If the full criteria are not currently met for a manic, mixed, or major depressive episode, *specify* the current clinical status of the bipolar I disorder or features of the most recent episode:

  In partial remission, in full remission

  With catatonic features

  With postpartum onset

Source: Reprinted with permission from the Diagnostic and Statistical Manual of Mental Disorders, Fourth Edition, Text Revision *(Copyright 2000). American Psychiatric Association. (Note that internal cross-references have been removed from the reprinted text.)*

DIAGNOSTIC CRITERIA FOR 296.40 BIPOLAR I DISORDER, MOST RECENT EPISODE HYPOMANIC

A. Currently (or most recently) in a hypomanic episode

B. There has previously been at least one manic episode or mixed episode.

C. The mood symptoms cause clinically significant distress or impairment in social, occupational, or other important areas of functioning.

D. The mood episodes in Criteria A and B are not better accounted for by schizoaffective disorder and are not superimposed on schizophrenia, schizophreniform disorder, delusional disorder, or psychotic disorder not otherwise specified.

Specify:

Longitudinal course specifiers (with and without interepisode recovery)

With seasonal pattern (applies only to the pattern of major depressive episodes)

With rapid cycling

Reprinted with permission from the Diagnostic and Statistical Manual of Mental Disorders, Fourth Edition, Text Revision *(Copyright 2000). American Psychiatric Association. (Note that internal cross-references have been removed from the reprinted text.)*

DIAGNOSTIC CRITERIA FOR 296.4X BIPOLAR I DISORDER, MOST RECENT EPISODE MANIC

    A. Currently (or most recently) in a manic episode

    B. There has previously been at least one major depressive episode, manic episode, or mixed episode.

    C. The mood episodes in Criteria A and B are not better accounted for by schizoaffective disorder and are not superimposed on schizophrenia, schizophreniform disorder, delusional disorder, or psychotic disorder not otherwise specified.

If the full criteria are currently met for a manic episode, *specify* its current clinical status and/or features:

Mild, moderate, severe without psychotic features/severe with psychotic features

With catatonic features

With postpartum onset

If the full criteria are not currently met for a manic episode, *specify* the current clinical status of the bipolar I disorder and/or features of the most recent manic episode:

In partial remission, in full remission

With catatonic features

With postpartum onset

Specify:

Longitudinal course specifiers (with and without interepisode recovery)

With seasonal pattern (applies only to the pattern of major depressive episodes)

With rapid cycling

Source: Reprinted with permission from the Diagnostic and Statistical Manual of Mental Disorders, Fourth Edition, Text Revision *(Copyright 2000). American Psychiatric Association. (Note that internal cross-references have been removed from the reprinted text.)*

DIAGNOSTIC CRITERIA FOR 296.6X BIPOLAR I DISORDER, MOST RECENT EPISODE MIXED

A. Currently (or most recently) in a mixed episode.

B. There has previously been at least one major depressive episode, manic episode, or mixed episode.

C. The mood episodes in Criteria A and B are not better accounted for by schizoaffective disorder and are not superimposed on schizophrenia, schizophreniform disorder, delusional disorder, or psychotic disorder not otherwise specified.

If the full criteria are currently met for a mixed episode, *specify* its current clinical status and/or features:

Mild, moderate, severe without psychotic features/severe with psychotic features

With catatonic features

With postpartum onset

If the full criteria are not currently met for a mixed episode, *specify* the current clinical status of the bipolar I disorder and/or features of the most recent mixed episode:

In partial remission, in full remission

With catatonic features

With postpartum onset

Specify:

Longitudinal course specifiers (with and without interepisode recovery)

With seasonal pattern (applies only to the pattern of major depressive episodes)

With rapid cycling

Source: Reprinted with permission from the Diagnostic and Statistical Manual of Mental Disorders, Fourth Edition, Text Revision *(Copyright 2000). American Psychiatric Association. (Note that internal cross-references have been removed from the reprinted text.)*

DIAGNOSTIC CRITERIA FOR 296.5X BIPOLAR I DISORDER, MOST RECENT EPISODE DEPRESSED

A. Currently (or most recently) in a major depressive episode.

B. There has previously been at least one manic episode or mixed episode.

C. The mood episodes in Criteria A and B are not better accounted for by schizoaffective disorder and are not superimposed on schizophrenia, schizophreniform disorder, delusional disorder, or psychotic disorder not otherwise specified.

If the full criteria are currently met for a major depressive episode, *specify* its current clinical status and/or features:

Mild, moderate, severe without psychotic features/severe with psychotic features

Chronic

With catatonic features

With melancholic features

With atypical features

With postpartum onset

If the full criteria are not currently met for a major depressive episode, *specify* the current clinical status of the bipolar I disorder and/or features of the most recent major depressive episode:

In partial remission, in full remission

Chronic

With catatonic features

With melancholic features

With atypical features

With postpartum onset

Specify:

Longitudinal course specifiers (with and without interepisode recovery)

With seasonal pattern (applies only to the pattern of major depressive episodes)

With rapid cycling

Source: Reprinted with permission from the Diagnostic and Statistical Manual of Mental Disorders, Fourth Edition, Text Revision *(Copyright 2000). American Psychiatric Association. (Note that internal cross-references have been removed from the reprinted text.)*

DIAGNOSTIC CRITERIA FOR 296.7 BIPOLAR I DISORDER, MOST RECENT EPISODE UNSPECIFIED

A. Criteria, except for duration, are currently (or most recently) met for a manic, a hypomanic, a mixed, or a major depressive episode.

B. There has previously been at least one manic episode or mixed episode.

C. The mood symptoms cause clinically significant distress or impairment in social, occupational, or other important areas of functioning.

D. The mood symptoms in Criteria A and B are not better accounted for by schizoaffective disorder and are not superimposed on schizophrenia, schizophreniform disorder, delusional disorder, or psychotic disorder not otherwise specified.

E. The mood symptoms in Criteria A and B are not due to the direct physiological effects of a substance (e.g., a drug of abuse, a medication, or other treatment) or a general medical condition (e.g., hyperthyroidism).

Specify:

Longitudinal course specifiers (with and without interepisode recovery)

With seasonal pattern (applies only to the pattern of major depressive episodes)

With rapid cycling

DIAGNOSTIC CRITERIA FOR 296.89 BIPOLAR II DISORDER

A. Presence (or history) of one or more major depressive episodes.

B. Presence (or history) of at least one hypomanic episode.

C. There has never been a manic episode or a mixed episode.

D. The mood symptoms in Criteria A and B are not better accounted for by schizoaffective disorder and are not superimposed on schizophrenia, schizophreniform disorder, delusional disorder, or psychotic disorder not otherwise specified.

E. The symptoms cause clinically significant distress or impairment in social, occupational, or other important areas of functioning.

Specify current or most recent episode:

Hypomanic: if currently (or most recently) in a hypomanic episode

Depressed: if currently (or most recently) in a major depressive episode

If the full criteria are currently met for a major depressive episode, *specify* its current clinical status and/or features:

Mild, moderate, severe without psychotic features/severe with psychotic features

Chronic

With catatonic features

With melancholic features

With atypical features

With postpartum onset

If the full criteria are not currently met for a hypomanic or major depressive episode, *specify* the clinical status of the bipolar II disorder and/or features of the most recent major depressive episode (only if it is the most recent type of mood episode):

In partial remission, in full remission

Chronic

With catatonic features

With melancholic features

With atypical features

With postpartum onset

Specify:

Longitudinal course specifiers (with and without interepisode recovery)

With seasonal pattern (applies only to the pattern of major depressive episodes)
With rapid cycling

Source: Reprinted with permission from the Diagnostic and Statistical Manual of Mental Disorders, Fourth Edition, Text Revision *(Copyright 2000). American Psychiatric Association. (Note that internal cross-references have been removed from the reprinted text.)*

DIAGNOSTIC CRITERIA FOR 301.13 CYCLOTHYMIC DISORDER

A. For at least 2 years, the presence of numerous periods with hypomanic symptoms and numerous periods with depressive symptoms that do not meet criteria for a major depressive episode. **Note:** In children and adolescents, the duration must be at least 1 year.

B. During the above 2-year period (1 year in children and adolescents), the person has not been without the symptoms in Criterion A for more than 2 months at a time.

C. No major depressive episode, manic episode, or mixed episode has been present during the first 2 years of the disturbance.
Note: After the initial 2 years (1 year in children and adolescents) of cyclothymic disorder, there may be superimposed manic or mixed episodes (in which case both bipolar I disorder and cyclothymic disorder may be diagnosed) or major depressive episodes (in which case both bipolar II disorder and cyclothymic disorder may be diagnosed).

D. The symptoms in Criterion A are not better accounted for by schizoaffective disorder and are not superimposed on schizophrenia, schizophreniform disorder, delusional disorder, or psychotic disorder not otherwise specified.

E. The symptoms are not due to the direct physiological effects of a substance (e.g., a drug of abuse, a medication) or a general medical condition (e.g., hyperthyroidism).

F. The symptoms cause clinically significant distress or impairment in social, occupational, or other important areas of functioning.

Source: Reprinted with permission from the Diagnostic and Statistical Manual of Mental Disorders, Fourth Edition, Text Revision *(Copyright 2000). American Psychiatric Association. (Note that internal cross-references have been removed from the reprinted text.)*

DIAGNOSTIC CRITERIA FOR 296.80 BIPOLAR DISORDER NOT OTHERWISE SPECIFIED

The bipolar disorder not otherwise specified category includes disorders with bipolar features that do not meet criteria for any specific bipolar disorder. Examples include

1. Very rapid alternation (over days) between manic symptoms and depressive symptoms that meet symptom threshold criteria but not minimal duration criteria for manic, hypomanic, or major depressive episodes

2. Recurrent hypomanic episodes without intercurrent depressive symptoms
3. A manic or mixed episode superimposed on delusional disorder, residual schizophrenia, or psychotic disorder not otherwise specified
4. Hypomanic episodes, along with chronic depressive symptoms, that are too infrequent to qualify for a diagnosis of cyclothymic disorder
5. Situations in which the clinician has concluded that a bipolar disorder is present but is unable to determine whether it is primary, due to a general medical condition, or substance induced.

Source: Reprinted with permission from the Diagnostic and Statistical Manual of Mental Disorders, Fourth Edition, Text Revision *(Copyright 2000). American Psychiatric Association. (Note that internal cross-references have been removed from the reprinted text.)*

DIAGNOSTIC CRITERIA FOR 293.83 MOOD DISORDER DUE TO. . . [INDICATE THE GENERAL MEDICAL CONDITION]

A. A prominent and persistent disturbance in mood predominates in the clinical picture and is characterized by either (or both) of the following:
1. depressed mood or markedly diminished interest or pleasure in all, or almost all, activities
2. elevated, expansive, or irritable mood

B. There is evidence from the history, physical examination, or laboratory findings that the disturbance is the direct physiological consequence of a general medical condition.

C. The disturbance is not better accounted for by another mental disorder (e.g., adjustment disorder with depressed mood in response to the stress of having a general medical condition).

D. The disturbance does not occur exclusively during the course of a delirium.

E. The symptoms cause clinically significant distress or impairment in social, occupational, or other important areas of functioning.

Specify type:

With depressive features: if the predominant mood is depressed but the full criteria are not met for a major depressive episode

With major depressive-like episode: if the full criteria are met (except Criterion D) for a major depressive episode

With manic features: if the predominant mood is elevated, euphoric, or irritable

With mixed features: if the symptoms of both mania and depression are present but neither predominates

Source: Reprinted with permission from the Diagnostic and Statistical Manual of Mental Disorders, Fourth Edition, Text Revision *(Copyright 2000). American Psychiatric Association. (Note that internal cross-references have been removed from the reprinted text.)*

DIAGNOSTIC CRITERIA FOR SUBSTANCE-INDUCED MOOD DISORDER

A. A prominent and persistent disturbance in mood predominates in the clinical picture and is characterized by either (or both) of the following:
   1. Depressed mood or markedly diminished interest or pleasure in all, or almost all, activities;
   2. Elevated, expansive, or irritable mood.

B. There is evidence from the history, physical examination, or laboratory findings of either (1) or (2):
   1. The symptoms in Criterion A developed during, or within a month of, substance intoxication or withdrawal.
   2. Medication use is etiologically related to the disturbance.

C. The disturbance is not better accounted for by a mood disorder that is not substance induced. Evidence that the symptoms are better accounted for by a mood disorder that is not substance induced might include the following: the symptoms precede the onset of the substance use (or medication use); the symptoms persist for a substantial period of time (e.g., about a month) after the cessation of acute withdrawal or severe intoxication or are substantially in excess of what would be expected given the type or amount of the substance used or the duration of use; or there is other evidence that suggests the existence of an independent non-substance-induced mood disorder (e.g., a history of recurrent major depressive episodes).

D. The disturbance does not occur exclusively during the course of a delirium.

E. The symptoms cause clinically significant distress or impairment in social, occupational, or other important areas of functioning.
   Note: This diagnosis should be made instead of a diagnosis of substance intoxication or substance withdrawal only when the mood symptoms are in excess of those usually associated with the intoxication or withdrawal syndrome and when the symptoms are sufficiently severe to warrant independent clinical attention.

Specify type:

With depressive features: if the predominant mood is depressed

With manic features: if the predominant mood is elevated, euphoric, or irritable

With mixed features: if symptoms of both mania and depression are present and neither predominates

Specify if:

With onset during intoxication: if the criteria are met for Intoxication with the substance and the symptoms develop during the intoxication syndrome

With onset during withdrawal: if criteria are met for withdrawal from the substance and the symptoms develop during, or shortly after, a withdrawal syndrome

BOX 6.4

DSM-IV-TR DIAGNOSTIC CRITERIA FOR MANIC, MIXED, AND HYPOMANIC EPISODES

A. A distinct period of abnormally and persistently elevated, expansive, or irritable mood, lasting at least 1 week (or any duration if hospitalization is necessary).

B. During the period of mood disturbance, three (or more) of the following symptoms have persisted (four if the mood is only irritable) and have been present to a significant degree:
    1. Inflated self-esteem or grandiosity
    2. Decreased need for sleep (e.g., feels rested after only 3 hours of sleep)
    3. More talkative than usual or pressure to keep talking
    4. Flight of ideas or subjective experience that thoughts are racing
    5. Distractibility (i.e., attention too easily drawn to unimportant or irrelevant external stimuli)
    6. Increase in goal-directed activity (either socially, at work or school, or sexually) or psychomotor agitation
    7. Excessive involvement in pleasurable activities that have a high potential for painful consequences (e.g., engaging in unrestrained buying sprees, sexual indiscretions, or foolish business investments)

C. The symptoms do not meet criteria for a mixed episode.

D. The mood disturbance is sufficiently severe to cause marked impairment in occupational functioning or in usual social activities or relationships with others, or to necessitate hospitalization to prevent harm to self or others, or there are psychotic features.

E. The symptoms are not due to the direct physiological effects of a substance (e.g., a drug of abuse, a medication, or other treatment) or a general medical condition (e.g., hyperthyroidism).

Note: Manic-like episodes that are clearly caused by somatic antidepressant treatment (e.g., medication, electroconvulsive therapy, light therapy) should not count towards a diagnosis of bipolar I disorder.

Source: Reprinted with permission from the Diagnostic and Statistical Manual of Mental Disorders, Fourth Edition, Text Revision, *(Copyright 2000). American Psychiatric Association. (Note that internal cross-references have been removed from the reprinted text.)*

CRITERIA FOR MIXED EPISODE

A. The criteria are met both for a manic episode and for a major depressive episode (except for duration) nearly every day during at least a 1-week period.

B. The mood disturbance is sufficiently severe to cause marked impairment in occupational functioning or in usual social activities or relationships with others, or to necessitate hospitalization to prevent harm to self or others, or there are psychotic features.

C. The symptoms are not due to the direct physiological effects of a substance (e.g., a drug of abuse, a medication, or other treatment) or a general medical condition (e.g., hyperthyroidism).

Note: Mixed-like episodes that are clearly caused by somatic antidepressant treatment (e.g., medication, electroconvulsive therapy, light therapy) should not count toward a diagnosis of bipolar I disorder.

Source: Reprinted with permission from the Diagnostic and Statistical Manual of Mental Disorders, Fourth Edition, Text Revision *(Copyright 2000). American Psychiatric Association. (Note that internal cross-references have been removed from the reprinted text.)*

CRITERIA FOR HYPOMANIC EPISODE

A. A distinct period of persistently elevated, expansive, or irritable mood, lasting throughout at least 4 days, that is clearly different from the usual nondepressed mood.

B. During the period of mood disturbance, three (or more) of the following symptoms have persisted (four if the mood is only irritable) and have been present to a significant degree:
1. Inflated self-esteem or grandiosity
2. Decreased need for sleep (e.g., feels rested after only 3 hours of sleep)
3. More talkative than usual or pressure to keep talking
4. Flight of ideas or subjective experience that thoughts are racing
5. Distractibility (i.e., attention too easily drawn to unimportant or irrelevant external stimuli)
6. Increase in goal-directed activity (either socially, at work or school, or sexually) or psychomotor agitation
7. Excessive involvement in pleasurable activities that have a high potential for painful consequences (e.g., the person engages in unrestrained buying sprees, sexual indiscretions, or foolish business investments)

C. The episode is associated with an unequivocal change in functioning that is uncharacteristic of the person when not symptomatic.

D. The disturbance in mood and the change in functioning are observable by others.

E. The episode is not severe enough to cause marked impairment in social or occupational functioning, or to necessitate hospitalization, and there are no psychotic features.

F. The symptoms are not due to the direct physiological effects of a substance (e.g., a drug of abuse, a medication, or other treatment) or a general medical condition (e.g., hyperthyroidism).

Note: Hypomanic-like episodes that are clearly caused by somatic antidepressant treatment (e.g., medication, electroconvulsive therapy, light therapy) should not count toward a diagnosis of bipolar II disorder.

Source: Reprinted with permission from the Diagnostic and Statistical Manual of Mental Disorders, Fourth Edition, Text Revision, *(Copyright 2000). American Psychiatric Association. (Note that internal cross-references have been removed from the reprinted text.)*

becomes magically filled with cosmic meaning and understanding. These exuberant and positive feelings, however, quickly pass and change into more pronounced psychiatric symptoms (Taylor, 2002, 2006).

A manic person's cognitive information-processing skills are disrupted by rapidly occurring thoughts that not only collide together, but form incomplete and incongruent ideas. Additionally, the ability to screen and judge the appropriateness of one's thoughts, behaviors, productivity, and quality of work largely disappears (Taylor, 2002, 2006). The previously elated mood, filled with self-confidence, grandiosity, and positive symbolic meaning, can turn into unexplained, almost random, anger and irritability or confusion and fear. While some individuals alternate between periods of elation and irritability, many slip into a state of mania dominated by dissatisfaction, frustration, intolerance, fear, and an unsettling irritated mood. A sizable minority of individuals experiencing a manic episode develop an internal rage that with almost no provocation can explode into verbal aggression or physical violence (Goodwin & Jamison, 2007; Post & Leverich, 2008; Taylor, 2002, 2006; Torrey & Knable, 2002). Mania also blunts and distorts learned social-cultural judgment, while simultaneously stimulating a need for increased activity and excitement. In an attempt to alleviate these pressured feelings of desire, anxiety, anger, and grandiosity, the person behaves and makes decisions that are erratic and often dangerous (Taylor, 2002). Without forethought or consideration of consequences, among other behaviors, individuals in a manic episode may

- run up large credit card debts;
- buy enormous quantities of a single and unusual item;
- spend endless hours at the computer or with a pad of paper writing a "secret" manifesto;
- think that they are famous or have answers to problems no one else can resolve;
- call every radio talk show or make an entry on countless computer blogs, protesting or warning of a coming disaster;
- be unusually talkative and talk at a fast rate;
- proclaim to have a special connection with God;
- engage in risky sexual activities with multiple unknown partners;
- drive recklessly;
- feel justified driving the wrong direction down a one-way street or disobeying traffic lights;
- indulge in large quantities of food and alcoholic drinks, or go without eating and sleeping;
- drive aimlessly until the car runs out of gas;

- lose inhibitions and speak crudely or go nude in public;
- take countless and thoughtless risks;
- dress bizarrely; or
- verbally and physically lash out at others.

Mania is always dangerous. As self-perceptions raging from grandiosity to paranoia are stimulated and judgment is severely suppressed, the manic person can become extremely reckless and can cause serious self-injury or death (Goodwin & Jamison, 2007; Post & Leverich, 2008; Taylor, 2002). The inability to foresee consequences and consider multiple solutions, along with impulsive, agitated thinking and anger, can induce rapid suicidal thoughts and behaviors. Depressed patients ruminate, plan, and deliberate the possibilities of suicide. For the depressed, death is often a means of ending mental anguish and hopelessness, or of stopping an unexplainable, constant drive and obsessive desire to die (Jamison, 1999). In contrast, manic individuals often kill themselves over poorly conceived, impulsive, almost momentary issues and feelings (Jamison, 1999; Taylor, 2006). Furthermore, for some clients, severe mania will trigger attempts to injure themselves or to take risks that have a high probability of physically hurting themselves or others. Similar thoughts, emotions, and impulses may also cause the client in a severe manic episode to unexpectedly destroy or damage property. The property may or may not belong to the manic person (Goodwin & Jamison, 2007; Taylor, 2002; Torrey & Knable, 2002).

As the severity of a manic episode increases to the severe state, thoughts can rush through a person's mind so fast that part way through a sentence the beginning point is forgotten. This occurs when manic symptoms disrupt or block the brain's working memory (Taylor, 2002, 2006). Under normal circumstances, working memory allows us to pull appropriate information from long-term memory, lock it in our mind, and manipulate the facts into interlinking complete thoughts and logical problem-solving models (Haight & Taylor, 2013). Severe mania can completely disrupt a person's working and short-term memory. Many clients find the loss of their working memory to be extremely frightening and disorienting (Taylor, 2002, 2006). A discussion of working memory can be found in Chapter 1.

In the most severe stages, mania can cause a person to experience psychotic hallucinations and delusions. It is important to note that not all individuals with severe mania evolve into a state of psychosis. Additionally, psychosis can also accompany depressive episodes. A primary difference between psychosis in schizophrenia and bipolar disorder is that the psychotic episodes for manic-depressive illness are generally shorter than those experienced by people with schizophrenia. Furthermore, clients with bipolar disorder usually respond more quickly to antipsychotic medication and return to, or closer to, their previous level of functioning than people recovering from schizophrenia-produced psychosis (Goodwin & Jamison, 2007; Post & Leverich, 2008; Taylor, 2002, 2006). Without medication, the person's manic hyperactivity and psychotic state will evolve into a stressful fatigue, and loss of psychological orientation to time and place. Without medication treatment, a manic client can decompensate and appear completely confused, bewildered, and stupefied (Goodwin & Jamison, 2007; Taylor, 2002, 2006). In the past this was referred to as "delirious mania" (Pies, 2007). Fortunately, today's modern medications and supportive treatments prevent most people with a manic-depressive disorder from reaching this level of severity. An exercise for gaining insights and some understanding of how clients experience mania is provided in Box 6.5.

BOX 6.5

THE EXPERIENCE OF MANIA

EXPLANATION

This is an exercise that the author uses with graduate students studying psychopathology. The idea is to help people recognize bits and pieces of manic behavior that have occurred in their own private lives, and mentally combine them into a simulation of mania. Obviously, a simulation cannot tell us what mania is like. One must live the experience to know and understand how it feels. The exercise, however, can help us to better understand the way that mania grows and takes over the mind. Most people will not relate to all of the suggested images. When an experience or image is suggested that does not match your past, simply accept that it is a factor that often occurs during a manic episode.

EXERCISE

Recall a time when exuberant energy caused a momentary lapse in judgment. Perhaps in excitement you embarrassingly overrated your work, claimed phantom skills, or exaggerated personal influence and relationships. Picture the time you acted silly, insulting, or hyperactive, or took physical risks that could have ended in disaster. Picture the time you took chances driving fast, weaving through traffic, accepted a dare that could have ended in death, or that time you had unprotected sex with a stranger. Perhaps after sleeping only a couple of hours for one or two nights you were over-talkative, found the unfunny comical, then suddenly became irritable, angry, and hurt over something that now makes no sense. Remember becoming verbally aggressive and making threatening remarks, perhaps shoving another person for no real reason. Finally, picture a time when, with friends, perhaps partly intoxicated, you insisted on weaving a conspiracy story. With no effort, one thought after another rushed into your head and out of your mouth. At the time, every fast-moving detail seamlessly fitted together. Today, embarrassment is still felt when friends joke about the improbable logic loosely knitted into an unbelievable fantasy.

Now, imagine all of these exaggerated thoughts, emotions, and behaviors coming together at once. The flood of ideas is welcomed until sleepless nights and unstoppable thinking turn self-assurance into fear and confusion. Unfinished thoughts start rapidly colliding, crashing like freight trains, and leaving you disorientated, irritated, and unsure how to end the madness. The feelings of understanding the unknowable are suddenly gone, creating a void filled only by never-ending unfinished, unthinkable thoughts. Feel the fear and confusion washing over you when no explanation for these emotions, thoughts, and behaviors is found. Picture yourself overwhelmed with anxiety, stressed beyond any point ever experienced, when a plan for escaping, returning to normalcy and sanity will not come into your mind. You now know that thinking your way back to reality is impossible.

You feel hopelessly alone, frightened, confused, unable to stop the noise in your mind, or to control your emotions, thoughts, and body. You are pacing, talking faster than ever, but saying nothing, thinking thoughts that have no meaning, crying, yelling for at people for no real reason. You want to run and hide and be found all at the same time. You feel hot and cold, want to take all your clothing off yet wear everything you own. You move about having no idea where you are going. You are not sure what you want or what to do. You are terrified with no answers. You are having a manic episode.

Euphoria and hyperactivity that create difficulties but do not reach the level of severity of manic episodes are the diagnostic hallmark of hypomania and the key indicator of bipolar II disorder (American Psychiatric Association, 2000). Emanuel Mendel, a German psychiatrist, is credited with being the first to describe bipolar II, in the late 1800s (Shorter, 2012), as a hypomanic mood, producing behavior that resembles the first phase of a full manic episode. The person has an elated mood, increased energy, rapid thinking and speaking, and reduced information-processing skills. While thoughts occur quickly, information is processed in a more narrow, concrete, and restricted manner (Goodwin & Jamison, 2007; Taylor, 2002). For example, one's abilities to form alternative solutions, empathize, consider input from others, or perform problem-solving that requires an exact sequential sequence is substantially reduced (Taylor, 2002, 2006). Additionally, hypomania causes problems perceiving, organizing, and analyzing fragmented social information and interpreting social cues that have multiple meanings. As a result, hypomanic individuals make impulsive decisions, fail to consider behavioral consequences, and seldom perceive how others experience their actions (Post & Leverich, 2008; Taylor, 2002, 2006). The symptoms may also include an inability to screen verbal communications. That is, the person feels an actual need or urge to voice almost every thought. When this symptom occurs, the individual interrupts others, talks incessantly, and has little concern if his or her words insult or upset the listener. Furthermore, hypomania, like the first phase of mania, can cause grandiose self-perceptions. During periods of grandiosity, individuals overvalue their skills, status, or personal magnetism, which can lead to behaviors like risky investments and business decisions, overspending and credit card debt, sexual experimentation and excess, and careless and reckless activities (Taylor, 2002, 2006).

A hypomanic person often displays seductive and addictive behaviors that may first appear as spontaneity or personality characteristics. A closer examination, however, will show that the individual's actions extend beyond the boundaries that are acceptable for most people within the same age and cultural group. Many times, individuals with hypomania are labeled by families, schools, and community agencies as immature or delinquent. This places the person at risk for not receiving a mental health referral. Individuals with hypomania, compared to manic clients, remain more organized, are less bizarre in their thinking and behavior, and become less cognitively and affectively impaired. Most often, hypomanic clients are able to minimally maintain their education or work responsibilities, in spite of reduced judgment, increased irritability, and decreased functioning (American Psychiatric Association, 2000; Taylor, 2002, 2006; Torrey & Knable, 2002).

Depression

Only a brief overview of depression symptoms is provided in this section. Readers are directed, however, to the separate chapter on the subject (Chapter 5) that is included in this textbook. Depression is different from sadness, grief and bereavement, feelings of loneliness and isolation, or disappointment. Each of these situations creates a normal, but nonetheless unpleasant, mood reaction to a real or perceived event. More important, one is able to shift away from the reaction, receive relief, and often block the feelings by engaging in non-related activities. That is, normal depressive feelings are mood reactions that seldom pervade every domain of our life for an extended period of time. Even when one's mood is lowered by a specific event, most individuals continue to experience a range of positive thoughts and feelings.

Unlike reactive sadness, depression is a downward spiraling or narrowing of feeling and emotional range across most major life domains for an extended period. Dulling and despondent feelings relentlessly occur from depression and prevent one from experiencing pleasure, accepting solace and praise, and finding emotional relief. Rumination over issues like regret, guilt, personal loss, shame, incompetency, disappointments, and hopelessness is often experienced as emotional stress and pain. Severe depression can also create a numbing emptiness and an inability to care about oneself, family, others, or the future. Additionally, during a depressive episode, most people with a bipolar disorder not only experience a feeling of gloom but also restrictions and deficits in their cognition, information-processing, motor, and perceptual skills. Concentration and working memory are always reduced by depression. Abstract thinking, along with simple social cognitive information processing, is greatly slowed (American Psychiatric Association, 2000). Other common symptoms include social withdrawal, insomnia or hypersomnia, weight loss or gain, fatigue, headaches, constipation, and loss of sexual drive and interest and enjoyment in past pleasures or life skills.

In severe depressive episodes, a bipolar disordered person may also develop delusional thinking, hallucinations, catatonic states, or other forms of psychotic symptoms (American Psychiatric Association, 2000). Approximately 50% of all people with a bipolar disorder will experience a period of psychosis (Goodwin & Jamison, 2007; Taylor, 2002, 2006). There is a higher probability that psychotic symptoms will occur during a severe manic episode than when the client is depressed. Nonetheless, psychosis is a possibility during mania and major depression, but not hypomania. As a result, clients with either bipolar I or bipolar II are at risk for developing psychosis (American Psychiatric Association, 2000; Goodwin & Jamison, 2007; Post & Leverich, 2008; Taylor, 2002, 2006). Additionally, even without entering a psychotic state, severe depression can usher in and maintain paranoid thinking for an extended period (Taylor, 2002, 2006). To stop the emotional pain stemming from hopelessness, lost cognitive skills, and hurt from burdening others or feeling unloved or undeserving of love, far too many bipolar disordered patients during a depressive episode make serious and deadly suicidal attempts.

MIXED AND RAPID BIPOLAR I EPISODES

Another cluster of bipolar symptoms forms the mixed affective mood states, or simply "mixed episodes." A small subgroup of individuals with bipolar disorders will, for a week or more, concurrently experience the symptoms required for diagnosing a major depressive and manic episode (American Psychiatric Association, 2000). This is a highly torturous state that simultaneously inflicts the rushing frenzy of mania and the restrictive negative sensations of depression. Even though the mood abnormality was first described by a seventeenth-century doctor, modern medicine continues to struggle and debate the exact characteristics that define a mixed state (Taylor, 2002). The prevailing symptoms can greatly vary for patients having a mixed episode. Some individuals, for example, will feature psychotic symptoms, while others become highly irritable, and yet others manifest more depressive behaviors. There is, however, growing evidence that a mixed state does not occur in all bipolar disorders. Consequently, many experts believe that mixed episodes need to be thought of as a form of bipolar disorder, or mixed mania, that is separate from both depression and mania (Taylor, 2002, 2006).

Dysphoric mania is similar to mixed episodes, but the symptoms are less severe, often have a shorter duration, and do not qualify as full depressive and manic episodes (American Psychiatric Association, 2000). Patients who rapidly cycle between depressed and manic or hypomanic states can appear, but are not technically in a mixed state.

The length of time between episodes of illness varies greatly among all patients with bipolar illness. For many people, the cycle lengths shorten, causing more frequent episodes, then plateau at approximately three to five episodes per year, and finally shift to episodes that more or less occur annually. This appears to be the natural course of the illness. As the interval between psychiatric crises lengthens, most patients will have extended periods when their mood, cognition, motor, and information-processing skills return to normal. Unfortunately, around 5%–20% of bipolar patients have at least four manic or depressive episodes per year. This is known as rapid cycling, and episodes may take place in any combination and order (Goodwin & Jamison, 2007; Taylor, 2002, 2006).

Diagnostically, rapid cycling episodes do not differ in criteria from those that take place in non-rapid cycling. The symptoms must meet the criteria required for a manic, hypomanic, mixed or major depressive episode. A smaller group of patients has ultra-rapid cycling in which a depressive, manic, or a hypomanic episode may last for only a day, or may trigger multiple episodes within a 24-hour period. Unlike rapid and ultra-rapid cycling, individuals with continuous cycling move through episodes without returning to their normal baseline or without feeling normal for a significant period of time (Goodwin & Jamison, 2007; Taylor, 2002, 2006). With these individuals one depressive, manic, or hypomanic episode melts into another. Correctly and promptly diagnosing this illness is extremely important. Rapid cycling appears to be related to morbidity, is pharmacologically difficult to treat, and requires a specific medication regimen. Studies show that these patients do not respond well to medications that are normally used with other bipolar disorders, like lithium and antidepressants. Moreover, antipsychotic drugs may actually stimulate or exacerbate the cycling process (Goodwin & Jamison, 2007; Post & Leverich, 2008; Taylor, 2006; Torrey & Knable, 2002).

TREATMENT ISSUES

When symptoms first start, an extensive physical exam from a qualified physician is immediately required. Both depression and manic symptoms can stem from problems ranging from vitamin deficiencies or excess to major autoimmune, cardiovascular, gastrointestinal, and endocrine malignancies, and hematologic, neurological, and pulmonary diseases (American Psychiatric Association, 2000; Goodwin & Jamison, 2007; Taylor, 2002, 2006). Additionally, a long list of medications and drug interactions can cause manic-depressive behaviors. Commonly, bipolar symptoms caused by medical problems other than a neuropsychiatric disorder will improve as the person recovers from the primary physical illness.

Once alternative explanations such as medical problems and substance abuse are ruled out and the person is diagnosed with a bipolar disorder, psychotropic medications become the first treatment method. Lithium and the anticonvulsant medications carbamazepine and valproic acid are widely used as mood stabilizers (Taylor, 2006). Lithium continues to be the most widely used drug for combating manic episodes and has also been found to relieve depressive symptoms for some individuals. Approximately 70% of bipolar patients experience significant benefits from taking lithium (Taylor, 2002, 2006). This, however, is not without a cost. Lithium can cause numerous transient cognitive and physiological side effects, which can become life-threatening if the amount accumulating in the blood becomes toxic. When taking lithium, blood must routinely be drawn to monitor the drug's blood level and ensure that toxicity does not occur.

As medication is stabilizing the person, social workers can work with the client and family to develop a comprehensive ecological treatment plan. While interventions are always tailored to a specific individual, it is generally helpful to provide education, psychotherapy for accepting the illness, problem-solving training, and support (Taylor, 2006). Ecologically, it is important to help the client and family learn how to manage symptoms across environmental settings. Clients may also need changes in their living situation. If, for example, the client cannot sleep and makes noise throughout the night, moving to a more private bedroom and not taking naps during the day may prove helpful. Furthermore, the home and work or school's social climates have a higher probability of helping a client if the key participants within these settings receive education about bipolar illness as well as support. Clients may come to you, as a social worker, wanting permission to stop their medication or requesting that you advocate to a doctor for a different drug. In these situations it is mandatory for the non-medical clinician in a caring but clear manner to instruct the client that social workers are not qualified to give advice about starting, changing, or stopping medications. We can, however, remind clients that there could be physical and emotional consequences of stopping or changing a drug treatment without medical oversight. Furthermore, social workers are encouraged to help clients discuss their medication concerns with a medical doctor. Before meeting with a physician, clinicians may want to ensure that they have a complete understanding of how medications are impacting the client. This can be accomplished with a brief client medication attitude and effectiveness interview, containing questions such as

- Have your symptoms changed over the past 2–3 months?
- How stable is your home and school or work life?
- How stressed have you been the past few months?
- Are you facing new family, financial, work, or other problems?
- What tasks do you find the most difficult to do on a daily basis?
- When was the last depressive or manic episode you experienced, and how many episodes have you had in the past year?
- Have there been changes in your functioning at home, work, or school?
- How does your ability to socialize, communicate, think, and work compare with before you had bipolar illness?
- Have you consistently taken the medication as prescribed by your doctor?
- Is your current medication causing side effects that concern you?
- Describe the medication side effects.
- How does the medication help you?
- What would you hope to gain by changing medications?
- How much have you discussed your hope to change medications with your medical doctor?
- Is there something that makes it hard for you to discuss these concerns with your doctor?
- Why do you think your doctor would not want to change your medication?
- How would you like for me to help you talk with your doctor about these concerns?

Depression in bipolar disorders often is difficult to treat. The fact that standard antidepressant medications can induce mania and rapid cycling presents a particular hazard for individuals with bipolar I or II. These individuals often present as having recurring severe depression. A person can have numerous repeated depressive episodes before manic symptoms appear. Furthermore, mild hypomania can be difficult for both the client and clinician to identify. When this occurs, the person is at risk of being incorrectly diagnosed, prescribed an antidepressant, and sent into a state of mania or rapid cycling. Therefore, best practice guidelines recommend that bipolar depression be treated first with a mood-stabilizing medication (Stahl, 2003). Lithium is reported to be effective for 30%–79% of bipolar depressed patients (Goodwin & Jamison, 2007; Stahl, 2003; Taylor, 2006; Gershon & Soares 1997). When the depressive episode is not reduced by lithium treatment, the medical doctor will add either an additional mood-stabilizing medication or an antidepressant. Because tricyclic medications are known to increase mania, physicians most often put the patient on a monoamine oxidase inhibitor (MAOI) or one of the newer serotonin-reuptake inhibitor (SSRI) antidepressants (Taylor, 2006; Torrey & Knable, 2002).

However, the effectiveness of antidepressants in decreasing bipolar depression has been questioned by researchers. A nationally funded long-term study reported that antidepressant medications were no more effective than a placebo for treating depression in clients with bipolar illness (Sachs et al., 2007). Reports on best practice methods for treating bipolar depression consistently emphasize that antidepressants generally must be co-administered with a standard antimanic medication. Furthermore, unlike unipolar depression, there is no evidence that maintaining a patient on an antidepressant after the bipolar depression ends prevents the recurrences of future episodes (Sachs et al., 2007; Stahl, 2003).

Psychotherapy is always part of the comprehensive treatment of manic-depressive illness. During severe depressive or manic episodes, therapy anchors the person by offering support, assurance, hope, and reflections of reality. As episodes lift and normal moods and thinking re-emerge, psychotherapy assists in logical and systematic problem-solving, reinforcing positive behaviors and cognition, and understanding one's self and world. More specifically, psychotherapy can help individuals who have bipolar illness better understand their disorder, remain on prescribed medications, learn to predict and prevent or soften recurring episodes, learn to not be afraid when experiencing normal sadness, grief, or joy, how and when to let others take charge of their decision-making, and how to better care for their significant others and friends. A combination of cognitive, behavioral, and supportive therapies can accomplish these goals with many individuals.

An important part of psychotherapy is recording in a chart or journal how moods change over time, are affected by medication, and react in differing environments. Methods of this type are also used to identify internal thoughts or cognitive non-verbal self-talk. The messages we silently give ourselves can highlight strengths, fears, and oncoming depressive and manic episodes. By knowing that the patient's cognition and behaviors are dangerously changing, the treatment team can take steps to prevent or reduce the severity of an approaching illness by adjusting the person's medication, providing additional psychological support, and reducing stress in the person's home and work environment. Moreover, psychotherapy can help individuals make sense and meaning of their physical and mental difficulties (Taylor, 2002, 2006).

Families can also provide important information concerning the patient's developmental history, illness onset, and current progress, but it is important to remember that they also need support, understanding, and assistance from the treatment team. Psychotherapists or other treatment team members can offer families psycho-social education, guided problem-solving sessions, and methods for managing anxieties and organizing their thoughts to assist with the stress and difficulty of living with an ill loved one. Psycho-social education provides the family with information about the cause, treatment, care, and prognoses of bipolar disorders. Family members need to understand that manic-depression is a biological illness that can be treated. They also often need assistance in learning how to relate to the ill family member and how to help with the ongoing treatment. With the onset of illness, families not only must learn how to once again live together and redistribute work tasks, but also concretely know how to respond to psychiatric emergencies. For example, members must know when and when not to call mental health professionals, police, clergy, and emergency rooms (Taylor, 2002, 2006).

Beyond medication, psychotherapy, and education, comprehensive treatment must also include concrete supports, such as helping patients and families gain real services and tangible resources. Bipolar disorders can greatly alter the patient's and family's ability to earn money and provide transportation, housing, food, medication, and access to medical services. Moreover, these disorders can severely limit opportunities to separate from each other and rest. This is a significant problem, as family members often remain with the patient continuously for an extended period of time to prevent suicide or other hazardous behaviors, which is extremely stressful and requires recovery time. Other family members take on additional employment to pay for medical and rehabilitation expenses, or spend countless hours coordinating services for the ill family member. Treatment teams need to not only understand the stressors experienced by families, but substantially assist in the resolution of these problems (Taylor, 2002, 2006).

STRESS AND ONSET

Stress does not appear to be a major factor in explaining why individuals develop a bipolar disorder (Goodwin & Jamison, 2007; Taylor, 2002, 2006). Additionally, research does not support the idea that the number of depressive or manic episodes experienced by a patient relates to that individual's pre-onset stress level (Goodwin & Jamison, 2007). There is, however, some evidence that unstable electrical stimulations in the brain, known as "kindling," may be triggered by stress in some, but not all, clients (Wyatt & Chew, 2005). Kindling refers to the brain, at the cellular level, learning from repeated episodes to trigger automatically an event such as a seizure or mania. Studies show that after a number of electrically stimulated seizures, spontaneous epilepsy will occur without introducing the electrical stimulation (Post & Leverich, 2008). A popular brain kindling and behavioral sensitization theory hypothesized that bipolar patients become highly aware of stress. Environmental and behavioral symbols for stress are then linked to repeated depressive and manic episodes. Eventually, the brain will automatically trigger a relapse with only the slightest perception of a stressful stimulus. While kindling has been shown to occur in laboratory animals, it has not been directly demonstrated in humans with bipolar illness. Nonetheless, retrospective research indicates that severe early hardships and trauma may increase how stress interacts and contributes to the recurrence of manic episodes. The relationship among stress, kindling, and manic episodes is thought to be increased when a child has both experienced negative life events and has early onset bipolar disorder (Dienes, Hammen, Henry, Cohen, & Daley, 2006). Before this hypothesis can be accepted as an assessment or practice fact, however, more research is needed with a greater diversity of subjects.

There is some evidence that the onset of the first episode may partially be triggered by a stressful experience. This appears to be less true for depressive and manic episodes occurring after the initial onset of the illness (Goodwin & Jamison, 2007; Taylor, 2002; Torrey & Knable, 2002). While stress may not explain why episodes occur, a strong relationship exists between the severity and frequency of symptoms and environmental stress (Goodwin & Jamison, 2007; Post & Leverich, 2008; Torrey & Knable, 2002). Reducing interpersonal, community, and work stressors often increases the patient's level of functioning and decreases the bipolar symptoms. This is one of the immediate benefits that some individuals gain from emergency hospitalizations and partial hospital programs. Stress management, however, is an adjunct therapy that serves as an enhancement to appropriate medication and psychotherapy treatment. Environmental manipulations cannot independently address and treat manic-depressive symptoms. Furthermore, people who are in the midst of an extremely severe episode may receive almost no relief from the reduction of stressors or from environmental enhancements (Goodwin & Jamison, 2007; Torrey & Knable, 2002).

NEUROSTRUCTURES AND NEUROCHEMISTRY

In the simplest terms, bipolar disorders occur from abnormalities in the brain's anatomy and chemistry. As a result, the brain is unable to orchestrate the dispatch and reception of chemical messages that direct, appropriately control, or modulate a person's mood (Dubovsky et al., 2003; Taylor, 2002, 2006). These are complex illnesses that cannot be explained by a single neurotransmitter or localized to one primary brain structure. Both abnormal brain structures and neurochemical functioning appear to play major roles in bipolar I and II episodes.

Imaging studies have identified in clients with bipolar disorder that their cerebellum, amygdala, basal ganglia, hippocampus, prefrontal cortex, temporal lobe, and third ventricle differ in volume or shape from individuals with no history of mental illness (Matsuo, Sanches, Brambilla, & Soares, 2012; McDonald et al., 2004; Rajkowska, Halaris, & Selemon, 2001). Additionally, researchers have found that there is sulcal widening and subcortical hyperintensities in patients with bipolar and unipolar depression (Ketter et al., 1997) Bipolar I clients, as a group, have a larger lateral ventricle than that found in people with bipolar II (Hauser et al., 2000). However, there is no meaningful difference in hippocampus or temporal lobe size between the two disorders (Narrow et al., 2002). Both bipolar I and II appear to create changes in the brain's gray and white matter (Gigante et al., 2010; Ha, Ha, Kim, & Choi, 2009; McDonald et al., 2004). Adolescents with bipolar I disorder have been found to have a smaller hippocampus and overall cerebral volume (Frazier et al., 2005). The decreased hippocampus size was particularly pronounced in adolescent girls, even though the abnormality occurred across both genders. These findings support suggestions that the hippocampus and perhaps the brain's entire limbic system play a major role in the pathology and physiological formation of adolescent bipolar disorder (Frazier et al., 2005).

Studies comparing brain regions of twins with bipolar I disorder and twins with schizophrenia discovered less structural damage to the bipolar clients' hippocampus and amygdala than those with schizophrenia (Torrey, Bowler, Taylor, & Gottesman, 1994). In addition, MRI studies have reported that people with schizophrenia have greater temporal lobe abnormalities and less gray matter in the left posterior superior temporal gyrus compared to clients with bipolar illness (Altshuler et al., 2000; Hirayasu et al., 1998). These structural differences may explain, in part, why, unlike clients with bipolar illness, individuals with schizophrenia fail to return to their social and cognitive functional baseline between episodes. There is also evidence that a person's genes may increase the risk for distributed gray matter volume deficits in the bilateral fronto-striato-thalamic and left lateral temporal regions in schizophrenia, but may be confined to gray matter deficits only in the right anterior cingulate gyrus and ventral striatum gray matter for bipolar I disorder (McDonald et al., 2004). However, it is thought that there is an association between genetic risk for both disorders and white matter volume reduction in the left frontal and temporoparietal regions. Left frontotemporal disconnectivity as a genetically controlled brain structural abnormality seems common to both schizophrenia and bipolar I disorders (McDonald et al., 2004). These findings are significant in that the imaging documents both similarities and differences between two illnesses that have the ability to create psychotic symptoms. Furthermore, the results provide support for the hypothesis that illnesses causing psychosis are spectrum disorders and may share some of the same genes (Lichtenstein et al., 2009).

There is also a relationship between neurostructure and how the brain chemically functions. Individuals with bipolar illness, for example, have a higher density of monoamine-releasing cells than people who do not have an affective disorder (Shastry, 2005). These specialized cells are responsible for controlling the discharge of norepinephrine, serotonin, and dopamine.

Computerized imaging devises like MRI are greatly increasing our knowledge of how the brain functions differently when attacked by bipolar illness. Among other things, we are starting to learn that, unlike unipolar depression, bipolar disorders I and II may cause a reduction in metabolism throughout the brain. This would indicate that while the behavioral symptoms of the two forms of depression appear similar, they are actually neurologically different. This global slowdown may also help explain why psychosis is more often seen in bipolar than unipolar depression. Further studies are required, however, before these explanations can be clinically accepted (Bearden, Hoffman, & Cannon, 2001; Lichtenstein et al., 2009).

In both unipolar and bipolar I and II depression, studies have consistently found reduced metabolism in the frontal cortex and increased activity in the limbic system (Bora & Pantelis, 2012; Ketter & Drevets, 2002; Ketter et al., 1997; Taylor, 2006). The combination of slowed cortical functioning and neuroanatomical abnormalities partially explains why clients with major depressive episodes experience a reduction in their skills and life activities. The brain's center for judgment, decision-making, interpreting abstractions, and producing and weighing alternative solutions is malfunctioning and not working properly. Moreover, it is understandable that when the limbic system, which contains the brain's emotional and anxiety circuitry, operates at an abnormal speed, mood-related responses will be negatively altered.

Early research in the 1950s demonstrated that imipramine medication used for treating depression inhibited the reuptake of increased levels of neurotransmitters known as neurogenicamines (neuroamines) (Stahl, 2003). Neurotransmitters are chemical messengers that carry electrical impulses between brain cells (Taylor, 2002, 2006). Reuptake is the process whereby chemicals that remain after a transmission from one cell to another are either stored in the neuron's presynaptic terminal or eliminated by glial cells (Stahl, 2003; Taylor, 2002, 2006). Neurotransmitters that move chemical messages throughout the brain have historically been known to play a role in bipolar disorders. This is particularly true for dopamine, serotonin (5-hydroxytryptamine), norepinephrine (noradrenaline), GABA (gamma-aminobutyric acid), and glutamate (Mayberg, Mahurin, & Brannan, 1997; Taylor, 2006). However, for many years norepinephrine and dopamine were considered the most important neurotransmitters for understanding bipolar disorders (Stahl, 2003). This led scientists to hypothesize that depression developed principally as norepinephrine decreased and that mania occurred when the reuptake system caused norepinephrine levels to overly increase. In the 1960s this concept became known as the catecholamine hypothesis (Stahl, 2003; Taylor, 2002). Both norepinephrine and dopamine are classified as catecholamines.

Dopaminergic pathways project throughout much of the brain, but are highly concentrated in the nigrostriatal region (Stahl, 2003). This area is most often associated with Parkinson's disease, stiffness, tremors, and other movement disorders. The nigrostriatal system ranges from the substantia nigra to the neostriatum, and is responsible for controlling complex muscular movements and posture. As part of the dopamine pathway, the system also plays a role in the coordination of voluntary movement (Goodwin & Jamison, 2007; Stahl, 2003). It is also thought that dopamine located in the basal ganglia helps individuals filter out unwanted or inappropriate verbal expressions. This may neurochemically explain why during periods of depression some individuals find word selection difficult, make distressed non-word sounds, walk with their head down, awkwardly swing arms, distort facial muscles, or fail to use complete sentences or speech structures. An overabundance of dopamine appears to be related to psychotic episodes, while lower levels are associated with Parkinson's disease (Goodwin & Jamison, 2007; Stahl, 2003). Unfortunately, dopamine's complete role in bipolar disorders is not yet understood. We do know that the neurotransmitter influences not only movement and verbal filtering, but is also involved in arousal, attention, mood, reality testing, and cerebral blood flow (Stahl, 2003).

Early research tended to focus on the actions and effects of a primary neurotransmitter, rather than the interactions occurring among neurochemicals and brain structures. Manic-depression was often described as a chemical imbalance primarily caused by changes in a person's norepinephrine level. Today we know that a disruption or change within a single reuptake system only partially explains why individuals uncontrollably cycle through states of depression and mania. There is, however, strong evidence that bipolar disorders involve defects in complex interplays among multiple neurotransmitters and physical changes in the brain's structure (Goodwin & Jamison, 2007; Post & Leverich, 2008; Stahl, 2003; Taylor, 2002). Chemically, moods appear to be controlled or destabilized by changes in the level and interaction of norepinephrine, serotonin, dopamine, and other neurochemical factors.

While norepinephrine cannot stand alone as an explanation for manic-depressive illness, it nonetheless continues to be viewed as a major contributor to the illness (Taylor, 2002, 2006). The neurotransmitter's circuitry illustrates why it is an important link in understanding bipolar disorders. Norepinephrine pathways originate in the brainstem and project through the limbic system and most major brain areas. The limbic system plays a significant role in the regulation and modulation of moods, emotions, memory, and how one responds to events in the external world (Haight & Taylor, 2013). Research has consistently found that individuals with bipolar disorders have reduced norepinephrine levels (Goodwin & Jamison, 2007; Stahl, 2003).

The idea that serotonin depletion triggers a change in norepinephrine or other neurochemical levels has become known as the permissive hypothesis and continues to receive attention among researchers (Durand & Barlow, 2013; Stahl, 2003). While the exact roles of these neurotransmitters remain unclear, there is no doubt that they both play important roles in bipolar illness. Scientists, for example, can measure the brain's serotonin level by the amount of a serotonin byproduct found in a person's cerebrospinal fluid. Studies of cerebrospinal fluid consistently find that the serotonin levels in the brain for depressed and suicidal individuals, as a group, are significantly below those found in populations with no history of mood disorders (Durand & Barlow, 2013; Goodwin & Jamison, 2007; Post & Leverich, 2008; Stahl, 2003). Additionally, postmortem studies report that compared to people with no history of a mood disorder, depressed and bipolar disordered individuals have an increased density of serotonin receptors (Goodwin & Jamison, 2007; Stahl, 2003; Taylor, 2002). This, like the increase of norepinephrine receptors, suggests that the brain may be attempting to compensate for extended periods of reduced serotonin in the neuron's synaptic cleft.

CONCLUSION

Manic-depression is a spectrum of neurobiological illnesses that involves abnormal changes in the brain's chemistry and cellular structures. The neurotransmitters serotonin, norepinephrine, and dopamine appear to play key roles in triggering manic-depressive episodes. Anatomical damage or changes have been documented in numerous brain domains. How bipolar disorders specifically start, however, is yet to be explained. Evidence from studies of family histories, adoptions, and twins strongly indicates that the disorders are largely, but not completely, genetically transmitted. There is growing evidence that some individuals may develop manic-depressive illness from an in utero neurovirus. Environmental stress does not appear to play a major role in the causation, but may contribute to brain kindling during manic episodes. Once individuals are in the midst of an episode, the reduction of environmental stress does appear to help reduce or soften the symptoms. Nonetheless, medications remain the principal treatment for bipolar disorders. Psychotherapy, psychosocial education, and environmental manipulation therapies serve as important adjuncts or additive components to treatment, but are never the primary or sole intervention. This is particularly true for bipolar I and II, and schizoaffective disorders. Approximately 70% of patients with bipolar I disorder significantly improve after taking lithium (Goodwin & Jamison, 2007). Psychotherapy alone seldom has a meaningful impact on severe manic-depressive episodes.

The future is extremely hopeful for individuals with bipolar disorder. New medications are currently being clinically studied, and our knowledge of how the brain functions is rapidly growing. Researchers are also learning to identify early risk factors and minor symptoms that signal the onset of illness. Unfortunately, bipolar disorder is an illness that cannot yet be prevented and continues to be misdiagnosed for many people. However, as knowledge of medications, brain functioning, ecological interaction factors, and early symptoms grows, science will be better positioned to effectively prevent and treat manic and depressive episodes.

REFERENCES

Altshuler, L. L., Bartzokis, G., T., G., Curran, J., Jimenez, T., Leight, K.,. . . Mintz, J. (2000). An MRI study of temporal lobe structures in men with bipolar disorder or schizophrenia. *Biological Psychiatry 2000, 48,* 147–162.

American Psychiatric Association. (2000). *Diagnostic and Statistical Manual of Mental Disorders* (4th ed., text rev.). Washington, DC: American Psychiatric Association.

American Psychiatric Association. (2013a). *Diagnostic and Statistical Manual of Mental Disorders.* (5th ed.). Arlington, VA: American Psychiatric Association.

American Psychiatric Association. (2013b). *Highlights of changes from DSM-IV-TR to DSM-5.* Arlington, VA: American Psychiatric Association. Retrieved June 24, 2014 from http://www.dsm5.org/Documents/changes%20from%20dsm-iv-tr%20to%20dsm-5.pdf.

Bearden, C. E., Hoffman, K. M., & Cannon, T. D. (2001). The neuropsychology and neuroanatomy of bipolar affective disorder: a critical review. *Bipolar Disorders, 3,* 106–150.

Bora, E., & Pantelis, C. (2012). The neurobiology of bipolar II disorder. In G. Parker (Ed.), *Bipolar II Disorder Modelling, Measuring and Managing* (2nd ed.). Cambridge, UK: Cambridge University Press.

Deutsch, A. (1949). *The Mentally Ill in America: A History of Their Care and Treatment From Colonial Times* (2nd ed.). New York: Columbia University Press.

Dienes, K. A., Hammen, C., Henry, R. M., Cohen, A. N., & Daley, S. E. (2006). The stress sensitization hypothesis: Understanding the course of bipolar disorder. *Journal of Affective Disorders, 95,* 43–49.

Dubovsky, S. L., Davies, R., & Dubovsky, A. (2003). Mood disorders. In R. E. Hales & S. C. Yudofsky (Eds.), *The American Psychiatric Publishing Textbook of Clinical Psychiatry* (4th ed., pp. 439–542). Washington, DC: American Psychiatric Publishing.

Durand, V. M., & Barlow, D. H. (2013). *Essentials of Abnormal Psychology* (6th ed.). Belmont, CA: Wadsworth Cengage Learning.

Frazier, J. A., Chiu, S., Breeze, J. L., Makris, N., Lange, N., Kennedy, D. N.,. . . Biederman, J. (2005). Structural brain magnetic resonance imaging of limbic and thalamic volumes in pediatric bipolar disorder. *American Journal of Psychiatry, 162*, 1256–1265.

Gershon, S. & Soares, J. (1997). Current therapeutic profile of lithium. *Archives of General Psychiatry, 54*(1), 16–20.

Gigante, A. D., Young, L. T., N., Y., Andreazza, A. C., Nery, F. G., Grinberg, L. T.,. . . Lafer, B. (2010). Morphometric post-mortem studies in bipolar disorder: Possible association with oxidative stress and apoptosis. *International Journal of Neuropsychopharmacology, 23*, 1–15.

Goodwin, F. K., & Jamison, K. R. (2007). *Manic-Depressive Illness Bipolar Disorders and Recurrent Depression* (2nd ed.). New York: Oxford University Press.

Ha, T. H., Ha, K., Kim, J. H., & Choi, J. E. (2009). Regional brain gray matter abnormalities in patients with bipolar II disorder: A comparison study with bipolar I patients and healthy controls. *Neuroscience Letters, 456*, 44–48.

Haight, W. L., & Taylor, E. H. (2013). *Human Behavior for Social Work Practice: A Developmental-Ecological Framework for Social Work*. Chicago: Lyceum Books.

Hauser, P., Matochik, J., Altshuler, L. L., Denicoff, K. D., Conrad, A., Li, X., & Post, R. M. (2000). MRI-based measurements of temporal lobe and ventricular structures in patients with bipolar I and bipolar II disorders. *Journal of Affective Disorders, 60*(1), 25–32.

Hirayasu, Y., Shenton, M. E., Salisbury, D. F., Dickey, C. C., Fischer, I. A., Mazzoni, P.,. . . Robert W. McCarley, R. W. (1998). Lower left temporal lobe MRI Volumes in patients with first-episode schizophrenia compared with psychotic patients with first-episode affective disorder and normal subjects. *American Journal of Psychiatry 155*, 1384–1391.

Jamison, K. R. (1999). *Night Falls Fast: Understanding Suicide*. New York: Alfred A. Knopf.

Kessler, R., McGonagle, K., Zhao, S., Nelson, C., Hughes, M., Eshleman, S.,. Kendler, K. (1994). Lifetime and 12-month prevalence of DSM-III-R psychiatric disorders in the United States: Results from the National Comorbidity Survey. *Achieves of General Psychiatry, 51*, 8–19.

Ketter, T. A., & Drevets, W. C. (2002). Neuroimaging studies of bipolar depression: Functional neuropathology, treatment effects, and predictors of clinical response. *Clinical Neuroscience Research, 2*, 182–192.

Ketter, T. A., George, M. S., Kimbrell, T. A., Willis, M. W., Benson, B. E., & Post, R. M. (1997). Neuroanatomical models and brain-imaging studies. In L. T Young & R. T. Joffe (eds.), *Bipolar Disorder-Biological Models and Their Clinical Application* (pp. 179–218). New York: Marcel Dekker.

Lewinsohn, P. M., Seeley, J. R., & Klein, D., N. (2003). Bipolar disorder in adolescents: Epidemiology and suicidal Behavior. In B. Geller & M. P. DelBello (Eds.), *Bipolar Disorder in Childhood and Early Adolescence* (pp. 1–6). New York: Guilford Press.

Lichtenstein, P., Yip, B. H., Björk, C., Pawitan, Y., Cannon, T. D., Sullivan, P. F., & Hultman, C. M. (2009). Common genetic determinants of schizophrenia and bipolar disorder in Swedish families: A population-based study. *Lancet, 373*, 234–239.

Matsuo, K., Sanches, M., Brambilla, P., & Soares, J. C. (2012). Structural brain abnormalities. In S. M. Strakowski (Ed.), *The Bipolar Brain: Integrating Neuroimaging and Genetics* (pp. 53–78). New York: Oxford University Press.

Mayberg, H. S., Mahurin, R. K., & Brannan, S. K. (1997). Neuropsychiatric aspects of mood and affective disorders. In S. C. Yudofsky & R. E. Hales (Eds.), *The American Psychiatric Press Textbook of Neuropsychiatry* (3rd ed., pp. 883–902). Washington, DC: American Psychiatric Press.

McDonald, C., Bullmore, E. T., Sham, P. C., Chitnis, X., Wickham, H., Bramon, E., & Murray, R. M. (2004). Association of genetic risks for schizophrenia and bipolar disorder with specific and generic brain structural endorphin. *Archives of General Psychiatry, 61*(10), 974–984.

McGuffin, P., Rijsdijk, F., Andrew, M., Sham, P., Katz, R., & Cardno, A. (2003). The heritability of bipolar affective disorder and the genetic relationship to unipolar depression. *Archives of General Psychiatry, 60*(5), 497–502.

Narrow, W. E., Rae, D. S., Robins, L. N., & Regier, D. A. (2002). Revised prevalence estimates of mental disorders in the United States: Using a clinical significance criterion to reconcile 2 surveys' estimates. *Archives of General Psychiatry, 59*, 115–123.

National Institute of Mental Health. (2001). National Institute of Mental Health Research Roundtable on Prepubertal Bipolar Disorder. *Journal of the American Academy of Child and Adolescent Psychiatry, 40*, 871–878.

Nurnberger, J. I., & Foroud, T. (2000). Genetics of bipolar affective disorder. *Current Psychiatry Reports, 2*(2), 147–157.

Parboosing, R., Bao, Y., Schaefer, C. A., & Brown, A. S. (2013). Gestational influenza and bipolar disorder in adult offspring. *JAMA Psychiatry*, 1–8. doi: 10.1001/jamapsychiatry.2013.896.

Pies, R. (2007). The historical roots of the "bipolar spectrum": Did Aristotle anticipate Kraepelin's broad concept of manic-depression? *Journal of Affective Disorders, 100*(1), 7–11.

Post, R. M., & Leverich, G. S. (2008). *Treatment of Bipolar Illness: A Casebook for Clinicians and Patients.* New York: W. W. Norton.

Rajkowska, G., Halaris, A., & Selemon, L. D. (2001). Reductions in neuronal and glial density characterize the dorsolateral prefrontal cortex in bipolar disorder. *Biological Psychiatry, 49*, 741–752.

Sachs, G., Nierenberg, A. A., Calabrese, J. R., Marangell, L. B., Wisniewski, S. R., Gyulai, L.,... Thase, M. E. (2007). Effectiveness of adjunctive antidepressant treatment for bipolar depression: A double-blind placebo-controlled study New England Journal of Medicine *New England Journal of Medicine, 356*(17), 1771–1773.

Shastry, B. S. (2005). Bipolar disorder: An update. *Neurochemistry International, 46*(4), 273–279.

Shorter, E. (2012). Bipolar disorders in history. In G. Parker (Ed.), *Bipolar II Disorder: Modelling, Measuring and Managing.* Cambridge, UK: Cambridge University Press.

Smoller, J. W., & Finn, C. (2003). Family, twin, and adoption studies of bipolar disorder. *American Journal of Medical Genetics 123C*, 48–58.

Stahl, S. M. (2003). *Essential Psychopharmacology Neuroscientific Basis and Practical Applications* (2nd ed.). New York: Cambridge University Press.

Taylor, E. H. (2002). Manic depression. In V. S. Ramachandran (Ed.), *Encyclopedia of the Human Brain* (Vol. 2, pp. 745–757). San Diego, CA: Academic Press.

Taylor, E. H. (2006). *Atlas of Bipolar Disorders.* London: Taylor & Francis Group.

Torrey, E. F., Bowler, A. E., Taylor, E. H., & Gottesman, I. I. (1994). *Schizophrenia and Manic Depressive Disorder: The Biological Roots of Mental Illness as Revealed by the Landmark study of Identical Twins.* New York: Basic Books.

Torrey, E. F., & Knable, M. B. (2002). *Surviving Manic Depression.* New York: Basic Books.

Wyatt, R. J., & Chew, R. (2005). *Wyatt's Practical Psychiatric Practice: Forms and Protocols For Clinical Use* (3rd ed.). Arlington, VA: American Psychiatric Publishing.

/// 7 /// ANXIETY DISORDERS

INTRODUCTION AND EPIDEMIOLOGY OF ANXIETY

Early Greek accounts of anxiety place the problem more in the professional purview of philosophers than medical doctors. Hippocrates, for example, had little to say about anxiety, and may not have viewed the problem as a biological disorder (Norman, Burrows, et al., 2003). Anxiety today remains a complex concept, as it overlaps and interacts with the emotion of fear. Because the treatment differs between these two, it is diagnostically important to separate fear from anxiety. Fear is part of our evolutionary development that alerts us to immediate dangers (Barlow, 2002). Anxiety is future oriented and strongly linked to uncontrollable neurobiological factors and learned perceptions that intensely project a coming danger (Barlow, 2002). Additionally, individuals generally not only know why they are experiencing fear, but can make sense and meaning of the emotional experience. Once the threat is over, fear usually subsides. In most cases, people experiencing anxiety are aware that their emotional state is not logical and that they are not truly in any type of immediate danger. Even this insight, however, fails to stop or prevent the psychological and physiological experience of anxiety.

For professional mental health workers and researchers, anxiety is a concept that serves as a framework for connecting vastly different disorders, which nevertheless share some similarities. Not counting anxiety due to medical, substance-induced, or the catch-all "not otherwise specified" causes, this diagnostic category of anxiety includes (American Psychiatric Association, 2000)

- panic attack;
- agoraphobia;
- panic disorder with and without agoraphobia;
- specific phobia;
- social phobia;
- obsessive-compulsive disorder;

- post-traumatic stress disorder;
- acute stress disorder; and
- generalized anxiety disorder.

Anxiety is a chronic long-term problem experienced by more individuals than any other neurobiological mental disorder. As with depression, anxiety appears to affect women more than men. Adult females have a lifetime prevalence of 30.5%, while the life time prevalence for males is 19.2%. A US Surgeon General's report using dates from the Epidemiologic Catchment Area study (Regier, Myers, et al., 1984) and the National Comorbidity Survey (Kessler, McGonalgle, et al., 1999) found a 12-month adult anxiety prevalence of 16.4% and a youth (ages 9–17) occurrence of 13% (US Department of Health and Human Services 1999). This means that within any 12-month period 16.4% of all adults 18 years of age or older and 13% of all children and adolescents struggle with one or more of the anxiety disorders listed above. The National Comorbidity Study (NCS) reported a lifetime combined prevalence in the United States of 25%. In Canada, about 12% of the population experience some form of anxiety in a 12-month period. Approximately 12% of Canadian women and 9% of Canadian men during any 12-month period have some form of diagnosable anxiety (Public Health Agency Canada, 2002; Regehr & Glancy, 2010). When inclusion criteria require stronger evidence of clinical symptoms, prevalence decreases. Table 7.1 represents 1-year prevalence rates for individuals with more severe anxiety (Narrow, Rae, et al., 2002).

There is most likely a significant difference between the number of people who could improve their quality of life by decreasing anxiety and those with symptoms requiring or greatly needing mental health treatment. A person who never has to speak or perform in front of a group may find workable ways of compensating for mild social

TABLE 7.1 One-Year Prevalence for Anxiety Disorders When Only Clinically Significant Criteria Are Used

Anxiety Disorder	One-Year Prevalence
Any anxiety disorder	11.8%
Social phobia	03.2%
Agoraphobia	02.1%
Panic disorder	01.4%
Obsessive-compulsive disorder	02.1%
General anxiety disorder	02.8%
Post-traumatic stress disorder	03.6%

anxiety, whereas a person who cannot talk to non-family members without anxiety will experience chronic discomfort and a significant decrease in her or his quality of life.

Anxiety, though, is more than numbers and uncontrolled nervousness. Both fear and anxiety increase the body's somatic and autonomic activity. Suddenly realizing that you are stepping in front of a fast-moving car will cause, for most of us, an increased heart rate, fast shallow breathing, and perhaps stomach churning or even pain. This is your autonomic nervous system reacting to fear, and the knowledge that you are in danger. The same physical reaction can be created by anxiety, without the stimulus of immediate danger. All fear and anxiety appear to consist of uncomfortable physical reactions and vague restless mental worries and alarm or apprehension (Sadock & Sadock, 2007; Regehr & Glancy, 2010). Numerous psychology textbooks have historically spoken of fear and anxiety as synonyms. Sadock and Sadock (2007) state that anxiety can be adaptive, causing people to work harder to prevent difficulties and disasters. For example, due to anxiety about failing an exam, students study more and longer in preparation. One could also argue, however, that this is fear rather than anxiety. Even though the exam is a future rather than an immediate event, such as stepping in front of a moving car, the consequences of not studying are known. Additionally, once the examination process is over, the fear ends. That is not to say that a new fear of parental disapproval from a failing grade does not follow, but the original fear of the exam is over.

As overlapping emotions, both fear and anxiety can cause one to make bad decisions, procrastinate, and even hide from reality. Furthermore, while the two are very similar, it is important from an assessment and treatment perspective to view them as different psychological emotions. Fear generally occurs from cues of environmental dangers, whereas anxiety appears in the absence of clear or realistic ecological factors. Consider again the example of the student facing an exam. Fear of failure may motivate a student to study, and receiving a rewarding grade may help the person face the next exam with less fear. If, however, the student has test anxiety, studying may feel overwhelming and may create more severe symptoms. Additionally, passing the exam seldom reduces the person's future anxiety. Perhaps more important, chronic anxiety is more emotionally, physically, and economically costly for clients than realistic fears. Barlow (2002) identifies the following human problems that directly result from an anxiety disorder:

- the frequency of suicide in clients with anxiety disorders and individuals with depression is equal;
- 20% of individuals with panic disorder make a suicidal attempt sometime in their life;

- high relationship between anxiety disorders and substance abuse;
- alcohol abuse and dependence often co-occur with anxiety disorders;
- anxiety occurs before alcoholism for some, but for others alcoholism predates anxiety symptoms;
- alcohol and other substances may be used to self-medicate and increase coping;
- depression occurs in episodes and tends to abate for about 80% of clients whether or not treated, but anxiety is chronic and remains to some degree even after treatment;
- anxiety accounts for about 31% of the total mental health costs in the United States;
- quality of life is decreased for individuals with anxiety disorders;
- individuals with anxiety disorders have higher rates of unemployment and under-employment.

While our understanding of anxiety has increased, scientists have yet to find the exact cause of these disorders. Perhaps more than any other disorder, anxiety illustrates the interactive bioecological model. Neither learning nor biological predisposition completely explains the development, progression, and chronicity of these disorders, though there certainly are exceptions in which biology is primary, requiring little or no environmental involvement. The person is simply neurologically wired to experience one of the major types of anxiety (Crowe 2004). This is illustrated in Figure 7.1. Infants who show unusually high levels of anxiety are most likely preprogrammed by genetics and brain development to show hypersensitivity to environmental stimuli.

The path to anxiety that may apply to far more individuals is a bioecological model consisting of interacting genetics, brain development, temperament, experiential learning, learned futuristic automatic thinking, and social stimuli (see Figure 7.2). There is evidence that family genetics play a role in the onset of anxiety. However, as

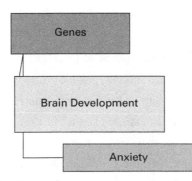

FIGURE 7.1 Direct Road to Anxiety.

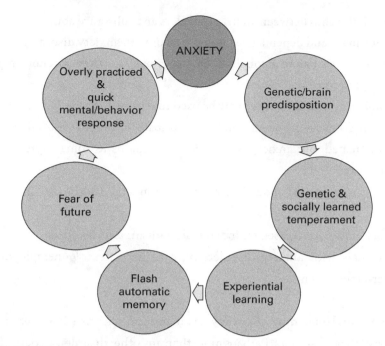

FIGURE 7.2 The Bioecological Route to Anxiety.

pointed out by Regehr and Glancy (2010), based on twins studies, genetics do not appear to contribute as robustly to the development of anxiety, as occurs with other major mental disorders. In bipolar disorder, about 60%–70% of cases are thought to relate directly to inherited genes; for schizophrenia, the concordance rate for twins is around 46%. Genetic twin studies for anxiety report concordance or heritability rates as follows: panic disorders = 28%–40%; agoraphobia = 36%; social anxiety = 10%; specific phobias = 24%; general anxiety = 15%–20%; and post-traumatic stress = 13.6% (Knowles, 2003; Regehr & Glancy, 2010). Interpreting heritability estimates for anxiety is also complicated by the lack of uniform definitions used for including or excluding research studies, and the differing methods by which data were collected (Barlow, 2002; Crowe, 2004). Studies of obsessive-compulsive disorder (OCD) serve as an excellent example of these issues.

There have been very few twin studies of OCD. One study that is often quoted found an 80% heritability in the monozygotic twin sample (Carey & Gottesman, 1981). Unfortunately, the study had only 15 sets of monozygotic twins. Five of the 15 were concordant for OCD. Another study of 14 monozygotic twins also found 5 OCD concordant pairs (Walkup, Leckman, et al., 1988). However, because of comorbidity (Tourette's syndrome) within the sample and the absence of zygosity documentation, the data cannot be interpreted with any certainty (Eley, Collier, et al., 2002).

Twin findings for post-traumatic stress must also be interpreted with caution. Not only are there very few studies, but the 13.6% twin concordant rate was developed through the use of self-report questionnaires (True, Rice, et al., 1993). The researchers used a database of twin pairs known to have been in the US Armed Forces during the Vietnam War. While the sample was large (4,042 males) it nonetheless leaves a number of questions unanswered. From the study we cannot determine if the concordance rate is equal for women, whether rates differ for non-war-related trauma, the importance of age groupings, the role that severity of trauma played, and how subjects interpreted survey items. Experts tend to believe that most anxiety disorders have a foundation of multiple genes that have only a small effect until they interact with a number of ecological factors (Walkup, Leckman, et al., 1988; Barlow, 2002; Crowe, 2004).

If genetics are only part of the story, then how do anxiety disorders start? As usual, this question cannot be completely answered. Some people see anxiety closely linked to personality. The most highly used screening scale for anxiety, for example, was developed based on the idea that each individual has a trait (personality) and state rate of anxiety (Spielberger, Gorsuch, et al., 1983). The trait or personality rate is constant and serves as a person's anxiety baseline. As stress increases or decreases, the individual's state rate moves above or below the trait baseline. Therefore, even with fluctuations, individuals develop a unique personality trait where their anxiety level is generally maintained. As our knowledge has grown, the model has become more complicated. More than personality, it is a combination of genes, temperament, experiential learning, automatic memory, and futuristic thinking that appears to drive the development of anxiety (Kagan, 1997; Kagan & Snidman, 1999; Barlow, 2002; Charney, 2004; Wehrenberg & Prinz, 2007).

Temperament is the automatic way in which one responds to unexpected or novel stimuli in the environment. Children, for example, when approached by a stranger or placed in an unknown environment, tend to either withdraw or energetically engage with the person or new situation (Kagan, 1997; Barlow, 2002). Studies indicate that up to 50% of temperament is genetically inherited. This leaves space for a child's anxiety to be equally influenced by environmental events, ecological stability, and the youth's overall physical and mental health. Current models hypothesize that one learns and constantly reinforces ideas that disaster or harm is about to occur. These thoughts of doom may be formed from actual negative experiences or neurologically produced perceptions that turn into automatic cognitive memories (Barlow, 2002; Himle, Fischer, et al., 2007; Hyman, 2007). Figure 7.3 illustrates the interaction required among experience/perception, cognition/memory, automatic thoughts (futuristic fears), and brain functioning.

All anxiety involves some form of physiological arousal or alerting, avoidance behavior, and perception of danger. These reactions are hypothesized by the author to come

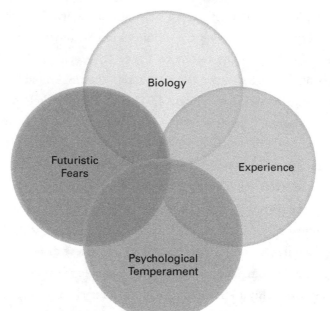

FIGURE 7.3 The Road to Anxiety.

from established abnormal brain functioning, the result of previously learned information that is now part of long-term memory. Additionally, the perception of danger invokes an overwhelming belief that the worst will occur; personal control and prevention of the perceived threat are extremely limited; a state of constant vigilance (anticipation) must be maintained; and it is necessary to focus attention and narrow one's concentration on the perceived danger (Dozois & Westra, 2004). These beliefs form the neuromechanism for futuristic automatic thoughts of danger, and stem from incorrectly labeled experiential learning and over-practiced cognitions and behaviors. Symbolically speaking, the beliefs are planted at the very top of the client's memory bank, ready to be triggered into action from the slightest environmental or neurochemical cue.

While the development of anxiety requires learning, reinforcement, and ecological input, it is important to help clients understand that pathological response patterns will not develop without the added presence of abnormal brain activity (Barlow, 2002; Wehrenberg & Prinz, 2007). The pathology does not develop out of choice or bad habits, but rather from a neurobiological foundation.

Anxiety and the Brain

Anxiety is sometimes explained as symbolic gates in the brain that are supposed to open when fear is appropriate and close immediately after the danger has passed. If in the middle of a conversation you step in front of an on-coming car, your brain's anxiety gates are expected to open and send an alarm for you to quickly step back onto the sidewalk. In cases like this, we do not want to process all possible information, such as calculating the speed of the car and its stopping ratios. We want our brain to simply scream, "get back, wake up." This is anxiety working for us. However, we also expect the anxiety gates to close once we are safe, and the incident to fade into distant memory. For individuals with anxiety disorders, the symbolic brain gates consistently remain open, creating fear, hypervigilance, and false futuristic beliefs, even when there is no danger and no reason for calculating possibilities for disaster.

The exact relationship of anxiety and brain functioning is not completely clear. Nonetheless, neuroscientists have hypothesized that the primary anxiety circuits are in a system linking the brain's orbito-frontal-limbic-basal ganglia (McGuire, Bench, et al., 1994; Hollander & Simeon, 2003). The prefrontal-orbital-cortex is located in the front area of the brain. An excess of metabolism (neurochemical activity) in this area results in an unrealistic emphasis on cleanliness, fears that one will behave inappropriately, increased general social worries, and unexplained feelings of guilt. Underactivity of the prefrontal-orbital-cortex is associated with a lack of feelings of inhibition and guilt (Amen & Routh, 2003; Hollander & Simeon, 2003; Charney & Bremner, 2004; Kent & Rauch, 2004; Swedo & Snider, 2004).

You may recall that the limbic system, among other things, includes the amygdala, which is the brain's emotional center, and the hippocampus, which stores short-term memory and helps with the learning process (Taylor 2002). If the amygdala is hyper-sensitive and gives false or over-reactive emotional responses, this results in the hippocampus storing, learning, and passing forward signals that fail to match the realities of the environment. Another important player in producing anxiety is the cingulate gyrus (Charney & Bremner, 2004; Kent & Rauch, 2004; Swedo & Snider, 2004). When working properly, the cingulate gyrus allows us to shift our attention to appropriate environmental cues and provides humans with cognitive flexibility. The reason you can quickly shift from one idea to another and identify social and personal options is largely because of a functioning cingulate gyrus. It also helps one accept the environment—that is, you can be comfortable not having every question answered, or knowing all the facts, or even agreeing with what is being said around you (Amen & Routh, 2003; Charney & Bremner, 2004). The cingulate gyrus is our "social zen" organ. Overactivity in this section of the brain results in obsessions, compulsions, worries, a lack of flexibility, and an inability to let go of fearful or angry thoughts.

The basal ganglia serve many purposes. For anxiety, however, they are somewhat the music conductor that integrates feelings and movement, and suppresses unwanted fine-motor behaviors. We also credit the basal ganglia with enhancing individual motivation. When the basal ganglia are functioning incorrectly, individuals experience panic attacks, nervousness, and muscle tension. Additionally, as the basal ganglia overactivate, personal motivation drops, and physical sensations such as headaches, fine motor problems, and tremors appear (Charney & Bremner, 2004; Kent & Rauch, 2004). Moreover, the caudate nucleus, which is part of the corpus striatum that is part of the basal ganglia, is extremely important in the brain's manufacturing of anxiety. This caudate nucleus is assigned the job of filtering signals (thoughts) coming from other brain sections, and is expected to manage or control habitual and repetitive behaviors (Amen & Routh, 2003; Charney & Bremner, 2004; Kent & Rauch, 2004). Remember the over-emotional reactions sent forward from the amygdala and hippocampus? They were supposed to first go through the thalamus for partial processing, and to undergo the brain's questioning if the proposed emotions are congruent with reality. However, the thalamus's main job is to hand the emotions off to the caudate nucleus, which, when working, looks at the emotions and says, "I don't think we want a repetitive reaction of this type." But if the caudate nucleus is overactive, the emotion is passed unfiltered to the frontal cortex. As stated earlier, the frontal cortex is our brain's center of judgment and reasoning. Under normal circumstances, the frontal cortex reviews the overstated emotions and slows the entire neuroprocess down. In other words, the brain's total system of checks and balances for errors functions correctly, and thus we do not embarrass ourselves. Unfortunately, overactivity in the cortex can block limbic system signals from being appropriately filtered for judgment, reasoning, and abstract thinking. Therefore, we can symbolically think of anxiety as fast-acting, encapsulated, and unprocessed cognition that, through practice, becomes embedded in long-term memory as automatic beliefs.

PANIC DISORDER

Experiencing Panic

Imagine yourself in a café, at peace with the world, enjoying wonderful food and conversation, when suddenly three people burst into the room, wielding guns and yelling that everyone was going to die. Most likely your heart races, your hands or entire body trembles, breathing seems harder, faster, and shallower than normal, tears and crying involuntarily occur, and the only thought registering in your mind at a locomotive speed is, "I will not get out of this alive, I am about to die." Most everyone in the café is having a similar experience. This is fear, stimulated by a real, immediate threat.

But how would it affect your daily life if waves of uncontrolled fearful emotions, physical reactions, and cognitive thoughts of doom randomly occurred when no threat was present? Furthermore, how would it shape your lifestyle if it was unpredictable when or where these reactions would take place? How would you react if your mind could not move from the thought that you were going to die—not figuratively, but actually, at any minute drop dead? Finally, what if you knew it made no logical sense to have waves of fear and thoughts of death. You are totally aware that no harm is lurking, yet no amount of positive self-talk, reassurance, or mental resolve to be strong prevents the next random wave of illogical breath-crushing emotions. This is panic (American Psychiatric Association, 2000; Barlow, 2002; Hollander & Simeon, 2003; Wehrenberg & Prinz, 2007). It makes no sense, but it is as frightening as experiencing a real life-or-death event. As a reader, take a moment, and contemplate how randomly occurring panic—that may happen at any time and in any place, public or private—would alter your lifestyle, economics, socialization, and quality of life. This is the difficult balancing act that clients with a panic disorder must face daily. Many clients, however, who cannot negotiate places and situations when alone can function within these environments and situations if accompanied by a significant friend or family member (Hollander & Simeon, 2003).

ASSESSING, DIAGNOSING, AND TREATING PANIC DISORDER

As with all disorders, early in the assessment process social workers must insist that the client receive a medical physical exam, specifically designed for ruling out a physiological explanation for the reported anxiety. A team approach that includes a physician is sometimes needed to help clients accept that they are not in a medical crisis and facing death or severe physical disabilities. Assessing functionality requires estimating the amount of abstract thinking, problem-solving, reality perspective, and self-care that is lost and maintained during panic attacks and between episodes. It is important to determine the severity of the panic and whether the client routinely restricts her or his life out of fear that an attack will occur. In addition to assessing whether the person meets *DSM-IV-TR* criteria, it is also helpful to evaluate

- the onset, frequency, severity and course of attacks;
- history and current psychiatric problems in client and family;
- past and current use of substance;
- behavior just before, during, and after an attack;
- amount of ruminating about possible future attacks;

- level of anticipatory anxiety;
- amount of time spent in phobic avoidance (preventing self from being in certain places or situations);
- methods used to try to prevent attacks;
- methods used to try to overcome an occurring attack;
- how the client has modified her or his life to accommodate for attacks; and
- how the person's panic disorder has impacted the family and work/education.

This assessment outline was developed from the author's experience and published recommendations (Cambell-Sills & Stein, 2006; Himle, Fischer, et al., 2007).

Another way of assessing panic and other anxiety disorders is to systematically evaluate specific domains (Antony & Rowa, 2005). Research is needed to better define the domains that are specific to each anxiety disorder versus those that are found across the spectrum. Nonetheless, Antony and Rowa (2005), based on a review of anxiety studies, suggest that clinicians focus their assessments in the following areas or domains:

- diagnostic features (which *DSM* criteria does the person meet, and to what degree or level of severity);
- anxiety cues and triggers;
- avoidance behaviors;
- physical symptoms and responses;
- skill deficits;
- compulsions and overprotective behaviors;
- associated distress and functional impairment;
- development and course of the problem;
- environmental and family factors;
- treatment history;
- medical and health issues; and
- associated problems and comorbidity.

While there is noticeable overlap between the two outlines, together they provide a comprehensive tool for interviewing and assessing clients for anxiety disorders.

In order to provide expert treatment, however, one must be able to differentiate among the anxiety disorders, despite the overlapping of many symptoms and domains. Having a panic attack, for example, does not in itself identify the specific anxiety disorder that should be targeted for treatment. A person can have a panic attack without having a diagnosable panic disorder. In addition, panic attacks may occur in relation to other forms of anxiety and diagnostic categories. Panic attacks are also commonly seen in clients with post-traumatic stress, specific phobias, and social phobias (Sadock & Sadock, 2007). Panic attacks, however, are always primary in a panic disorder. Furthermore, as discussed below, panic disorders may or may not include the added diagnostic dimension of agoraphobia. The *DSM-IV-TR* criteria for a panic attack are provided in Box 7.1. The attack can be completely unexpected, triggered by an environmental cue, or predisposed by a specific situation (American Psychiatric Association, 2000).

As suggested by the term, an *unexpected panic attack* occurs without warning and is not attached to any conscious trigger or stimulus. *Situationally bound cued attacks* are directly triggered by an environmental situation or an anticipated event. Therefore, the cue can be either an actual ecological factor or internally developed. Regardless of the trigger, a panic attack occurs immediately after cues are perceived. Simply anticipating a triggering event can cause panic to emotionally sweep through the person. A person who has *situationally bound cued attacks* need only be placed within the threatening

---

BOX 7.1

DSM-IV-TR CRITERIA FOR PANIC ATTACK

A discrete period of intense fear or discomfort, in which four (or more) of the following symptoms developed abruptly and reached a peak within 10 minutes:

1. Palpitations, pounding heart, or accelerated heart rate;
2. Sweating;
3. Trembling or shaking;
4. Sensations of shortness of breath or smothering;
5. Feeling of choking;
6. Chest pain or discomfort;
7. Nausea or abdominal distress;
8. Feeling dizzy, unsteady, lightheaded, or faint;
9. Derealization (feelings of unreality) or depersonalization (being detached from oneself);
10. Fear of losing control or going crazy;
11. Fear of dying;
12. Paresthesias (numbness or tingling sensations);
13. Chills or hot flushes.

Source: Reprinted with permission from the Diagnostic and Statistical Manual of Mental Disorders, Fourth Edition, Text Revision *(Copyright 2000). American Psychiatric Association. (Note that internal cross-references have been removed from the reprinted text.)*

environment, visualize a past frightful situation, or imagine an unknown never experienced fearful situation for panic to happen. In contrast, *situationally predisposed panic attacks* are not always directly related to a specific perceived cue, and reactions are most often delayed; that is, the person is more ambiguously than specifically cued, and the attack does not always take place while the client is directly facing or feeling apprehensive about a fearful situation (Katerndahl & Realini, 1993). Clients who have situationally predisposed panic attacks and who fear looking down from heights may find that, at times, observing from a high place produces no attack. However, on another visit to the same location, the person may start looking down from a height with no difficulty, but as time passes, and for no known reason to the client, a wave of anxiety and fear from looking down rushes through the person. In this example it is difficult to pinpoint the environmental or internal cue, and to explain why panic occurred on this visit but not at first, and not at all during the previous visit (Katerndahl & Realini, 1993; American Psychiatric Association, 2000; Wehrenberg & Prinz, 2007).

Panic disorder most often starts when people are in their early thirties. Late onset is defined as meeting criteria for the illness from age 60 forward. When the disorder starts late in life, social workers must assess for factors such as decreased cognitive functioning, mild undiagnosed anxiety occurring earlier in life, deterioration of health, medication or substance reactions, deaths of significant individuals, loss of physical skills or privileges such as driving, and decreased economic independence (Wehrenberg & Prinz, 2007). Panic disorder often coexists with other forms of anxiety. Currently it is thought that 15%–30% of people with panic disorder also have generalized anxiety disorder or social phobia, 2%–20% suffer from specific phobia, and another 10% have a comorbid obsessive-compulsive disorder (American Psychiatric Association, 2000). At a minimum, between 2% and 10% of clients with panic disorder are or will also be diagnosed with post-traumatic stress disorder (American Psychiatric Association, 2000). Most authorities, however, believe that future research will prove that the actual number of people with comorbid panic and post-traumatic disorders is much higher than presently estimated (American Psychiatric Association, 2000; Barlow, 2002). When a client has panic or any other anxiety disorder, clinicians must also perform a comprehensive assessment and rule out depression. Between 10% and 65% of individuals with a panic diagnosis will also have major depressive episodes (American Psychiatric Association, 2000; Barlow, 2002). The first panic attack of panic disorder often takes place while performing a routine task. The onset is frightening and overwhelming, often creating physical symptoms that can resemble a heart attack. The client may report to an emergency facility complaining of heart palpitations, chest pain, breathing difficulties, and dizziness.

A common symptom seen across clients with panic disorder who are seeking treatment is hyperventilation (Hollander & Simeon, 2003). Fundamentally, hyperventilation is breathing that is excessively rapid or deep. It can also consist of a combination of excessively fast and deep, or extremely rapid and shallow, breathing. The person's respiration rate is far greater than that needed by the body (Ayd, 1995). Social workers often see this as simply part of the overall symptom package that accompanies clients who have panic attacks, despite the fact that it has major psychiatric and physiological consequences. The rapid shallow breathing causes a decrease in the blood's hydrogen ion (carbon dioxide) concentration. This in turn will cause blood vessels to narrow, creating a condition known as vasoconstriction. As the client's blood vessels constrict, the body's metabolism slows and the person experiences dizziness, faintness, and visual problems. Some clients with severe hyperventilation develop tetany and paraesthesia (tingling sensations). Tenany causes muscle cramps in the hands and feet. In more advanced, serious cases, the client experiences twitching and larynx spasms. The spasms can trigger breathing difficulties, vomiting, and, in extreme cases, convulsions (Macefield & Burke, 1991; Cambell-Sills & Stein, 2006). From a psychiatric perspective, hyperventilation decreases cerebral blood flow in the brain. The reduced cerebral metabolism decreases judgment and problem-solving skills, and accounts for the confusion and feelings of derealization that often accompany panic attacks (Hollander & Simeon, 2003).

General panic attack symptoms may also include hot and cold flashes and trembling. Clients often fear that death is imminent, or experience a temporary state of psychological depersonalization and derealization (Katerndahl & Realini, 1993; Barlow, 2002; Regehr & Glancy, 2010). These are forms of altered reality in which an individual feels a loss of personal identity, or that the environment and his or her body are different or no longer real. Depersonalization refers more to an altered reality of the body, mind, and personal self, while derealization refers more to a sense that the environment has changed or is no longer real. The combination of panic, depersonalization, or other highly charged emotions can quickly trigger mood changes, problems organizing thoughts and processing information, as well as preventing normal word retrieval and creating a feeling that one's brain is simply not working.

In rare cases, a panic attack can last up to an hour, but most will often subside in 5 to 20 minutes. Clients reporting day-long or extended panic attacks may actually have emotional side effects such as agitation once the panic has ended, waves of panic rather than a single continuous attack, or an additional comorbid form of anxiety or other disorder such as depression (Katerndahl & Realini, 1993). As seen in Box 7.2, the main feature of panic disorder without agoraphobia is reasonably frequent, recurring, unexpected panic attacks (American Psychiatric Association, 2000). This does not mean

---

DSM-IV CRITERIA FOR PANIC DISORDER WITHOUT AGORAPHOBIA

DIAGNOSTIC CRITERIA FOR 300.01 PANIC DISORDER WITHOUT AGORAPHOBIA

A. Both (1) and (2):

1. Recurrent unexpected Panic Attacks
2. At least one of the attacks has been followed by 1 month (or more) of one (or more) of the following:
   a. Persistent concern about having additional attacks
   b. Worry about the implications of the attack or its consequences (e.g., losing control, having a heart attack, "going crazy")
   c. A significant change in behavior related to the attacks.

B. Absence of agoraphobia

C. The panic attacks are not due to the direct physiological effects of a substance (e.g., a drug of abuse, a medication) or a general medical condition (e.g., hyperthyroidism).

D. The panic attacks are not better accounted for by another mental disorder, such as social phobia (e.g., occurring on exposure to feared social situations), specific phobia (e.g., on exposure to a specific phobic situation), obsessive-compulsive disorder (e.g., on exposure to dirt in someone with an obsession about contamination), posttraumatic stress disorder (e.g., in response to stimuli associated with a severe stressor), or separation anxiety disorder (e.g., in response to being away from home or close relatives).

Source: Reprinted with permission from the Diagnostic and Statistical Manual of Mental Disorders, Fourth Edition, Text Revision *(Copyright 2000). American Psychiatric Association. (Note that internal cross-references have been removed from the reprinted text.)*

---

that a person cannot learn anticipatory fears and panic responses. If clients consistently have a panic attack when looking down from elevated places, they will start feeling anxiety from the expectation that an attack will occur. For some clients, the anticipation creates dread and automatic hypervigilance and hyperactivity that mimics the discomfort experienced during an actual panic attack (Katerndahl & Realini, 1993). This may also cause the person to believe that the panic attack is extended and not unexpected. In reality the client is suffering from fears that the attack will occur, in addition to an actual panic attack that occurs at some point.

Agoraphobia is a fear of being trapped in certain places or situations, along with a belief that escape will be emotionally costly and embarrassing (American Psychiatric Association, 2000; Himle, Fischer, et al., 2007). Typically, clients report an extreme fear focused on issues such as leaving home alone, being in a crowd, waiting in line, or being on a bridge, in an elevator, or on an escalator. Approximately twice as many women as men are found in community and clinical studies to have a panic disorder with agoraphobia (see Box 7.3) (Wittchen, Essau, et al., 1992; Katerndahl & Realini, 1993; Barlow, 2002; Himle, Fischer, et al., 2007). While agoraphobia can precede the onset of a panic attack, it more often starts after the client has had several or more panic experiences (Hollander & Simeon, 2003). The focus of the client's fear varies, but often relates to a location or event where a panic attack previously occurred. That is, the person defines a place or activity as a trigger, but the actual stimulus for the phobia is the spontaneous repeated panic occurring in similar situations. Clients learn to

---

BOX 7.3

DSM-IV CRITERIA FOR PANIC DISORDER WITH AGORAPHOBIA

DIAGNOSTIC CRITERIA FOR 300.21 PANIC DISORDER WITH AGORAPHOBIA

A. Both (1) and (2):
  1. Recurrent unexpected Panic Attacks
  2. At least one of the attacks has been followed by 1 month (or more) of one (or more) of the following:
    a. Persistent concern about having additional attacks
    b. Worry about the implications of the attack or its consequences (e.g., losing control, having a heart attack, "going crazy")
    c. A significant change in behavior related to the attacks.
B. The presence of agoraphobia
C. The panic attacks are not due to the direct physiological effects of a substance (e.g., a drug of abuse, a medication) or a general medical condition (e.g., hyperthyroidism).
D. The panic attacks are not better accounted for by another mental disorder, such as social phobia (e.g., occurring on exposure to feared social situations), specific phobia (e.g., on exposure to a specific phobic situation), obsessive-compulsive disorder (e.g., on exposure to dirt in someone with an obsession about contamination), post-traumatic stress disorder (e.g., in response to stimuli associated with a severe stressor), or separation anxiety disorder (e.g., in response to being away from home or close relatives).

Source: Reprinted with permission from the Diagnostic and Statistical Manual of Mental Disorders, Fourth Edition, Text Revision *(Copyright 2000). American Psychiatric Association. (Note that internal cross-references have been removed from the reprinted text.)*

anticipate and fear that an attack will start if they return to the self-labeled location or event (Barlow, 2002). Hollander and Simeon (2003) report that most agoraphobia fears center around the following three themes: (1) fear of leaving home, (2) fear of being alone, and (3) fear of being in a situation away from home and experiencing a feeling of being trapped, embarrassed, or helpless.

In trying to avoid the phobia-triggered terror, people often alter major work, social, and family routines. For example, they may refuse to shop and go to social events with friends, or insist on doing their grocery shopping between midnight and 5:00 AM when few people are in the stores. For some, driving to unknown places or on overly crowded freeways can become an impossible task. Clients can also associate the onset of attacks with consumption of specific products or participation in physical activities (Hyman, 2007). These clients, fearing they will initiate an attack, rigidly refrain from associated items such as caffeine, alcohol, cosmetics, scented products, or over-the-counter drugs. In some cases, even sexual activity, exercise, and other events requiring exertion are zealously avoided. Clients affected with agoraphobia are also embarrassingly aware that their fears and beliefs make no sense. Instead of knowledge providing relief, it serves to reinforce the use of avoidance strategies and to move people further into social isolation. Clients soon learn not to expose and defend beliefs, fears, and behaviors that are not logical even to themselves. Consequently, the anticipation of having to explain the unexplainable can serve both as a cue to limit social engagement and to once again cognitively practice, revisit, and reinforce one's beliefs of futuristic doom.

There currently is a debate concerning whether agoraphobia without a history of panic disorder should remain as a *DSM-IV-TR* diagnosable disorder. New epidemiology studies report that many people categorized as having agoraphobia without history of panic disorder actually had a specific phobia, rather than agoraphobia (American Psychiatric Association, 2000; Hyman, 2007). Box 7.4 provides the *DSM-IV-TR* criteria for diagnosing agoraphobia without history of panic disorder. The brief requirements primarily direct clinicians to assure that there is no history of panic disorder; that the fears do not stem from using a substance; and that phobic fears related to a medical disorder are more excessive than generally found in people with the same physical problem.

OBSESSIVE-COMPULSIVE DISORDER

Obsessive-compulsive disorder (OCD) affects clients differently from most other forms of anxiety. Even so, like the other anxiety disorders, OCD is a neurobiological disorder causing false beliefs, futuristic fears, and practiced mental or physical activities that are

BOX 7.4

DSM-IV CRITERIA FOR AGORAPHOBIA WITHOUT A HISTORY OF PANIC DISORDER

DIAGNOSTIC CRITERIA FOR 300.22 AGORAPHOBIA WITHOUT HISTORY OF PANIC DISORDER

A. The presence of agoraphobia related to fear of developing panic-like symptoms (e.g., dizziness or diarrhea).

B. Criteria have never been met for panic disorder.

C. The disturbance is not due to the direct physiological effects of a substance (e.g., a drug of abuse, a medication) or a general medical condition.

D. If an associated general medical condition is present, the fear described in Criterion A is clearly in excess of that usually associated with the condition.

Source: Reprinted with permission from the Diagnostic and Statistical Manual of Mental Disorders, Fourth Edition, Text Revision *(Copyright 2000). American Psychiatric Association. (Note that internal cross-references have been removed from the reprinted text.)*

disturbing, unrealistic, and socially embarrassing. OCD is an illness that causes recurring obsessive thoughts or compulsive behaviors that are distressful, interfere with personal obligations, or take time away from the client (American Psychiatric Association, 2000). For the client however, OCD is an overwhelming sense of being controlled and powerless to stop invading thoughts that drive unwanted and even hated behavior. Most OCD symptoms take the form of

- cognitive thoughts, images, or sounds that intermittently occur and cannot be willfully stopped;
- an overwhelming mental requirement to perform specific physical movements, rituals, or repetitive tasks; or structured unspoken mental activities such as silently and repeatedly counting or calculating;
- excessive and continuous questioning or expressions of doubt about important and unimportant issues and events.

As symptoms occur, the client feels required to perform the dictated physical or mental task, and experiences an increase in anxiety.

Unlike other forms of anxiety disorders, OCD is found equally in adult men and women (American Psychiatric Association, 2000; Sadock & Sadock, 2007). Onset of illness can be in childhood or early adulthood. Approximately 31% of the first episodes appear in youths 10–15 years of age, and the majority of adult onsets (75%) develop by age 25–30. Only about 15% of clients experience OCD onset after the age of 35 (Hollander & Simeon, 2003; Sadock & Sadock, 2007). The average age of onset is approximately 19 years for both genders (Conybeare & Behar, 2012). OCD is found in nearly every culture and nation. While the research supports a hypothesis of family genetic causation, experts, nonetheless, consider the evidence to be rather weak (Eley, Collier, et al., 2002). As with other disorders, epidemiological studies have reported different prevalence rates within the United States. This was considered to be a rare mental disorder until around the mid-1980s (First & Tasman, 2004). Today, OCD is the fourth largest mental disorder, with a 2.5% lifetime prevalence rate. OCD cases do not greatly differ among racial groups within the United States (Karno, Goldberg, et al., 1989; Barlow, 2002). At least one study, however, indicated that the illness is seen slightly less frequently in African-Americans than European-Americans (Karno, Golding, et al., 1988). This is a rather outdated finding in need of replication. It is important to remember that societal and cultural changes have the ability to reshape epidemiological findings. Consider, for example, how economics, stressors, and racism have impacted differing groups of African-Americans. From a bioecological perspective, we would not be surprised if the prevalence rate had changed.

As suggested by the disorder's name, the primary symptoms and discomfort centers around unwanted, obsessive thoughts and/or compulsive behavioral actions. Obsessions are recurrent and persistent thoughts, impulses, or images that are recognized by the client as a product of one's own mind but are experienced as intrusive and inappropriate (American Psychiatric Association, 2000). The most common obsessions include fear of contamination, repeated doubt, fears of becoming ill or having a deadly physical disorder, need for symmetry and exactness, thoughts of aggression, and sexual thoughts (Rasmussen & Eisen 1990; Van Noppen, Himle, et al., 2007).

Compulsions are repetitive behaviors or mental thoughts performed to reduce or stop anxiety. The behavior or mental activity is consistently done by a set of rigid rules or in response to an obsession. The person is literally driven to do the compulsive act in order to relieve the distress caused by obsessive thoughts, or to prevent some form of disaster or tragedy (American Psychiatric Association, 2000). There is also often, but not always, a connection between obsessions and compulsions. For example, one may obsessively think about having sinned, and compulsively develop a ritual requiring a prayer for forgiveness that must be done at a specific time, in a defined manner, and with the exact same words. Common compulsive behaviors often include various rigidly performed rituals. Washing compulsions, including hand, body, and clothes washing, for example, account for 25%–50% of compulsions treated in clinics and accounted for in epidemiological sampling (Hollander & Simeon, 2003; Sadock & Sadock, 2007). Other common compulsions include cleaning, touching, checking, repeating certain acts, hoarding, counting, requiring items to be symmetrical or in a set order, and a need to ask questions or confess (Yaryura-Tobias & Neziroglu, 1997; American Psychiatric Association, 2000; Hollander &Simeon, 2003; Sadock & Sadock, 2007). Clinicians also see compulsive verbal aggression and self-mutilation not as a result of anger, but from a need to stop the pain caused by obsessive thoughts (Yaryura-Tobias & Neziroglu, 1997).

Assessing and Diagnosing OCD

Diagnosing OCD requires assurance that the symptoms are not part of a medical or alternative psychiatric disorder, and that the *DSM-IV-TR* criteria can be documented (see Box 7.5). Numerous physical and mental conditions can cause symptoms similar to those seen in clients with OCD. It is not unusual to see obsessive thinking and

---

BOX 7.5

DSM-IV-TR CRITERIA FOR DIAGNOSING OCD

DIAGNOSTIC CRITERIA FOR 300.3 OBSESSIVE-COMPULSIVE DISORDER

A. Either obsessions or compulsions:

Obsessions as defined by (1), (2), (3), and (4):

1. Recurrent and persistent thoughts, impulses, or images that are experienced, at some time during the disturbance, as intrusive and inappropriate and that cause marked anxiety or distress;
2. The thoughts, impulses, or images are not simply excessive worries about real-life problems;
3. The person attempts to ignore or suppress such thoughts, impulses, or images, or to neutralize them with some other thought or action;
4. The person recognizes that the obsessional thoughts, impulses, or images are a product of his or her own mind (not imposed from without as in thought insertion).

Compulsions as defined by (1) and (2):

1. Repetitive behaviors (e.g., hand washing, ordering, checking) or mental acts (e.g., praying, counting, repeating words silently) that the person feels driven to perform in response to an obsession, or according to rules that must be applied rigidly;

2. The behaviors or mental acts are aimed at preventing or reducing distress or preventing some dreaded event or situation; however, these behaviors or mental acts either are not connected in a realistic way with what they are designed to neutralize or prevent or are clearly excessive.

B. At some point during the course of the disorder, the person has recognized that the obsessions or compulsions are excessive or unreasonable. **Note:** This does not apply to children.

C. The obsessions or compulsions cause marked distress, are time consuming (take more than 1 hour a day), or significantly interfere with the person's normal routine, occupational (or academic) functioning, or usual social activities or relationships.

D. If another Axis I disorder is present, the content of the obsessions or compulsions is not restricted to it (e.g., preoccupation with food in the presence of an eating disorder; hair pulling in the presence of trichotillomania; concern with appearance in the presence of body dysmorphic disorder; preoccupation with drugs in the presence of a substance use disorder; preoccupation with having a serious illness in the presence of hypochondriasis; preoccupation with sexual urges or fantasies in the presence of a paraphilia; or guilty ruminations in the presence of major depressive disorder).

E. The disturbance is not due to the direct physiological effects of a substance (e.g., a drug of abuse, a medication) or a general medical condition.

Specify if:

With poor insight: if, for most of the time during the current episode, the person does not recognize that the obsessions and compulsions are excessive or unreasonable

---

Source: Reprinted with permission from the Diagnostic and Statistical Manual of Mental Disorders, Fourth Edition, Text Revision *(Copyright 2000). American Psychiatric Association. (Note that internal cross-references have been removed from the reprinted text.)*

compulsive behaviors in clients with Parkinson's disease, schizophrenia, major depression, attention deficit disorders, and brain trauma.

As illustrated in Figure 7.4, the central focus for assessing OCD is documenting that a person has either obsessions or compulsions, or both. Additionally, the symptoms must take a significant amount of time away from the client and must be experienced as stressful. To fully meet *DSM-IV-TR* criteria, the person is also required to exhibit awareness of the obsessions or compulsions and to attempt to suppress or ignore or neutralize the recurring thoughts (American Psychiatric Association, 2000). In most

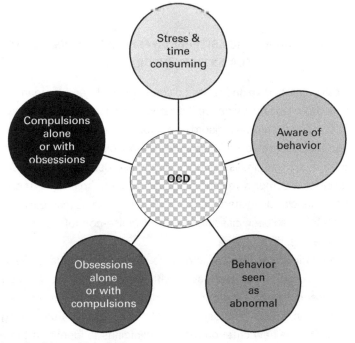

FIGURE 7.4 Keys for Diagnosing OCD.

cases, the client not only understands the link between a specific obsessive thought and compulsion, but is also aware that the compulsive behaviors are abnormal and excessive. There are, however, a minority of clients who lack insight into their personal and interpersonal actions and fail to experience their obsessions and compulsions as abnormal (Yaryura-Tobias & Neziroglu, 1997; Barlow, 2002). *DSM-5* placed OCD in a separate chapter, but as shown in Box 7.6, only minor changes were made in the overall diagnostic criteria

ACUTE AND POST-TRAUMATIC STRESS

Throughout our life, we experience periods of mild and severe stress. Our mind and bodies are shocked by deaths, economic problems, natural disasters, crime, major disappointments, betrayals, illnesses, and future uncertainties. How we identify and respond to distressing events is highly differential. What one person experiences as psychological pain may go almost unnoticed by a different individual. Fortunately, even when an event is traumatic, the brain most often finds a means to resolve the stress and return to a normal state. Otherwise people would be in a constant state of stress-related anxiety. As social workers, it is helpful to keep in mind that short-term states of stress are normal. Events such as work demands, parenting, loneliness, debt, worry, and strained

DSM-5 DIAGNOSTIC CRITERIA DIFFERING FROM *DSM-IV-TR* FOR ANXIETY DISORDERS

- Obsessive-compulsive and related disorders have been placed in a chapter separate from anxiety. Evidence indicates that obsessive-compulsive disorder; body dysmorphic disorder; hoarding disorder; trichotillomania (hair-pulling) disorder; excoriation (skin-picking) disorder; substance/medication-induced obsessive-compulsive disorder and related disorder; and obsessive-compulsive and related disorder due to another medical condition are closely related problems. Trichotillomania (hair-pulling) disorder in *DSM-IV-TR* had been classified as an "impulse-control disorder not elsewhere classified."

- Posttraumatic stress disorder and acute stress disorder have been removed from the anxiety chapter and placed with a separate chapter entitled Trauma-and-Stressor Related Disorders. Criterion A for acute stress disorder and posttraumatic stress disorder in *DSM-5* has significantly changed from *DSM-IV-TR*. The new criterion requires clinicians to identify if the traumatic events were experienced directly, witnessed, or experienced through hearing repeated or extreme details about an upsetting (traumatic) event. The ability to develop posttraumatic stress disorder indirectly (hearing repeated or extreme details of an event) significantly widens the scope of the diagnosis. *DSM-5* has also discontinued using a *DSM-IV-TR* criterion requiring clients to have had a fearful, helpless, or horrified response to the event causing stress. This was done because research indicates that reactions to traumatic events are highly unpredictable.

- *DSM-5* rejected the *DSM-IV-TR* requirement for adult clients with agoraphobia, specific phobia, and social anxiety disorders to self-identify that their anxiety symptoms are unwarranted or unreasonable.

- The *DSM-5* criteria for panic attack mirror those found in *DSM-IV-TR*.

- Panic disorder and agoraphobia are now two independent diagnoses. There no longer are the *DSM-IV-TR* diagnoses of panic disorder with agoraphobia, panic disorder without agoraphobia, and agoraphobia without history of panic disorder. There are now separate criteria for panic disorder and agoraphobia disorder. Clients experiencing both disorders will now receive two independent diagnoses.

- The criteria for social anxiety disorder are not significantly changed from those found in *DSM-IV-TR*. However, as stated above, clients do not have to have insight or a belief that their symptoms are excessive or unreasonable.

Source: The above information is paraphrased from DSM-5 and a web report (American Psychiatric Association 2013a, 2013b).

interpersonal relationships can result in extreme tiredness and stress. Even positive occasions such as promotions, births, marriage, and new-found money can create stress reactions. The distance between normal stress and trauma is extremely close for some and distant for others. Consequently, a major role for social work clinicians is helping to prevent people from moving from stress into an acute or post-traumatic stress disorder.

Every year an unknown number of people annually slip from a state of worried stress and to experience days or weeks of what *DSM-IV-TR* defines as acute stress disorder (American Psychiatric Association, 2000). While the total number of people with this disorder is unknown, a study reports that acute stress reactions are found in 13%–21% of car accident victims; 16%–19% of individuals who are physically assaulted; 16% of people experiencing a traumatic loss; 6%–12% of individuals after an industrial accident; approximately 33% of people following a mass shooting; and 7% of people who were in a typhoon (Bryant, 2004). Clearly, different types of traumatic events cause lesser or greater stress within the population.

Clients experiencing acute stress disorder display an array of symptoms that can include emotional numbing, dissociative behaviors, an inability to experience pleasure, blunted affect and decreased emotions, and feelings of guilt when trying to continue their normal life pattern. They may additionally report an inability to concentrate, and experience being detached from their bodies, or that the environment is unreal (Otto, Pollack, et al., 1999; American Psychiatric Association, 2000; Sadock & Sadock, 2007). The symptoms follow a traumatic event, cause decreased functioning, and last at least 2 days, but no more than 4 weeks. Clinicians generally diagnose symptoms lasting more than 4 weeks as post-traumatic stress disorder (PTSD). As with other anxiety disorders, before diagnosing acute stress or PTSD, one must rule out that the reported problems are not resulting from a medical condition or the use of a legal or illegal substance (American Psychiatric Association, 2000). The symptoms of acute stress disorder may appear immediately or within a month of a traumatic experience (Bryant, 2004). The specific *DSM-IV-TR* criteria for acute stress disorder are provided in Box 7.7.

Bryant (2004) states that assessing acute stress disorder is complicated because the *DSM-IV-TR* criteria are extremely similar to PTSD symptoms. Additionally, there is a lack of diagnostic clarity. *DSM-IV*, for example, globally allows a client's dissociation to take place during or after the traumatic experience (Bryant, 2004). Bryant explains that dissociation during an event may serve to prevent or limit how many of the threatening and stressful factors are experienced. Perhaps the most important clinical factor in diagnosing acute stress disorder is that it dissipates relatively quickly with little or no professional assistance and does not transition into PTSD.

BOX 7.7
DSM-IV CRITERIA FOR ACUTE STRESS DISORDER

DIAGNOSTIC CRITERIA FOR 308.3 ACUTE STRESS DISORDER

A. The person has been exposed to a traumatic event in which both of the following were present:

1. The person experienced, witnessed, or was confronted with an event or events that involved actual or threatened death or serious injury, or a threat to the physical integrity of self or others.

2. The person's response involved intense fear, helplessness, or horror.

B. Either while experiencing or after experiencing the distressing event, the individual has three (or more) of the following dissociative symptoms:

1. A subjective sense of numbing, detachment, or absence of emotional responsiveness;

2. A reduction in awareness of his or her surroundings (e.g., "being in a daze");

3. Derealization;

4. Depersonalization;

5. Dissociative amnesia (i.e., inability to recall an important aspect of the trauma).

C. The traumatic event is persistently re-experiencing in at least one of the following ways: recurrent images, thoughts, dreams, illusions, flashback episodes, or a sense of reliving the experience; or distress on exposure to reminders of the traumatic event.

D. Marked avoidance of stimuli that arouse recollections of the trauma (e.g., thoughts, feelings, conversations, activities, places, people).

E. Marked symptoms of anxiety or increased arousal (e.g., difficulty sleeping, irritability, poor concentration, hypervigilance, exaggerated startle response, motor restlessness).

F. The disturbance causes clinically significant distress or impairment in social, occupational, or other important areas of functioning or impairs the individual's ability to pursue some necessary task, such as obtaining necessary assistance or mobilizing personal resources by telling family members about the traumatic experience.

G. The disturbance lasts for a minimum of 2 days and a maximum of 4 weeks and occurs within 4 weeks of the traumatic event.

H. The disturbance is not due to the direct physiological effects of a substance (e.g., a drug of abuse, a medication) or a general medical condition, is not better accounted for by brief psychotic disorder, and is not merely an exacerbation of a preexisting Axis I or Axis II disorder.

Source: Reprinted with permission from the Diagnostic and Statistical Manual of Mental Disorders, Fourth Edition, Text Revision *(Copyright 2000). American Psychiatric Association.*

Unlike acute stress, post-traumatic stress disorder (PTSD) does not disappear in 2 to 30 days, and requires expert and extensive treatment. PTSD is found in about 8% of the population. The disorder can occur in both children and adults. Symptoms often appear within months after a traumatic event is experienced (American Psychiatric Association, 2000). However, Barlow (2002) underscores that trauma experienced years in the past can be hidden in memory and triggered by a similar or dissimilar current event. That is, old, forgotten trauma can be rekindled, moved into active memory, and relived when associated with a recent stressful incident. The person does not have to be involved in the event, nor does the terror have to parallel the individual's experience for stress symptoms to start.

Once developed, PTSD can become chronic, cause multiple types of symptoms, and last for years. Additionally, PTSD is a neurobiological illness that for unknown reasons often co-occurs along with other psychiatric disorders (Cahill & Foa, 2007). In clinics we often see PTSD combined with depression, self-harm, substance abuse, anxiety, or combinations of these disorders. PTSD occurs from experiencing, observing, or learning about one or more traumatic events, which triggers a sense of fear, helplessness, or horror. Also, diagnostically the events must be perceived as having caused or having potential for causing death or injury to one's self or others (American Psychiatric Association, 2000). While terrible events such as rape, terrorist attacks, automobile accidents, murders, and unexpected death of loved ones are triggering elements, they alone do not explain why a person develops PTSD. Exactly why some individuals involved in a crisis situation are vulnerable to the disorder while others in the same situation do not develop PTSD remains unknown. However, research indicates that as traumatic events become more severe, brutal, or life-threatening, and exposure time increases, the probability for psychological distress increases, and personal risk factors explain less of the causality (Barlow, 2002). Findings of this type help social workers better understand that extended abuse within a family, community, or country can override internal strengths and create PTSD in people who otherwise would have a natural or genetic resistance to stress and anxiety. The *DSM-IV-TR* criteria for diagnosing PTSD are provided in Box 7.8.

Immediately following a traumatic event, support, education, and case management can be helpful for acutely traumatized clients (Ursano, Bell, et al., 2006). As with all forms of anxiety disorders, a treatment plan must consider the person's age, comorbid disorders, ethnic status, and total trauma history. Several cognitive-behavioral interventions have been found helpful in working with clients who experience PTSD. However, most evidence currently points to the use of exposure therapies (Barlow, 2002; Ursano, Bell, et al., 2006). This is a cognitive-behavioral intervention that helps

BOX 7.8
DSM-IV DIAGNOSTIC CRITERIA FOR PTSD

DIAGNOSTIC CRITERIA FOR 309.81 POST-TRAUMATIC STRESS DISORDER

A. The person has been exposed to a traumatic event in which both of the following were present:
   1. The person experienced, witnessed, or was confronted with an event or events that involved actual or threatened death or serious injury, or a threat to the physical integrity of self or others.
   2. The person's response involved intense fear, helplessness, or horror. **Note:** In children, this may be expressed instead by disorganized or agitated behavior.

B. The traumatic event is persistently re-experienced in one (or more) of the following ways:
   1. Recurrent and intrusive distressing recollections of the event, including images, thoughts, or perceptions. **Note:** In young children, repetitive play may occur in which themes or aspects of the trauma are expressed.
   2. Recurrent distressing dreams of the event. **Note:** In children, there may be frightening dreams without recognizable content.
   3. Acting or feeling as if the traumatic event were recurring (includes a sense of reliving the experience, illusions, hallucinations, and dissociative flashback episodes, including those that occur on awakening or when intoxicated). **Note:** In young children, trauma-specific re-enactment may occur.
   4. Intense psychological distress at exposure to internal or external cues that symbolize or resemble an aspect of the traumatic event.
   5. Physiological reactivity on exposure to internal or external cues that symbolize or resemble an aspect of the traumatic event.

C. Persistent avoidance of stimuli associated with the trauma and numbing of general responsiveness (not present before the trauma), as indicated by three (or more) of the following:
   1. Efforts to avoid thoughts, feelings, or conversations associated with the trauma;
   2. Efforts to avoid activities, places, or people that arouse recollections of the trauma;
   3. Inability to recall an important aspect of the trauma;
   4. Markedly diminished interest or participation in significant activities;
   5. Feeling of detachment or estrangement from others;
   6. Restricted range of affect (e.g., unable to have loving feelings);
   7. Sense of a foreshortened future (e.g., does not expect to have a career, marriage, children, or a normal life span).

D. Persistent symptoms of increased arousal (not present before the trauma),
as indicated by two (or more) of the following:
1. Difficulty falling or staying asleep;
2. Irritability or outbursts of anger;
3. Difficulty concentrating;
4. Hypervigilance;
5. Exaggerated startle response.
E. Duration of the disturbance (symptoms in Criteria B, C, and D) is more than
1 month.
F. The disturbance causes clinically significant distress or impairment in social,
occupational, or other important areas of functioning.

Specify if:

Acute: if duration of symptoms is less than 3 months

Chronic: if duration of symptoms is 3 months or more

Specify if:

With delayed onset: if onset of symptoms is at least 6 months after the stressor

---

Source: Reprinted with permission from the Diagnostic and Statistical Manual of Mental
Disorders, Fourth Edition, Text Revision *(Copyright 2000). American Psychiatric Association.*

clients identify environmental triggers and reduces their fear of places, things, actions, smells, sounds, and so on, that trigger memories of the traumatic event. However, other cognitive therapies, such as eye movement desensitization and reprocessing (EMDR), have also demonstrated efficacy with PTSD (Ursano, Bell, et al., 2006). In general, all support, education, and psychotherapy are aimed at helping the person recall the trauma without having a negative emotional and anxious reaction. We do not want the person to forget the event, but rather to be able to recall the traumatic circumstances with little or no symptoms of anxiety or depression.

GENERALIZED ANXIETY DISORDER

We all have worries about the future. However, people with generalized anxiety disorder find it difficult to stop feeling frightened and concerned about everyday life events. These individuals worry excessively, on an almost daily basis, about routine work, family, financial, health, and other issues. Some clients focus on multiple perceived distresses, while others limit their fear obsessively to a single concern. The disorder is more frequently seen in women, and is often reported to have started in childhood (American Psychiatric Association, 2000). However, as pointed out by the *DSM-IV-TR* (2000), it is not unusual for the first symptoms to appear between 20 and 30 years of age. Additionally, like other forms of anxiety, this disorder is often found in clients suffering with other diagnosable psychiatric problems, such as depression, other anxiety disorders, or substance abuse or addiction (American Psychiatric Association, 2000; Cassano, Rossi, et al., 2003). There is even some evidence that generalized anxiety disorder may be the foundation or trigger for the formation of other disorders (Barlow, 2002).

Diagnostically it is important to clarify that the client has feelings of apprehension nearly every day, cannot control the worrisome thoughts, and has experienced symptoms for at least 6 months. Children and teenagers often demonstrate perfectionist symptoms. That is, they excessively focus on personal mistakes, self-imperfections, and general concerns of either not being "perfect," good enough, or as good as peers (Flannery-Schroeder, 2004). The specific *DSM-IV* criteria for the disorder are provided in Box 7.9.

Because generalized anxiety disorder most often occurs periodically throughout the day and in response to multiple stimuli and situations, a single therapeutic method

---

BOX 7.9

DSM CRITERIA FOR GENERALIZED ANXIETY DISORDER

DIAGNOSTIC CRITERIA FOR 300.02 GENERALIZED ANXIETY DISORDER

A. Excessive anxiety and worry (apprehensive expectation), occurring more days than not for at least 6 months, about a number of events or activities (such as work or school performance).

B. The person finds it difficult to control the worry.

C. The anxiety and worry are associated with three (or more) of the following six symptoms (with at least some symptoms present for more days than not for the past 6 months). **Note:** Only one item is required in children.

1. Restlessness or feeling keyed up or on edge;
2. Being easily fatigued;
3. Difficulty concentrating or mind going blank;
4. Irritability;
5. Muscle tension;
6. Sleep disturbance (difficulty falling or staying asleep, or restless unsatisfying sleep).

D. The focus of the anxiety and worry is not confined to features of an Axis I disorder, e.g., the anxiety or worry is not about having a panic attack (as in panic disorder), being embarrassed in public (as in social phobia), being contaminated (as in obsessive-compulsive disorder), being away from home or close relatives (as in separation anxiety disorder), gaining weight (as in anorexia nervosa), having multiple physical complaints (as in somatization disorder), or having a serious illness (as in hypochondriasis), and the anxiety and worry do not occur exclusively during post-traumatic stress disorder.

E. The anxiety, worry, or physical symptoms cause clinically significant distress or impairment in social, occupational, or other important areas of functioning.

F. The disturbance is not due to the direct physiological effects of a substance (e.g., a drugs of abuse, a medication) or a general medical condition (e.g., hyperthyroidism) and does not occur exclusively during a mood disorder, a psychotic disorder, or a pervasive developmental disorder.

Source: Reprinted with permission from the Diagnostic and Statistical Manual of Mental Disorders, Fourth Edition, Text Revision *(Copyright 2000). American Psychiatric Association.*

used in isolation may not benefit a client. Wehrenberg and Prinz (2007) recommend developing a treatment plan with the client that addresses the person's physiological stress, behavior, and cognition. There is obviously no single combination of interventions that fits every client. However, treatment planning for this disorder often includes psychosocial education, systematic relaxation training, self-hypnosis induction, thought stopping, cognitive reframing, breathing exercises, imaging and role rehearsal, and exposure therapy (Cambell-Sills & Stein, 2006; Wehrenberg & Prinz, 2007). Additionally, social workers may need to help educate family members and work associates about the disorder. It is also extremely helpful if the person can have private space at work or school to perform breathing and relaxation exercises immediately when anxiety symptoms first start to increase. While this may create a mild burden for the employer or school, it may also reduce absenteeism and increase the person's work quality. When ecologically treating generalized anxiety or other disorders, a social worker must assess and understand how the illness impacts the client and the systems and people around the client. In a very real sense, the client, surrounding systems, and people involved with the client must be supported and helped to adequately understand and address the psychiatric symptoms.

REFERENCES

Amen, D. G., & Routh, L. C. (2003). *Healing Anxiety and Depression*. New York: Berkley Books.
American Psychiatric Association. (2000). *Diagnostic and Statistical Manual of Mental Disorders* (4th ed.). Washington, DC: American Psychiatric Association.

American Psychiatric Association. (2013a). *Diagnostic and Statistical Manual of Mental Disorders* (5th ed.). Arlington, VA: American Psychiatric Association.

American Psychiatric Association. (2013b). *Highlights of changes from DSM-IV-TR to DSM-5*. Retrieved August 2013 from http://www.dsm5.org/Documents/changes%20from%20dsm-iv-tr%20to%20dsm-5.pdf.

Antony, M. M., & Rowa, K. (2005). Evidence-based assessment of anxiety disorders in adults. *Psychological Assessment, 17*(3): 256–266.

Ayd, F. J. J. (1995). *Lexicon of Psychiatric, Neurology, and the Neurosciences*. Baltimore, MD: Williams & Wilkins.

Barlow, D. H. (2002). *Anxiety and Its Disorders*. New York: The Guilford Press.

Bryant, R. A. (2004). Assessing Acute Stress Disorder. In J. P. Wilson & T. M. Keane (Eds.), *Assessing Psychological Trauma and PTSD* (pp. 45–60). New York: The Guilford Press.

Cahill, S. P., & Foa, E. B. (2007). Psychological theories of PTSD. In M. J. Friedman, T. M. Keane, & P. A. Resick (Eds.), *Handbook of PTSD Science and Practice* (pp. 55–77). New York: The Guilford Press.

Cambell-Sills, L., & Stein, M. B. (2006). Guideline watch: Practice guideline for the treatment of patients with panic disorder. In J. S. McIntyre & S. C. Charles (Eds.), *American Psychiatric Association Practice Guidelines for the Treatment of Psychiatric Disorders* (pp. 933–1003). Arlington, VA: American Psychiatric Association.

Carey, G., & Gottesman, I. I. (1981). Twin and family studies of anxiety, phobic, and obsessive disorders. In D. F. Klein & J. Rabkin (Eds.), *Anxiety: New Research and Changing Concepts* (pp. 117–136). New York: Raven.

Cassano, G. B., Rossi, N. B., et al. (2003). Comorbidity of depression and anxiety. In S. Kasper, J. A. Den Boer, & J. M. Ad Sitsen (Eds.), *Handbook of Depression and Anxiety* (pp. 69–90). New York: Marcel Dekker.

Charney, D. S. (2004). Anxiety disorders. In D. S. Charney & E. J. Nestler (Eds.), *Neurobiology of Mental Illness* (pp. 523–524). New York: Oxford University Press.

Charney, D. S., & Bremner, D. (2004). The neurobiology of anxiety disorders. In D. S. Charney & E. J. Nestler (Eds.), *Neurobiology of Mental Illness* (pp. 605–627). New York: Oxford University Press.

Conybeare, D., & Behar, E. (2012). Generalized anxiety disorder, posttraumatic stress disorder, and obsessive-compulsive disorder. In M. Hersen & D. C. Beidel (Eds.), *Adult Psychopathology and Diagnosis* (pp. 433–470). Hoboken, NJ: John Wiley & Sons.

Crowe, R. R. (2004). Molecular genetics of anxiety. In D. S. Charney & E. J. Nestler (Eds.), *Neurobiology of Mental Illness* (pp. 535–545). New York: Oxford University Press.

Dozois, D. J. A., & Westra, H. A. (2004). The nature of anxiety and depression: Implications for prevention. In D. J. A. Dozois & K. S. Dobson (Eds.), *The Prevention of Anxiety and Depression Theory, Research, and Practice* (pp. 9–41). Washington, DC: American Psychological Association.

Eley, T., Collier, D., et al. (2002). Anxiety and eating disorders. In P. McGuffin, M. J. Owen, & I. I. Gottesman (Eds.), *Psychiatric Genetics and Genomics* (pp. 303–340). New York: Oxford University Press.

First, M. B., & Tasman, A. (2004). *DSM-IV Mental Disorders Diagnosis, Etiology and Treatment*. Hoboken, NJ: John Wiley & Sons.

Flannery-Schroeder, E. C. (2004). Generalized anxiety disorder. In T. L. Morris & J. S. March (Eds.), *Anxiety Disorders in Children and Adolescents* (pp. 125–140). New York: The Guilford Press.

Himle, J. A., Fischer, D. J., et al. (2007). Panic disorder and agoraphobia. In B. A. Thyer & J. S. Wodarski (Eds.), *Social Work in Mental Health: An Evidence-Based Approach* (pp. 331–349). Hoboken, NJ: John Wiley & Sons.

Hollander, E., & Simeon, D. (2003). Anxiety disorders. In R. E. Hales & S. C. Yudofsky (Eds.), *The American Psychiatric Publishing Textbook of Clinical Psychiatry* (pp. 543–630). Washington, DC: American Psychiatric Publishing.

Hyman, B. M. (2007). Agoraphobia without history of panic disorder. In B. A. Thyer & J. S. Wodarski (Eds.), *Social Work in Mental Health: An Evidence-Based Approach* (pp. 351–375). Hoboken, NJ: John Wiley & Sons.

Kagan, J. (1997). Temperament and the reaction to unfamiliarity. *Child Development, 68*, 139–143.

Kagan, J., & Snidman, N. (1999). Early childhood predictors of adult anxiety disorders. *Biological Psychiatry, 46*, 1536–1541.

Karno, M., Goldberg, J. M., et al. (1989). Anxiety disorders among Mexican Americans and non-Hispanic whites in Los Angeles. *Journal of Nervous and Mental Disease, 177*, 202–209.

Karno, M., Golding, J. M., et al. (1988). The epidemiology of obsessive-compulsive disorder in five U.S. communities. *Archives of General Psychiatry, 45*, 1094–1099.

Katerndahl, D. A., & Realini, J. P. (1993). Lifetime prevalence of panic states. *American Journal of Psychiatry, 150*, 246–249.

Kent, J. M., & Rauch, S. L. (2004). Neuroimaging studies of anxiety disorders. In D. S. Charney & E. J. Nestler (Eds.), *Neurobiology of Mental Illness* (pp. 639–660). New York: Oxford University Press.

Kessler, R. C., McGonalgle, K. A., et al. (1999). Lifetime and 12 month prevalence of DSM-III-R psychiatric disorders in the United States. *Archives of General Psychiatry, 51*, 8–19.

Knowles, J. (2003). Genetics. In R. E. Hales & S. C. Yudofsky (Eds.), The American Psychiatric Publishing Textbook of Clinical Psychiatry (pp. 3–63). Washington, DC: American Psychiatric Publishing.

Macefield, G., & Burke, D. (1991). Paraesthesiae and tetany induced by voluntary hyperventilation increased excitability of human cutaneous and motor axons. *Brain, 114*(1), 527–540.

McGuire, P. K., Bench, C. J., et al. (1994). Functional anatomy of obsessive-compulsive phenomena. *British Journal of Psychiatry, 164*(4), 459–468.

Narrow, W. E., Rae, D. S., et al. (2002). Revised prevalence estimates of mental disorders in the United States using a clinical significance criterion to reconcile 2 surveys' estimates. *Archives of General Psychiatry, 59*(2), 115–123.

Norman, T., Burrows, G. D., et al. (2003). Theories of the etiology of anxiety. In S. Kasper, J. A. den Boer, & J. M. Ad Sitsen (Eds.), *Handbook of Depression and Anxiety* (pp. 657–679). New York: Marcel Dekker.

Otto, M. W., Pollack, M. H., et al. (1999). Anxiety disorders and their treatment. In A. M. Nicholi Jr. (Ed.), *The Harvard Guide To Psychiatry* (pp. 220–239). Cambridge, MA: The Belknap Press of Harvard University Press.

Public Health Agency Canada. (2002). *A Report on Mental Illnesses in Canada*. Ottawa: Health Canada.

Rasmussen, S., & Eisen, J. (1990). Epidemiology and clinical features of obsessive compulsive disorder. In M. A. Jenike, L. Baer, & W. E. Minichiello (Eds.), *Obsessive Compulsive Disorders: Theory and Management* (pp. 10–27). Chicago: Year Book Medical.

Regehr, C., & Glancy, G. (2010). *Mental Health Social Work Practice in Canada*. New York: Oxford University Press.

Regier, D. A., Myers, J. K., et al. (1984). The NIMH Epidemiologic Catchment Area Program: Historical context, major objectives, and study population characteristics. *Archives of General Psychiatry, 41*(10), 934–941.

Sadock, B. J., & Sadock, V. A. (2007). *Synopsis of Psychiatry*. Philadelphia: Wolters Kluwer/Lippincott Williams & Wilkins.

Spielberger, C. D., Gorsuch, R. L., et al. (1983). *Manual for the State-Trait Anxiety Inventory (Form Y Self-Evaluation Questionnaire)*. Palo Alto, CA: Consulting Psychologists Press.

Swedo, S. E., & Snider, L. A. (2004). The neurobiology and treatment of obsessive-compulsive disorder. In D. S. Charney & E. J. Nestler (Eds.), *Neurobiology of Mental Illness* (pp. 628–638). New York: Oxford University Press.

Taylor, E. H. (2002). Manic-depressive illness. In V. S. Ramachandran (Ed.), *Encyclopedia of the Human Brain* (Vol. 2, pp. 745–757). San Diego, CA: Academic Press.

True, W. R., Rice, J., et al. (1993). A twin study of genetic and environmental contributions to liability for posttraumatic stress symptoms. *Archives of General Psychiatry, 50*(4), 257–264.

US Department of Health and Human Services. (1999). *Mental Health: A Report of the Surgeon General*. Rockville, MD: US Department of Health and Human Services, Substance Abuse and Mental Health Services Administration, Center for Mental Health Services, National Institutes of Health, National Institute of Mental Health.

Ursano, R. J., Bell, C., et al. (2006). Practice guideline for the treatment of patients with acute stress disorder and posttraumatic stress disorder. In J. S. McIntyre & S. C. Charles (Eds.), *American Psychiatric Association Practice Guidelines for the Treatment of Psychiatric Disorders* (pp. 1003–1095). Arlington, VA: American Psychiatric Association.

Van Noppen, B., Himle, J. A., et al. (2007). Obsessive-compulsive disorder. In B. A. Thyer & J. S. Wodarski (Eds.), *Social Work in Mental Health: An Evidence-Based Approach* (pp. 377–400). Hoboken, NJ: John Wiley & Sons.

Walkup, J. T., Leckman, J. E., et al. (1988). The relationship between obsessive-compulsive disorder and Tourette's syndrome: A twin study. *Psychopharmacology Bulletin, 24*(3), 375–379.

Wehrenberg, M., & Prinz, S. M. (2007). *The Anxious Brain.* New York: W. W. Norton.

Wittchen, H. U., Essau, C. A., et al. (1992). Lifetime and six-month prevalence of mental disorders in the Munich follow-up study. *European Archives of Psychiatry and Clinical Neuroscience, 241,* 247–258.

Yaryura-Tobias, J., & Neziroglu, F. (1997). *Obsessive-Compulsive Spectrum Disorder.* New York: W. W. Norton.

/// 8 /// PERSONALITY DISORDERS

HISTORICAL PERSPECTIVE

Interest in subtyping personality goes back at least to Hippocrates. The early Greeks related personality to four humors or body fluids. It was thought that blood imbalances explained the development of highly optimistic extraverted people, while black bile accounted for the development of a serious-minded, pessimistic, or sad nature. Yellow bile related to a life lived in an upset or hostile-irritable state, and lymph, the clear liquid in tissue, when out of balance resulted in apathy or an unemotional personality (First & Tasman, 2004; Hopwood & Thomas, 2012; Oldham, 2005; Oldham, Skodol, & Bender, 2005; Woo & Keatinge, 2008).

The idea of personality traits dates back to at least Aristotle, who taught that internal dispositions determine moral and immoral behaviors (Livesley, 2001; Seager, 2007; van der Eijk, 2005). His dispositions, or personality characteristics, included vanity, modesty, and cowardice. Aristotle's student Theophrastus described 30 "characters" or personality types/traits (Saucier, 2003; van der Eijk, 2005). Starting with Aristotle and continuing today, many theorists, researchers, and the popular press conceptualize personality as consisting of (Cervone & Pervin, 2008; Cloninger, 2004; Livesley, 2001)

- good and bad traits of character that can be isolated and studied;
- traits that are stable over time;
- traits that directly influence behavior and cognition;
- traits that allow prediction of behavior and cognition;
- traits that explain behavior;
- traits that describe behavior and cognition.

Beginning with the work of Sigmund Freud, Western theoretical concepts for assessing personality disorders have largely evolved from psychoanalytic, trait, learning, social-cultural, and behavioral theories. Interestingly, much of the *DSM* personality disorders are founded more on historical psychodynamic frameworks than on cultural or social-psychological theories. Therefore, a brief overview of selected psychoanalytic personality models is provided. Each of the theories is far more complex than presented. Additionally, while the personality conceptualizations are rejected for lack of empirical evidence, it must be noted that each pioneered pathways for thinking about personality. Over many years, the psychoanalytic community also developed numerous assessment and treatment protocols. Since there is no single unified psychodynamic theory, and psychoanalytic thought varies, there are numerous psychoanalytic personality theories. Though they all share a common belief that the unconscious is the foundation of most personality development, the definition of "unconscious" varies according to each theorist. However, they generally share a belief that the unconscious is dynamic, has hidden memories that create conflicts and fears, and is formed if not in infancy, then early in life.

Freud conceptualized the unconscious as generating sexual and aggressive motivations that are neither understood nor wanted by the conscious mind (Brenner, 1957; Freud, 1995). Carl Jung developed a much broader model, casting the unconscious as an overall universal source of motivation that included common behaviors and spirituality. He founded the concept of the collective unconsciousness, and theorized that infants are born with an unconscious inherited knowledge (Jung, 2001). This specialized part of the mind has universal archetypes or models of key personality and behavioral expectations. The unconscious universal archetypes of mother and father therefore guide parent-child relationships (Jung, 2001). Adler was perhaps the first psychoanalytically trained theorist to move away from the conflict model of personality formation. He prescribed that the conscious and unconscious work together, creating a unified state. In a global sense, personality for Adler rises from how an individual perceives, describes, and thinks of oneself (Abnsbacher & Abnsbacher, 1956). The psychology of Melanie Klein connected unconscious conflicts to primitive or undeveloped ideas of the "self," in relationship to others. The mother, as the first object, or other, in an infant's life was, for Klein, a primary source of unconscious development (Grosskurth, 1986; Klein, 1984). Her conceptualization of unconscious conflict starting in infancy led to what later became known as Kleinian play therapy (Grosskurth, 1986). The problem with these theories is that they were developed from limited case observations, discussions, and reasoning, rather than evidence-based research. They may on some level inform normal development, but offer little to the understanding and treatment of personality disorders.

In the late 1960s, a group of theorists challenged whether personality, as a long-term, concrete component of human development and behavior, existed. For these academics and researchers, personality was viewed as situational and related to the shifting context of environmental forces. In other words, people did not have a more or less stable personality (Mischel, 1968; Widiger, 2012). This is a good example of theories that overly focus on a single element, such as environment, without consideration of interacting factors. Today, most researchers agree that personality is an internal characteristic that is subject to situational pressures, but that nonetheless establishes a consistent tone for how an individual will perceive and react to events. Furthermore, there is little argument that personality is a developmental process resulting from cultural and environmental influences, ecological systems structures, personal experiences, genetics, and physical and mental health interactions (Widiger, 2012).

Identifying which innate and ecological factors drive a person's personality and behavior is difficult. Researchers have yet to find practical ways for clinicians to separate inherited from environmental behavioral forces. From an observational perspective, most human actions appear to have combinations of personal and environmental elements. Even one's social position and power within a setting most often reflect both innate and ecological indicators. We most often think of the internal and external influences interacting and working together. This certainly is one of the themes in this book. However, when considering personality, neurobiological mental disorders, and behavior, it is helpful to remember that this model does not always apply. Situational and biological factors can both simultaneously exist, yet the way in which an observed behavior is shaped by one of these elements may have no relationship to how the same behavior is affected by the other variable (Wagerman & Funder, 2009). The coexistence of factors may not explain the person's behavior. This is one reason that accurately understanding a person's personality or state of mental health is so complex and difficult.

Personality theory today is mostly researched from what has become known as the five factor model (FFM), or the "big five" (Skodol, 2012). This is a trait model that attempts to identify key characteristics that form the underpinning for the expression of personality. Historically, theorists have thought that common behavioral, cognitive, temperament, and self-lifestyle elements existed across cultures and nations. Gordon Allport and Raymond Cattell established foundational trait models that continue to inform theorists. The FFM reflects Cattell's idea that, through statistical factor analysis, one can identify core universal personality factors. An important difference between FFM from psychoanalytic personality theories is that no attempt is made to explain what causes personality development (McCrae & Costa, 1987; Rolland, 2002; Skodol, 2012). FFM research and assessments are designed only to describe personality characteristics. Therefore, one cannot address causation with this model. The model is widely used for researching personality, but just recently has evolved into an assessment framework for diagnosing personality disorders.

There have been various synonyms used for the characteristics, or five factors, repeatedly found to broadly define personality. The most often used and agreed-upon terms thought to make up personality's core are (1) extraversion, (2) agreeableness, (3) neuroticism, (4) openness, and (5) conscientiousness (Skodol, 2012). Each of the factors are expressed and measured in bipolarity extremes. People are assumed to fall on a continuum from high to low for each of the five factors. Extraversion can range from extreme extraversion (dominance) to a low of introversion (submissiveness) (John, 1990). A unique feature of the FFM is that a high or low score can indicate personality strengths and deficits for both high and low scores. The five factors are not interpreted as a positive or negative (Reynolds & Clark, 2001). Agreeableness is helpful for gaining cooperation in a work committee, yet it can become a deficit in a social situation requiring critical analysis and concrete objective feedback. A social worker, for example, may appreciate supervisors who provide friendly feedback and are very friendly. The social worker's client may end up wishing that the supervisors had offered challenging and critical oversight. Within each of these five factors are six facets or sub-traits. The facets provide added appraisal dimensions that are assessed independently or as part of the larger factor that they accompany (RMcCrae & John, 1992; Reynolds & Clark, 2001; Skodol, 2012). Assertiveness as an extraversion facet, for example, could be either positive or negative, depending on the amount, consistency, and context in which it is expressed. The factors and facets create similarities across populations and individual uniqueness within cultures.

Evolution, genetic selection, and social learning most likely play major roles in how personalities develop universally, yet can be expressed in countless personal manners (Dall, Houston, & McNamara, 2004). From an ecological-evolutionary perspective, individuals and society must learn when assertive or aggressive behavior versus disengagement and non-confrontational behaviors have a higher probability for succeeding. Macro and micro systems establish rules that dictate whether flexibility or rigidity, group identity or individualism, is best for one's welfare (Dall et al., 2004). Additionally, the environment molds much of our interactions and reciprocity actions. These repeated behaviors, as we develop, become automatic cognition and personality traits (Haight & Taylor, 2013). Furthermore, ecological factors dynamically interact with neurodevelopment, inherited dispositions, and learned or genetically predisposed psychological factors (Cloninger, 2009; DeYoung & Gray, 2009; Dall et al., 2004).

Studies have consistently found that the big five factors generally cross-culturally identify personality structures (McCrae & Costa, 1987; Rolland, 2002; Saulsman &

Page, 2004). There has additionally been validation for using the model with mental disorders; however, the majority of psychometric studies have been on basic personality rather than illnesses (Lynam & Widiger, 2001; Saulsman & Page, 2004). The FFM appears hopeful as a tool for better understanding personality characteristics and disorders. As with any framework for understanding people, the model has limitations. Two issues important for social work clinicians is that the FFM can only address functioning associated with traits, and the model pays little attention to social context and human conditions (McAdams, 1992).

AN OVERVIEW OF *DSM* PERSONALITY DISORDERS

DSM-IV and *DSM-5* define personality disorders as a pattern of stable or persistent internal experiences and observable behaviors that diverge from a person's culture, and partially begin in adolescence or late childhood. To qualify as a disorder, the internal abnormalities and behavior must also endure over time, lack flexibility across a number of settings, and create distress or difficulties in relationships, work, school, or other areas of functioning. The specific *DSM-IV-TR* criteria for problems to qualify as a personality disorder are provided in Box 8.1.

The *DSM* somewhat arbitrarily divides personality disorders into three groups or clusters. The only requirement for cluster membership is to broadly have similarities in how each disorder is described (American Psychiatric Association, 2000). The cluster system sounds logical and helpful. Cluster A consist of paranoid, schizoid, and schizotypal personality disorders, while Cluster B contains antisocial, borderline, histrionic, and narcissistic disorders. Cluster C is made-up of avoidant, dependent, and obsessive-compulsive personality disorders (American Psychiatric Association, 2000). From an empirical perspective, however, the highest overlap of similarities is not found within the same cluster (Blashfield & McElroy, 1995; Grant, Stinson, Dawson, Chou, & Ruan, 2005; Reich, Yates, & Nduaguba, 1989; Torgersen et al., 2008). Additionally, knowing which cluster a disorder falls into does not help the clinician diagnose or select treatments for a client.

WHAT CAUSES PERSONALITY DISORDERS

Based on *DSM* standards, it is estimated that 10%–15% of Americans meet the criteria for one or more personality disorders (First & Tasman, 2004; Woo & Keatinge, 2008). However, estimating the actual number of people with personality disorders in a general population is difficult. Often the studies are not randomized, and may suffer from

> ### BOX 8.1
>
> ### GENERAL *DSM-IV-TR* DIAGNOSTIC CRITERIA FOR A PERSONALITY DISORDER
>
> A. An enduring pattern of inner experience and behavior that deviates markedly from the expectations of the individual's culture. This pattern is manifested in two (or more) of the following areas:
>   1. Cognition (i.e., ways of perceiving and interpreting self, other people, and events);
>   2. Affectivity (i.e., the range, intensity, lability, and appropriateness of emotional response);
>   3. Interpersonal functioning;
>   4. Impulse control.
> B. The enduring pattern is inflexible and pervasive across a broad range of personal and social situations.
> C. The enduring pattern leads to clinically significant distress or impairment in social, occupational, or other important areas of functioning.
> D. The pattern is stable and of long duration, and its onset can be traced back at least to adolescence or early adulthood.
> E. The enduring pattern is not better accounted for as a manifestation or consequence of another mental disorder.
> F. The enduring pattern is not due to the direct physiological effects of a substance (e.g., a drug of abuse, a medication) or a general medical condition (e.g., head trauma).
>
> ---
>
> *Source: Reprinted with permission from the* Diagnostic and Statistical Manual of Mental Disorders, Fourth Edition, Text Revision *(Copyright 2000). American Psychiatric Association.*

research selection bias. Moreover, individuals with personality disorders are known not to seek treatment (Woo & Keatinge, 2008). Therefore, most epidemiological studies focusing on personality disorders are at best limited estimations.

A review of epidemiological studies reported by Woo and Keatinge (2008) found that the 10 *DSM* personality disorders are most often found in poorly educated urban citizens who live alone and routinely face social and occupational difficulties. Findings of this type, however, invite the consideration of numerous alternative hypotheses. One can ask, for example, whether the researchers are measuring environmental impact, subcultures and social learning, depression and anxiety, unique personalities and habits, or actual *DSM* personality disorders? As one would expect, considering the lack of agreement among theories, the continuing search for universal traits, and the *DSM*'s classification difficulties, the causation of personality disorders remains largely unknown.

There is growing agreement that if personality problems are in fact illnesses separate from other disorders, they stem from interactions among multiple genetic and environmental factors (Paris, 2005). However, as Paris (2005) points out, there has been only minor success in identifying genes that relate to personality traits. Furthermore, considering environmental variables along with genetic findings does not provide an overly robust causation explanation. Half of the variance or difference among traits is explained by environment. However, the ecological influence almost always comes from unshared environmental factors (Crabbe, 2003; Paris, 2005; Plomin & Bergeman, 1991). In other words, living in a certain family environment does not strongly predict personality traits (Paris, 2005). This may, in part, explain why culture and social circumstances set the context for development, and provide interactional factors, but do not directly shape a person's mind or personality (Millon & Grossman, 2005). No one factor such as biology, psychology, social context, or life experience is responsible for causing disorders related to personality (Paris, 2012). Nonetheless, twin, family, and adoption research repeatedly finds a genetic component for both personality and personality disorders (Roussos & Siever, 2012).

Attachment problems during early life are also often cited as a possible cause for personality disorders. However, when examined closely, attachment, like other factors, does not clearly explain any of the disorders. This is largely because there are most often variables that cannot be accounted for in retrospective studies. Separating existing symptoms and adult personality traits from findings on attachment measurements becomes an impossible task (Fonagy & Bateman, 2005). We also know, for example, that anxious attachment is found in a majority of working-class non-clinical samples. Additionally, anxious attachment in infancy does not appear to disrupt or prevent adult relationships (Fonagy & Bateman, 2005). Furthermore, studies of maltreatment seldom indicate robust personality effects (Fonagy & Bateman, 2005). This is not to minimize the role of attachment, abuse, or traumatic events in development, but rather to underscore that simple one-dimensional models fail to fully explain personality disorders. Additionally, attachment problems for some youths may originate less in relation to parental actions and more from developing neurobiological problems, distorted social-perceptions, and behavioral management difficulties. Early symptoms signaling that a major mental disorder is forming can appear as poor attachment responses. In addition, social workers are reminded that studies are mixed concerning the role of attachment in causing personality disorders. The child's temperament, rather than attachment, has also been identified as a major factor for explaining borderline symptoms (Woo & Keatinge, 2008). There is, however, research supporting the hypothesis that personal experiences during childhood and adolescence play a role in personality development (J. G. Johnson, Bromley, & McGeoch, 2005).

Child physical, sexual, and emotional abuse, as well as neglect, does correlate with the development of adult personality disorders. After viewing the literature, Johnson, Bromley, and McGeoch (2005) hypothesized that youths are at an increased risk for personality disorders if they are subject to any of these experiences. What the literature has not clarified is whether abuse and neglect independently disrupt personality, or play a role in illness onset by triggering gene switches, or interacting with genetic and developing brain structures. Regardless, social workers cannot automatically assume that abuse and family trauma are the root or a primary interacting component of their client's borderline personality disorder. Evidence suggests that genetics, neurobiology, and abuse or other traumatic events have the possibility of causing or becoming interacting factors for triggering that disorder (American Psychiatric Association, 2006; Woo & Keatinge, 2008).

Neurobiological evidence for personality disorders is less robust than that found in other forms of mental disorders, and most often is focused on borderline personality disorder. Even within the more vigorous studies, however, the findings often overlap with abnormalities seen in other *DSM*-Axis I disorders. In clients who have borderline personality disorder, both structural and functional irregularities have been discovered in the amygdala, hippocampus, and prefrontal cortex (DeYoung & Gray, 2009; Paris, 2012; Teicher, Ito, Glod, Schiffer, & Gelbard, 1994; Teicher, Glod, Surrey, & Swett, 1993). As noted elsewhere in this book, these areas also show changes in clients with depression, mania, anxiety, and schizophrenia.

There are, however, clues as to why this disorder causes extreme behavioral and emotional fluctuations. Imaging, for example, indicates that the prefrontal cortex and limbic system of individuals with borderline personality disorder may contain fewer serotonin neurotransmitters (American Psychiatric Association, 2006; P. A. Johnson, Hurley, Benkelfat, Herpertz, & Taber, 2003). Unfortunately, there are far fewer imaging studies of *DSM* personality disorders, including borderline personality disorder, than found for other mental illnesses. Furthermore, the neurobiological studies that are published generally have small samples, and their findings often are either inconclusive or have weak statistical power (American Psychiatric Association, 2006). Nonetheless, as interest in understanding personality disorders from an bioecological perspective grows, it is predictable that brain imaging and environmental functioning studies will increase. This is especially true for those personality mental illnesses that are suspected to be part of a *DSM* Axis I spectrum disorder.

THE PROBLEM WITH *DSM* PERSONALITY DISORDERS

Personality as part of human nature is completely accepted throughout this textbook. However, the validity of *DSM* personality disorders representing separate illnesses stemming from irregularities in personality is less clear and convincing. This is because *DSM* personality disorders have not been developed from personality research. They have come from clinician treatment experience and psychiatric studies of clinical populations. None of the disorders historically is founded in basic scientific research or general personality structures (Widiger, 2005). Moreover, these personality disorders fail to distinguish normal personality from maladaptive personality functioning, do not adequately specify problematic personality functioning, and share many common symptoms with other mental disorders. Additionally, how these disorders impact individuals is often highly diversified within the same personality disorder (Widiger, 2005).

There are at least three competing hypotheses for explaining personality deviations and symptoms. It can be argued that most *DSM* personality disorders (1) are basically correct as currently stated and need only minor changes; (2) are more related to other spectrum disorders than personality; or (3) are not mental disorders but rather issues of well-being. Clinical observations certainly document the logic and indicators for *DSM* personality-defined disorders. Clinical reasoning and observed symptoms that fit a set of criteria, however, do not document causation or diagnostic accuracy. Interestingly, from the start of the *DSM* series, personality disorders have been defined and criteria formulated more on clinical judgment and bias than empirical findings. *DSM-I* and *DSM-II* personality disorders were largely based on psychoanalytic theory and concepts (Spitzer, Williams, & Skodol, 1980; Widiger, 2012). This set the stage for psychodynamic language and thought to continue through each revision. One could argue that psychoanalytic theory has been acculturated into the concepts of personality disorders.

This bias toward a psychodynamic perspective has continued, despite the *DSM-III* and *DSM-IV*'s attempts to be far more theoretically neutral. As the *DSM-III* was prepared and published, there were voices that raised concern about the lack of empirical support for the personality disorders (Widiger, 2012). Because there was little or no research to support decisions on which personality disorders to include in *DSM-III*, the selections were primarily based on the agreement of expert clinical panels (Gunderson, 1983). The development of *DSM-IV* was more rigorous and included intricately monitored and planned literature reviews and some field testing. Among other things, the writers had to document where there were differing points of view, and were not permitted to simply provide references supporting personal points of view (Widiger,

2012). Field trials were designed to test controversial recommendations and concerns found in the literature (Widiger, 2012). These steps resulted in substantial revisions, leaving only 10 of the 93 *DSM-III-R* personality disorders unchanged. Fifty-two of the disorders received major modifications, 10 were completely removed, and 9 were added (Widiger, 2012). Nonetheless, empirical evidence that personality disorders exist, or are correctly represented by *DSM-IV-TR*, is extremely limited. This was highlighted when the *DSM-5* study group suggested that half of the existing personality disorders should be eliminated (Widiger, 2012). Even though these disorders have been clinically treated and followed for years, they simply lack the empirical evidence or clinical usefulness to remain part of a diagnostic system (Pilkonis, Hallquist, Morse, & Stepp, 2011; Widiger, 2011, 2012). Partly because of the actual or perceived psychodynamic orientation of personality disorders, as well as the lack of empirical evidence, this working group in fact seriously considered removing the entire personality section from *DSM-5* (Widiger, 2012).

A major hypothesis of this textbook is that most personality abnormalities may not exist as independent disorders. Perhaps personality difficulties stem from other mental health spectrum disorders, rather than discrete disorders; that is, one's temperament, stimulus response, and behaviors are more shaped by chronic symptoms fostered by mood, anxiety, or psychotic disorders than deficits in personality development. There has been consideration of moving borderline personality disorder to the mood spectrum category and including schizoid and schizotypal personality disorders with schizophrenia (Skodol, 2012; Widiger, 2012). Avoidant personality disorder and anxiety, particularly social phobias, are another example of illnesses that share similar symptoms and may be part of a single spectrum (Widiger, 2001, 2012). Additionally, recommendations have been made to move antisocial behavior from a personality nomenclature and into a *DSM* Axis I adult conduct disorder (Widiger, 2012). Moving the primary personality disorders to existing *DSM* Axis I categories could help better define treatment alternatives, remove unproven psychoanalytic connotations from the disorders, reduce stigma, and advance research.

The mental health professions must also consider whether all *DSM* personality profiles and difficulties are best categorized as disorders. One can question whether some *DSM* personality disorders are more social-fit issues that impact well-being, satisfaction, and interpersonal relationships, rather than mental disorders. Is a flaw in personality in fact a mental disorder, or a personal challenge? How societies define self and individuals within cultural groups and perceive and promote themselves can greatly differ. Historically, there is little doubt that the concept of "ill" personalities has come from Western thought and has developed from less than scientific methods (Mulder,

2012). Furthermore, there is ample evidence that not only have the personality disorder categories failed to consider social-cultural context, but additionally are based largely on middle-class values (Mulder, 2012).

Culture, along with genetics, can shape how a person is motivated, selects goals, and generally defines the personal self. Self-determination theory speculates that universally, personality is formed based on a psychological need for autonomy, competence, and relatedness. Furthermore, these basic needs, interacting with learned culture and ecological systems, shape one's motivation, self-expression, and personal goals (Deci & Ryan, 2009).

Suggesting that personality disorders may not exist, or occur differently than described in the *DSM*, is not intended to minimize the hardships, pain, and social-economic problems caused when a lack of fit exists between a person's personality and environment. It is, however, questioning whether a disservice is made to individuals and society when problems with no clear neurobiological underpinnings are classified as mental disorders. The line between a lack of personality well-being and mental disorder is admittedly difficult to define. In the broadest sense, the impact of a definition between the two concepts on clients may be minor. However, from a practical perspective, not having a "disorder" places individuals in a different societal category and reduces stigma. It also widens treatment possibilities and allows far more environmental, educational, and self-help alternatives to psychiatric interventions. One can also hypothesize that if borderline personality disorder were moved into the mood spectrum, clients would face less social and professional rejection and their families would experience less guilt. Similarly, shifting clients with the currently labeled schizotypal and schizoid disorders into the schizophrenia spectrum may help them more quickly receive evidence-based interventions and may allow the families to be more empathetically assisted.

The suggestion for incorporating some personality disorders into Axis I spectrum disorders and declassifying others entirely became highly controversial among clinicians and researchers. Those advocating for increased neurobiological criteria standards across all disorders largely favored the proposal, while professionals dedicated to not abandoning personality disorders as distinct illnesses objected to the plan (Widiger, 2012). Common ground within the *DSM* working groups for how to modify personality disorders could not be reached. As a result, *DSM-IV-TR* personality disorders and criteria were simply transferred into *DSM-5*. The American Psychiatric Association did, however, include an alternative approach for helping clinicians to conduct an evidence-based assessment. Still, the model is based on limited field experience and psychometric research (Skodol, 2012; Widiger, 2012).

The new assessment method was developed from a literature review and is thought to help clinicians measure personality functioning and more empirically identify personality disorders. The experimental assessment or alternative model does consistently define diagnostic criteria across *DSM-5* personality disorders. Additionally, the criteria are anchored by empirically identified personality functioning impairments and pathological personality traits. This is a dimensional assessment that resembles the five factor model (FFM). Skodol (2012), however, points out that the new diagnostic framework incorporates a limited number of personality traits and does not use bipolarity factors. The trait scores only indicate if a maladaptive personality factor is present within the specified domain. A low score does not inform clinicians if deficits exist at the opposite trait within a domain. The FFM, on the other hand, scores traits in both directions Therefore, the opposite of antagonism in the FFM is agreeability, which is a positive unless the person's agreeability causes gullibility or other self-defacing behaviors (Skodol, 2012). Psychometric studies indicate that the construct validity for the FFM is much more robust than found for the *DSM-IV-TR* personality disorders (McCrae & Costa, 2003; Widiger, 2005). The *DSM* personality diagnoses also fall behind the FFM in discriminant validity. Using the standard *DSM* criteria, it is not unusual to identify within a client not one, but numerous personality disorders (Widiger, 2005). Nonetheless, regardless of the weaknesses in the model currently used, the inclusion of this assessment model represents a positive step for the *DSM* system.

How then does a social worker relate to the *DSM* concept of personality disorders if the hypotheses that the disorders do not exist as defined by *DSM*, may be part of other spectrum disorders, or may represent a social-quality of life problem rather than a disorder are all accepted? This is not an easy question to answer, considering the dominance of the *DSM*. Perhaps the most professional way of answering is to accept that

1. Our main task is not to argue with a diagnostic manual, but rather to help our client;
2. Whether *DSM* definitions of personality disorders are correct remains an open question, and a question that an individual clinician cannot independently answer;
3. We must consequently neither accept nor reject the possibility that personality disorders exist;
4. Anytime a client is labeled as having a personality disorder, there is an ethical obligation to continue assessing and ensure that the person does not have a *DSM-IV* Axis I spectrum disorder, or a problem in quality of life, rather than a disorder;

5. If a client has reduced quality of life related to personality characteristics, we reframe the diagnosis away from pathology and disorders, and offer assistance through education, socialization, economic support, skills training, or environmental changes.

CLUSTER A

Paranoid Personality Disorder

Throughout a number of planning meetings for the development of the *DSM-5*, committee members had planned to drop both paranoid and schizoid personality disorders (Hopwood & Thomas, 2012). Research evidence simply does not currently support their inclusion as mental illnesses that stem from personality. No one questions that the behaviors and emotions of these disorders are troublesome for the clients and deserve professional attention. Considering the lack of concrete linkage to personality, the symptoms may more appropriately belong with a *DSM* Axis I disorder, or need labeling as quality-of-life problems rather than as a disorder. The planning committee, however, was swayed by arguments from traditional theoretical alignments and the lack of research directing how to define the disorders. As a result, the two disorders found their way into the new diagnostic manual. Hopwood and Thomas (2012) state that, before either of these two disorders can be validated as separate diagnostic categories, the following questions need to be addressed:

- Is paranoia a normal developmental process that can be derailed by environmental or other factors and disrupt adaptive functioning and cognitive processing?
- Do symptoms such as aloofness stem from personality development, or are the symptoms more related to fear, concern, and anxiety about interpersonal relationships?
- Are the symptoms secondary consequences of a specific constellation of normative traits or other factors?
- How adequate is the *DSM* paranoid (schizoid) personality disorder syndrome model to represent paranoid or schizoid behaviors as explained in other theories?

The cause of non-psychotic paranoid symptoms is uncertain. Family studies suggest a possible genetic overlap among schizotypal, paranoid personality disorders and schizophrenia (McGuffin, Moffitt, & Thapar, 2002). These findings generally support, but do not document, the hypothesis that the symptoms are more associated with *DSM*

Axis I disorders rather than personality deficits. One must, however, underscore that according to First and Tasman (2004) the genetic findings cannot always be replicated. There is also an assumption that learning in part perpetuates the disorder once it has started. Beliefs accepted without evidence and reinforced from limited events requiring no verification can increase in scope and content and become automatic cognitions (First & Tasman, 2004; Haight & Taylor, 2013). An association among paranoid, schizoid, and schizotypal symptoms and childhood physical abuse has been documented (J. G. Johnson et al., 2005). The difficulty with trauma is that researchers cannot determine if the abuse is a primary cause, an interacting variable, a predictor of severity, or an independent co-occurring psychological event. From an epidemiological perspective, paranoid personality disorder is found in only 0.5%–2.5% of the general population, yet up to 30% of inpatient and 10% of outpatient clients carry a diagnosis of paranoid personality disorder (American Psychiatric Association, 2000; First & Tasman, 2004). Inpatient units may assign this disorder because of the rather global *DSM* criteria and the difficulty of diagnosing individuals who are unquestionably experiencing mental pain, but do not clearly meet *DSM* criteria for mood, schizophrenia, or other Axis I disorders. For example, clients with paranoid personality disorders can become psychotic; however, the episodes, unlike schizophrenia, are brief, and the personality symptoms must be identified before the onset of psychosis and continue after the psychotic episode ends. This can be difficult to correctly document in short-term inpatient services. The *DSM-IV-TR* warns clinicians to take extra care when assessing clients from minority, refugee, immigrant, and ethnic communities. Individuals who have experienced discrimination, political or police brutality, or oppression, or who are unfamiliar with the majority society, may have suspicions and behaviors that are clinically misinterpreted (American Psychiatric Association, 2000).

The primary behavior that defines clients with paranoid personality disorder is a persistent suspiciousness of others that is documented across settings and situations, and is an identifiable lifestyle theme (American Psychiatric Association, 2000). An important point to keep in mind is that paranoia is not psychosis, yet the paranoid thinking found in paranoid personality disorder highly resembles psychotic paranoia. Unlike symptoms seen in psychotic episodes, paranoia associated with personality is not illogical or irrational, implausible, or bizarre. Additionally, the paranoia is not mixed with hallucinations and other symptoms known to be part of psychosis. Nonetheless, similar to psychotic paranoia, beliefs are not easily changed, regardless of confronting evidence and the fact that suspicions are inconsistent with a culture's prevailing reality (American Psychiatric Association, 2000; First & Tasman, 2004). A key diagnostic factor is the timing of symptom onset: whether the paranoid symptoms started in late childhood or early adolescence (American Psychiatric Association, 2000). Paranoia related to personality first appears during late childhood or adolescence, whereas the same symptoms in schizophrenia and other psychotic disorders most often are not present until early adulthood. The required criteria for diagnosing paranoid personality disorder are provided in Box 8.2.

Individuals with this disorder are often difficult to get along with and, as a result, close meaningful interpersonal relationships can be problematic. Additionally, people with paranoid personality disorder prevent others from getting too personally close. They purposely do not share information out of fear that the friend or family member will betray

---

BOX 8.2

DSM-IV-TR DIAGNOSTIC CRITERIA FOR 301.0 PARANOID PERSONALITY DISORDER

A. A pervasive distrust and suspiciousness of others such that their motives are interpreted as malevolent, beginning by early adulthood and present in a variety of contexts, as indicated by four (or more) of the following:

1. Suspects, without sufficient basis, that others are exploiting, harming, or deceiving him or her;
2. Is preoccupied with unjustified doubts about the loyalty or trustworthiness of friends or associates;
3. Is reluctant to confide in others because of unwarranted fear that the information will be used maliciously against him or her;
4. Reads hidden demeaning or threatening meanings into benign remarks or events;
5. Persistently bears grudges, i.e., is unforgiving of insults, injuries, or slights;
6. Perceives attacks on his or her character or reputation that are not apparent to others and is quick to react angrily or to counterattack;
7. Has recurrent suspicions, without justification, regarding fidelity of spouse or sexual partner.

B. Does not occur exclusively during the course of schizophrenia, a mood disorder with psychotic features, or another psychotic disorder and is not due to the direct physiological effects of a general medical condition.

Note: If criteria are met prior to the onset of schizophrenia, add "premorbid," e.g., "paranoid personality disorder (premorbid)."

---

them (American Psychiatric Association, 2000; First & Tasman, 2004). Clients may also become upset and push away people who do not accept that their suspicions are real. In some cases, clients suspect partners of sexually cheating or doing secretive things against them. Throughout adulthood they are hypersensitive to criticism and on guard for signs that businesses, institutions, and people are going to financially, emotionally, or even physically injure them (Woo & Keatinge, 2008). Because of the ongoing suspicion, maintaining employment is possible, but often difficult for the client, coworkers, and supervisor.

People with paranoid personality disorder seldom appear in community clinics requesting treatment for delusional thinking. When opportunities for treating these clients occur, a major task for the clinician is to win the person's trust. Therapists will be unsuccessful in attempting to simply talk or reason the individual out of paranoid thinking. Social workers are encouraged to modify the cognitive technique explained in Chapter 4 for overcoming suspicious obsessions. First and Tasman (2004) emphasize that process groups or any form of group intervention may cause the client to flee treatment. Using supportive non-confrontational methods to address feelings of vulnerability and fear that others are trying to control the client, including the therapist, may slowly change the automatic cognitive paranoid structures. In the beginning of therapy, even kind words and encouragement can cause clients to fear that the clinician is using seduction to control their awareness of what is actually happening in the treatment session. Therefore, one must employ interpretations and engagement methods carefully and must accept that the client will likely make unfounded accusations about the therapist and the session (Appelbaum, 2005). Furthermore, as with all therapy, frustration and defensiveness will greatly damage, if not end, the therapeutic relationship.

Schizoid Personality Disorder

Individuals diagnosed with schizoid personality disorder have a lifelong history of social withdrawal. As children, they were socially isolated and withdrawn. They not only internally find human relationships difficult, but also have limited or constricted emotions when forced to interact with people (American Psychiatric Association, 2000). While engaging others, a person with schizoid personality disorder tends to act emotionally cold and detached. Even close relationships with family members are most often not enjoyed. However, individuals with schizoid personality disorder have difficulty expressing anger (American Psychiatric Association, 2000). Therefore, peers and family may not know that internally the person is upset Additionally, neither praise nor criticism from others seems to create emotional responses, and observers may come to believe that the client is incapable of feeling pleasure. There is evidence, though, that pleasure can be gained from a few activities. However, sexual pleasure, when it occurs, mostly takes place in fantasy, and mature sexuality is often never achieved (Sadock & Sadock, 2007). Individuals with this disorder like to see themselves as observers rather than participants. A strength found in these clients is that, unlike individuals with paranoid and schizotypal disorders, they do not have unusual thoughts that mimic psychotic symptoms (American Psychiatric Association, 2000; First & Tasman, 2004). However, their inability to socialize and their need to isolate makes clients with schizoid symptoms at risk for homelessness.

Prevalence is largely unknown, and the disorder is seldom diagnosed in clinical settings. As stated in the section on paranoid personality disorder, there is no genetic data explaining causation, and the associations with childhood abuse are difficult to interpret. There is an increased prevalence in people who have relatives with schizophrenia or schizoid personality disorder. Box 8.3 details the *DSM-IV-TR* criteria for diagnosing the disorder.

BOX 8.3

DSM-IV-TR DIAGNOSTIC CRITERIA FOR 301.20 SCHIZOID PERSONALITY DISORDER

A. A pervasive pattern of detachment from social relationships and a restricted range of expression of emotions in interpersonal settings, beginning by early adulthood and present in a variety of contexts, as indicated by four (or more) of the following:
   1. Neither desires nor enjoys close relationships, including being part of a family;
   2. Almost always chooses solitary activities;
   3. Has little, if any, interest in having sexual experiences with another person;
   4. Takes pleasure in few, if any, activities;
   5. Lacks close friends or confidants other than first-degree relatives;
   6. Appears indifferent to the praise or criticism of others;
   7. Shows emotional coldness, detachment, or flattened affectivity.
B. Does not occur exclusively during the course of schizophrenia, a mood disorder with psychotic features, another psychotic disorder, or a pervasive developmental disorder and is not due to the direct physiological effects of a general medical condition.

Note: If criteria are met prior to the onset of schizophrenia, add "premorbid," e.g., "schizoid personality disorder (premorbid)."

Source: Reprinted with permission from the Diagnostic and Statistical Manual of Mental Disorders, Fourth Edition, Text Revision *(Copyright 2000). American Psychiatric Association.*

There are no evidence-based or best practice guidelines for treating clients with schizoid personality disorder. A supportive therapeutic relationship may grow if the person's need for privacy, non-emotional responses, and need for not being involved with others is respected and not directly confronted (Appelbaum, 2005).

Schizotypal Personality Disorder

Clients with schizotypal personality disorder have difficulty connecting interpersonally, experience cognitive and perceptual abnormalities, and exhibit odd and eccentric behaviors (American Psychiatric Association, 2000). Their odd behaviors stand out and are viewed as unusual by most community standards. One does not need professional training to know that the person's behavior is different. Their speech pattern is often vague and idiosyncratic (American Psychiatric Association, 2000; Sadock & Sadock, 2007). A listener can track the individual's verbal reasoning and generally understands the content, but is not completely sure what the person is saying or actually means. Magical thinking, peculiar notions, unusual perceptions, and ideas of reference are common symptoms (American Psychiatric Association, 2000).

Ideas of reference refer to distorted beliefs in which clients think environmental events or media information relate specifically to them. Both a person with schizophrenia and another with schizotypal personality disorder may report that everyone in the waiting room is telepathically transmitting thoughts to them. However, unlike the individual with schizophrenia, a client with schizotypal personality disorder can often acknowledge that these thoughts and feelings may not be valid. A person with schizophrenia would rarely personally question or accept suggestions to question internal perceptions. Even though clients with this disorder approach the dividing line for disordered thinking, their ability to not cross into psychosis separates them from clients with schizophrenia. During periods of intense stress, a person with schizotypal symptoms can deteriorate into a state of psychosis. This, however, is rare, and the psychotic symptoms are fragmented and last only for a short period of time (Sadock & Sadock, 2007).

Magical thinking and belief in unusual abilities is often part of this disorder. The client may express beliefs in an ability to control others or a gift of telepathic perception or clairvoyant skills. Once trust is built with the social worker, clients may confide unusual or unconventional thoughts. They often think of themselves as psychic and predict events ranging from rather commonly shared fears such as "another shooting will take place," to a more idiosyncratic idea that the world is going to end by a certain date (American Psychiatric Association, 2000; Sadock & Sadock, 2007). Underneath the claims of special insights is a combination of distorted perceptions and excessive social anxiety. Much like behavior seen in people with schizophrenia, their anxiety is not decreased by becoming familiar with the setting and the people interacting with them (American Psychiatric Association, 2000; Sadock & Sadock, 2007). Along with the anxiety, clients with schizotypal personality disorder experience paranoid thoughts and are suspicious of people and reported events. A client, for example, may question whether humans have really gone to the moon or if the government is just tricking us to get more taxes. In certain social situations, such as in the social worker's office, however, most people with this disorder can control their unusual thoughts and withhold responses that would expose their beliefs and emotions (American Psychiatric Association, 2000; Sadock & Sadock, 2007). Nonetheless, it is difficult for them over an extended period of time to hide their isolated lifestyle and their lack of joy and motivation. The *DSM-IV-TR* diagnostic criteria for schizotypal personality disorder are provided in Box 8.4.

The characteristics of this disorder are so similar to schizophrenia that researchers have divided the symptoms into positive and negative categories. Similar to schizophrenia, positive symptoms consist of perceptual-cognitive abnormalities. Social fears or aversions, along with isolation or withdrawal, represent the negative symptoms or social-interpersonal dimension (Squires-Wheeler et al., 1997). The parallel among schizophrenia and schizotypal symptoms and behaviors is illustrated by the following case overview.

Everyone Is Dumb

Mike is 39 years old and has a bachelor's degree in journalism. He lives with his mother and father in a rural semi-poor area. After completing his degree, Mike got a federal job, but within 9 months abruptly announced that he was resigning. To this day, he states that he had to leave the federal position because everyone was "stupid," especially his boss. After leaving federal service, Mike was mostly supported by his parents. However, he spends about half of most days trying to sell business advertising for a catalog company. Over the years, he has been modestly successful at this endeavor, but not to the point where he is self-supporting. Therefore, Mike has never moved from his parents' home. He pays no rent, nor does he buy any groceries. He sometimes makes enough money to buy gas for his car.

Mike was persuaded to see me by his parents. They had several concerns. The father reported that it is impossible for his son to throw out any newspapers, and that he is always worried about germs. If newspapers are put in the trash, he becomes upset. Mike refuses to eat at restaurants, fearing that they are not clean. He only wants to eat food

---

DSM-IV-TR DIAGNOSTIC CRITERIA FOR 301.22 SCHIZOTYPAL PERSONALITY DISORDER

A. A pervasive pattern of social and interpersonal deficits marked by acute discomfort with, and reduced capacity for, close relationships as well as by cognitive or perceptual distortions and eccentricities of behavior, beginning by early adulthood and present in a variety of contexts, as indicated by five (or more) of the following:

1. Ideas of reference (excluding delusions of reference);
2. Odd beliefs or magical thinking that influences behavior and is inconsistent with subcultural norms (e.g., superstitiousness, belief in clairvoyance, telepathy, or "sixth sense"; in children and adolescents, bizarre fantasies or preoccupations);
3. Unusual perceptual experiences, including bodily illusions;
4. Odd thinking and speech (e.g., vague, circumstantial, metaphorical, overelaborate, or stereotyped);
5. Suspiciousness or paranoid ideation;
6. Inappropriate or constricted affect;
7. Behavior or appearance that is odd, eccentric, or peculiar;
8. Lack of close friends or confidants other than first-degree relatives;
9. Excessive social anxiety that does not diminish with familiarity and tends to be associated with paranoid fears rather than negative judgments about self.

B. Does not occur exclusively during the course of schizophrenia, a mood disorder with psychotic features, another psychotic disorder, or a pervasive developmental disorder.

Note: If criteria are met prior to the onset of schizophrenia, add "premorbid," e.g., "schizotypal personality disorder (premorbid)."

Source: Reprinted with permission from the Diagnostic and Statistical Manual of Mental Disorders, Fourth Edition, Text Revision *(Copyright 2000). American Psychiatric Association.*

---

prepared by his mother. Interestingly, these behaviors do not concern or embarrass Mike. He does not see himself or his behaviors as abnormal or a problem.

Mike always sees special meaning in events and often interprets accidental meetings as signs that something good or bad is going to happen. He is highly superstitious and spends much of his time studying horoscopes and Tarot cards. Additionally, he believes that a Ouija board has the ability to predict the future by picking up human vibrations and receiving messages from spirits. In short, Mike believes that he has the power to "sense" events before they happen.

It is often hard to interpret exactly what Mike is talking about. He tends to speak in a global manner, and often declares people, government agencies, and organizations to be "dumb." When asked what "dumb" means, he states, "They are just stupid." While Mike has never been in trouble with law enforcement, he considers all police personnel and police departments to be "dumb." He is also fond of stating that the nation's intelligence agencies do not know what they are doing, and that if given the chance he could straighten them out. He is also certain that the intelligence agencies periodically check everyone's mail and randomly listen to phone conversations. Mike openly speaks about not trusting government, law enforcement, intelligence, or big corporations. He will not elaborate or explain what he believes the agencies are doing wrong. He also changes the subject or avoids the conversation when asked how he would change the agencies. Nonetheless, based on his affect and serious statements, it appears that these are real beliefs and not simply a general statement.

Mike's affect is most often either flat or somewhat angry. However, once in a while he will smile or even laugh at a joke. In private, his parents state that Mike has no friends, and has not really socialized since completing college. They noticed his behavior changing and becoming less social and more suspicious of government during his junior year of college. At home Mike will visit for a short time with his parents and select family members, but not with anyone outside the family. When family comes to the house, he most often refuses to sit in a chair. Mike will stand and sway while visiting the family. After visiting for a very short period, he goes to his room. When people who are not family come to the house, Mike goes immediately to his room.

The mother states that even as a child Mike was nervous in social situations. She also admits that his nervousness is even more obvious, because he insists on wearing old clothing and seems to care nothing about his appearance. This worries the family, but over the years they have accepted it as simply Mike's way of living.

This brief case sketch typifies the concrete symptoms of odd thinking and beliefs found in both schizophrenia and schizotypal personality disorder. One cannot know for certain, for example, what Mike really means when he states that everyone at his job was stupid, or that the government is dumb. The symptom of lost motivation becomes clear as we learn that he has lived continuously with his parents, and attempts only to do sales for about half of each day. You may recall from Chapter 4 on schizophrenia that loss of motivation is a neurobiological symptom caused by the illness, rather than a choice. Paranoia and odd beliefs are highlighted by only wanting to eat food prepared by the mother and an inability to discard newspaper. It is tempting to call the collection of newspapers an indication of obsessive-compulsive disorder. However, as a whole, the person does not meet OCD criteria. The symptoms document eccentric and odd behavior. Magical thinking, constricted affect, social anxiety, and ideas of reference are part of Mike's routine life. One does not need a lot of information to understand that Mike experiences the world differently from most people. Additionally, while he certainly is not psychotic, Mike nonetheless has symptoms that mimic what is seen in many people with schizophrenia.

About 3% of the general public meets the *DSM-IV-TR* criteria for schizotypal personality disorder. The disorder is more often found in families that also have members with schizophrenia (American Psychiatric Association, 2000; Sadock & Sadock, 2007). There appears to be little evidence that psychosocial factors explain the causation for the disorder (First & Tasman, 2004). A number of studies have associated the schizotypal symptoms with child physical and sexual abuse, but do not directly address causation (J. G. Johnson et al., 2005). Treatment recommendations are identical to those for schizoid personality disorder. Antipsychotic medications are recommended if the client has more severe ideas of reference, and antidepressants are prescribed when a person has a highly depressive or withdrawn presentation (First & Tasman, 2004; Sadock & Sadock, 2007).

CLUSTER B

Borderline Personality Disorder

Borderline personality disorder is thought to be present in 1%–2% of the population (American Psychiatric Association, 2000; First & Tasman, 2004). The majority of individuals with this diagnosis in treatment are women, and some epidemiology studies estimate that approximately 75% of individuals with borderline personality disorder are female (First & Tasman, 2006). There is evidence, however, that the overwhelming female findings may simply reflect a clinical treatment sampling bias. When samples are taken from communities rather than clinic populations, the prevalence rates do not differ between genders (Woo & Keatinge, 2008). In addition, a large Norwegian study found that borderline personality disorder was equally distributed between males and females (Torgersen, Kringlen, & Cramer, 2001).

These clients face difficulty regulating their emotions, perceptions of the environment, and interpersonal relationships. The specific criteria for assessing borderline personality disorder are provided in Box 8.5.

For many with this disorder, life is a constant struggle for finding and managing close friendships and romantic partnerships. These clients consistently worry and

BOX 8.5

DSM-IV-TR DIAGNOSTIC CRITERIA FOR 301.83 BORDERLINE
PERSONALITY DISORDER

A pervasive pattern of instability of interpersonal relationships, self-image, and affects, and marked impulsivity beginning by early adulthood and present in a variety of contexts, as indicated by five (or more) of the following:

1. Frantic efforts to avoid real or imagined abandonment. **Note:** Do not include suicidal or self-mutilating behavior covered in Criterion 5.
2. A pattern of unstable and intense interpersonal relationships characterized by alternating between extremes of idealization and devaluation;
3. Identity disturbance: markedly and persistently unstable self-image or sense of self;
4. Impulsivity in at least two areas that are potentially self-damaging (e.g., spending, sex, substance abuse, reckless driving, binge eating). **Note:** Do not include suicidal or self-mutilating behavior covered in Criterion 5.
5. Recurrent suicidal behavior, gestures, or threats, or self-mutilating behavior;
6. Affective instability due to a marked reactivity of mood (e.g., intense episodic dysphoria, irritability, or anxiety usually lasting a few hours and only rarely more than a few days);
7. Chronic feelings of emptiness;
8. Inappropriate, intense anger or difficulty controlling anger (e.g., frequent displays of temper, constant anger, recurrent physical fights);
9. Transient, stress-related paranoid ideation or severe dissociative symptoms.

Source: Reprinted with permission from the Diagnostic and Statistical Manual of Mental Disorders, Fourth Edition, Text Revision *(Copyright 2000). American Psychiatric Association.*

fantasize that they will be emotionally hurt, taken advantage of, and abandoned. These emotions can trigger unrealistic hopes and intense periods of anger. The person may fall desperately in love after a single casual meeting, and become enraged, hurt, or highly manipulative upon discovering that the feelings are not shared by the other individual. At one point the client may declare unending friendship, only to misinterpret a meaningless event and emotionally express intense accusatory anger. Expressions of verbal hostility and tones of irritation are routine when one has borderline symptoms. Some clients, in the midst of high emotions, can display irresponsible sexual and aggressive behaviors. To prevent loneliness, the person may treat a stranger at a bar as if the person were a good friend, or behave sexually promiscuously.

Friends and loved ones find life, or even extended time frames, with an individual who has borderline symptoms to be stressful and unpredictable. The behaviors unfortunately often set into motion the client's worst fear of being rejected and abandoned. Therefore, clinicians, in addition to treating the client and supporting family members, may need to help couples find ways to have individual respites, discover reasons for remaining together, or permanently separate. In addition to doing almost anything to avoid real or imagined abandonment, clients with this disorder have a disturbed and unstable sense of self. In clinics we hear clients expressing a feeling of nonexistence, self-guilt, and hatred, and casting themselves as evil. They may also typically express feeling empty, bored, or having no identity. These are extremely strong emotions and repetitive thoughts that can result in recurring suicidal or self-harm behaviors (such as cutting or burning oneself). Thoughts of self-violence may be acted on to gain help, express anger, or numb an overwhelming mental pain. Professionals, out of their own frustration and inability to help, may declare that the person is self-harming only to seek attention. This is a dangerous attitude that can cause slow professional help, decrease family vigilance, and reinforce the client's destructive thinking. Moreover, a punitive one-dimensional attitude belittles a client's anguish, fails to recognize how depression limits a person's choices, and overly frames the problem as under the person's control and self-will.

An assessment of a client with borderline personality disorder will reveal reduced impulse control, depression, anxiety, and, for some, psychotic symptoms. Reckless, impulsive acts during periods of joyful jubilation and disappointment are commonly reported. However, individuals who experience a psychotic episode generally respond to antipsychotic medications and recover their former baseline of functioning faster than seen in bipolar and schizophrenia disorders. The term "borderline" actually came about because the clients were described as standing between neurosis and psychosis. This depiction is no longer used because neurosis is a poorly defined concept, many clients never develop psychosis, and psychotic symptoms are found in a few clients across many *DSM* disorders, including depression, bipolar, schizophrenia, schizoaffective, schizotypal, and substance abuse disorders. While psychotic symptoms are often averted, paranoid thinking is common. Dissociative symptoms can also be observed with some, but not all, clients. As with all mental disorders, borderline personality symptoms range from extremely mild to highly severe.

Treating Borderline Personality Disorder

All personality disorders require long-term interventions, multiple forms of intervention, education, and support for the family and client. In addition, because borderline personality disorder is a chronic illness that distorts social judgment and causes one to destroy interpersonal relationships, support and education for community and work peers are also recommended. An important dimension of treatment, to the maximum extent a client will allow, is to provide proactive ecological case management across the client's social network and primary settings. Clients can benefit from people, in addition to family members, understanding borderline personality disorder, responding therapeutically to unexpected and sometimes explosive behaviors, and maintaining positive, supportive connections in spite of difficult conduct. People disengage when an individual fears loneliness, expresses eternal dedication only to become hostile and intensively angry, threatens or attempts self-harm, or when his or her emotions quickly turn from euphoria to depression. Remaining in a roller-coaster relationship without support or a reason for sustaining contact is difficult for families and almost impossible for coworkers, peers, and casual community acquaintances. As individuals disengage from the client, fantasies of abandonment are reinforced, and, predictably, anxiety and other symptoms increase. Stress is thought to play a role in the disorder's etiology and symptom intensity (American Psychiatric Association, 2006; First & Tasman, 2004). Therefore, case management and community supportive interventions become paramount. A primary goal when working within the community is to help establish social climates that are stable and consistent, yet have an element of flexibility within and across ecological settings. Ideally, it is helpful if peers and authority figures within each setting foster a balance between acceptance, inclusion, and realistic expectations. Additionally, family and community individuals will find that if they correctly engage and disengage with the client, relationships will be more productive.

Considering that it is estimated that 30%–50% of individuals with borderline personality disorder have co-occurring problems with alcohol or other drugs, assessments and treatment plans must include appropriate interventions for substance use disorders (American Psychiatric Association, 2006; Trull, Sher, Minks-Brown, Durbin, & Burr, 2000). There is also evidence that *DSM* Axis I and II disorders have poorer recovery rates when a person has co-occurring substance problems (Trull et al., 2000). Clients with borderline personality disorder tend to hide and deny their involvement with alcohol and drugs. Without information from sources other than the client, early detection and diagnosis of substance problems are difficult. Furthermore, once correctly assessed, talk therapies that are not nested within a more complete substance-treatment program most often are not effective (American Psychiatric Association, 2006). Individuals with severe substance problems who do not respond to outpatient services may need inpatient treatment (American Psychiatric Association, 2006).

Psychotherapy continues to be the primary intervention for treating borderline personality disorder (American Psychiatric Association, 2006). Evidence supports cognitive-behavioral therapy in general and dialectical behavior therapy (DBT) specifically for treating borderline personality disorder (American Psychiatric Association, 2006; First & Tasman, 2006; Koons, 2001; M. M.. Linehan et al., 1999; Verheul et al., 2003; Woo & Keatinge, 2008). It is impressive that DBT has been more effective in treating borderline personality disorder and preventing suicide than other forms of psychotherapy conducted by experts (M. M. Linehan et al., 2006). Regardless of the method employed, treating clients with borderline symptoms requires a flexible intervention plan and an ability to quickly respond to changing behaviors (American Psychiatric Association, 2006). Moreover, it is imperative for clinicians to accept that (1) clients would change and control their behaviors if they could; (2) treatment in isolation, without including the family and community, is questionable; (3) expressions of suicide cannot be left unattended and simply declared an act of manipulation; (4) clinician frustration will only increase problems for the client and the social worker; and (5) treatment must be planned and systematic, using a therapy model such as DBT.

Medication is seldom used as a single treatment for clients with borderline personality disorders. Treatment for this disorder requires psychotherapy, support, education, community case management, and in some cases medication (American Psychiatric Association, 2006; First & Tasman, 2004; Woo & Keatinge, 2008). Before starting treatment, social workers are advised to immediately have a client with borderline symptoms see a psychiatrist for a medication consultation. Mild controlled behaviors can suddenly become severe, requiring medication or hospitalization. Medical doctors generally prescribe an antipsychotic medication to control psychotic and aggressive behaviors (Simeon & Hollander, 2004; Stahl, 2000). In addition, cognitive and perceptual symptoms that do not qualify as a psychosis, but that signal problems with reality or thought, may warrant a low-dose antipsychotic drug trial (American Psychiatric Association, 2006). Mood swings, emotional dysregulation, and impulsivity are commonly treated with one of the newer SSRI antidepressant medications. Lithium and anticonvulsant medications are prescribed in some cases for controlling mood, anger, irritability, and other behavioral stability symptoms (Simeon & Hollander, 2004). However, much of the research on lithium with clients who have borderline personality disorder is rather old, and only a few studies have been conducted with anticonvulsant drugs (Simeon & Hollander, 2004). As a result, evidence-based guidelines are currently cautious in endorsing anticonvulsant medications (American Psychiatric Association, 2006). When clients do not respond or have severe side effects to accepted medication protocols, doctors are forced to prescribe drugs that are not as well researched. Therefore, social workers should not, without medical consultation, immediately assume that there is a more effective drug for a client who is not receiving the most highly or widely recommended prescription.

Antisocial Personality Disorder

Antisocial personality disorder's prevalence rate is approximately 3% in men and 1% in women (Sadock & Sadock, 2007). There is agreement among most researchers that this is a disorder resulting from genetic and ecological interactions (Sutker & Allain). Twin and adoption studies indicate that there is a moderate genetic contribution to antisocial development. Research in North America, Japan, and Europe indicate a 50%–52% concordance rate for criminality among identical twins, but only about 23% for fraternal twins (McGuffin et al., 2002). This suggest that a number of people have a genetic predisposition for developing criminal behavior. However, shared environments may account for as much as 20% of the explained variance for criminality (McGuffin et al., 2002). A Swedish study indicated that multiple placements during a person's youth and residing in a low socioeconomic status home increased the risk for criminality for men. Women were less affected by these factors, but had increased risk for antisocial behaviors if as a youth they experienced prolonged institutional care and were raised in an urban environment (McGuffin et al., 2002).

The hallmark of this disorder is an inability to consistently conform to social rules, legal laws, family expectations, and values that are generally accepted by the culture. Individuals with this disorder demonstrate a persistent pattern of disregard for the rights of others (American Psychiatric Association, 2000). In addition, they knowingly break laws, contracts, and interpersonal obligations without remorse. *DSM-IV-TR* criteria require that conduct problems, along with deficits in social sensitivity and respect, will have started by the person's 15th birthday (American Psychiatric Association, 2000). Primary characteristics found in individuals with antisocial personality disorder include (Hare, Neumann, & Widiger, 2012)

- self-grandiosity and glibness, yet an ability to charm others for the purposes of deception and manipulation;
- shallow, superficial affect that does not reflect cognitive or emotional guilt or remorse;
- manifestation of little or no empathy for others, and seldom acceptance of responsibility for actions;
- feelings of boredom and time spent in search of stimulation;
- few, if any, long-term goals, and impulsive and irresponsible responses to life;

- opportunistic tendencies and a parasitic lifestyle;
- behavioral problems demonstrated from mid-adolescence; because of an inability to assert behavioral controls, person has often had youthful confrontations with the legal and educational systems;
- short-term relationships;
- promiscuous and self-centered sexual behavior; and
- a tendency to live violent lives.

Individuals with antisocial personality disorder, as a group, can commit many kinds of violence toward others, engage in partner domestic violence, and take little or no parenting responsibility. Statistically they are also known to die early and have a higher probability than the general public of dying violently or spending much of their adult life in prison (Woo & Keatinge, 2008).

Diagnosing the disorder is based largely on documenting the lifestyle that disregards concern for others without feeling regret. The complete *DSM-IV-TR* assessment criteria are provided in Box 8.6.

Strangely, individuals under 18 years of age are not given a diagnosis of antisocial personality disorder, even though conduct problems must have started by the age of 15. The two age requirements are puzzling in that they do not correspond to what is known about neurological development. Brain maturation is uneven from one individual to another and continues to evolve and change over the life span. There usually are great differences in judgment and problem-solving skills among youths of the same age. In addition, we know that the brain goes through a number of physical and functional changes during adolescence and early adulthood (Haight & Taylor, 2013). The fact that 18 is the legal turning point from youth to adult is not justification for a psychiatric diagnostic starting point.

Treatment of individuals with antisocial personality disorder is difficult, but not impossible (First & Tasman, 2006). The very best intervention is prevention treatment for elementary schoolchildren at risk for, or who have, conduct problems (Woo & Keatinge, 2008). Insight therapies seldom work with this population. Reality-grounded interventions that employ concrete cognitive-behavioral methods, along with anger management, are thought to be the most effective when working with clients demonstrating antisocial symptoms (First & Tasman, 2006; Kraus & Reynolds, 2001; Woo & Keatinge, 2008). Once a relationship is even loosely cemented, clinicians strive to help the client identify that behaviors have either costs or rewards and that everyone must make a clear choice. This is not a quick or assured method. Clients with antisocial personality disorder resist accepting responsibility, have difficulty taking responsibility for

BOX 8.6

DSM-IV-TR DIAGNOSTIC CRITERIA FOR 301.7 ANTISOCIAL
PERSONALITY DISORDER

A. There is a pervasive pattern of disregard for and violation of the rights of others occurring since age 15 years, as indicated by three (or more) of the following:
   1. Failure to conform to social norms with respect to lawful behaviors as indicated by repeatedly performing acts that are grounds for arrest;
   2. Deceitfulness, as indicated by repeated lying, use of aliases, or conning others for personal profit or pleasure;
   3. Impulsivity or failure to plan ahead;
   4. Irritability and aggressiveness, as indicated by repeated physical fights or assaults;
   5. Reckless disregard for safety of self or others;
   6. Consistent irresponsibility, as indicated by repeated failure to sustain consistent work behavior or honor financial obligations;
   7. Lack of remorse, as indicated by being indifferent to or rationalizing having hurt, mistreated, or stolen from another.
B. The individual is at least 18 years old.
C. There is evidence of conduct disorder with onset before age 15 years.
D. The occurrence of antisocial behavior is not exclusively during the course of schizophrenia or a manic episode.

Source: Reprinted with permission from the Diagnostic and Statistical Manual of Mental Disorders, Fourth Edition, Text Revision *(Copyright 2000). American Psychiatric Association. (Note that internal cross-references have been removed from the reprinted text.)*

their destiny, and often do not want to conform. Additionally, researched evidence for how to clinically treat this population is very thin. Woo and Keatinge (2008) suggest that treatment plans to overcome antisocial behavior must include multiple approaches. In addition to reality-based methods, family therapy, residential treatment, and wilderness programs have shown some success in reducing antisocial actions. However, wilderness programs work best for individuals with milder symptoms, and family therapy can increase unwanted behaviors when not professionally managed (Woo & Keatinge, 2008). Because of the nature and complexity of clients with antisocial personality disorder, it is strongly recommended for social workers to either specialize in forensic services and interventions or refer cases to an expert. When clinicians only occasionally treat antisocial symptoms, they risk unknowingly increasing or reinforcing the client's destructive thoughts and behaviors.

Histrionic Personality Disorder

Histrionic personality disorder has stereotypically over many years been associ-ated with women (Sprock, Blashfield, & Smith, 1990). Perhaps, more specifically, the disorder in the past was applied from a male orientation to females who were weak, emotional, superficial, appearance focused, seductive, and sexually manipu-lative (Kaplan, 1983). Prevalence rates were reported as high as 19% in the general population and up to 40% in clinic studies (Schotte, De Doncker, Maes, Cluydts, & Cosyns, 1993). These high rates occurred in part because theorists, with no empirical evidence, incorrectly hypothesized that the disorder was caused by a combination of domineering mothers with fathers who vacillated between sexual seductiveness and strict moral authoritarian behaviors (Bornstein, 1999; First & Tasman, 2004; Kernberg, 1991). Estimates today, thanks to less sexist theories, narrower defini-tions, and better controlled epidemiology studies, report that approximately 2%–3% of the general population and 10%–15% of mental health clients meet the criteria for histrionic personality disorder (American Psychiatric Association, 2000; First & Tasman, 2004). Even though the finding is considered highly controversial, more women than men continue to receive a histrionic diagnosis (American Psychiatric Association, 2000; First & Tasman, 2004; Woo & Keatinge, 2008). This is not overly surprising, considering that the diagnostic criteria in *DSM III, DSM-IV,* and *DSM-5* have remained virtually unchanged. Furthermore, one can argue that the current criteria remain overly focused on female stereotypes and have few male equivalents (Woo & Keatinge, 2008).

Individuals with histrionic personality disorder make their way through life by employing unwarranted high levels of emotionality, and constantly have a goal to be the center of attention. The disorder starts in early adulthood. However, little is known about early youthful behaviors or how the disorder changes as the young adult ages (First & Tasman, 2004). There are minor reports indicating that symptoms decrease during the person's senior years (Sadock & Sadock, 2007). Box 8.7 provides the *DSM-IV-TR* criteria for diagnosing the disorder. It is thought that even though individuals with this disorder easily fall in love, they find it difficult to maintain close relationships. Like individuals with borderline personality disorder, these individuals seek attention, have high voltage emotions that can quickly change, and employ manipulative behaviors to win what they want. Unlike borderline characteristics, however, individuals with his-trionic symptoms do not feel empty or angry, and are not self-destructive. In addition, they differ from narcissistic personality disorder in that, while longing for attention, it is nonetheless permissible to be fragile or dependent. Clients with narcissistic problems

BOX 8.7

DSM-IV-TR DIAGNOSTIC CRITERIA FOR 301.50 HISTRIONIC PERSONALITY DISORDER

A pervasive pattern of excessive emotionality and attention seeking, beginning by early adulthood and present in a variety of contexts, as indicated by five (or more) of the following:

1. Is uncomfortable in situations in which he or she is not the center of attention;
2. Interaction with others is often characterized by inappropriate sexually seductive or provocative behavior;
3. Displays rapidly shifting and shallow expression of emotions;
4. Consistently uses physical appearance to draw attention to self;
5. Has a style of speech that is excessively impressionistic and lacking in detail;
6. Shows self-dramatization, theatricality, and exaggerated expression of emotion;
7. Is suggestible, i.e., easily influenced by others or circumstances;
8. Considers relationships to be more intimate than they actually are.

Source: Reprinted with permission from the Diagnostic and Statistical Manual of Mental Disorders, Fourth Edition, Text Revision *(Copyright 2000). American Psychiatric Association.*

generally want to be seen as strong and in charge, rather than vulnerable (American Psychiatric Association, 2000; First & Tasman, 2004).

As can be seen in Box 8.7, the *DSM-IV-TR* diagnostic criteria are extremely broad and subjective. Therefore, social workers must understand their own social and gender biases before attempting to assess this disorder. Additionally, before assigning a diagnosis of histrionic personality disorder, one has to know that the client's emotions, cognitions, and behaviors are measurably beyond the person's historical and acceptable cultural boundaries. We must also ensure that the person's current culture is not conflicting with the historical culture of origin, and either creating or adding to the observed behaviors.

There is little in the way of evidence to guide treatment planning. There is a general clinical bias that individuals with this disorder respond best to group therapy. A highly trained therapist is required, however, to prevent a client with histrionic personality disorder from controlling and manipulating the group (First & Tasman, 2004).

Narcissistic Personality Disorder

Individuals with narcissistic personality disorder are described as self-centered, with overinflated beliefs of self-importance, and little or no concern about others. They are generally characterized as lacking empathy, yet they become upset when their "specialness" is overlooked or not validated by others. Criticism from others is either experienced as a crushing blow, and countered with enraged anger, or is disregarded as obviously an incorrect appraisal (American Psychiatric Association, 2000; Sadock & Sadock, 2007). The core cognitive and emotional content of individuals with narcissistic personality disorder is grandiosity, self-importance, envy, and obsession for respect and admiration from others. Though these individuals in reality may have no substantial personal achievements, they perceive themselves as surpassing the contributions of peers, coworkers, and leaders. Like clients with borderline and antisocial diagnoses, people with narcissistic personality disorder are willing to exploit and manipulate others to reach their goals and receive praise (American Psychiatric Association, 2000; First & Tasman, 2006). The *DSM-IV-TR* diagnostic criteria are provided in Box 8.8.

There are numerous inheritability theories hypothesizing how narcissism starts. However, there are no specific genetic data supporting that the disorder is passed biologically within and across family generations (First & Tasman, 2004; Jang & Vernon, 2001). Additionally, while narcissistic personality disorder is reported in 2%–16% of clinical populations, the symptoms are found in less than 1% of the general public (American Psychiatric Association, 2000; First & Tasman, 2004). This is a disorder founded almost completely on psychoanalytic, sociological, and interpersonal assumptions, logic, and limited clinical observations, rather than evidence (First & Tasman, 2004; Woo & Keatinge, 2008). Moreover, the disorder is not included in the European diagnostic manual (*International Classification of Diseases*). Evidence is also lacking for how to best help clients with narcissism. Clinical wisdom directs social workers to consider group interventions for helping the clients become more realistic about their grandiosity, lack of empathy, and self-centered approach to life. Individual cognitive treatment may help clients label and understand their automatic thoughts, cognitive distortions, and self-defeating interpersonal strategies (Cottraux & Blackburn, 2001; First & Tasman, 2004; Hopwood & Thomas, 2012). However, considering the lack of etiology evidence, and the fact that the diagnostic criteria are seldom found in the general population, one must question whether narcissistic personality disorder is a mental disorder, and if it is, whether we realistically know how the symptoms are best treated.

BOX 8.8

DSM-IV-TR DIAGNOSTIC CRITERIA FOR 301.81 NARCISSISTIC PERSONALITY DISORDER

A pervasive pattern of grandiosity (in fantasy or behavior), need for admiration, and lack of empathy, beginning by early adulthood and present in a variety of contexts, as indicated by five (or more) of the following:

1. Has a grandiose sense of self-importance (e.g., exaggerates achievements and talents, expects to be recognized as superior without commensurate achievements);
2. Is preoccupied with fantasies of unlimited success, power, brilliance, beauty, or ideal love;
3. Believes that he or she is "special" and unique and can only be understood by, or should associate with, other special or high-status people (or institutions);
4. Requires excessive admiration;
5. Has a sense of entitlement, i.e., unreasonable expectations of especially favorable treatment or automatic compliance with his or her expectations;
6. Is interpersonally exploitative, i.e., takes advantage of others to achieve his or her own ends;
7. Lacks empathy: is unwilling to recognize or identify with the feelings and needs of others;
8. Is often envious of others or believes that others are envious of him or her;
9. Shows arrogant, haughty behaviors or attitudes.

Source: Reprinted with permission from the Diagnostic and Statistical Manual of Mental Disorders, Fourth Edition, Text Revision *(Copyright 2000). American Psychiatric Association.*

CLUSTER C

Avoidant Personality Disorder

Avoidant personality disorder was first introduced in the *DSM-III* and closely followed the psychoanalytic concept of phobic character (Phillips & Gunderson, 1999). In the *DSM*'s fourth edition, attempts were made to better separate avoidant symptoms from Axis I illnesses, but little or no changes were made to the disorder's theoretical underpinnings (Phillips & Gunderson, 1999). The *DSM-5* simply carried forward the constructs and criteria from the previous edition. The disorder occurs in around 0.5%–1.0% of the general public, and is diagnosed in clinics for about 10% of the clients (American

Psychiatric Association, 2000). Avoidant personality disorder is seldom studied by researchers, and little is known about the underlying factors from the environment and biology. There have been no significant imaging studies done on the disorder (Sanislow, da Cruz, Gianoli, & Reagan, 2012). However, a growing number of neurobiological studies have been conducted on social phobia. These explorations may in the future help inform clinicians about avoidant personality disorder. It is thought that avoidant symptoms start in early infancy or childhood as forms of shyness. Additionally, shyness in children is expected to largely dissipate or improve with advancing age. However, people with this disorder experience increasing difficulty with shyness as they mature (Phillips & Gunderson, 1999).

Individuals diagnosed with this disorder are extremely socially inhibited, express or demonstrate feelings of inadequacy, have low self-esteem, and are highly sensitive to criticism or negative personal feedback from others (American Psychiatric Association, 2000). As a result, making new friends is difficult, and they gravitate to individuals they feel certain will provide acceptance. Attempts are always made by these clients to avoid interpersonal activities and group activities. It is thought that the withdrawal from socialization is mostly driven by fear of receiving disapproval or complete rejection (American Psychiatric Association, 2000). The issue of fear of rejection is a dominant theme in their lives. They very much want warm and meaningful relationships but cannot risk allowing themselves to share enough of themselves to develop the desired personal relationships (Sadock & Sadock, 2007). Box 8.9 contains the *DSM-IV-TR* diagnostic criteria.

When reading the criteria, one is struck by how closely they reflect Axis I anxiety disorders, and how global the items are. The criteria make it difficult to identify the line between shyness or a need for quality of life improvement from a documented and defined neurobiological disorder. Treatment often consists of supportive psychotherapy. Once a therapeutic alliance is cemented, therapists may want to introduce assertiveness and social skills training, along with other cognitive-behavioral interventions. Ideally, the therapy is designed to allow the client to experience being accepted and supported in risking more and more social interactions outside the treatment room (Phillips & Gunderson, 1999; Sadock & Sadock, 2007).

Dependent Personality Disorder

Adult individuals who believe they must be guided, helped, and taken care of beyond what is considered acceptable within their individual culture are considered to have dependent personality disorder (American Psychiatric Association, 2000; Sadock & Sadock, 2007).

BOX 8.9

DSM-IV-TR DIAGNOSTIC CRITERIA FOR 301.82 AVOIDANT PERSONALITY DISORDER

A pervasive pattern of social inhibition, feelings of inadequacy, and hypersensitivity to negative evaluation, beginning by early adulthood and present in a variety of contexts, as indicated by four (or more) of the following:

1. Avoids occupational activities that involve significant interpersonal contact, because of fears of criticism, disapproval, or rejection;
2. Is unwilling to get involved with people unless certain of being liked;
3. Shows restraint within intimate relationships because of the fear of being shamed or ridiculed;
4. Is preoccupied with being criticized or rejected in social situations;
5. Is inhibited in new interpersonal situations because of feelings of inadequacy;
6. Views self as socially inept, personally unappealing, or inferior to others
7. Is unusually reluctant to take personal risks or to engage in any new activities because they may prove embarrassing.

Source: Reprinted with permission from the Diagnostic and Statistical Manual of Mental Disorders, Fourth Edition, Text Revision *(Copyright 2000). American Psychiatric Association.*

In order to secure the security and oversight needed to emotionally feel safe, they are often submissive, clingy, and self-critical. The fear of separation is so overwhelming that being alone can feel intolerable. To prevent these internal feelings and thoughts of abandonment, individuals with dependent personality disorder are known to accept demands of submission, and in some cases endure physical or sexual abuse (American Psychiatric Association, 2000). They psychologically survive by ensuring that the person they are dependent upon does not leave. These behaviors can lead to the person becoming unusually self-sacrificing (American Psychiatric Association, 2000; First & Tasman, 2004).

Clients are thought to perceive themselves as weak, but consistently maintain a belief that someone will care for them, as long as the caregiver is adequately pacified (Bornstein, 1999). When death, divorce, or relocation ends a relationship, the client often makes irrationally quick decisions and immediately attaches to another individual (American Psychiatric Association, 2000). Persons with dependent personality disorder are able to hold a job but almost never accept leadership roles, independent decision-making opportunities, or supervisory positions (American Psychiatric Association, 2000). It is generally thought that clients with this disorder do not want to overly advance within the workplace or social organizations, and may purposefully make themselves appear less competent (American Psychiatric Association, 2000; First & Tasman, 2004; Sadock & Sadock, 2007). The specific DSM-IV-TR criteria for assessing dependent personality disorder are found in Box 8.10.

Dependent personality disorder occurs in approximately 5%–30% of clinic individuals with a personality disorder, but only about 2%–5% of the general population (First & Tasman, 2004). Studies using more narrow criteria report that 5%–15% of clinic clients are diagnosed with the disorder (Bornstein, 1999). The wide range within clinic populations alerts us that various inclusion criteria and sampling methods have been used in the epidemiology studies. Therefore, one must question the accuracy of the research and diagnostic validity. The disorder is most often assessed in females.

BOX 8.10

DSM-IV-TR DIAGNOSTIC CRITERIA FOR 301.6 DEPENDENT PERSONALITY DISORDER

A pervasive and excessive need to be taken care of that leads to submissive and clinging behavior and fears of separation, beginning by early adulthood and present in a variety of contexts, as indicated by five (or more) of the following:

1. Has difficulty making everyday decisions without an excessive amount of advice and reassurance from others;
2. Needs others to assume responsibility for most major areas of his or her life;
3. Has difficulty expressing disagreement with others because of fear of loss of support or approval. **Note:** Do not include realistic fears of retribution.
4. Has difficulty initiating projects or doing things on his or her own (because of a lack of self-confidence in judgment or abilities rather than a lack of motivation or energy);
5. Goes to excessive lengths to obtain nurturance and support from others, to the point of volunteering to do things that are unpleasant;
6. Feels uncomfortable or helpless when alone because of exaggerated fears of being unable to care for himself or herself;
7. Urgently seeks another relationship as a source of care and support when a close relationship ends;
8. Is unrealistically preoccupied with fears of being left to take care of himself or herself.

Source: Reprinted with permission from the Diagnostic and Statistical Manual of Mental Disorders, Fourth Edition, Text Revision (Copyright 2000). American Psychiatric Association.

However, there is some evidence that this may occur because of a criteria and sampling bias that prevents the disorder from being discovered in males (American Psychiatric Association, 2000; Bornstein, 1999; First & Tasman, 2004; Widiger, 1998). The lack of ongoing robust studies has allowed outdated, limited findings and poorly designed research to leave questionable gender beliefs unchallenged across the personality disorder spectrum.

Causation hypotheses have focused on insecure attachments. There is also a belief that the disorder may occur when a child has an anxious temperament that interacts with inconsistent or overprotective parenting (First & Tasman, 2004). There has also been limited documentation that dependent personality disorder may result from parental neglect (J. G. Johnson et al., 2005). However, it is not clear if there are critical developmental periods, a specific length of exposure, or a certain severity of neglect needed to trigger dependent personality disorder. Currently, limited attention is being focused on the inheritability of the disorder. Newer genetic studies are suggesting that dependent symptoms exist within families and can be passed across generations (Bornstein, 1999). As with other personality disorders, there is little or no evidence to guide treatment choices. Researchers and therapists report at least limited success when using support and cognitive-behavioral interventions. Additionally, supportive group therapy may provide meaningful feedback and role modeling, and help in overcoming anxious dependent feelings (Bornstein, 1999; First & Tasman, 2004).

Obsessive-Compulsive Personality Disorder

A person with obsessive-compulsive personality disorder is driven by an overpowering need for perfection, orderliness, and control of self and others (American Psychiatric Association, 2000). These desires and beliefs can cause people to be highly inflexible, and in some cases to dedicate themselves excessively to work. In severe cases, clients will forgo friendships and leisure to reach or work toward their perfectionistic goals (American Psychiatric Association, 2000; Sadock & Sadock, 2007). However, some individuals report that the disorder can cause indecisiveness and an inability to make decisions (American Psychiatric Association, 2000). Delegating tasks is not only difficult, but often impossible. Other people simply cannot be trusted to complete a task with the degree of perfection required by the client. Individuals with obsessive-compulsive personality disorder find themselves overly burdened, with a need for developing lists, along with ordering and organizing personal and work items (American Psychiatric Association, 2000). They additionally are often overly preoccupied with assuring that every nuance of laws and rules is known and followed. Furthermore, they find it extremely upsetting and concerning when there are no concrete procedures to guide one's actions or decisions (American Psychiatric Association, 2000). The *DSM-IV-TR* diagnostic criteria is for the disorder are provided in Box 8.11

Epidemiology studies report that about 1%–2% of the general population meet the disorder's diagnostic criteria, whereas within psychiatric inpatient units 3%–10% of the clients receive a diagnosis of obsessive-compulsive personality disorder (First & Tasman, 2004; Samuels & Costa, 2012). Studies indicate that the symptoms of obsessionality are passed within families (First & Tasman, 2004). However, the relationship between obsessive-compulsive disorder and obsessive-compulsive personality disorder is not predictable (Dolan-Sewell, Krueger, & Shea, 2001). A small amount of research

---

BOX 8.11

DSM-IV-TR DIAGNOSTIC CRITERIA FOR 301.4 OBSESSIVE-COMPULSIVE PERSONALITY DISORDER

A pervasive pattern of preoccupation with orderliness, perfectionism, and mental and interpersonal control, at the expense of flexibility, openness, and efficiency, beginning by early adulthood and present in a variety of contexts, as indicated by four (or more) of the following:

1. Is preoccupied with details, rules, lists, order, organization, or schedules to the extent that the major point of the activity is lost;
2. Shows perfectionism that interferes with task completion (e.g., is unable to complete a project because his or her own overly strict standards are not met);
3. Is excessively devoted to work and productivity to the exclusion of leisure activities and friendships (not accounted for by obvious economic necessity);
4. Is overconscientious, scrupulous, and inflexible about matters of morality, ethics, or values (not accounted for by cultural or religious identification);
5. Is unable to discard worn-out or worthless objects even when they have no sentimental value;
6. Is reluctant to delegate tasks or to work with others unless they submit to exactly his or her way of doing things;
7. Adopts a miserly spending style toward both self and others; money is viewed as something to be hoarded for future catastrophes;
8. Shows rigidity and stubbornness.

---

has indicated that the disorder may result from parental emotional abuse (J. G. Johnson et al., 2005). In theory, emotional abuse is thought to increase a child's maladaptive thoughts and feelings of guilt, shame, social anxiety, and mistrust (J. G. Johnson et al., 2005). Psychoanalytic theorists have hypothesized that obsessive-compulsive personality disorder stems from unconscious issues such as guilt, shame, insecurity, identification with authoritarian parents, and a need for infallibility (First & Tasman, 2004). However, there are only limited and somewhat older data supporting these concepts (First & Tasman, 2004). As with all mental illness, science has yet to discover exactly what causes and triggers the symptoms. Furthermore, there are no evidence-based guidelines for directing treatment planning. First and Tasman (2004) recommend supportive therapy coupled with cognitive-behavioral methods. The same authors report that group therapy is problematic for clients with this disorder. They have found that clients with obsessive-compulsive personality disorder tend to be judgemental and overbearing when in group therapy. Currently there is no medication specifically designed or known to be effective in reducing obsessive-compulsive personality symptoms (First & Tasman, 2004; Lee & Coccaro, 2004).

REFERENCES

Abnsbacher, H. L., & Abnsbacher, R. R. (1956). Individual psychology in its larger setting. In H. L. Abnsbacher & R. R. Abnsbacher (Eds.), The Individual Psychology of Alfred Adler. (pp. 1–9). New York: Basic Books.

American Psychiatric Association. (2000). *Diagnostic and Statistical Manual of Mental Disorders* (4th ed., text rev.). Washington, DC: American Psychiatric Association.

American Psychiatric Association. (2006). Practice guidelines for the treatment of psychiatric disorders. In *Compendium* (pp. 349–563). Arlington, VA: American Psychiatric Association.

Appelbaum, A. H. (2005). Supportive psychotherapy. In J. M. Oldham, A. E. Skodol, & D. Bender (Eds.), *The American Psychiatric Publishing Textbook of Personality Disorders* (pp. 335–346). Washington, DC: American Psychiatric Publishing.

Blashfield, R. K., & McElroy, R. A. (1995). Confusions in the terminology used for classification models. In W. J. Livesley (Ed.), *The DSM-IV Personality Disorders* (pp. 407–416). New York: Guilford Press.

Bornstein, R. F. (1999). Dependent and histrionic personality disorders. In T. Milton, P. H. Blaney, & D. R. D. (Eds.), *Oxford Textbook of Psychopathology* (pp. 535–554). New York: Oxford University Press.

Brenner, C. (1957). The nature and development of the concept of repression in Freud's writings. *The Psychoanalytic Study of the Child, 12,* 19–46.

Cervone, D., & Pervin, L. A. (2008). *Personality Theory and Research.* Hoboken, NJ: John Wiley & Sons.

Cloninger, S. (2004). *Theories of Personality: Understanding Persons* (4th ed.). Upper Saddle River, NJ: Pearson/Prentice Hall.

Cloninger, S. (2009). Conceptual issues in personality theory. In P. J. Corr & G. Matthews (Eds.), *The Cambridge Handbook of Personality Psychology* (pp. 4–26). Cambridge, UK: Cambridge University Press.

Cottraux, J., & Blackburn, I.-M. (2001). Cognitive therapy. In W. J. Livesley (Ed.), *Handbook of Personality Disorders* (pp. 377–399). New York: Guilford Press.

Crabbe, J. C. (2003). Finding genes for complex behaviors: Progress in mouse models of the addictions. In R. Plomin, J. C. DeFries, I. W. Craig, & P. McGuffin (Eds.), *Behavioral Genetics in the Postgenomic Era* (pp. 291–308). Washington, DC: American Psychological Association.

Dall, S. R. X., Houston, A. I., & McNamara, J. M. (2004). The behavioural ecology of personality: Consistent individual differences from an adaptive perspective. *Ecological Letters, 7*(8), 734–739.

Deci, E. L., & Ryan, R. M. (2009). Self-determination theory: A consideration of human motivational universals. In P. J. Corr & G. Matthews (Eds.), *The Cambridge Handbook of Personality Psychology* (pp. 441–456). New York: Cambridge University Press.

DeYoung, C. G., & Gray, J. R. (2009). Personality neuroscience: Explaining individual differences in affect, behaviour and cognition. In P. J. Corr & G. Matthews (Eds.), *The Cambridge Handbook of Personality Psychology* (pp. 323–346). Cambridge, UK: Cambridge University Press 2009.

Dolan-Sewell, R. T., Krueger, R. F., & Shea, M. T. (2001). Co-occurrence with syndrome disorders. In W. J. Livesley (Ed.), *Handbook of Personality Disorders: Theory, Research, and Treatment* (pp. 84–104). New York: Guilford Press.

First, M. B., & Tasman, A. (2004). *DSM-IV-TR Mental Disorders Diagnosis, Etiology and Treatment.* West Sussex, UK: John Wiley & Sons.

First, M. B., & Tasman, A. (2006). *Clinical Guide to the Diagnosis and Treatment of Mental Disorders.* New York: John Wiley & Sons.

Fonagy, P., & Bateman, A. W. (2005). Attachment theory and mentalization-oriented model of borderline personality disorder. In J. M. Oldham, A. E. Skodol, & D. Bender (Eds.), *Textbook of Personality Disorders* (pp. 187–207). Washington, DC: American Psychiatric Publishing.

Freud, S. (1995). *The Basic Writings of Sigmund Freud* (A. A. Brill, Trans.). New York: Modern Library.

Grant, B. F., Stinson, F. S., Dawson, D. A., Chou, S. P., & Ruan, W. J. (2005). Co-occurrence of DSM-IV personality disorders in the United States: Results from the National Epidemiologic Survey on Alcohol and Related Conditions. *Comprehensive Psychiatry, 46*(1), 1–5.

Grosskurth, P. (1986). *Melanie Klein: Her World and Her Work.* New York: Knopf.

Gunderson, J. G. (1983). DSM-III diagnoses of personality disorders. In J. Frosch (Ed.), *Current Perspectives on Personality Disorders* (pp. 20–39). Washington, DC: American Psychiatric Press.

Haight, W. L., & Taylor, E. H. (2013). *Human Behavior for Social Work Practice: A Developmental-Ecological Framework* (2nd ed.). Chicago: Lyceum Books.

Hare, R. D., Neumann, C. S., & Widiger, T. A. (2012). Psychopathy. In T. A. Widger (Ed.), *The Oxford Handbook of Personality Disorders* (pp. 478–504). New York: Oxford University Press.

Hopwood, C., & Thomas, K. M. (2012). Personality disorders. In M. Hersen & D. C. Beidel (Eds.), *Adult Psychopathology and Diagnosis* (6th ed., pp. 681–716). Hoboken, NJ: John Wiley & Sons.

Hopwood, C. J., & Thomas, K. M. (2012). Paranoid and schizoid personality disorders. In T. A. Widiger (Ed.), *The Oxford Handbook of Personality Disorders* (pp. 582–602). New York: Oxford University Press.

Hopwood, C. J., & Thomas, K. M. (2012). Personality disorders. In M. Hersen & D. C. Beidel (Eds.), *Adult Psychopathology and Diagnosis* (6th ed., pp. 681–716). Hoboken, NJ: John Wiley and Sons.

Jang, K. L., & Vernon, P. A. (2001). Genetics. In W. J. Lively (Ed.), *Handbook of Personality Disorders* (pp. 177–195). New York: Guilford Press.

John, O. P. (1990). The "Big Five" factor taxonomy: Dimensions of personality in natural language and in questionnaires. In L. A. Pervin (Ed.), *Handbook of Personality: Theory and Research* (pp. 66–100). New York: Guilford Press.

Johnson, J. G., Bromley, E., & McGeoch, P. G. (2005). Role of childhood experiences in the development of maladaptive and adaptive personality traits. In J. M. Oldham, A. E. Skodol, & D. Bender (Eds.), *Textbook of Personality Disorders* (pp. 209–221). Washington, DC: American Psychiatric Publishing.

Johnson, P. A., Hurley, R. A., Benkelfat, C., Herpertz, S. C., & Taber, K. H. (2003). Understanding emotion regulation in borderline personality disorder: Contributions of neuroimaging. *The Journal of Neuropsychiatry & Clinical Neurosciences, 15*, 397–402.

Jung, C. G. (2001). *On the Nature of the Psyche* (2nd ed.). London: Routledge

Kaplan, M. (1983). A woman's view of DSM-III. *American Psychologist, 38*(7), 786–792.

Kernberg, O. F. (1991). Hysterical and histrionic personality disorders. In R. Michels (Ed.), *Psychiatry* (Vol. 1, pp. 1–11). Philadelphia: J. B. Lippincott.

Klein, M. (1984). The psycho-analysis of children (A. Strachey, Trans.). In R. Money-Kyrle (Ed.), *The Writings of Melanie Klein* (Vol. 2). New York: Free Press.

Koons, C. R. (2001). Efficacy of dialectical behavior therapy in women veterans with borderline personality disorder. *Behavior Therapy, 32*(2), 371–390.

Kraus, G., & Reynolds, D. J. (2001). The A-B-C's of the cluster B's: Identifying, understanding and treating cluster B personality disorders. *Clinical Psychology Review, 21*(3), 345–373.

Lee, R., & Coccaro, E. F. (2004). Biology of personality disorder. In A. F. Schatzberg & C. B. Nemeroff (Eds.), *The American Psychiatric Publishing Textbook of Psychopharmacology* (3rd ed., pp. 833–844). Washington, DC: American Psychiatric Publishing.

Linehan, M. M., Schmidt, H., Dimeff, III, L. A., Craft, C. J., Kanter, J., & Comtois, K. A. (1999). Dialectical behavior therapy for patients with borderline personality disorder and drug-dependence. *The American Journal on Addictions, 8*(4), 279–292.

Linehan, M. M., Comtois, K. A., Murray, A. M., Brown, M. Z., Gallop, R. J., Heard, H., . . . Lindenboim, N. (2006). Two-year randomized controlled trial and follow-up of dialectical behavior therapy vs therapy by experts for suicidal behaviors and borderline personality disorder. *Archives of General Psychiatry 63*(7), 757–766.

Livesley, W. J. (2001). Conceptual and taxonomic issues. In W. J. Livesley (Ed.), *Handbook of Personality Disorders Theory, Research, and Treatment* (pp. 3–38). New York: The Guilford Press.

Lynam, D. R., & Widiger, T. A. (2001). Using the five-factor model to represent the DSM-IV personality disorders: An expert consensus approach. *Journal of Abnormal Psychology, 110*(3), 401–412.

McAdams, D. P. (1992). The five-factor model in personality: A critical appraisal. *Journal of Personality, 60*(2), 329–361.

McCrae, R. R., & Costa, P. T. (1987). Validation of the five-factor model of personality across instruments and observers. *Journal of Personality and Social Psychology, 52*(1), 81–90.

McCrae, R. R., & Costa, P. T. (2003). *Personality in Adulthood: A Five-Factor Theory Perspective* (2nd ed.). New York: Guilford Press.

McCrae, R. R., & John, O. P. (1992). An introduction to the five-factor model and its applications. *Journal of Personality and Social Psychology, 60*(2), 175–215.

McGuffin, P., Moffitt, T., & Thapar, A. (2002). Personality Disorders. In P. McGuffin, M. J. Owen, & I. I. Gottesman (Eds.), *Psychiatric Genetics and Genomics* (pp. 183–210). New York: Oxford University Press.

Millon, T., & Grossman, S. D. (2005). Sociocultural factors. In J. M. Oldham, A. E. Skodol, & D. Bender (Eds.), *Textbook of Personality Disorders* (pp. 223–235). Washington. DC: American Psychiatric Publishing.

Mischel, W. (1968). *Personality and Assessment*. New York: Wiley.

Mulder, R. T. (2012). Cultural aspects of personality disorder. In T. Widiger (Ed.), *The Oxford Handbook of Personality Disorders* (pp. 260–273). New York: Oxford University Press.

Oldham, J. M. (2005). Personality disorders recent history and future directions. In J. M. Oldham, A. E. Skodol, & D. S. Bender (Eds.), *The American Psychiatric Publishing Textbook of Personality Disorders* (pp. 3–16). Washington, DC: American Psychiatric Publishing.

Oldham, J. M., Skodol, A. E., & Bender, D. S. (2005). Introduction. In J. M. Oldham, A. E. Skodol, & D. S. Bender (Eds.), *The American Psychiatric Publishing Textbook of Personality Disorders* (pp. xvii–xx). Washington, DC: American Psychiatric Publishing.

Paris, J. (2005). A current perspective on personality disorders. In J. M. Oldham, A. E. Skodol, & D. Bender (Eds.), *The American Psychiatric Publishing Textbook of Personality Disorders* (pp. 119–128). Washington, DC: American Psychiatric Publishing.

Paris, J. (2012). Pathology of personality disorder: An integrative conceptualization. In T. A. Widiger (Ed.), *The Oxford Handbook of Personality Disorders* (pp. 399–406). New York: Oxford University Press.

Phillips, K., & Gunderson, J. G. (1999). Personality disorders. In R. E. Hales, S. C. Yudofsky, & J. A. Talbott (Eds.), *The American Psychiatric Press Textbook of Psychiatry* (3rd ed., pp. 795–823). Washington, DC: American Psychiatric Press.

Pilkonis, P., Hallquist, M. N., Morse, J. Q., & Stepp, S. D. (2011). Striking the (im)proper balance between scientific advances and clinical utility: Commentary on the DSM-5 proposal for personality disorders. *Personality Disorders: Theory, Research, and Treatment, 2*, 68–82.

Plomin, R., & Bergeman, C. S. (1991). The nature of nurture: Genetic influence on "environmental" measures. *Behavioral Brain Sciences, 14*, 373–427.

Reich, J., Yates, W., & Nduaguba, M. (1989). Prevalence of DSM-III personality disorders in the community. *Social Psychiatry and Psychiatric Epidemiology, 24*(1), 12–16.

Reynolds, S. K., & Clark, L. A. (2001). Predicting dimensions of personality disorder from domains and facets of the five factor model. *Journal of Personality, 69*(2), 199–222.

Rolland, J.-P. (2002). Cross-cultural generalizability of the five-factor model of personality. In R. R. McCrae & J. Allik (Eds.), *The Five-Factor Model of Personality Across Cultures* (pp. 7–28). New York: Springer.

Roussos, P., & Siever, L. J. (2012). Neurobiological contribution. In T. A. Widiger (Ed.), *The Oxford Handbook of Personality Disorders* (pp. 299–324). New York: Oxford University Press.

Sadock, B. J., & Sadock, V. A. (2007). *Kaplan and Sadock's Synopsis of Psychiatry* (10th ed.). Philadelphia: Wolters Kluwer/Lippincott Williams & Wilkins.

Samuels, J., & Costa, P. T. (2012). Obsessive-compulsive personality disorder. In T. A. Widiger (Ed.), *The Oxford Handbook of Personality Disorders* (pp. 566–581). New York: Oxford University Press.

Sanislow, C. A., da Cruz, K. L., Gianoli, M. O., & Reagan, E. M. (2012). Avoidant personality disorder, traits, and type. In T. A. Widiger (Ed.), *The Oxford Handbook of Personality Disorders* (pp. 549–565). New York: Oxford University Press.

Saucier, G. (2003). Factor structure of English-language personality type-nouns. *Journal of Personality and Social Psychology, 85*(4), 695–708.

Saulsman, L. A., & Page, A. C. (2004). The five-factor model and personality disorder empirical literature: A meta-analytic review. *Clinical Psychology Review, 23*, 1055–1085.

Schotte, C., De Doncker, D., Maes, M., Cluydts, R., & Cosyns, P. (1993). MMPI assessment of the DSM-III-R histrionic personality disorder. *Journal of Personality Assessment, 60*(3), 500–510.

Seager, W. (2007). A brief history of the philosophical problems of consciousness. In P. D. Zelazo, M. Moscovitch, & E. Thompson (Eds.), *The Cambridge Handbook of Consciousness* (pp. 9–33). Cambridge, UK: Cambridge University Press.

Simeon, D., & Hollander, E. (2004). Treatment of personality disorders. In A. F. Schatzberg & C. B. Nemeroff (Eds.), *The American Psychiatric Publishing Textbook of Psychopharmacology* (3rd ed., pp. 1049–1066). Washington, DC: American Psychiatric Publishing

Skodol, A. E. (2012). Diagnosis and DSM-5: Work in progress. In T. Widiger (Ed.), *The Oxford Handbook of Personality Disorders* (pp. 35–57). New York: Oxford University Press.

Spitzer, R. L., Williams, J. B. W., & Skodol, A. E. (1980). DSM-III: The major achievements and an overview. *American Journal of Psychiatry, 137*, 151–164.

Sprock, J., Blashfield, R. K., & Smith, B. (1990). Gender weighting of DSM-III-R personality disorder criteria. *American Journal of Psychiatry, 147*(5), 586–590.

Squires-Wheeler, E., Friedman, D., Amminger, G. P., Skodol, A., Looser-Ott, S., Roberts, S., & Erlenmeyer-Kimling, L. (1997). Negative and positive dimensions of schizotypal personality disorder. *Journal of Personality Disorders, 11*(3), 285–300.

Stahl, S. (2000). *Essential Psychopharmacology: Neuroscientific Basis and Practical Applications.* New York: Cambridge University Press.

Sutker, P. B., & Allain, A. N., Jr. Antisocial personality disorder. In H. E. Adams & P. B. Sutker (Eds.), *Comprehensive Handbook of Psychopathology* (3rd ed., pp. 445–490). New York: Kluwer Academic/Plenum Publishers.

Teicher, M. H., Glod C. A., Surrey J., & Swett C. Jr. (1993). Early childhood abuse and limbic system ratings in adult psychiatric outpatients. *Journal of Neuropsychiatry and Clinical Neuroscience*, 5, 301–306.

Teicher M. H., Ito Y. N., Glod C. A., Schiffer F., & Gelbard H. A. (1994). Early abuse, limbic system dysfunction, and borderline personality disorder. In K. R. Silk (Ed.), *Biological and Neurobehavioral Studies of Borderline Personality* (pp. 177–207). Washington, DC: American Psychiatric Press.

Torgersen, S., Czajkowski, N., Jacobson, K., Reichborn-Kjennerud, T., Røysamb, E., Neale, M. C., & Kendler, K. S. (2008). Dimensional representations of DSM-IV cluster B personality disorders in a population-based sample of Norwegian twins: A multivariate study. *Psychological Medicine*, 38(11), 1617–1625.

Torgersen, S., Kringlen, E., & Cramer, V. (2001). The prevalence of personality disorders in community sample. *Archives of General Psychiatry*, 58, 590–596.

Trull, T. J., Sher, K., Minks-Brown, J. C., Durbin, J., & Burr, R. (2000). Borderline personality disorder and substance use disorders: A review and integration. *Clinical Psychology Review*, 20(2), 235–253.

van der Eijk, P. J. (2005). Between the Hippocratics and the Alexandrians: Medicine, philosophy and science in the fourth century BCE. In R. W. Sharples (Ed.), *Philosophy and the Sciences in Antiquity* (pp. 72–109). London: Ashgate Publishing.

Verheul, R., Van den Bosch, L. M. C., Koeter, M. W. J., De Ridder, M. A. J., Stijnen, T., & Van den Brink, W. (2003). Dialectical behaviour therapy for women with borderline personality disorder 12-month, randomised clinical trial in The Netherlands. *The British Journal of Psychiatry*, 182, 135–140.

Wagerman, S. A., & Funder, D. C. (2009). Personality psychology of situations. In P. J. Corr & G. Matthews (Eds.), *The Cambridge Handbook of Personality Psychology* (pp. 27–41). Cambridge, UK: Cambridge University Press.

Widiger, T. A. (1998). Sex bias in the diagnosis of personality disorders. *Journal of Personality Disorders*, 12, 95–118.

Widiger, T. A. (2001). Social anxiety, social phobia, and avoidant personality disorder. In W. R. Corzier & L. Alden (Eds.), *International Handbook of Social Anxiety* (pp. 335–356). New York: John Wiley & Sons.

Widiger, T. A. (2005). Five factor model of personality disorder: Integrating science and practice. *Journal of Research in Personality*, 39, 67–83.

Widiger, T. A. (2011). A shaky future for personality disorders. *Personality Disorders: Theory, Research, and Treatment*, 2, 54–67.

Widiger, T. A. (2012). Historical developments and current issues. In T. A. Widiger (Ed.), *The Oxford Handbook of Personality Disorders* (pp. 13–34). New York: Oxford University Press.

Woo, S. M., & Keatinge, C. (2008). *Diagnosis and Treatment of Mental Disorders Across the Lifespan*. Hoboken, NJ: John Wiley & Sons.

9

CHILD AND ADOLESCENT MENTAL DISORDERS

An Overview

Why worry about children and mental disorders? After all, during this developmental stage of life almost every individual picks up some skills more quickly and others more slowly than expected. Additionally, the stereotype is to anticipate that teens will know everything about everything, except how to control their emotions and behaviors, a frequent indicator of mental disorder. Ultimately, many people easily and frequently argue that there is no "normal" when talking about children and adolescents. The difficulty is that we have historically followed this paradigm and have failed to consider that up to 20% of youths in the United States and at least 15% of Canada's children have a measurable mental health problem, and 50% of adults with a mental disorder developed it before or by the age of 13 (Centers for Disease Control and Prevention, 2013b; Government of Canada, 2009; Mash, 2006). Because neurobiological disorders can start in childhood and follow one into adulthood, the *DSM-5* does not have a separate section for early childhood problems, as did the *DSM-IV*. Criteria for early onset illnesses are nested in the individual descriptions of the neurodevelopmental disorders that can follow individuals across the life span (American Psychiatric Association, 2013; Paris, 2013). As with adults, the causation and development of these disorders are not clear. However, children provide peeks into the diversity of pathways that most likely play a role in the onset of mental disorders. The purpose of this chapter is to provide an overview of a few diagnostic categories and mental health issues impacting today's youths. In addition to the material in this chapter, information about child and adolescent disorders has been integrated into most of the previous chapters.

Because a child has had fewer life experiences and because genetic histories are often available, clinical hypotheses and insights are marginally easy to formulate. Children and adolescents particularly serve as models for understanding how ecological interactions between environments and biology may provide at least one explanation for the onset of mental disorders. Animal research over many years has indicated that enhanced environments are often protective, while stressful and impoverished milieus can negatively affect a youth's behavior and brain development (Eiland, Ramroop, Hill, Manley, & McEwen, 2012; E. H. Taylor & Cadet, 1989). A recent prospective longitudinal study employing MRI scans over a 3- to 6-year period discovered that living in poverty can change key areas of a child's developing brain. The researchers documented that experiencing poverty early in childhood is associated with smaller white and cortical gray matter, and smaller hippocampal and amygdala volumes. Additionally, hippocampal changes, though not others, appear to be mediated positively by caregiving support and negatively by parental hostility and stressful life events (Luby et al., 2013). What the study does not tell us is the extent to which environment and biology account for the changes and mediating factors. For example, one does not know when the brain abnormalities were triggered, or the actual role played by biology and environmental events such as poor prenatal care, nutrition, sample selection, and parental psychopathology (Luby et al., 2013). In addition, the study oversampled preschoolers known to have depression. This presents a sampling error and limits the study's generalizability (Luby et al., 2013). Therefore, while the study illustrates bioecological interactions, it fails to define whether both biological and environmental factors are required and whether one must be primary for triggering or mediating mental disorders (Luby et al., 2013).

DIFFERENTIATING AMONG DISRUPTIVE MOOD DYSREGULATION, BIPOLAR, CONDUCT, AND OPPOSITIONAL DEFIANT DISORDERS

There is a growing concern that children and young adolescents are over-diagnosed and over-treated for bipolar disorders (Paris, 2013). Inappropriately labeling a child with any disorder can trigger a chain of negative and potentially dangerous events. A misdiagnosis of bipolar illness, however, most often results in immediate medication treatment. Each time this happens, a child improperly receives an antimanic, antiseizure, or antipsychotic drug that has been researched, tested, and approved not for youths, but for adults. To address the potential for over-diagnosing childhood bipolar illness, the *DSM-5* panels created a new disorder called disruptive mood dysregulation disorder (DMDD; American Psychiatric Association, 2013). Even though the disorder causes symptoms that resemble conduct and impulse problems, it has been placed in the *DSM-5* section addressing depression (Paris, 2013). This is because a small amount of research indicates that many of these children convert, in their adolescence or young adulthood, to unipolar depression or anxiety rather than bipolar illness (American Psychiatric Association, 2013). Some mental health clinicians and researchers, however, worry that the new diagnoses will increase the number of children given a mental illness label, and will increase rather than decrease the use of psychotropic medications (Frances, 2011). This fear is partially supported by a study of 706 children between the ages of 6 and 12 years. Twenty-six percent, or 184 of the participants, met *DSM-5* criteria for DMDD, but could not be clinically distinguished from children with oppositional defiant disorder and conduct disorder (Axelson et al., 2012).

Disruptive mood dysregulation disorder (DMDD) is diagnosed when a child demonstrates severe age-inappropriate verbal temper outbursts or physical aggression toward individuals or property, and the symptoms occur before the age of 10 years (American Psychiatric Association, 2013). Once it has been documented that the behaviors and mood dysregulation started before the age of 10, the diagnoses can be given up to an adolescent's 18th birthday. Generally, a diagnosis of DMDD is not given before the age of 6 or after one turns 18 (American Psychiatric Association, 2013). Additionally, the child generally demonstrates chronic and persistent irritability and has three or more tantrums per week (American Psychiatric Association, 2013). Furthermore, as with all diagnoses, the symptoms must not reflect cultural learning. Additionally, this disorder is most often seen in boys, whereas bipolar illness occurs equally in males and females (American Psychiatric Association, 2013).

One may think of DMDD as uncontrolled emotion driven by irritability and possibly an undercurrent of depression. Unlike childhood bipolar irritability or anger, DMDD symptoms are more chronic than episodical (American Psychiatric Association, 2013). Childhood, adolescent, and adult onset bipolar disorder I and II tend to have more clearly defined episodical boundaries. Moreover, bipolar mania often includes increased cognitive, behavioral, and physical symptoms that return to their normal baseline once the episode ends (American Psychiatric Association, 2013; Finnerty, 2013). However, one of the difficulties in differentiating between the two disorders is identifying chronic activity from short-term rapid cycling. Separating an episode from chronic behaviors that ebb and flow requires close observation and documentation at home, school, and after-care programs. This is not a natural process for parents, teachers, or care providers, so it is therefore an important role for social workers to train the supporting adults how to specifically observe, log, and behaviorally describe positive and troublesome child events. In addition, recent research indicates that childhood bipolar illness largely mimics adult symptoms (Finnerty, 2013; National Institute of Mental Health, 2013; Paris, 2013). Rapid cycling for adults is defined as four or more episodes in a 12-month period (American Psychiatric Association, 2013). Consequently, caution and extra assessment care is needed before labeling multiple behavioral changes or events in a single day as manic or depressive episodes (Finnerty, 2013). The dilemma that psychiatrists face is that there is growing evidence that early treatment of childhood bipolar mania and depression can possibly decrease the severity of symptoms and lengthen the time between episodes (K. Chang, Gallelli, & Howe, 2007). Longitudinal studies are needed to clarify which medications, given at what point or points in time and to which children, will delay the onset and severity of bipolar symptoms. One study, for example, found that the early use of mood stabilizers, but not antidepressants or stimulant medications, delayed the onset of mania in children and adolescents with full or subsyndromal bipolar illness (K. D. Chang, Saxena, Howe, & Simeonova, 2010). While it is unknown whether adding DMDD to *DSM-5* is a progressive step, it does underscore the growing tendency to over-diagnose childhood bipolar disorder, and to prescribe major psychiatric medications for controlling aggression.

Oppositional defiant disorder (ODD) has many similar symptoms to those found in DMDD. Youths with ODD often lose their temper, become touchy and quickly annoyed, and speak in angry or resentful tones. They are also infamous for claiming that their mistakes and misbehaviors occurred only in response to someone else's incorrect actions or unreasonable demands. In addition, they can be defiant, refuse to follow rules, and quickly become robustly argumentative with parents, teachers, and other authority figures (American Psychiatric Association, 2013). These same behaviors can also be seen in many children with DMDD. The principle that separates the two diagnostic groups is that children with DMDD experience persistent disturbances in mood after or between severe behavioral outbursts, unlike those with ODD. Furthermore, DMDD causes severe decreases in social functioning within at least one setting and mild to moderate impairment when interacting in a second setting. Children with ODD do not show the same degree of functional impairment within and across settings (American Psychiatric Association, 2013).

Both DMDD and ODD are differentiated from conduct disorder by the level of aggression expressed toward others. Children and adolescents with conduct disorders have behaviors such as purposefully breaking rules and routinely lying in order to gain material items and favors, or to avoid obligations. They may also freely steal from others, and can be violent to people and animals or destructive to property (American Psychiatric Association, 2013). The *DSM-5* lists 15 major behavioral misconducts that violate the rights of people or go against basic social values. To qualify for a diagnosis of conduct disorder, the youth must have demonstrated at least 3 of the 15 behaviors within the past 12 months (American Psychiatric Association, 2013).

In the past few years, prescription of antipsychotic medications for treating child and adolescent aggression resulting from DMDD, bipolar, conduct, and oppositional defiant disorders has risen at an alarming rate. The use of second generation antipsychotic medications (SGAm) increased approximately fourfold for British Columbia males 6 to 18 years of age between 1996 and 2010 (more for older youths and somewhat less for those under 13) (Horn et al., 2012). There is no doubt that psychiatric medication treatment is appropriate for many children and adolescents. However, a growing number of children and adolescents with no history of psychosis or prodromal psychotic symptoms are being prescribed antipsychotic medications (Doey, Handelman, Seabrook, & Steele, 2007; Panagiotopoulos, Ronsley, Elbe, Davidson, & Smith, 2010; Patel et al., 2005). A comprehensive review of antipsychotic medication prescribed to youths across the United States documented that the drugs are mostly given to treat disruptive behavior rather than psychosis (Penfold et al., 2013). Little is known about who these youths are, whether they are correctly diagnosed, if treatments other than SGAm are systematically employed, how the medications are monitored, and what education and support are provided to the families.

While approximately 13%–18% of Canada's youths have a mental disorder, very few ever experience a psychotic episode (British Columbia Ministry of Child and Family Development, 2003; Spenrath & Kutcher, 2011). Epidemiologic studies report that the most common disorders found in youths are attention deficit hyperactivity disorder (ADHD), conduct disorder, and depressive disorders (Olfson, Blanco, Iiu, Moreno, & Laje, 2006; Spenrath & Kutcher, 2011). These disorders do not generally result in psychotic episodes. In British Columbia it is estimated that 60,900 youths have an anxiety disorder, 30,900 deal with a conduct disorder, another 30,900 deal with ADHD, and 19,700 experience some form of depression. However, the number of youths with schizophrenia and bipolar disorders, illnesses known to cause psychosis, in British Columbia is estimated to be less than 2,000. Adding youths with pervasive developmental disorders, which can cause psychotic episodes (though not always), increases the population known to benefit from SGAm by another 2,800 (British Columbia Ministry of Child and Family Development, 2003). That is, only 4,800 British Columbia youths, approximately, have symptoms that unquestionably warrant antipsychotic medication treatment.

On a broader scale, a nationwide Canadian survey found that SGAm were prescribed for youths for the treatment of psychosis, mood, anxiety, impulse (externalization), and pervasive developmental disorders. The researchers also discovered that 20%

of all prescriptions were for children under 9 years old, and that wide variations occur in how children on SGAm are clinically monitored (Doey et al., 2007). The researchers concluded that despite a lack of approved indicators, SGAm were increasingly prescribed to youths for off-label treatment of aggression, low frustration tolerance, and affective or mood dysregulation (Doey et al., 2007). This increase is taking place even though Canada has no approved indicators for SGAm use in children and adolescents. Additionally, no evidence-based guidelines for systematically monitoring youths receiving antipsychotic medications has been nationally adopted (Doey et al., 2007). Studies in the United States have similarly concluded that SGAm are being commonly used with children and young adolescents even though only limited evidence supports their efficacy with pediatric populations (Aparasu & Bhatara, 2007; Curtis et al., 2005; Olfson et al., 2006; Patel et al., 2005; Rani, Murray, Byrne, & Wong, 2008; Rawal, Lyons, MacIntyre II, & Hunter, 2004). Moreover, children in foster care and certain racial minorities in the United States are more often treated with SGAm than majority youths living with their families (Patel et al., 2005; Raghavan, Zima, Andersen, Leibowitz, & Landsverk, 2005; Zito et al., 2008).

These findings are concerning because the use of antipsychotic medications with children and adolescents carries some health and developmental risks. We know very little about the long-term impact of these medications on the developing brain (Rani et al., 2008). Furthermore, SGAm can trigger weight gain, tiredness, agitation, insomnia, confusion, difficulty concentrating, difficulty remembering, and increased dreaming (Byrne et al., 2010; Correll, 2008; Stigler, Potenza, Posey, & McDougle, 2004; Walter et al., 2008). In addition, weight gain increases a youth's risk for diabetes, cardiac problems, and other chronic illnesses (Stigler et al., 2004). We do not know what support and social interventions children prescribed SGAm routinely receive, or the effectiveness of these interventions. Studies are needed to identify which children are best treated with antipsychotic medications and how the drug intervention should be systematically monitored.

ATTENTION DEFICIT HYPERACTIVITY DISORDER

Attention deficit hyperactivity disorder (ADHD) affects 5%–11% of America's children between the ages of 4 and 17 years (Centers for Disease Control and Prevention, 2013a). Boys are more likely to have ADHD than girls, and the average age of diagnosis is 7 years old. However, children with more severe symptoms tend to be diagnosed at an even younger age (Centers for Disease Control and Prevention, 2013a). The increased learning and attending responsibilities of school may account for the identification of ADHD around the age of 7. ADHD consists of a persistent pattern of inattention, hyperactivity, or combinations of attention, hyperactivity, or impulse control problems that decrease the child's age-appropriate functioning or ongoing development (American Psychiatric Association, 2013). Youths with ADHD are generally found to have altered neurobiological structures and functioning, along with motor and language difficulties or delays that are similar to those found in pervasive developmental disorders, learning disabilities, and Tourette disorders (E. Taylor & Sonuga-Barke, 2008). As a result, a child with ADHD is at risk or has a higher probability for developing co-occurring disorders (E. Taylor & Sonuga-Barke, 2008). Studies indicate a high association between ADHD and executive or frontal cortex brain functioning (Huang-Pollock & Nigg, 2003; E. Taylor & Sonuga-Barke, 2008). This may in part explain why children with ADHD have difficulty systematically problem-solving, and executing good age-appropriate judgment. Moreover, individuals with ADHD have reduced brain volume, with a larger decrease of white and grey matter in the right hemisphere (Seidman, Valera, & Makris, 2005; E. Taylor & Sonuga-Barke, 2008). These similarities in neurodevelopment with other disorders can create diagnostic dilemmas. Therefore, it is important for social work clinicians to differentiate between ADHD and oppositional/defiant or conduct, learning, and other disorders. While these disorders can co-occur, it becomes easy to either label misconduct as ADHD rather than defiance, or to suppose that a youth is simply oppositional and difficult when the behaviors, in reality, are symptoms of an attention deficit (E. Taylor & Sonuga-Barke, 2008).

The *DSM-5* defines hyperactivity as ". . . excessive motor activity (such as a child running about) when it is not appropriate, or excessive motor fidgeting, tapping, or talkativeness" (American Psychiatric Association, 2013). The disorder cannot be diagnosed if several attention deficit symptoms are not reported before the age of 12, and if the identified problems occur in only one setting (American Psychiatric Association, 2013). Hyperactivity that is primarily observed in only one environment signals a decrease in personal wellness triggered by specific ecological factors that are unique to the identified setting, rather than an ADHD disorder. A youth with ADHD will have a cluster of symptoms that cause difficulties and problems in the following areas:

- Attending to multiple, simultaneous, or sequential details and requirements; as a result, he or she makes careless errors that are obvious to others;
- Focusing or maintaining attention and interest in games, activities, or lectures, and he or she is easily distracted by noticeable surrounding stimuli or almost random unrelated thoughts occurring while in the midst of another activity;

- Paying attention to others because his or her mind wanders, even when there are no obvious environmental distractions, and additionally may avoid tasks or work requiring concentration and extended systematic thinking;
- Organizing, losing things frequently, and failing many times to finish an agreed-upon task, or forgetting to perform common activities such as appointments, homework, or routine courtesies;
- Sitting for an extended period without leaving the seat; squirming or fidgeting when remaining seated is expected;
- Restlessness, talking excessively, interrupting others, and blurting a response or answer before the question or statement by another person can be completed;
- Waiting and taking turns; appears to stay in motion and always going or doing something, including, in some cases, moving around or climbing on things when it is not appropriate (American Psychiatric Association, 2013).

A child or adolescent who has attention and concentration problems but few symptoms of hyperactivity or impulse control is diagnosed as having ADHD with predominantly an inattentive presentation (American Psychiatric Association, 2013). The popular press and others often refer to these children as simply having attention deficit disorder (ADD). There are also youths who exhibit hyperactivity, but no real attention problems. The *DSM-5* specifier for these clients is ADHD with predominantly a hyperactivity and impulse presentation (American Psychiatric Association, 2013).

ANXIETY AND DEPRESSION

Anxiety and depression in youths were overviewed in previous chapters. However, as with ADHD and conduct problems, children and adolescents are constantly referred to clinics and school mental health workers for the assessment and treatment of these two disorders. Additionally, anxiety, depression, ADHD, and conduct problems often share similar or overlapping symptoms. We know that anxiety is one of the most common disorders found in children and adolescents, and depression in youths is a major public health problem (Clarke & Lewinsohn, 2003; Kendall, Aschenbrand, & Hudson, 2003). As illustrated in Chapter 7, anxiety involves neurobiological alterations, experiential learning, and futuristic thinking. That is, the child is either predisposed, or events change the brain, causing the youth to become hypersensitive to the environment. As a result, experiences that may or may not be traumatic to others become magnified in the child or adolescent's mind. Once the person is overly attending to the surroundings, fear or anxiety sets in as futuristic thoughts predict doom.

The clinical presentation of anxiety to include obsessive compulsive disorder largely mimics the symptoms found in adults (American Psychiatric Association, 2013; Freeman et al., 2004). The *DSM-5* criteria for all types of anxiety, including separation anxiety, are identical for children, adolescents, and adults. However, the symptoms are expressed according to the emotional age of the individual. Children, for example, with separation anxiety may cling and find it impossible to go to a different room of the house without a parent or sibling, whereas adults report difficulty traveling and staying in a hotel alone. Both children and adults may experience nightmares and sleep problems (American Psychiatric Association, 2013). Figure 9.1 illustrates the age at which children and adolescents most often start to experience differing types of anxiety. However, clinic workers see some young children with types of anxiety disorders that are known to most often start in late childhood and adolescence. Thus one should not automatically rule out any particular type of anxiety simply because of the child's age.

Clinicians and others routinely assertively state that anxiety, at least for many children, is caused by economic, traumatic, or other environmental events. This, however, is less evident from a research perspective. The most consistent risk factor for a child to develop some form of anxiety is gender. Girls continue to develop the disorder at a higher rate than boys (Pine & Klein, 2008). Researchers are not able to come to an agreement concerning how and to what extent environment plays a role in causing or triggering anxiety disorders. There is no doubt that anxiety in children and adolescents has been linked to poverty, abuse and other trauma, school failure, numerous life stressors, family and parenting dysfunction, parental mental health problems, low parental education, and single parenting. However, none of these ecological events

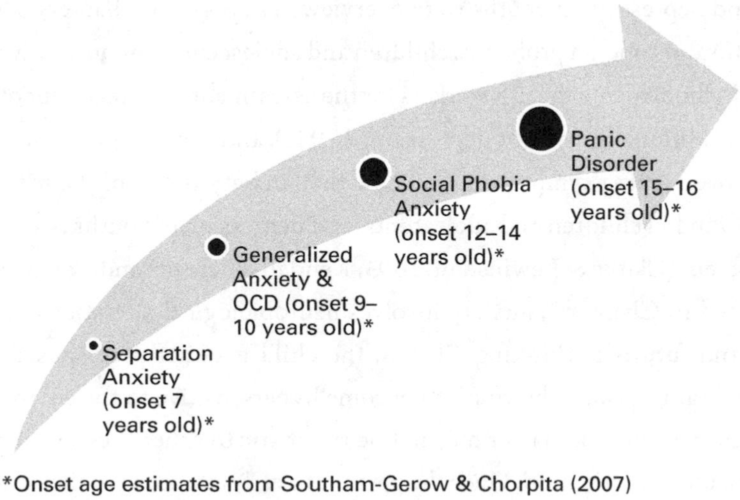

Panic Disorder (onset 15–16 years old)*

Social Phobia Anxiety (onset 12–14 years old)*

Generalized Anxiety & OCD (onset 9–10 years old)*

Separation Anxiety (onset 7 years old)*

*Onset age estimates from Southam-Gerow & Chorpita (2007)

FIGURE 9.1 Child and Adolescent Anxiety Onset by Age and Disorder.

creates a consistent causation pattern. Even changes in social welfare are not associated with changes in the rates of anxiety (Costello, Compton, Keller, & Angold, 2003; Pine & Klein, 2008). Furthermore, when associations among family, environment, and child-adolescent onset anxiety are statistically found, causation remains elusive.

There are still, however, reasons to suspect that ecology plays a significant role in the formation and triggering of anxiety. As has been stated in several parts of this book, animal studies indicate that stressful environments can alter brain structures and functioning. Furthermore, there is growing evidence that neuro-circuitry responsible for stabilizing anxiety is altered in infant rats when parental attachment is disrupted (Moriceau & Sullivan, 2005). Moreover, children who experience trauma consistently demonstrate anxiety symptoms that include, but are not limited to, post-traumatic stress disorder (PTSD). Whether trauma will result in PSTD, a different category of anxiety, or no disorder is not predictable on an individual basis. We also know that an enriched home environment can for some reduce anxiety related to a learning disorder, lessen the severity of learning problems, and possibly help develop new neuro pathways (Haight & Taylor, 2013).

While the question of causation cannot be answered, there is substantial evidence that environment plays an interacting role in the causation of child and adult anxiety. Consequently, a healthy ecological fit within the home, school, and community will often improve the youth and significant others' quality of life, and may substantially reduce mental health symptoms. Nonetheless, social workers and other clinicians can best serve children and families when parents, home environments, or life experiences are not automatically seen as the explanation for an anxiety disorder. It is important for us to keep in mind that science has not quantified how much environment creates, interacts, or triggers child onset anxiety. Social workers will therefore want to offer interventions that improve a child's environmental fit without implying causation or blaming. Manualized exposure and other forms of cognitive therapy have become a primary treatment for most forms of early onset anxiety (Chorpita, 2007). Though there are many different forms and protocols for cognitive therapy, at the heart of the methods is the belief that to a large extent people can decide to shape and change themselves and their environments. A key belief is that a client must decide to change. This is both a positive and negative factor in using cognitive therapy with children and adolescents. Change is thought to occur when a client identifies, challenges, and changes faulty misconceptions, beliefs, distorted ideas, irrational self-talk, and unhealthy or destructive behaviors.

Cognitive treatment thus requires a high level of collaboration with the client, and a relationship that empowers the therapist to guide the exploration and make suggestions that sound factual. If clinical suggestions do not sound genuine, the client will find collaborating and completing practice exercises meaningless. As a result, it is almost impossible to initiate cognitive treatment if the child or adolescent does not feel connected to the therapist, or for any reason is not willing to participate. Cognitive treatment for anxiety or depression will consequently fail if the clinician does not first engage and educate the child. However, relationship alone seldom resolves anxiety symptoms. A major problem observed in clinics is that social workers and other clinicians never move from relationship building and positive engagement to cognitively treating the anxious child (Chorpita, 2007). To move from relationship building to intervention, cognitive therapy teaches clients to identify, evaluate, and respond differently to dysfunctional thoughts and beliefs. To accomplish this, therapists use a number of tools or methods with young clients that include the following:

- Education about the targeted disorder, and how cognitive therapy works;
- Clarification of thoughts and emotions;
- Emphasis on the present, with little attention to the past;
- Collaboration to identify emotions creating dysfunctional thoughts, and thoughts causing difficult emotions;
- Identification and change of negative self-talk;
- Reframing of automatic negative thinking to a more positive perspective;
- Restructuring of harmful or dysfunctional thoughts and emotions into permanent constructive concepts;
- Use of exposure to end fears and behaviors preventing a greater quality of life;
- Homework aimed at stopping and changing automatic negative thoughts;
- Testing and practicing of healthy thoughts and emotions;
- Continuous evaluation of symptom and functional change.

Though exposure therapy is one of the most effective and widely used interventions for working with anxious children and adolescents (Chorpita, 2007), other forms of cognitive treatment have also been found helpful. Guided self-help cognitive therapy has shown promise for helping anxious youths. This intervention teaches parents to deliver specific interventions with their children. A study in the United Kingdom found that the manualized full parent guided method was superior when compared to wait-list youths, and parents receiving a shorter version of the intervention (Thirlwall et al., 2013).

Anxiety is often, though not always, accompanied by depression. Clinic studies indicate that depressed children are at a higher risk for developing a co-occurring disorder. It is not clear if the comorbidity results from shared genetic and neurobiological factors, or is triggered by depression (Brent & Weersing, 2008). There is growing evidence that pre-natal exposure to tobacco smoke may disrupt the brain's regulatory processes and may increase the risk for depression and anxiety (Schuetze, Lopez, Granger, & Eiden, 2008). Additionally, alterations in cortisol levels have also been found in infants of depressed and anxious mothers (Azak, Murison, Wentzel-Larsen, Smith, & Gunnar, 2013). The biological foundation for depression and anxiety may be rooted in genetics. One twins study discovered that genes increasing the risk for anxiety also boost the probability for experiencing higher levels of sensitivity, and exposure to depressogenic (substances or factors) life events (Brent & Weersing, 2008; Eaves, Silberg, & Erkanli, 2003). The role that family and parenting styles play in causing depression is unclear. There is evidence, however, that family discord and expressed emotion focused on the child predicted onset or recurrence of depression if the child was already at risk for a mood disorder (Asarnow, Goldstein, Tompson, & Guthrie, 1993; Brent & Weersing, 2008). Considering that the study was done with inpatient youths and a brief assessment instrument, one must be careful in how the study is interpreted and applied in practice. Bullying is also an ecological interacting force in the development or triggering of depressive symptoms. Interestingly, research shows that both youths who are bullied and children or adolescents who do the bullying have a higher rate of depression than that found in the general population (Brent & Weersing, 2008). This suggests that assessments specifically for depression and anxiety are needed for both the bullied and the tormentor.

Like anxiety, depression is often treated with planned cognitive therapy. When a child is severely depressed, the treatment may need to simply consist of reduction of stress, with support and relationship building, for an extended period. Once recovery starts, however, it is important to move from a simple supportive relationship into a cognitive-behavioral, problem-solving, or other active therapeutic modality. Social workers need to constantly screen and assess for suicidal thoughts. This is true for all disorders, but particularly when a youth has depression. The National Institute of Mental health lists the following indicators as risk factors for suicide (National Institute of Mental Health, 2014):

- Threatening to hurt or kill oneself or talking about wanting to hurt or kill oneself;
- Looking for ways to kill oneself by seeking access to firearms, available pills, or other means;
- Talking or writing about death, dying, or suicide when these actions are out of the ordinary for the person;
- Feeling hopeless;
- Feeling rage or uncontrolled anger or seeking revenge;

- Acting reckless or engaging in risky activities—seemingly without thinking;
- Feeling trapped—like there's no way out;
- Increasing alcohol or drug use;
- Withdrawing from friends, family, and society;
- Feeling anxious, agitated, or unable to sleep or sleeping all the time;
- Experiencing dramatic mood changes;
- Seeing no reason for living or having no sense of purpose in life.

After completing a literature review, Hawton and Fortune (2008) found that the following behaviors are often seen specifically in children and adolescents who make a suicide attempt:

- Hopelessness;
- All or nothing thinking (as an example, I can never pass this course, or I will never be happy);
- Belief that one has no control over what will happen personally to him or her;
- Difficulty with or incorrect problem-solving skills;
- Over-generalized personal memories (nothing good ever happens in our family, every time something bad happens in the family, it happens to me);
- Substance abuse, including cigarette smoking;
- Difficult parent-child relationships and attachment problems;
- Family history of suicide and non-fatal attempts of suicide by family members;
- Having a friend commit suicide;
- A gay, lesbian, or bisexual orientation (most likely related to stress created by cultural and societal rejection);
- Exposure to rejection, conflict, or breakup in relationships;
- Dropping out of school.

Together, the NIMH and Hawton and Fortune indicators provide a more comprehensive view of youthful suicidal behavior or thinking, and can make assessments more robust. The role that media and the Internet play in child and adolescent suicides is not clear. There is some evidence, however, that depressed boys are heavy users of the Internet. In addition, depressed youths are more likely to participate in chat-rooms than children and adolescents who are free of depressive symptoms (Hawton & Fortune, 2008; Ybarra, Alexander, & Mitchell, 2005).

Social workers can play an important role in helping youths and their parents better interpret and understand how overuse of the Internet can at best simply remove a person from more stimulating social events, and at worst may be an indicator of dangerous depression. Hawton and Fortune (2008) report that school-based prevention programs can be helpful, but they also quote research documenting that older school suicidal programs are questionable. They were referring specifically to programs that identify suicide as a reaction to life stress, which emphasize that it could happen to anyone, and that fail to underscore the mental illness realities of suicidal behavior. Additionally, school-based programs do not routinely include youths with high rates of absenteeism or who have dropped out of school completely (Hawton & Fortune, 2008). A new program focusing on training parents to prevent suicide, entitled Resourceful Adolescent Program (RAP-P), is showing promising results. The RAP-P consists of four manualized parental educational sessions that do not include the at-risk adolescent. This is a brief strengths-based intervention. Families receiving RAP-P showed a significant decrease in their child's suicidal behaviors compared to parents and youths receiving usual community care (Pineda & Dadds, 2013).

In addition to prevention, every effort must be made to provide immediate ongoing treatment and support to the youth and family once a suicidal attempt is made and survived. Evidence shows that the child or adolescent is at added risk for repeating suicidal behaviors for the first 12 months following an actual attempt (Hawton & Fortune, 2008). In most cases, antidepressant treatment requires ongoing planned psychosocial interventions including cognitive-behavioral therapy, support, education, and family-parental education (Hawton & Fortune, 2008). Though antidepressants were once thought to increase the risk of adolescent suicide, current studies no longer support this hypothesis (Isacsson & Rich, 2014). A Swedish study reviewed all youths 10–19 years of age who committed suicide during a 2-year period. During the period studied, prescriptions for antidepressants to adolescents increased, but the rise did not significantly explain suicidal behaviors. Only 20% of the youths who committed suicide had received medication treatment in the previous 6 months (Isacsson & Ahlner, 2013). As with adults, the determination of whether medication treatment is needed is dependent on the severity of the illness and a complete assessment by a qualified medical doctor. Social workers are not in a position to make medication recommendations; however, social workers' ecological, functional, and diagnostic assessments can significantly help medical personnel more accurately identify whether antidepressant drugs would be helpful.

CHILD AND ADOLESCENT PSYCHOSIS

Recent research has made progress in identifying many of the major symptoms related to youth psychoses. Nonetheless, our ability for assessing, diagnosing, and treating psychotic youths relies largely on practice wisdom and clinical judgment rather than evidence (McGorry, Yung, & Phillips, 2002). Empirical studies document that psychotic symptoms are the result of neurobiological disorders. Nonetheless, very little is known about how these symptoms vary across gender, culture/race, age, and differing neurodevelopment (Kumra, Nicolson, & Rapoport, 2002). We have only rudimentary knowledge of how genetics, brain development, social-cognitive maturation, and ecological factors impact illness severity.

Studies indicate that psychotic symptoms in childhood are heritable and are linked to many of the risk factors found in adult schizophrenia (Moffitt, Polanczyk, Arseneault, Cannon, et al., 2010). In addition, youths with psychosis are often born with low birth weight and have early academic difficulties, speech and language problems, and numerous developmental delays (McClellan & Werry, 2001). The largest study to date of monozygotic twins discordant for schizophrenia documented that deficits in social cognition, gross and fine motor skills, and social-emotional behaviors occurred in 30% of the ill twins by their fifth birthday. The study also found that delivery and birth abnormalities occurred more often in the ill than well twins, and that social-economic status did not explain differences in the course of illness (McNeil et al., 1994; Torrey, Bowler, Taylor, & Gottesman, 1994; Torrey, Taylor, et al., 1994). While the twins had many indicators found in youths with psychosis the subjects did not develop schizophrenia until their early adulthood. The failure to find significant social-economic factors may reflect the study's limited sampling or may illustrate an important question for future research.

Other studies indicate that children with psychotic episodes reside at a higher rate than non-psychotic youths in chaotic homes, and experience significantly more maltreatment (Moffitt et al., 2010; Mortensen et al., 1999; Read, 1997). Current assessment skills, however, cannot predict which of these children will overcome brief psychotic episodes and which will develop a lifetime diagnosis of schizophrenia. Additionally, many of the abuse studies rely on retrospective self-reports from young adults who continue to have psychotic episodes. The causal relationship between maltreatment, trauma, and possible psychosis also remains unresolved (Kelleher et al., 2013). Therefore, social work and child welfare researchers need to more empirically study how ecological and family factors relate to psychosis. It certainly is possible that ecological factors play a larger role in some forms of early onset psychosis and less in other types.

Our inability to predict outcome across the entire psychosis spectrum occurs partly because the indicators grossly overlap with non-psychotic disorders such as learning and attention disorders (E. H. Taylor, 1998, 2003). In addition, a review of literature found wide variability in youth psychosis morbidity patterns and outcome predictors (Bromet,

Mojtabai, & Fennig, 2002). Treatment effectiveness research for helping youths with psychoses is also lacking. A study from the National Institute of Mental Health reports that few youths treated for psychosis with antipsychotic medications benefited from their initial treatment choice over the long term (National Institute of Mental Health, 2010). The findings suggest that few youths continue treatment on the same antipsychotic medication over an extended period of time. The primary reasons given for stopping the medications were (1) the drugs were not effective, and (2) the medication caused adverse effects. Those who dropped out of the study often reported having intolerable side effects. There continues to be a need for research that clarifies when antipsychotic medications should be used for psychosis, and which types of psychosis positively respond to drug treatments. Social work research can strive to clarify when all forms of medications increase functioning and how to help children and adolescents better comply to beneficial prescriptions.

REFERENCES

American Psychiatric Association. (2013). *Diagnostic and Statistical Manual of Mental Disorders* (5th ed.). Arlington, VA: American Psychiatric Association.

Aparasu, R. R., & Bhatara, V. (2007). Patterns and determinants of antipsychotic prescribing in children and adolescents, 2003–2004. *Current Medical Research and Opinion, 23*(1), 49–56.

Asarnow, J. R., Goldstein, M. J., Tompson, M., & Guthrie, D. (1993). One-year outcomes of depressive disorders in child psychiatric in-patients: Evaluation of the prognostic power of a brief measure of expressed emotion. *Journal of Child Psychology and Psychiatry, 34*, 129–137.

Axelson, D., Findling, R. L., Fristad, M. A., Kowatch, R. A., Youngstrom, E. A., Horwitz, S. M., . . . Birmaher, B. (2012). Examining the proposed disruptive mood dysregulation disorder diagnosis in children in the Longitudinal Assessment of Manic Symptoms study. *Journal of Clinical Psychiatry, 73*(10), 1342–1350.

Azak, S., Murison, R., Wentzel-Larsen, T., Smith, L., & Gunnar, M. R. (2013). Maternal depression and infant daytime cortisol. *Developmental Psychobiology, 55*(4), 334–351.

Brent, D., & Weersing, R. (2008). Depression disorders in childhood and adolescence. In M. Rutter, D. Bishop, D. Pine, S. Scott, J. Stevenson, E. Taylor, & A. Thapar (Eds.), *Rutter's Child and Adolescent Psychiatry* (pp. 587–612). Oxford, UK: Wiley-Blackwell.

British Columbia Ministry of Child and Family Development. (2003). *Child and Youth Mental Health Plan for British Columbia* (pp. 1–45). Victoria, BC: British Columbia, Ministry of Child and Family Development. Retrieved June 23, 2004, from http://www.mcf.gov.bc.ca/mental_health/pdf/cymh_plan.pdf.

Bromet, E. J., Mojtabai, R., & Fennig, S. (2002). Epidemiology of first-episode schizophrenia. In R. Zipursky & C. S. Schulz (Eds.), *The Early Stages of Schizophrenia* (pp. 33–54). Washington, DC: American Psychiatric Publishing.

Byrne, S., Walter, G., Hunt, G., Soh, N., Cleary, M., Duffy, P., . . . Malhi, G. (2010). Self-reported side effects in children and adolescents taking Risperidone. *Australasian Psychiatry, 18*(1), 42–45.

Centers for Disease Control and Prevention. (2013a, November). *Data and Statistics*. Retrieved January 2014 from www.cdc.gov/ncddd/adhd/data.html.

Centers for Disease Control and Prevention. (2013b). *Mental Health Surveillance Among Children—United States, 2005–2011 (Supplement 2)*. Morbidity and Mortality Weekly Report, 62, 1–35. Atlanta, GA: Office of Survellance, Epidemiology Services.

Chang, K., Gallelli, K., & Howe, M. (2007). Early identification and prevention of early-onset bipolar disorder. In D. Romer & E. F. Walker (Eds.), *Adolescent Psychopathology and the Developing Brain: Integrating Brain and Prevention Science* (pp. 315–514). New York: Oxford University Press.

Chang, K. D., Saxena, K., Howe, M., & Simeonova, D. (2010). Psychotropic medication exposure and age at onset of bipolar disorder in offspring of parents with bipolar disorder. *Journal of Child and Adolescent Psychopharmacology, 20*(1), 25–32.

Chorpita, B. F. (2007). *Modular Cognitive-Behavior Therapy.* New York: Guilford Press.

Clarke, G. D., Lynn L., & Lewinsohn. (2003). Cognitive-behavioral group treatment for adolescent depression. In A. E. Kazdin & J. R. Weisz (Eds.), *Evidence-Based Psychotherapies for Children and Adolescents* (pp. 120–134). New York: Guilford Press.

Correll, C. U. (2008). Antipsychotic use in children and adolescents: Minimizing adverse effects to maximize outcomes. *Journal of the American Academy of Child and Adolescent Psychiatry, 47*(1), 9–20.

Costello, E. J., Compton, F. N., Keller, G., & Angole, A. (2003). Relationships between poverty and psychopathology: A natural experiment. *Journal of the American Medical Association, 290*(15), 2023–2029.

Curtis, L. H., Masselink, L. E., Østbye, T., Hutchison, S., Dans, P. E., Wright, A.,. . . Suchulman, K. A. (2005). Prevalence of atypical antipsychotic drug use among commercially insured youths in the United States. *Archives of Pediatrics and Adolescent Medicine, 159*(4), 362–366.

Doey, T., Handelman, K., Seabrook, J., & Steele, M. (2007). Survey of atypical antipsychotic prescribing by Canadian child psychiatrists and developmental pediatricians for patients under 18 years. *The Canadian Journal of Psychiatry, 52*(6), 363–368.

Eaves, L., Silberg, J., & Erkanli, A. (2003). Resolving multiple epigenetic pathways to adolescent depression. *Journal of Child Psychology and Psychiatry, 44*, 1006–1014.

Eiland, l., Ramroop, J., Hill, M. N., Manley, J., & McEwen, B. S. (2012). Chronic juvenile stress produces corticolimbic dendritic architectural remodeling and modulates emotional behavior in male and female rats. *Psychoneuroendocrinology, 37*(1), 39–47.

Finnerty, T. (2013). *Disruptive Mood Dysregulation Disorder (DMDD), ADHD and the Bipolar Child Under DSM-5.* Columbus, OH: PsychContinuingEd.com.

Frances, A. (Producer). (2011). DSM-5 approves new fad diagnosis for child psychiatry: Antipsychotic use likely to rise. *Psychiatric Times.* Retrieved from http://www.psychiatrictimes.com/articles/dsm-5-approves-new-fad-diagnosis-child-psychiatry-antipsychotic-use-likely-rise.

Freeman, J. B., Garcia, A. M., Swedo, S. E., Rapport, J. L., Fucci, C. M., & L., L. H. (2004). Obsessive-compulsive disorder. In J. M. Wiener & M. K. Dulcan (Eds.), *The American Psychiatric Publishing Textbook of Child and Adolescent Psychiatry* (3rd ed., pp. 575–588). Washington, DC: American Psychiatric Publishing.

Government of Canada. (2009). The Chief Public Health Officer's Report on the State of Public Health in Canada 2009. In Public Health Agency of Canada (Ed.), *State of Mental Health in Canada* (pp. 1–112). Ottawa: Public Health Agency of Canada.

Haight, W. L., & Taylor, E. H. (2013). *Human Behavior for Social Work Practice: A Developmental-Ecological Framework.* Chicago: Lyceum Books.

Hawton, K., & Fortune, S. (2008). Suicidal behavior and deliberate self-harm. In M. Rutter, D. Bishop, D. Pine, S. Scott, J. Stevenson, E. Taylor & A. Thapar (Eds.), *Rutter's Child and Adolescent Psychiatry* (pp. 648–669). Oxford, UK: Wiley-Blackwell.

Horn, M., Procyshyn, R. M., Warburton, W. P., Tregillus, V., Cavers, B., & Davidson, J. (2012). Prescribing second-generation antipsychotic medications: Practice guidelines for general practitioners. *BC Medical Journal, 54*(2), 75–82.

Huang-Pollock, C. L., & Nigg, J. T. (2003). Searching for the attention deficit in attention deficit hyperactivity disorder: The case of visuospatial orienting. *Clinical Psychology Review, 23*, 801–830.

Isacsson, G., & Ahlner, J. (2013). Antidepressants and the risk of suicide in young persons: Prescription trends and toxicological analyses. *Acta Psychiatrica Scandinavica.* doi: 10.111/acp. 12160.

Isacsson, G., & Rich, C. L. (2014). Antidepressant drugs and the risk of suicide in children and adolescents. *Pediatric Drugs*. doi: 10.1007/s40272-013-0061-1.

Pineda, J., & Dadds, M. R. (2013). Family intervention for adolescents with suicidal behavior: A randomized controlled trial and mediation analysis. *Journal of the American Academy of Child and Adolescent Psychiatry, 52*(8), 851–862.

Kelleher, I., Keeley, H., Corcoran, P., Ramsay, H., Wasserman, C., Carli, V.,. . . Cannon, M. (2013). Childhood trauma and psychosis in a prospective cohort study: Cause, effect, and directionality. *American Journal of Psychiatry, 170*, 734–741. doi: 10.1176/appi.ajp.2012.12091169.

Kendall, P. C., Aschenbrand, S., & Hudson, J. L. (2003). Child-focused treatment of anxiety. In A. E. Kazdin & J. R. Weisz (Eds.), *Evidence-Based Psychotherapies for Children and Adolescents* (pp. 81–100). New York: Guilford Press.

Kumra, S., Nicolson, R., & Rapoport, J. (2002). Childhood-onset schizophrenia: Research update. In R. Zipursky & C. S. Schulz (Eds.), *The Early Stages of Schizophrenia* (pp. 161–190). Washington, DC: American Psychiatric Publishing.

Luby, J., Belden, A., Botteron, K., Marrus, N., Harms, M., Babb, C.,. . . Barch, D. (2013). The effects of poverty on childhood brain development: The mediating effect of caregiving and stressful life events. *Journal of the American Medical Association Pediatrics, 167*(12), 1135–1142.

Mash, E. J. (2006). Treatment of child and family disturbance. In E. J. Mash & R. A. Barkley (Eds.), *Treatment of Childhood Disorders* (3rd ed., pp. 3–62). New York: Guilford Press.

McClellan, J., & Werry, J. S. (2001). Practice parameter for the assessment and treatment of children and adolescents with schizophrenia. *Journal of the American Academy of Child and Adolescent Psychiatry, 40*(Supplement), 48–238.

McGorry, P. D., Yung, A. R., & Phillips, L. J. (2002). What features predict the onset of first-episode psychosis within an ultra-high-risk group? In R. Zipursky & C. S. Schulz (Eds.), *The Early Stages of Schizophrenia* (pp. 3–32). Washington, D.C.: American Psychiatric Publishing.

McNeil, T. F., Cantor-Graae, E., Torrey, E. F., Sjostrom, K., Bowler, A. E., Taylor, E. H.,. . . Higgins, E. S. (1994). Obstetric complications in histories of monozygotic twins discordant and concordant for schizophrenia. *Acta Psychiatrica Scandinavica, 89*, 196–204.

Moffitt, G., Polanczyk, T., Arseneault, L., Cannon, M., & et al. (2010). Etiological and clinical features of childhood psychotic symptoms: Results from a birth cohort. *Archives of General Psychiatry, 67*, 328–338.

Moriceau, S., & Sullivan, R. M. (2005). Neurobiology of infant attachment. *Developmental Psychobiology, 47*(3), 230–242.

Mortensen, P. B., Pedersen, C. B., Westergaard, T., Wohlfahrt, J., Ewald, H., Mors, O.,. . . Melbye, M. (1999). Effects of family history and place and season of birth on risk of schizophrenia. *New England Journal of Medicine, 340*(8), 603–608.

National Institute of Mental Health. (2010). Effectiveness of long-term use of antipsychotic medication to treat childhood schizophrenia is limited. *Science News*. Retrieved June 23, 2014 from http://www.nimh.nih.gov/news/science-news/2010/effectiveness-of-long-term-use-of-antipsychotic-medication-to-treat-childhood-schizophrenia-is-limited.shtml.

National Institute of Mental Health. (2013). *Bipolar Disorder in Children and Teens*. Retrieved January 6, 2014, from http://www.nimh.nih.gov/health/publications/bipolar-disorder-in-children-and-teens-easy-to-read/index.shtml.

National Institute of Mental Health. (2014). *Warning Signs of Suicide*. http://www.nimh.nih.gov/health/topics/suicide-prevention/suicide-prevention-studies/warning-signs-of-suicide.shtml.

Olfson, M., Blanco, C., Liu, L., Moreno, C., & Laje, G. (2006). National trends in the outpatient treatment of children and adolescents with antipsychotic drugs. *Archives of General Psychiatry, 63*(6), 679–685.

Panagiotopoulos, C., Ronsley, R., Elbe, D., Davidson, J., & Smith, D. H. (2010). First do no harm: Promoting an evidence-based approach to atypical antipsychotic use in children and adolescents. *Journal of the Canadian Academy of Child and Adolescent Psychiatry, 19*(2), 124–137.

Paris, J. (2013). *The Intelligent Clinician's Guide to the DSM-5*. New York: Oxford University Press.

Patel, N. C., Crismon, M. L., Hoagwood, K., Johnsrud, M. T., Rascati, K. L., Wilson, J. P., & Jensen, P. S. (2005). Trends in the use of typical and atypical antipsychotics in children and adolescents. *Journal of the American Academy of Child and Adolescent Psychiatry, 44*(6), 548–556.

Penfold, R. B., Stewart, C., Hunkeler, E. M., Madden, J. M., Cummings, J. R., Owen-smith, A. A.,. . . Ahmedani, B. K. (2013). Use of antipsychotic medication in pediatric populations: What do the data say? *Current Psychiatry Reports, 15*, 1–10. doi: 10.1007/s11920-013-0426-8.

Pine, D. S., & Klein, R. G. (2008). Anxiety disorders. In M. Rutter, D. Bishop, D. Pine, S. Scott, J. Stevenson, E. Taylor, & A. Thapar (Eds.), *Rutter's Child and Adolescent Psychology* (5th ed., pp. 628–647). Oxford, UK: Wiley-Blackwell.

Raghavan, R., Zima, B. T., Andersen, R. M., Leibowitz, A. A., & Landsverk, J. (2005). Psychotropic medication used in a national probability sample in the child welfare system. *Journal of Child and Adolescent Psychopharmacology, 15*(1), 97–106.

Rani, F., Murray, M. L., Byrne, P. J., & Wong, I. C. K. (2008). Epidemiologic features of antipsychotic prescribing to children and adolescents in primary care in the United Kingdom. *Pediatrics, 121*(5), 1002–1009.

Rawal, P. H., Lyons, J. S., MacIntyre, J. C., II, & Hunter, J. C. (2004). Regional variations and clinical indicators of antipsychotic use in residential treatment: A four-state comparison. *Journal of Behavioral Health Services and Research, 31*(2), 178–188.

Read, J. (1997). Child abuse and psychosis: Literature review and implications for professional practice. *Professional Psychology: Research and Practice, 28*(5), 448–456.

Schuetze, P., Lopez, F. A., Granger, D. A., & Eiden, R. D. (2008). The association between prenatal exposure to cigarettes and cortisol reactivity and regulation in 7-month old infants. *Developmental Psychobiology, 50*(8), 819–834.

Seidman, L. J., Valera, E. M., & Makris, N. (2005). Structural brain imaging or attention-deficit/hyperactivity disorder. *Biological Psychiatry, 57*, 1263–1272.

Southam-Gerow, M. A., & Chorpita, B. F. (2007). Anxiety in children and adolescents. In E. J. Mash & R. A. Barkley (Eds.), *Assessment of Childhood Disorders* (pp. 347–397). New York: Guilford Press.

Spenrath, M. A., & Kutcher, S. (2011). The science of brain and biological development: Implications for mental health research, practice and policy. *Journal of Canadian Academy of Child and Adolescent Psychiatry, 20*(4), 298–304.

Stigler, K. A., Potenza, M. N., Posey, D. J., & McDougle, C. J. (2004). Weight gain associated with atypical antipsychotic use in children and adolescents: Prevalence, clinical relevance, and management. *Pediatric Drugs, 6*(1), 33–44.

Taylor, E., & Sonuga-Barke, E. (2008). Disorders of attention and activity. In M. Rutter, D. Bishop, D. Pine, S. Scott, J. Stevenson, E. Tayor, & A. Thapar (Eds.), *Rutter's Child and Adolescent Psychiatry* (5th ed., pp. 521–542). Oxford, UK: Wiley-Blackwell Publishing.

Taylor, E. H. (1998). Advances in the diagnosis and treatment of children with serious mental illness. *Child Welfare, 77*(3), 311–332.

Taylor, E. H. (2003). Practice methods for working with children who have biologically based disorders: A bioecological model. *Families in Society, 84*, 39–50.

Taylor, E. H., & Cadet, J. L. (1989). Social intelligence, a neurological system? *Psychological Reports, 64*, 423–444.

Thirlwall, K., Cooper, P. J., Karalus, J., Voysey, M., Willetts, L., & Creswell, C. (2013). Treatment of child anxiety disorder via guided parent-delivery cognitive-behavioral therapy: Random controlled trail. *British Journal of Psychiatry, 203*(6), 436–444.

Torrey, E. F., Bowler, A. E., Taylor, E. H., & Gottesman, I. I. (1994). *Schizophrenia and Manic Depressive Disorder: The Biological Roots of Mental Illness as Revealed by the Landmark Study of Identical Twins*. New York: Basic Books.

Torrey, E. F., Taylor, E. H., Bracha, S., Bowler, A. E., McNeil, T. F., Rawlings, R. R., . . . Gottesman, I. I. (1994). Prenatal origin of schizophrenia in a subgroup of discordant monozygotic twins. *Schizophrenia Bulletin, 20*, 423–432.

Walter, G., DeLaroche, A., Soh, N., Hunt, G., Cleary, M., Malhi, G.,. . . Rey, J. (2008). Side effects of second-generation antipsychotics: The experiences, views and monitoring practices of Australian child psychiatrists. *Australasian Psychiatry, 16*(4), 253–262.

Ybarra, M. L., Alexander, C., & Mitchell, K. J. (2005). Depressive symptomatology, youth Internet use, and online interactions: A national survey. *Journal of Adolescent Health, 36,* 9–18.

Zito, J. M., Safer, D. J., Sai, D., Gardner, J. F., Thomas, D., Coombes, P.,. . . Maria, M.-L. (2008). Psychotropic medication patterns among youth in foster care. *Pediatrics, 121*(1), 157–163.

10

INTO THE FUTURE

In the last days of 2013, with much publicity, the fifth edition of the *Diagnostic and Statistical Manual of Mental Disorders* (*DSM-5*) was released. The new edition made only minor changes to the diagnostic criteria for most mental disorders found in *DSM-IV-TR*. While the manual has been important in classifying, discussing, and treating mental disorders, its limitations, recognized in this book and elsewhere, indicate how little we know about the nature, causes, and appropriate treatments of mental disorders. The new *DSM* manual reinforces and documents that after years of academic inquiry, we cannot identify the causation for most mental disorders. Certainly the brain and environment are complicated and difficult to define, let alone research. Nonetheless, considering the ongoing advances in medical science, one wonders why so little is known about the causation and treatment of mental disorders. Like most complex questions, there is no single answer. It is easy to blame limited government and private foundation research funding and inconsistent sponsorship of ongoing lines of research. Additionally, the fact that the brain is protected by a difficult to penetrate bony skull hindered observation and understanding until imaging and functional measurements became possible. These tools are beginning to unlock the secrets of the brain's structures, chemical messaging, and networking systems. Moreover, the fact that the brain interacts with, and can only be interpreted within, the context of diverse evolving cultural-social-political-economic ecological systems increases the probability for false starts and spurious scientific findings. All of these factors contribute to our lack of knowledge about the causation of mental illness. However, social work and other helping professions, reflecting the current state of society at large, have also played a role in delaying the discovery of what causes, triggers, and supports the onset of mental disorders. The necessary richness and diversity of thought that engenders discoveries and new knowledge can easily unravel, becoming entangled with individual biases and yielding strongly held opposing positions. The result is that some texts may address the neurobiological understanding of mental illness, while others might go so far as to declare mental illness a myth. The resulting conflict is counterproductive and destructive to the goals of discovery. The vilification of science in the name of righting social wrongs or supporting a specific political agenda does a disservice to the social work profession and to the people it is dedicated to serving. Without unifying theoretical constructs for defining and guiding our teaching, research, and policy advocacy about mental health and illness, it is difficult to move forward. As a result, our ability to maintain a consistent voice in advocating how mental health research and service dollars are spent is compromised.

ASSESSMENT

Discovering the causation of mental illness is a critical step in developing prevention strategies. As medical and neurological sciences advance in this regard, social work can develop expertise in the assessment and measurement of environment and ecological systems. Though social work educators and clinicians consistently talk about the role of environment, we have developed very few tools for assessing how ecological settings differentially affect individuals across the life span. Books produced for reporting and reprinting clinical instruments often do not have a section for specific environmental measurement scales, and contain few newly developed ecological tools (Corcoran & Fischer, 2013; Rush, First, & Blacker, 2008). The lack of instruments in part occurs because researchers, academics, and clinicians have yet to reach an agreement on a primary lens for studying multidimensional and complex ecological systems. A school of social work could support vital research development, perhaps beginning with hosting an international conference for experts to set an agenda and a theoretical model for comprehensively studying ecological factors, mental disorders, decrease in wellness, and brain activity.

In addition to tools for measuring how environments affect clients, there is an urgency for social work research to participate with other mental health professionals in advancing clinical diagnostic and assessment methods. The mental health professions require instruments that have the ability to accurately

- screen, assess, and diagnose precursors to major mental disorders;
- provide a system for continuous linked assessment throughout the client's illness;
- determine a person's mental health diagnoses and needs across age, gender, and cultures in a timely manner;

- guide medical teams in personalizing interventions to include psychotherapy, environmental, and medication treatment for children, adolescents, and adults across age, gender, and cultural groups; and
- identify how long-term use of antipsychotic and other medications differentially alters neurodevelopment, cognition, emotion, social development, and productivity over time, within and across diagnostic and cultural-social-economic groups.

We also need a new generation of assessment tools built upon a bioecological foundation that is sensitive to cultural, gender, and age differences. Often, psychometric concepts like neurobiology, cognition, emotion, and gender-social-cultural factors are either explored as separate unrelated diagnostic and treatment issues, or are largely overlooked. As a result, assessment information over time can become contradictory, founded upon differing theoretical perspectives, poorly organized, and forgotten. Clients with long-term disorders seldom have assessment findings over time integrated into a gestalt that systematically guides clinical decisions and provides an accurate historical picture of the individual's illness and strengths. Without scientifically proven, continuous, integrated mental health assessment, treatment progress becomes less certain. A new generation of assessment and diagnostic tools are needed that continuously connect and update (1) screening, (2) diagnostic assessments, (3) assessments for personalizing treatment, and (4) assessments for measuring the developmental impact and effectiveness of medication, social, psychological, and environmental treatments over time. An innovative mental health system requires empirical stepwise instruments that link and maintain a flow of information, from the most simplistic screening to diagnosis, treatment, neurobiological and behavioral changes, and outcome evaluations. Our existing assessment instruments are disconnected from one another, fail to reflect current scientific findings, and are neither comprehensive nor truly continuous throughout the screening, diagnostic, and treatment process. Because the assessment process is disjointed, actualizing the axiom of continuous multidimensional assessment is hindered or completely lost, and evidence-based practice suffers in the process.

It is predictable that the publication of *DSM-5* will create a rush to revise standard assessment instruments. However, simple updates to match minor *DSM* changes will produce instruments that are much the same as today's tools. The time has come to psychometrically design tools that incorporate new findings from brain imaging, biochemistry, human development, genetics, cognitive development and functional skills, environmental-social-cultural evidence, and computer science. Moreover, the next generation of instruments hopefully will be computer integrated, allowing for an ongoing reassessment of continuous client information and integration of client changes, discoveries, and information. In this manner, no information is ever lost, and from the beginning to the end, patient data are continuously computer analyzed. This "forward-backward" data assessment analysis would have the ability to highlight contradictive or changing information, isolated or hidden factors, and interacting variables.

LINKING ASSESSMENT AND TREATMENT

There is growing agreement that some forms of psychosis, such as schizophrenia, are neurodevelopmental and degenerative. Unfortunately, the acute symptoms may not appear until late adolescence. We must develop diagnostic assessment methods that more accurately identify which youths are in a hidden pre-psychotic state. Evidence suggests that antipsychotic medications decrease early onset psychotic symptoms and aggression. Unfortunately, we are just starting to learn how to use neurobiological medications with children and young adolescents. Currently, parents and mental health practitioners cannot be advised how, when, and what type of antipsychotic medication treatments are appropriate and optimal for children and adolescents. That is, even when it is clear that neuroleptic medication treatment is needed, medical doctors cannot quickly and easily personalize the prescribed drug selection and dosage. Furthermore, it is unknown if medication effectiveness and side effects vary within and across age, gender, and cultural groups. Numerous assessment questions around antipsychotic treatment for children and young adolescents remain unanswered. We do not know if personalizing the medication treatment process would result in decreased drug side effects and increased effectiveness. Additionally, it is unknown whether there are acceptable alternatives to antipsychotic medication treatment, or if the "right-personalized" neuroleptic drug is empirically our best-practice model for treating asymptomatic pre-psychosis and non-psychotic youths who are exhibiting aggression. Moreover, we have yet to document the developmental protections and consequences related to early child and adolescent use of antipsychotic medications.

In addition, personalized bioecological treatment requires clinicians to more robustly involve themselves with the families of adults, adolescents, and children with mental disorders. Family education and support has consistently been identified as an important element of evidence-based treatment (Beecher, 2009). Individuals with schizophrenia often have improved mental health outcomes when the family receives supportive education and become clinical treatment partners. However, studies indicate that most families are not directly involved in the clinical decision-making and team-treatment process (Beecher, 2009; Marshall & Solomon, 2004; Doornbos, 2002).

Social work interventions are not truly bioecological until assessments, treatments, and support include consideration of the client's neurobiology and overall health, family, community, and vital systems that support or present barriers to the ill person and that individual's family.

SOME CURRENT CHALLENGES

For some youths, aggression is an early indicator announcing the coming onset of bipolar disorders, schizophrenia, depression, attention disorders, substance addiction, substance-related psychosis, or conduct disorder. Unfortunately, our current assessment tools have almost no ability to efficiently and within a brief time span predict which child exhibiting aggression will in time develop a major lifelong mental disorder. Furthermore, aggressive behavior may appear long before other symptoms that clarify a youth's diagnosis. Unfortunately, most aggression research focuses on treating or improving behavior. While this is important, these studies treat aggression as the primary difficulty or explanatory-variable, rather than a complex indicator of a possible oncoming neurobiological disorder. Therefore, it is essential for research to develop assessment instruments that psychometrically and biologically determine whether a youth's aggression is reflecting a hidden neurobiological disorder. We must also identify the effectiveness of antipsychotic medications across diagnostic categories. A new literature review found efficacy in using risperidone and aripiprazole for treating irritability in youths with pervasive developmental disorders (PDD). However, the authors concluded that the same usefulness has not been established for the majority of antipsychotic medications presently used for treating PDD irritability and aggression. It was not, however, within the study's scope to measure long-term developmental issues (Politte & McDougle, 2014).

"Personalized medicine" refers to using an individual's genetic markers for diagnosing and identifying therapies that best match the person's molecular profile. In the future, diagnostic and treatment decisions will be partly determined by genomics information. However, a person's genetics are also linked to environmental realities and bioecological interactions (Ginsburg & McCarthy, 2001). Recent research has argued that personalized medicine discoveries depend upon assessing and understanding the person and the environmental factors that contextually influence the individual (Kohane, 2009). Therefore, research must empirically determine whether bioecological factors such as birthweight, gender, poverty, diet, education, and so on, interact with a person's genetics and predict treatment selections and outcomes (Kohane, 2009).

Personalized medicine also requires an ability to know when a youth or young adult who is aggressive but has no psychotic symptoms should be placed on an antipsychotic medication. There is no doubt that psychiatric medication treatment is appropriate for many children and adolescents. However, a growing number of children and adolescents with no history of psychosis or prodromal psychotic symptoms are annually prescribed antipsychotic medications (Doey, Handelman, Seabrook, & Steele, 2007; Panagiotopoulos, Ronsley, Elbe, Davidson, & Smith, 2010; Patel et al., 2005). While the number of youths prescribed antipsychotics has increased, little is known about who these youths are, the accuracy of the diagnoses, if treatments other than drugs are systematically employed, how the medications are monitored, and what education and supports are provided to the families.

This same upward trend of using medication that has limited research with children may also be occurring for the treatment of depression and anxiety. A Danish study of 23,547 youths found that between 1995 and 2011 prescriptions for antidepressant medications for children and adolescents had increased from 0.57 per 1,000 youths to 2.55 per 1,000 individuals. Furthermore, a significant number of those treated with antidepressant medications also were using other psychotropic medications; 12%–28% of the youths were taking both an SSRI antidepressant and an antipsychotic medication. The researchers additionally found that the largest increase of antidepressant medication was among adolescents (Pottegard, Zoëga, & Damkier, 2014). The purpose for highlighting the use of psychiatric medications with children and adolescents is not to pass judgment on the practice, but rather to underscore the immediate need for research. It is important for social work to neither endorse nor advocate against treatment trends without empirical evidence. For example, we do not currently know if these increases are occurring because of population changes, better assessments resulting in the identification of more children in need of medication treatment, or a disturbing unfounded and unneeded practice.

As discussed in Chapter 8, the mental health professions know very little about what actually constitutes the difference between the wide range found in culturally accepted personality styles and personality disorders. There continues to be speculation that many of the *DSM-5* personality disorders are part of the spectrum of other disorders, rather than an independent illness. However, much more definite findings are needed before a decision for reclassifying the disorders into other categories can occur. A major task for social workers and other mental health professionals is to better link personality disorders to an evidence-based theory, and to determine where normalcy ends and pathology begins. A major dilemma across all disorders, but paramount with personality disorders, is that clinicians cannot concretely state where a problem that decreases mental wellness, but does not stem from a neurobiological foundation, ends and where a mental disorder begins. In other words, where is the line between personality-driven behaviors that are not healthy and a personality disorder in the mildest form? In addition, we know very little about how to effectively and differentially treat personality behaviors that are primarily linked to ecological factors rather than neurobiological development. Furthermore, this author argues that we have neither instruments nor interviewing standards for assessing when unique or unacceptable personality behaviors are learned responses to perceived environmental dangers, rather than a core part of the person's temperament and cognitive structures. Bad habits are annoying to others and often hurtful for the individual, but they should be assessed, labeled, and treated differently from personality disorders. This is equally true for all mental illness. Social work can greatly serve society by helping to develop means for identifying clients who have a decrease in their personal wellness from those individuals with an actual neurobiological disorder.

IMPLICATIONS FOR RESEARCH, TEACHING, AND TRAINING

There is hope and concrete indications that new approaches for understanding and treating mental disorders are on the horizon. Schools of social work across the United States and Canada have initiated creative teaching and research programs that emphasize empirical studies and the evaluation of evidence-based interventions. In addition, the National Institute of Mental Health has funded a number of research centers in schools of social work. Researchers at the School of Social Work, University of British Columbia, Okanagan Campus, are currently funded to study whether psychotropic drugs given to children and adolescents for aggression can be reduced by providing collaborative cognitive therapy, education, information, and case management. Additionally, each time the child or adolescent is seen, one or both parents are provided support and information. The parent session allows the clinic team to receive and give updates and to work with the family around parenting and community resource needs. An important part of this study is monitoring which youths respond to the treatment. The researchers are attempting to develop a bioecological profile from the cumulative data that predicts which children not only benefit from comprehensive services, but also are able to have their medications reduced. While we basically know that cognitive behavioral therapy and case management can reduce aggression, it is not known which variables most predict that a child has a high probability of needing medications along with supportive services.

Studies of this type have the potential for identifying which aggressive youths benefit from highly comprehensive but costly services. It is possible that some children whose aggression is out of control are best served with medication therapy and support. However, we will not know who these individuals are until research develops improved assessment methods. As assessment instruments and new methods are discovered, both social work students and clinicians who are already in the field will require in-depth training. These individuals also deserve to know exactly how much one can trust the research supporting the new diagnostic and treatment directions.

Finally, the theoretical understanding, assessment, and treatment of mental health versus mental disorders have become extremely complicated. As a result, schools of social work and other academic programs training mental health professionals must critically examine their clinical curriculum and field education methods. Most Canadian and US schools of social work at best offer a concentration in mental health, and have limited course offerings focusing on how ecological and neurobiological factors interact. Considering that a clinician is required to understand fundamental brain functioning, basic genetics, social-cultural-political forces, mental health policies, *DSM-5* disorders, assessment techniques, diagnostic and treatment integration or conceptualization, evidence-based interventions, and treatment evaluation, MSW education may want to move from organizing academics around concentrations to highly defined mental health specializations. We must also question whether our current form of field education supervision is effective.

The time has come to research whether students gain more from actual client contact or intense computer simulations, or a combination of both. The University of British Columbia, Okanagan Campus, is attempting to improve field education by co-sponsoring a mental health clinic with the Department of Psychology and the School of Nursing. The students not only receive more supervision than most community programs can provide, but actually become the treatment team. That is, there is one senior clinician, hired by the school, who serves as the team leader, but all assessments, treatment decisions, and interventions are determined by the students. To accomplish this, the students are expected to conduct weekly research, find instruments and methods, and report on their discoveries each Friday. In this way they prepare for the coming week and consolidate their combined knowledge. The team leader provides supervision and guidance, and ensures that evidence-based assessments and interventions are always employed. Interventions used in the clinic include different forms of psychotherapy, psychosocial education, case management, advocacy, and information or problem-solving parent meetings. A differential treatment plan that includes assessing the client and community is developed for each client. Future training plans include the introduction of computer simulations.

How social work frames and works with clients suffering from mental disorders is in the process of changing. We have moved from simple concepts based on untested logic to models and frameworks founded on empirical evidence. Social work is now, however, faced with a difficult balancing act of incorporating basic neurobiological information and maintaining a focus on the role that environment plays in the process of a person moving toward or away from mental illness. Our job is not to become junior neuroscientists, but rather to understand how environmental forces interact and affect neurobiological factors related to mental disorders. We also have to keep in mind, as stated earlier in this book, that all theories, treatment frameworks, and interventions bias us as clinicians. Therefore, while the social work profession must robustly research and document the boundaries of evidence-based interventions, new clinicians have the responsibility to ensure that they remain open-minded, questioning, and constantly studying. Accepting the honor of becoming a clinical social worker obligates a person to remain a lifetime student, open to new findings and willing to face and manage personal biases. This is a wonderful time to be entering the profession and the study of mental disorders. One of the author's greatest satisfaction is having served mental health clients, and having seen our profession move from blaming clients and families to understanding mental disorders as having a neurobiological foundation. However, the real understanding and treatment of mental illness wait to be discovered. As a social worker, you can play a vital role in advancing our knowledge of how ecological forces interact with brain factors and either propel individuals toward a meaningful quality of life or send them spinning into painful mental illness. The future is before us. What will you make of it, what will you contribute to better the mentally ill and increase our empirical treatment knowledge? The urgency to move mental health knowledge from opinion to replicated, research-supported evidence cannot be understated.

REFERENCES

Beecher, B. (2009). Mental health practitioners' views of families of individuals with schizophrenia and barriers to collaboration: A mixed methods study. *Journal of Family Social Work, 12*(3), 264–282.

Corcoran, K., & Fischer, J. (2013). *Measures for Clinical Practice and Research: A Sourcebook* (5th ed., Vol. 1–2). New York: Oxford University Press.

Doey, T., Handelman, K., Seabrook, J., & Steele, M. (2007). Survey of atypical antipsychotic prescribing by Canadian child psychiatrists and developmental pediatricians for patients under 18 years. *The Canadian Journal of Psychiatry, 52*(6), 363–368.

Doornbos, M. M. (2002). Family caregivers and the mental health care system: Reality and dreams. *Archives of Psychiatric Nursing, 51*(1), 39–46.

Ginsburg, G. S., & McCarthy, J. J. (2001). Personalized medicine: Revolutionizing drug discovery and patient care. *Trends in Biotechnology, 19*(12), 491–496.

Kohane, I. S. (2009). The twin questions of personalized medicine: Who are you and whom do you most resemble? *Genome Medicine, 1*(1), 1–4.

Marshall, T., & Solomon, P. (2004). Confidentiality intervention: Effects on provider-consumer-family collaboration. *Research on Social Work Practice, 14*(1), 3–13.

Panagiotopoulos, C., Ronsley, R., Elbe, D., Davidson, J., & Smith, D. H. (2010). First do no harm: Promoting an evidence-based approach to atypical antipsychotic use in children and adolescents. *Journal of the Canadian Academy of Child and Adolescent Psychiatry, 19*(2), 124–137.

Patel, N. C., Crismon, M. L., Hoagwood, K., Johnsrud, M. T., Rascati, K. L., Wilson, J. P., & Jensen, P. S. (2005). Trends in the use of typical and atypical antipsychotics in children and adolescents. *Journal of the American Academy of Child and Adolescent Psychiatry, 44*(6), 548–556.

Politte, L., & McDougle, C. (2014). Atypical antipsychotics in the treatment of children and adolescents with pervasive developmental disorders. *Psychopharmacology, 23*(6), 1023–36.

Pottegard, A., Zoëga, H., & Damkier, P. (2014). Use of SSRIs among Danish children: A nationwide study. *European Child and Adolescent Psychiatry*, 1–8. doi: 10.1007/s00787-014-0523-1.

Rush, J. A. J., First, M. B., & Blacker, D. (2008). *Handbook of Psychiatric Measures* (2nd ed.). Washington, DC: American Psychiatric Publishing.

INDEX

abuse, 8, 10, 15, 85, 90; and personality, 319; and
personality disorders, 320, 334, 347
acute stress disorder, 303–05
adolescents. *See* youth
advocacy, 52
agoraphobia, 294–95, 296
amygdala, 20, 206, 273, 287, 320, 357
anxiety disorders, 4, 23, 26; assessment of, 282,
290; cause of, 283, 285–86; and depression,
292; epidemiology of, 280–86; and gender,
281, 364; causes of, 364–65; and environment, 365; onset, 354 fig. 9.1; and personality,
285; symptoms of, 290; treatment of, 282,
290, 305, 365, 366. *See also* generalized anxiety disorder; obsessive compulsive disorder;
panic disorder; youth: and anxiety
assessments: agency, 54; cultural, 9, 34, 35,
76–78, 97; and causation of mental illness, 83;
conducting, 89–93,and clinical beliefs, 93–99;
ecological 18–19; 45, 88–89, 155, 169, 377;
errors in, 94; and evidence-based measurement instruments, 95, 377–78; gestalt, 84
fig.3.1; goals, 79, 88; hazards in, 90, 96; for
mental illness, 9, 19, 20, 28, 164, 168, 194;
observational, 153; planning process, 92 fig
3.3; preparing to conduct, 84, 86–87; process,
44, 83–88, 378; skills for, 98; and social work,
30, 35, 79–80, 97–98, 377, 195; of symptoms,
45, and theoretical frameworks, 79; and treatment, 89, 98, 378, 379–80
assessment tools, 34
attention deficits, 23, 26
attention deficit hyperactive disorder (ADHD),
361–63

baby blues, 231
basal ganglia, 195, 208–09, 273, 275, 287–88
biecological assessment model, 14 fig. 1.1

bioecological framework, 1, 7, 16–25, 17 box
1.1, 29–46; and assessment tools, 378; and
depression, 190; and epidemiology, 298;
and environment, 9, 10; and environmental
theory, 26–29 and social work, 2, 9, 10, 28, 40,
46, 89; and treatment of mental disorders, 18,
379–80; and the unconscious, 14
biology first perspective, 3–4, 8–11, 26
bipolar disorders, 231, 241–243, 247–50, 271–77;
assessment of, 217, 245–46, 250; and family,
268, 271; treatment of, 267, 268–71. *See also*
bipolar-I disorder; bipolar-II disorder; cyclothymia; schizoaffective disorder
bipolar-I disorder, 242, 243–244, 249, 251–55,
273, 273–74; episodes of, 266–67
bipolar-II disorder, 244, 255–56, 264, 273
Bonet, Theophile, 240
Bleuler, Eugene, 113, 165, 240
Bronfenbrenner, Uri, 1, 31–32, 36

Cade, John F. J., 241
catatonia, 129–31, 161
case formulation, 91–92, 91 fig. 3.2
change agents, 45–46
children. *See* youth
cingulate gyrus, 208, 273, 287
clients, 7, 9, 71–72, 94; rights of, 4, 86, 96, 137,
153
clinical assumptions, 88
clinical models, 63
clinicians. *See* social workers
cognitive assessments, 18–19
cognitive blocking, 26
cognitive theories, 28
cognitive treatment, 365–67
compulsions, 126, 127
concrete support, 51–52, 174, 222, 224
conduct disorder, 359–60

critical analysis, 24
culture, 32–33, 34–35
cyclothymia, 244, 246, 256

delusions, 26, 123–24, 149, 167; assessing, 124, 125–26, 127–28, 128 box 4.2, 137–38; and environment, 127; forms of, 125; and schizophrenia, 109, 113, 114, 124, 127, 156, 162–64; structure of, 127
dementia praecox, 112, 113, 240. *See also* schizophrenia
depression, 26, 85, 235–36; 243; and age, 190; assessment of, 207, 208, 214–16; and the brain, 206–10; cause of, 189–90, 210; diagnosis of, 184, 185, 186; epidemiology of, 190–91; and family, 188–89, 195, 191, 208, 209, 221; and gender, 185, 190; historical overview of, 185–86; and memory, 200–02; early onset of, 217–29; onset of, 189, 190; and personal experience, 186; and problem-solving skills, 205 fig 5.2; psychotic, 164; and sadness, 186–87; screening instruments for, 218; symptom identification, 188; treatment of, 186, 187, 189, 190, 219–28, 269. *See also*, bipolar disorders; cyclothymia; disruptive mood dysregulation disorder; dysthymia; major depressive disorder (MDD); premenstrual dysphoric disorder; postpartum depression; youth: and depression
depression, symptoms of, 187, 191, 203, 206, 218, 265–66; anhedonia, 194; and the cognitive domain, 202–206; and the emotional-affective domain, 191–94; and the information-processing domain, 196; and gender, 190; and the physical domain, 194–96; prodromal, 190
diminished reality, 115–38, 116 fig. 4.1, 156; mental disorganization, 129; summary of, 134 box 4.4. *See also* delusions; hallucinations; schizophrenia, symptoms of
disruptive mood dysregulation disorder (DDMD), 184, 357–58
dopamine, 146, 210, 275
DSM (Diagnostic and Statistical Manual of Mental Disorders), 5, 96, 359, 376; and anxiety disorders, 302; and bipolar disorders, 249–250, 251–58; and delusions, 134; and depression, 184–185; and manic episodes, 259–260; and personality, 317, 318, 321–25; 381; and schizophrenia, 13, 148, 156–168; and youth, 356, 357
dysthymia, 190, 220, 228–29, 230

ecological learning experience, 16
ecological systems, 32
ecological theory, 14, 28–29, 36, 46, 76
emotion, 20, 133, 192, 206
emotional-cognitive support, 52, 53 box 2.2
empty speech. *See* poverty of content of speech
encapsulation, 15–16, 23
environment, 1, 9, 26
environmental intervention, 36, 39
Erikson, Erik, 11
Falret, Jean-Pierre, 240

family, 72; assessment 53, 56, 57, 58–59, 78; and clinical framework 62–66; and confidentiality, 71, 76; and culture, 51, 76–78; differential attention to, 60; education, 60, 61–62, 94, 197, 200, 220; educational assessment questions 62; intervention, 49–50, 53; pain, 58; knowledge and strengths, 66–69; negative behavior of, 66; response to mental illness, 55, 64–65; and treatment participation, 72; and treatment team, 55, 69–71; reactions to mental illness 50–51 box 2.1. *See also* concrete support; advocacy; emotional-cognitive support
family-bioecological-relationship-model, 59
Freud, Sigmund, 11, 15, 185, 241, 313, 314; concept of the unconscious, 14–15, 314
frontal cortex, 24, 192, 199, 209, 288

Gibson, Eleanor J., 39
generalized anxiety disorder, 292, 307–09
Germain, Carol, 29–30, 31
Germain and Gitterman model, 29, 30
group think, 96

hallucinations, 26, 116, 149, 167, 326; assessment of, 118, 119, 120, 121–122 box 4.1, 122, 137–38; auditory, 119, 162; and children, 117; command, 119–20; and diagnosis, 117; gustatory, 119; olfactory, 119; pseudohallucinations, 117; and religion, 120, 122–23; and schizophrenia, 109, 113, 114, 156, 162, 164; and stress, 119; treating, 173–74; and violence, 120; visual, 119
hippocampus, 206, 273, 287, 320, 357
Hudson, Walter, 95
hyperventilation, 293
hypomania, 264–65
illusion, 118
information processing, 21–22, 25–26; 188 fig 5.1, 196; alerting and attending, 197; assessment of, 198, 200; cognitive steps of, 21–22;

and culture 22–23; decoding into schema, 198–200; encoding, 197–98; and memory, 200; testing and adjusting schema, 200

Johnson, Harriette, 29
Jung, Carl, 314

Klein, Melanie, 314
Kraepelin, Emil, 112–13, 147, 148, 240–41

learning disorders, 23
limbic system, 20, 82, 144, 199, 206, 273, 274, 276, 287, 320
Luria, Alexander, 38

major depression disorder (MDD), 190, 210–14;
major depressive episodes, 85
mania, 26, 239, 243, 250, 261–64. See also DSM: and manic episodes
manic-depression. See bipolar-I disorder
manic-depressive disorders. See bipolar disorders
memory: declarative, 206; long term, 23, 200, 201; short-term, 200–01, 206; social-cultural, 23–24, 25; working 15, 23, 26, 166, 197, 201, 207, 262; verbal, 202
mental disorders: causation, 2, 7, 8, 10, 13, 35, 80, 89, 118, 376; explanation, 29; diagnosis of, 92, 115; impact on cognitive functioning, 23; and mental gestalts, 25; and neurobiology, 2, 7, 16, 41
mental disorder, treatment of, 2, 7, 30, 46; causes of failure, 27; choice of, 19; goals of, 18, 30, 31; planning process 92 fig. 3.3, 153. See also specific conditions
Meyer, Carol, 29
mood disorders, 23, 187. See also depression

neurobiology, 1, 7, 10
neurobiological disorder, 8 table 1.1, 13, 86; See also mental disorders
norepinephrine, 210, 275

obsessive-compulsive disorder (OCD), 126, 167, 199–200, 284, 292, 296–301; 334
oppositional defiant disorder (ODD), 359
outcome measurement, 30
Palo Alto Group: and Bateson, Gregory, 113
panic, 288–89
panic attack, 290–292, 293
panic disorder: 289–96

paranoia, 26, 326; and depression, 203
perceived variance, 42–43; assessing and changing, 43–44
personality, 5, 16, 315; development of, 316; and the five factor model (FFM), 315–17, 324
personality disorders, 381–382; antisocial, 339–42; assessment of, 324, 326, 336, 337; avoidant, 345–46; borderline, 320, 334–39, 342; causes of, 317–21; dependent, 346–49; historical perspective on, 313–17; histrionic, 342–43; narcissistic, 342, 344–45; and neurobiology, 320; obsessive-compulsive, 349–51; paranoid, 325–28, 329; problems with DSM categorization, 321–25; schizoid, 325, 328–30; and schizophrenia, 322, 326; schizotypal, 329, 330–34; treatment of, 318, 328, 330, 337, 340, 343, 344, 346
personalized medicine, 380–81
phobia, 292
postpartum depression, 229, 231–34
post-traumatic stress, 10, 285, 291, 301–03
post-traumatic stress disorder (PTSD), 38, 83, 292, 303–07, 365
poverty, 8, 10, 151
premenstrual dysphoric disorder, 184
psychoanalytic model. See psychodynamic framework.
psychodynamic interventions, 11
psychodynamic framework, 3, 28; and depression, 185; and environment, 13; and neurobiology, 3; and personality, 314, 315, 321; problems with, 11–14, 17 box 1.1; and schizophrenia, 113–114, 175
psychosis, 4, 12, 30, 203, 262, 266, 274, 379; and bipolar-I disorder, 243, 244; and personality disorders, 326, 330, 336; and schizoaffective disorder, 247; symptoms of, 114–15, 370
psychosocial framework. See psychodynamic framework

reciprocal interaction, 36
Richmond, Mary, 59

schizoaffective disorder, 243, 247
schizophrenia, 3, 8, 23, 26, 38, 85, 273, 370; biology of, 140–47; and children, 118; diagnosing, 117, 119, 143, 144, 149, 153–56; elements of, 139 fig. 4.2; epidemiology of, 147–52; and ethnicity, 151–52; and family, 68, 111, 139, 177–79, 178 fig. 4.4; and gender, 151; historical overview of, 111–14; indicators of, 154;

levels of severity, 111; risk factors, 148, 150; social and economic effects of, 152–53; and substance abuse, 141; and stress, 110; Vermont Longitudinal Study, 147; worldwide rates of incidence, 150–51

schizophrenia, onset: 149; adult, 117, 143; early 117–18, 142, 149–50; and gender, 151. *See also* youth: and schizophrenia

schizophrenia, subtypes of, 159–60, 167; catatonic, 160–61; disorganized, 164–67; paranoid, 162–64; residual, 168–69; undifferentiated, 167–68

schizophrenia, symptoms of, 109, 114, 132, 139, 148, 159, 193; blocking, 166; derailment, 166; measurement of, 154–155; negative/ type II, 114, 138–40, 146, 154; positive/ type I, 114–15, 146, 154; poverty of content of speech, 165–66; poverty of speech, 165; word salad, 132. *See also* catatonia; delusions; diminished reality; empty speech; hallucinations; psychosis; youth: and schizophrenia

schizophrenia, treatment of, 110, 143, 148, 150, 154, 156, 160, 169–70; clubhouse movement, 176–77; cognitive therapy, 174; medication, 170–73; personal therapy (PT), 175–76; social skill training, 175. *See also* hallucinations: treating; schizophrenia: and family

serotonin, 210, 225, 275–76, 320

sign tools, 37

social climate, 44–45

social cognitive theory, 20,

social density, 33

social intelligence, 203

social learning, 16, 20

social learning theories, 28, 76

social workers, 11, 22, 33; and anxiety, 365; beliefs of, 4, 40–42, 74–75; and bias, 19, 34, 41, 96–97, 384; and depression, 188–89, 194, 196, 204–05, 207, 218–19, 224; and family, 51, 52, 54–57, 66–67, 82; and family education 62, 72–76; and family meetings, 60–61, 73; and medication treatment, 170–73, 224–25; 268–69, 369; needed skills, 71; and personality disorders, 324–25; preparing for assessments, 79; record keeping process, 93 fig. 3.4; and schizophrenia, 110, 115, 153, 174; and suicide, 209–10; and theoretical frameworks, 9–10, 11–12; and unconscious mental activity,

15. *See also* assessments

social workers, roles and responsibilities of, 1, 7, 9, 24, 27, 39, 41, 42, 43, 56, 68, 69, 70, 75, 77, 83, 96, 120, 123, 137, 170, 384

social work education, 1, 2, 10, 383

social work interventions, 30

social work strengths model, 29, 30

strengths interventions, 30–31

suicide, 8, 73, 128, 152–53, 204, 209, 244, 262; assessing intentions for, 219; prevention of, 338, 368–69; risk factors for, 367–68

symptoms (general), 9, 45, 196

Szasz, Thomas, 114

tartive dyscanesia, 172

technical tools, 37

temperament, 285

terminology for mental illness, 8

thalamus, 207, 288

theoretical frameworks, 3, 9–10, 99, 384

Torrey, E. Fuller, 147, 170

trauma, 8, 15, 85, 285, 305, 365

treatment plan, 9, 33, 76, 91, 91 fig. 3.2, 92

treatment team, 55, 83

Vygotsky, Lev Semyonovich, 36–38, 39

youth, 117; and aggression, 380, 382–83; and antipsychotic treatment, 379, 381; and anxiety, 281, 283, 285, 308, 363–66; 381; and bipolar disorder, 247, 248, 357–58, 359; and depression, 193, 359, 366–69, 381; and medication, 357, 360–61, 369, 371, 379, 380, 382; and mental illness, 10, 38, 41, 85, 356; and mental illness onset, 356; and personality development, 319–20; and obsessive-compulsive disorder, 298; and personality disorders, 319–20, 339, 340; and post-traumatic stress disorder, 305, 365; and poverty, 357; and psychosis, 360, 369–71; and schizophrenia, 118, 149; and suicide, 367–69; treatment of, 365–66. *See also individual conditions*

zone of proximal development (ZPD), 37–38

9 780195 324792